FOCUS IN PHOTOGRAPHY

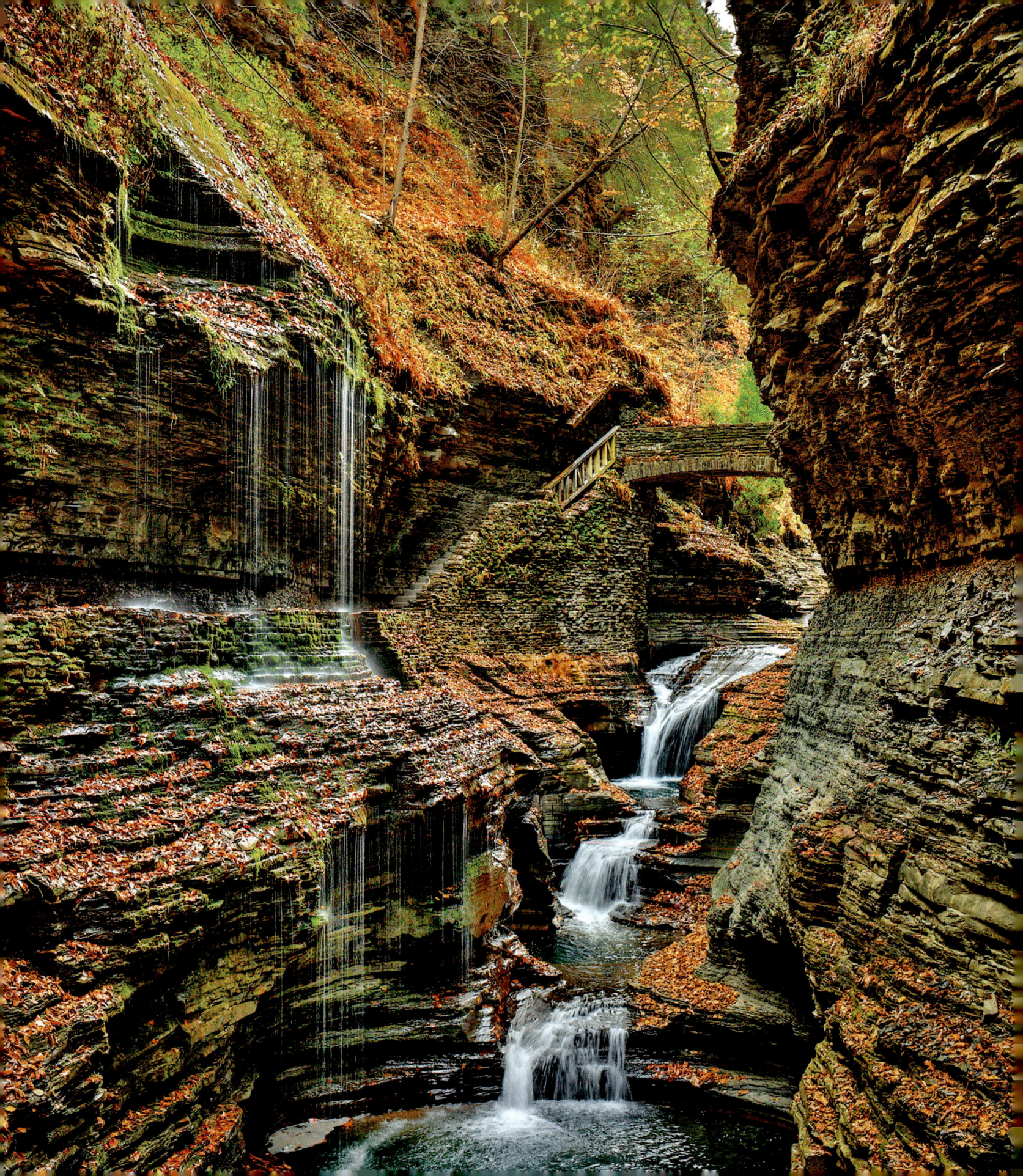

FOCUS IN PHOTOGRAPHY

Master the fundamental photographic method,
open up a new world of creativity

JOHN NEEL

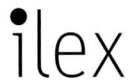

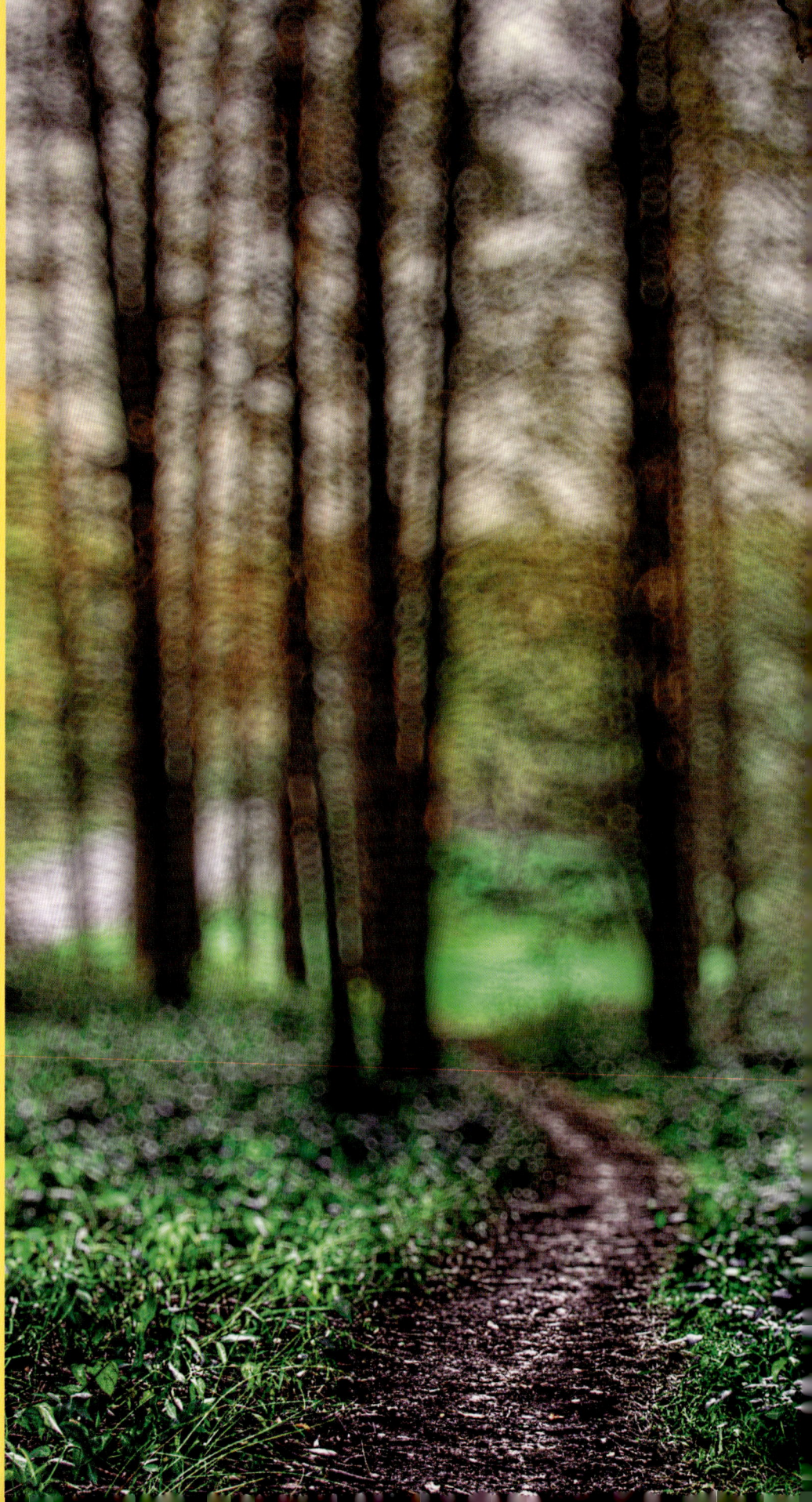

An Hachette UK Company
www.hachette.co.uk

First published in the United Kingdom in 2016 by
ILEX, a division of Octopus Publishing Group Ltd
Octopus Publishing Group
Carmelite House
50 Victoria Embankment
London, EC4Y 0DZ
www.octopusbooks.co.uk

Design, layout, and text copyright
© Octopus Publishing Group 2016

Publisher: Roly Allen
Associate Publisher: Adam Juniper
Managing Specialist Editor: Frank Gallaugher
Senior Project Editor: Natalia Price-Cabrera
Editors: Rachel Silverlight & Francesca Leung
Art Director: Julie Weir
Designer: Kate Haynes
Production Controller: Sarah Kulasek-Boyd

All rights reserved. No part of this work may be reproduced or utilized in any form or by any means, electronic or mechanical, including photocopying, recording or by any information storage and retrieval system, without the prior written permission of the publisher.

John Neel asserts the moral right to be identified as the author of this work.

ISBN 978-1-78157-238-2

A CIP catalogue record for this book is available from the British Library

Printed and bound in China

10 9 8 7 6 5 4 3 2 1

Contents

INTRODUCTION	06	**BOKEH**	50	**CLOSEUP**	104
The Zen of Focus	8	What Is Bokeh?	52	Getting Up Close	106
Think Outside the Box		Bokeh Size & Detail	53	Macro Lenses	
Another Kind of Focus	12	**Characteristics of Bokeh**	54	Extension Tubes	108
About This Book	13	Oval Bokeh	55	Lens Reversal	110
Focus Is More Than It Seems	14	Cat's Eye Bokeh		Two-Lens Macro	
Focus As A Creative Tool		Spiral Bokeh	56	Focusing Rails	112
Creation As Play		**How Lens Design Affects Bokeh**	58	Gallery	114
Gallery	16	Fast-Aperture Bokeh			
		Catadioptric Bokeh	60	**FOCUS STACKING**	116
LIGHT	18	Blade Shape & Bokeh	62	Focus Stacking Explained	118
Light Is Our Palette	20	Natural Bokeh	63	Image-Stacking	
Properties Of Light		**Utilizing Bokeh**	64	Software	119
Color Theory Of Light		**Shaped Bokeh**	66	**Focus Stacking**	
Light & Lenses	21	Cut-Out Bokeh	67	**In Practice**	120
Why We See The Colors We See	22	Faking Bokeh	68	Focus Stacking Walkthroughs	124
How Optical Systems Work	24	Bokeh Brushes	69	Gallery	128
A Pinhole & Light		Layering Bokeh			
How A Lens Sees	26	Pinhole Bokeh	70	**PANORAMAS**	132
Human Vision	28	Gallery	72	What Is A Panorama?	134
Focus is Relative	30			Image Stitching	
The Image Circle	31	**OPTICS & EQUIPMENT**	74	In-Camera Panoramas	136
Collecting Light	32	Placing Sharpness	76	Multi-Shot Panorama	138
Aberrations	34	The Art Of Defocusing	77	Parallax	140
Lens Flare		**Focal Length**	78	No Parallax Point	
Chromatic Aberration	35	Wide-Angle Lenses		Panoramic Equipment	142
Barrel Distortion		Telephoto Lenses		GigaPan Panoramas	144
Pincushion Distortion		**Mirrorless Cameras**	82	Gallery	146
Circles Of Confusion	36	**Large-Format Cameras**	84		
Depth of Field	38	Lens Movements	86	**SOFTWARE**	148
Hyperfocal Distance	40	Rising Front	88	Alien Skin	
Focus Peaking	41	Scheimpflug Principle	89	Exposure X	150
Filters	42	**Tilt-Shift Lenses**	90	Tonality Pro	
Soft Focus		Miniaturization	92	& Intensify Pro	154
Polarizing Filters	43	**DIY Lenses**	94	Noiseless	156
Neutral Density Filters	44	**Freelensing**	96	Piccure+	158
Variable ND Filters	45	**Tripods**	100	Photoshop	
Graduated ND Filters	46	Gallery	102	Bokeh Effects	160
Color Gradient Filters	47			Gallery	164
Colored Filters					
Gallery	48			**APPENDICES**	168
				Glossary	170
				Index	174
				Acknowledgments	176

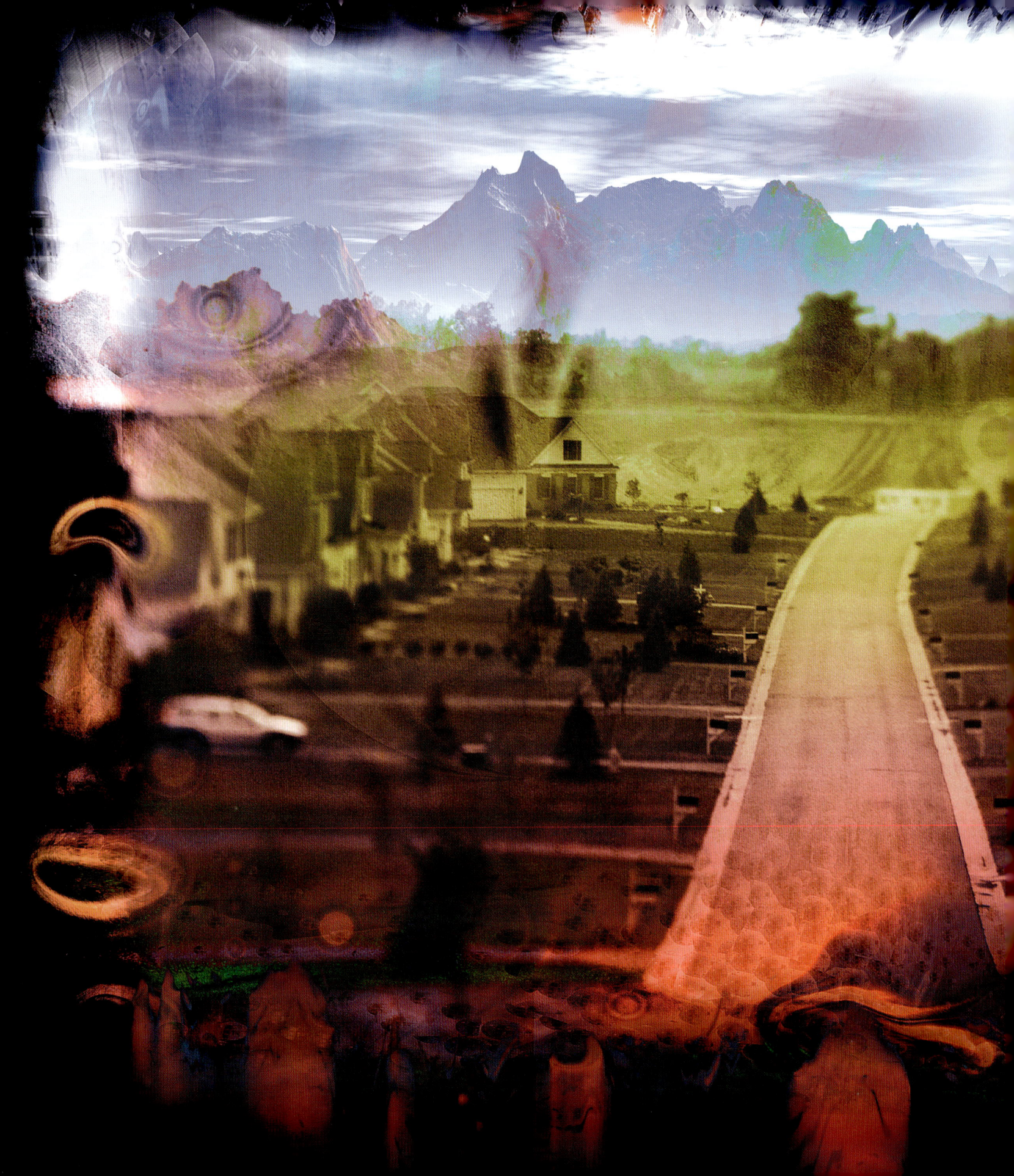

INTRODUCTION

The Zen of Focus

Photography is about light. Without it, photography would not exist. Everything I know about photography has to do with the properties of light, the subjects we can see and photograph, and the details that we both see and fail to see. But of all the concepts that I have explored, focus is always the primary concern.

Think Outside the Box

There is a saying in the corporate world; "think outside the box." This implies seeing beyond the horizon and being open-minded. I approach photography in a similar way, so that I am never trapped inside a box. I want to see what is outside the box, because that is where life happens.

For a period of time, I played in the corporate design department at Eastman Kodak Company as a graphic designer and illustrator. I use the word "played" (rather than "worked") because, to me, it was anything but work. I was assigned to the research labs as a concept visualization artist where I was allowed to experiment with many great toys and on many great projects for digital imaging.

Together with the Kodak engineers and scientists, I became involved with research, concept development, and invention. My play led to ownership of at least seven patents for digital cameras and digital imaging, not to mention hundreds of great concepts that for some managerial reason or another did not make it to the patent process. Play can be rewarding.

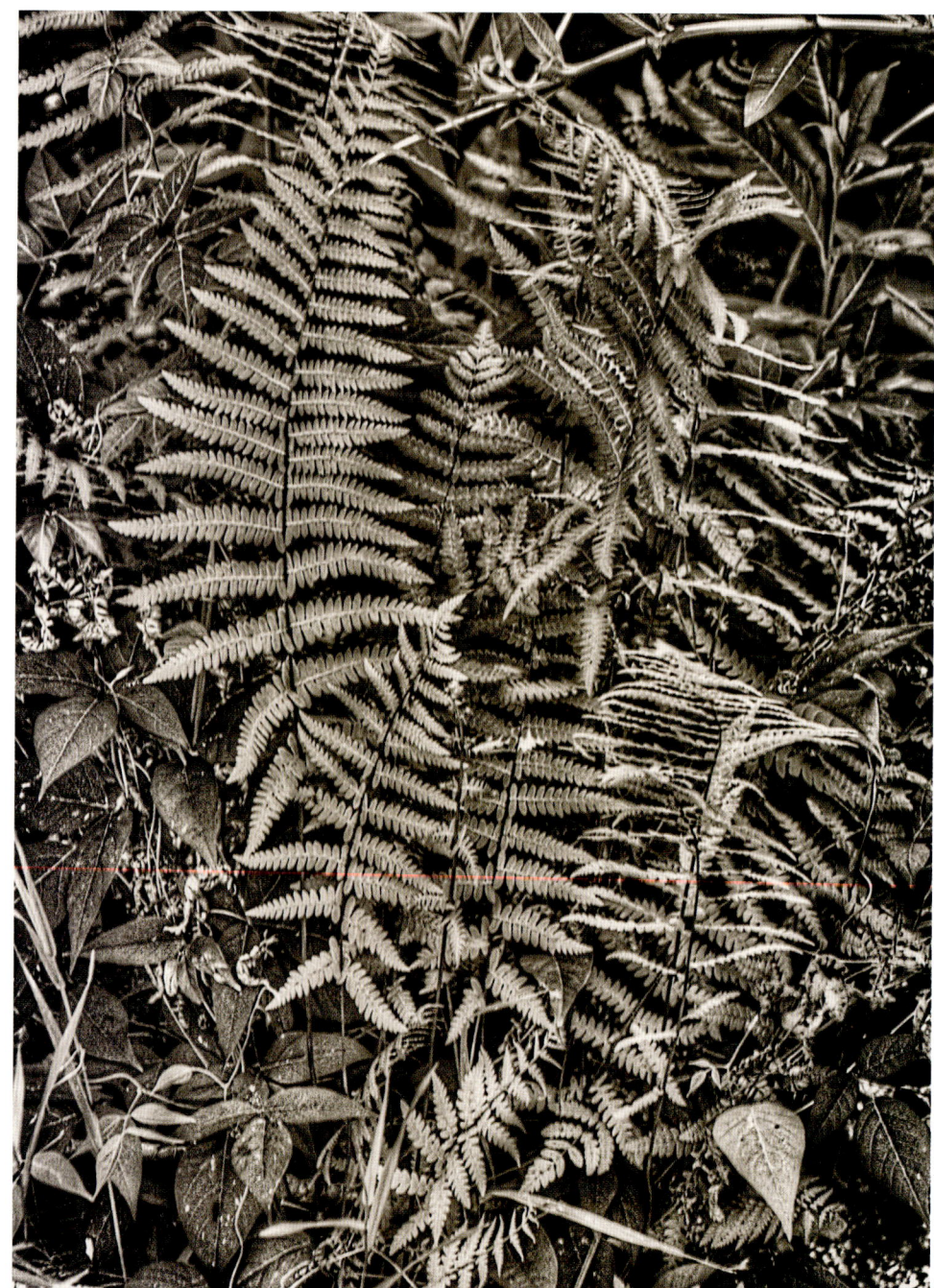

RIGHT: *A combination of subject focus and image contrast helps to bring out the form of these plants.*

FAR RIGHT: *These experimental slit-image landscapes were created using preset focusing.*

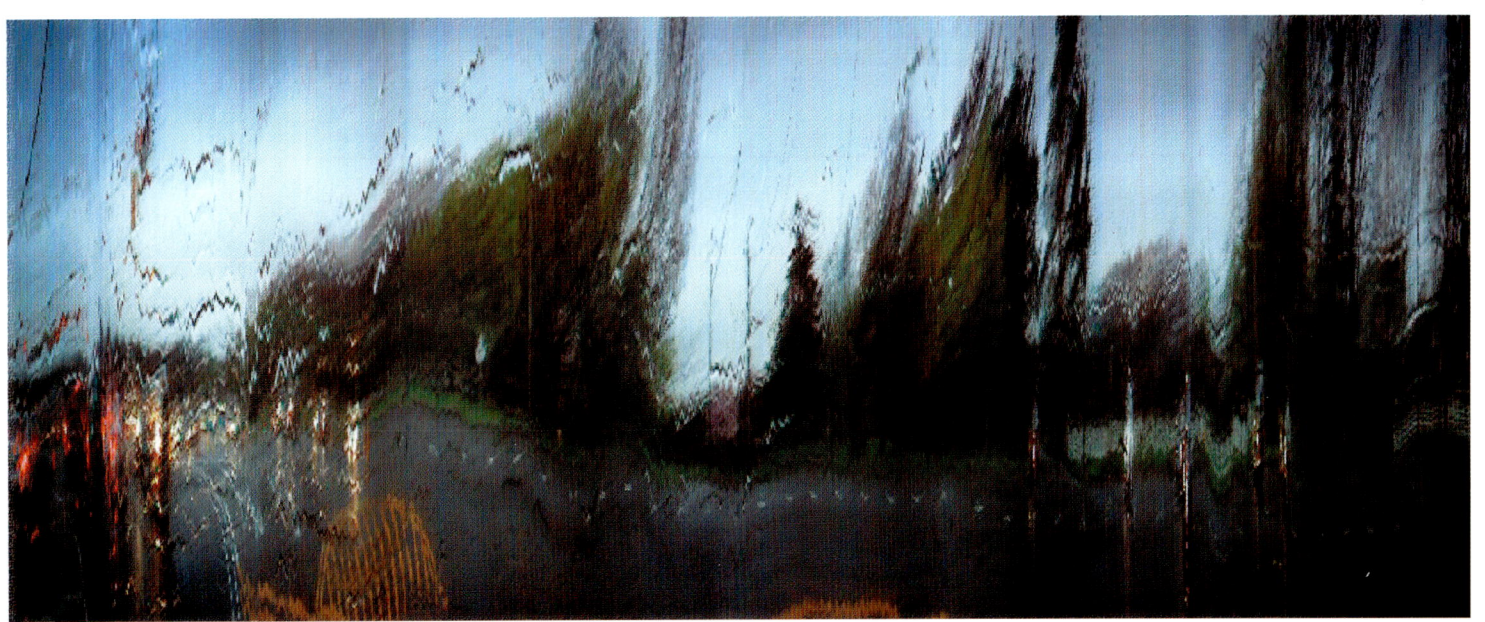

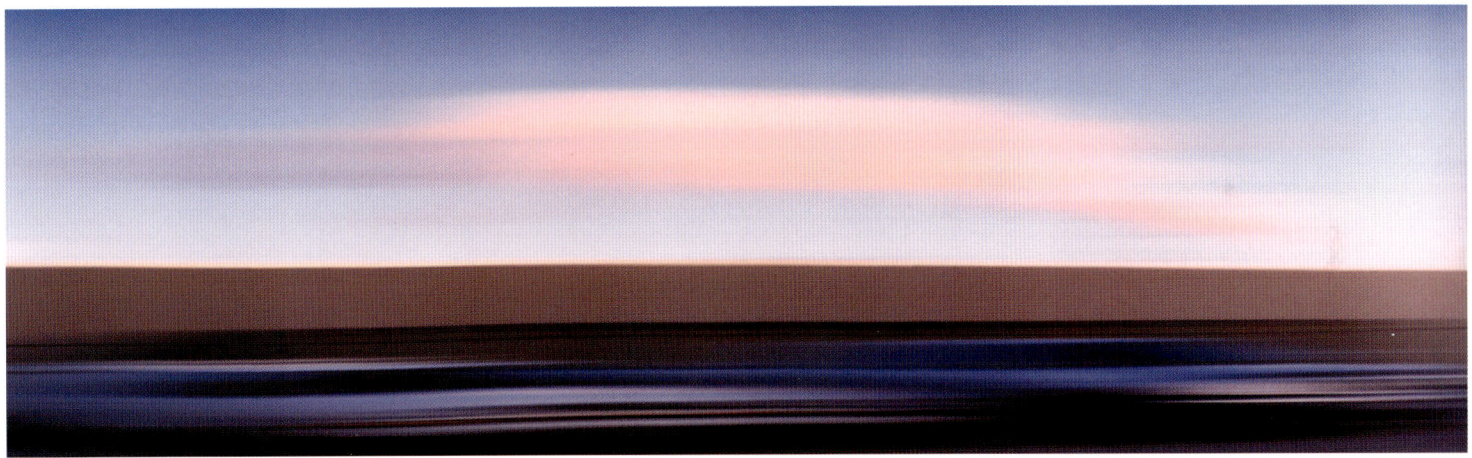

"Our job is to record, each in his own way, this world of light and shadow and time that will never come again exactly as it is today." —EDWARD ABBEY

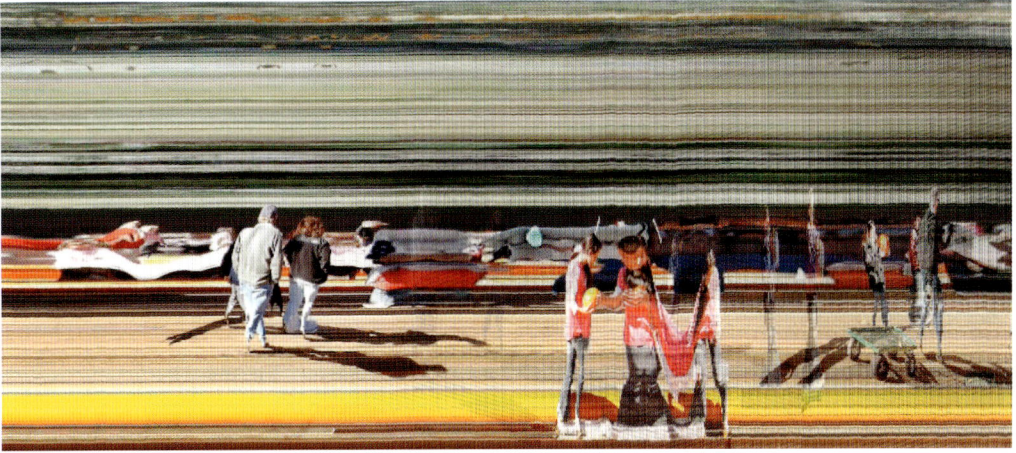

During that time, one of my personal goals was to look at film-based technologies, and find as many ways as I could in which film differed from digital imaging. I researched the tools and the methods, as well as the kinds of image that could be produced.

Although almost any look can be simulated through image-editing software, I specifically wanted to discover creative ways to produce images without the help of computer programs. Among many other things, I was looking for creative inspiration. My goals were to develop fresh ways to make digital images and new types of fun digital cameras, and to further my own concepts about photography.

For example, to date there are no digital cameras that can image on irregular surfaces such as a curve; all sensors are flat. Film, on the other hand, can easily produce images on a curve. Indeed, for many years, a large number of inexpensive cameras employed curved film planes in order to capture the sharpest image possible from a simple lens.

The problem is that lenses do not normally focus on a flat surface, so camera manufacturers have to design lenses with extra elements to make the lens focus the light onto a flat field, such as a digital sensor. However, corrected lenses are more expensive to produce, so a curved plane would allow for a cheaper focusing solution. At the time of writing, Sony has announced a patent for a curved sensor.

During my years at Kodak, I also explored new ways that people might have fun with cameras. I looked at toy cameras, pinhole cameras, phone cameras, stereo cameras, infrared cameras, large- and medium-format cameras, miniature cameras, slit cameras, historical cameras, and futuristic concept cameras. The aim here was to possibly invent (or reinvent) a new breed of image-making tool.

I also looked at camera paraphernalia, alternative imaging methods, and numerous 3D, fractal generation, image paint, and animation software packages. I even looked

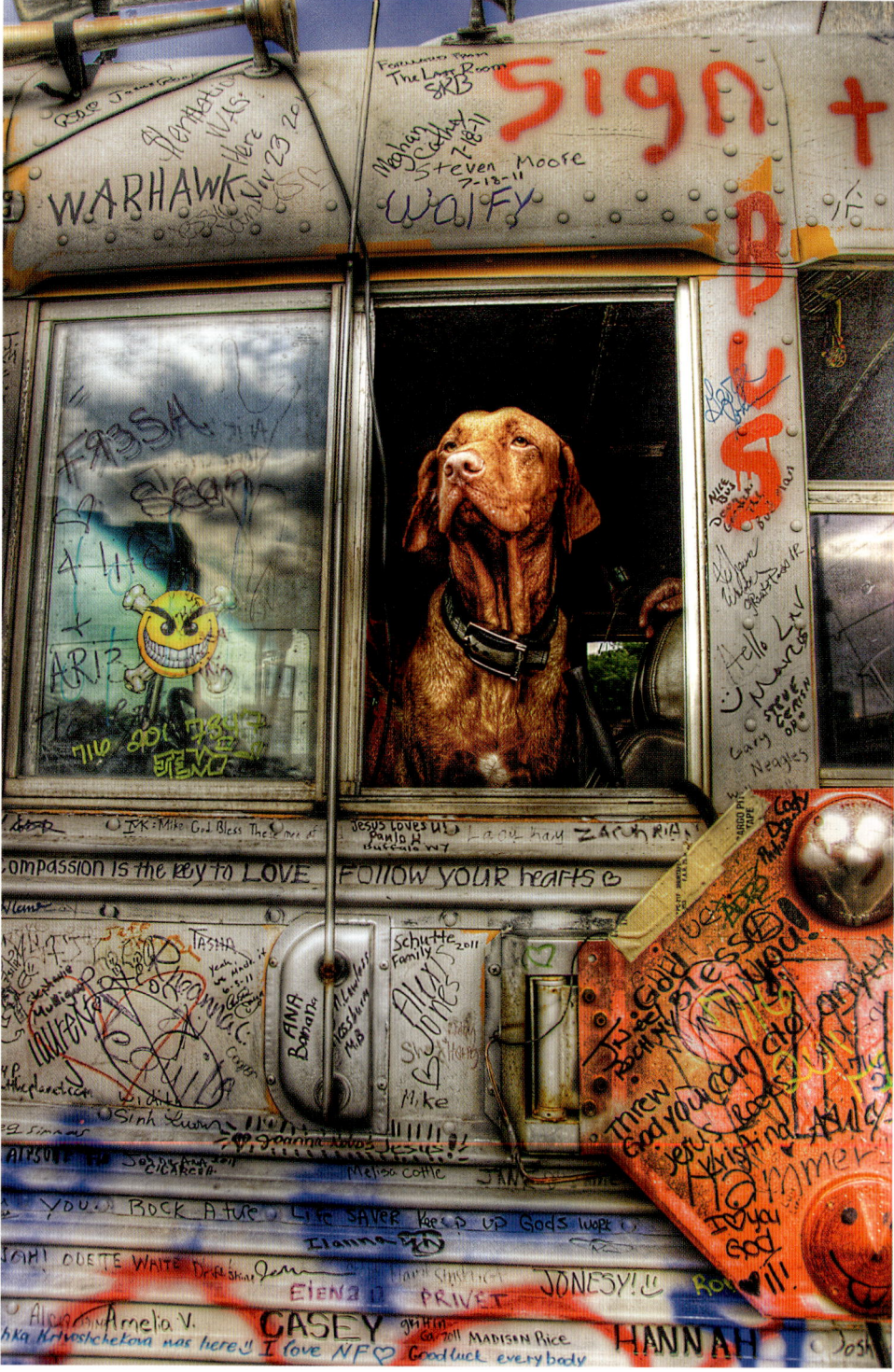

ABOVE: *Aperture settings are important when considering the subject, as well as the surrounding details. The writing on this bus is as important to the reading of this image as the dog.*

THE ZEN OF FOCUS // INTRODUCTION

at ways in which sound could be potentially used alongside images.

As a result of my research and experimentation, I realized that digital imaging had much to learn from film, and I began to see numerous analog opportunities that might be reproduced through digital means. More importantly, I discovered many creative approaches to photography that I personally wanted to explore for my own creative expression. Much of this book is a result of that continued search.

LEFT: *Pinhole images have a distinct soft-focus effect that makes them almost painterly. Pinhole photography has become very popular with those who want to get back to the basics of photography. This image was produced using a digital camera with a Micro Four Thirds sensor and a 0.2mm pinhole.*

BELOW: *It was very important to maintain the same focus throughout this 360 x 180° panoramic landscape photograph.*

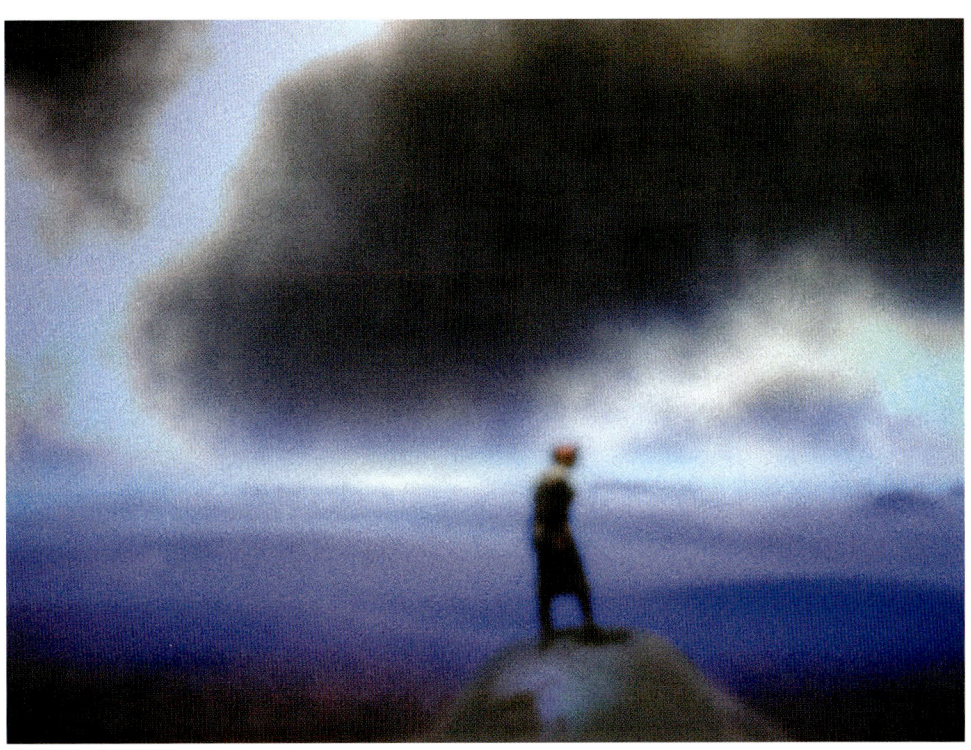

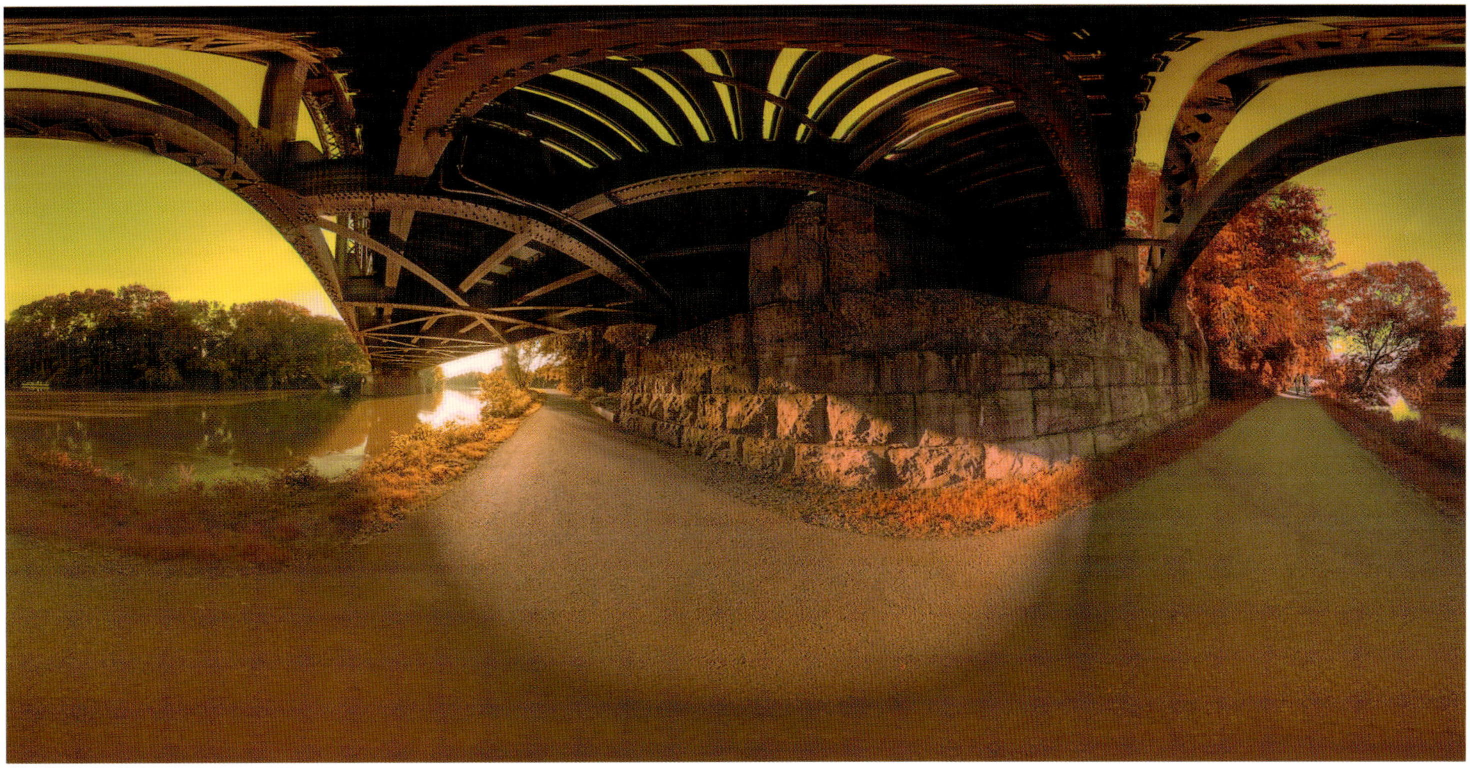

Another Kind of Focus

Focusing is an art, especially in photography. However, this time I'm only making a partial reference to its expected photographic meaning. In this instance, I am more interested in the subject matter, rather than the way it is rendered by a lens.

focus: *the center of interest or activity • an act of concentrating interest or activity on something.* – APPLE DICTIONARY

I think that focus implies a sense of subject. Focus is the "what" of an image; it is what you want the viewer to see and hopefully understand. Therefore, focus comes first from having an interest in a specific thing—an idea or a point of departure.

A point of departure is the point at which a journey begins. In art and photography, it is a learning process used to discover something, explore an idea, gain knowledge, and provoke thought and realization.

Creativity is the act of focusing on a concept or an idea. It is what happens when our subjects absorb us. It is an awareness of something that will make us better for having seen it. It is an understanding.

Focus is what all good photographers do. It is the act of imaging an idea or a metaphor, and of creatively transforming a subject. Focus can be compassionate, sympathetic, questioning, argumentative, and meditative. It is a way of transforming your thinking into a tangible form, and broadening your understanding of your world.

As communication, it tells others who and what you are, so focus is also rather like a window into the self. It is what you see, what you believe, what you learn, and what you are. How well you focus can also have the power to influence the thinking of others.

The theme for your journey and your capacity for focus is up to you, but it is worth remembering at all times that the worth of your vision will be determined by your ability to focus.

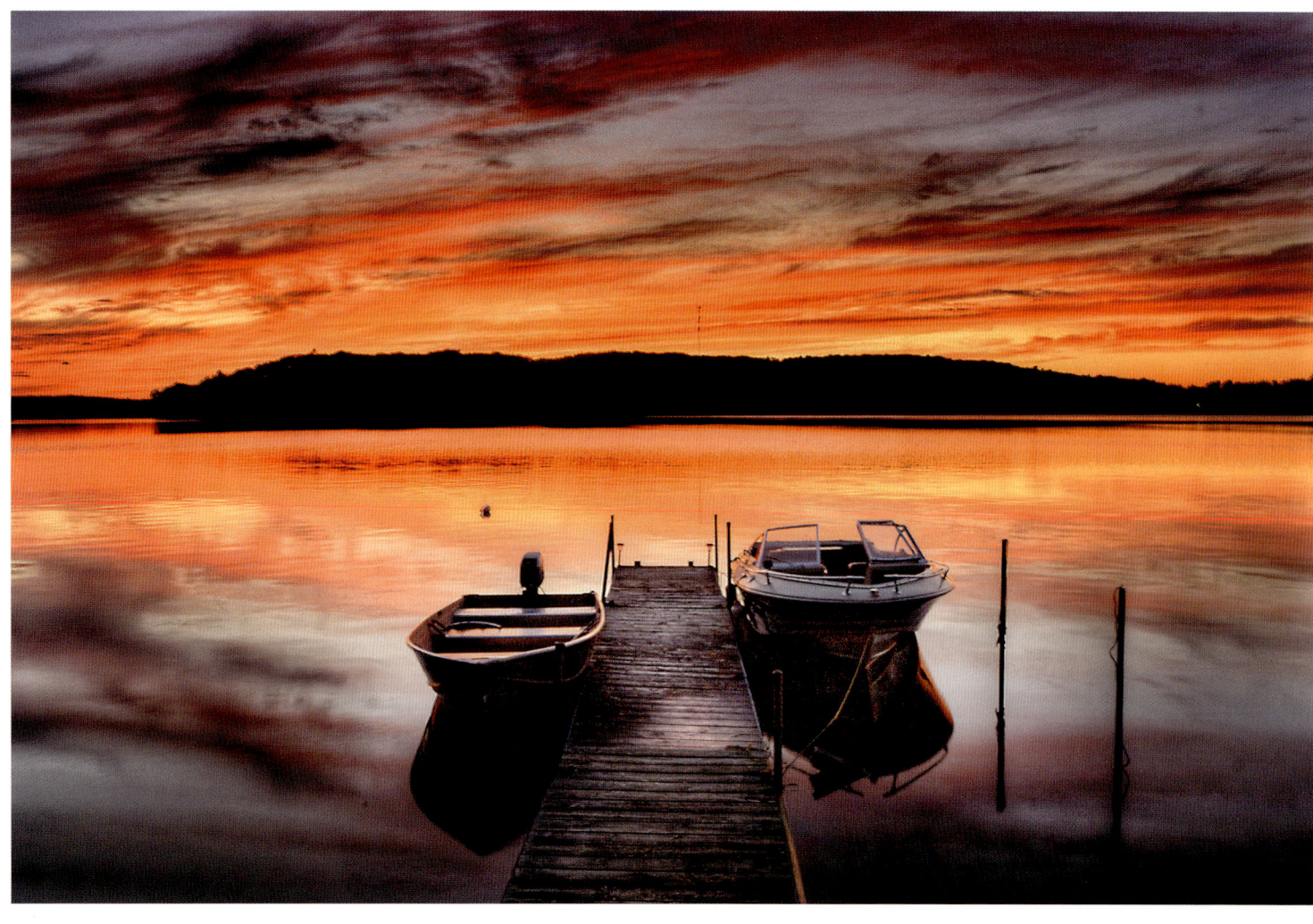

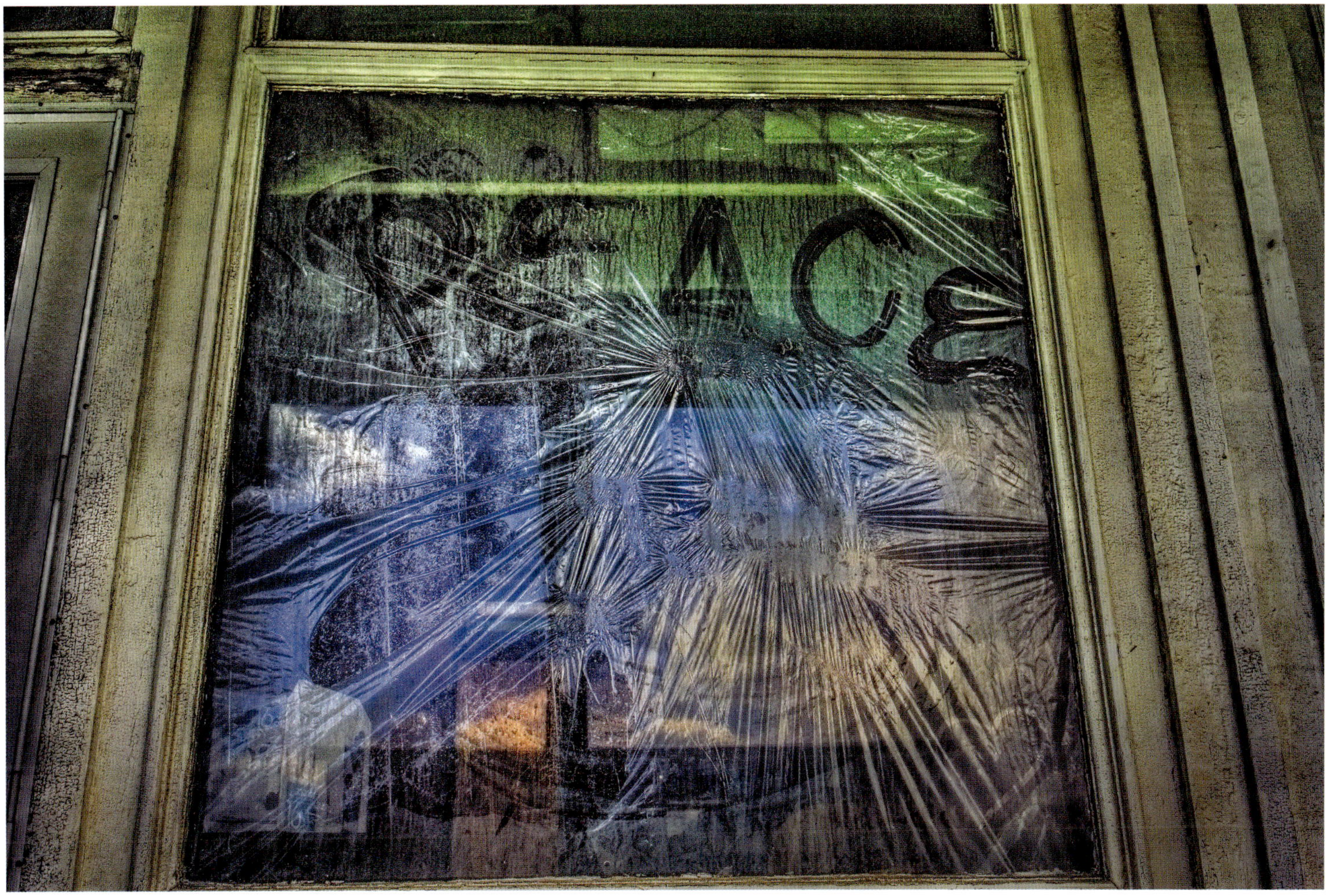

ABOVE: *A small aperture setting made everything in this shot appear sharply focused.*

RIGHT: *A combination of a small aperture and slow shutter speed produced the blurring effect of the water, while ensuring the image was sharp from the near foreground to the background.*

LEFT: *Using a small aperture extended both the depth of field and exposure duration, which gave me the time required to streak the water.*

About This Book

With this book, my goal is to inspire personal exploration and creativity utilizing any and all of the options available in a world that has "gone digital." However, more than anything else, this book is about the creative potential of focusing, in the broadest sense of the word.

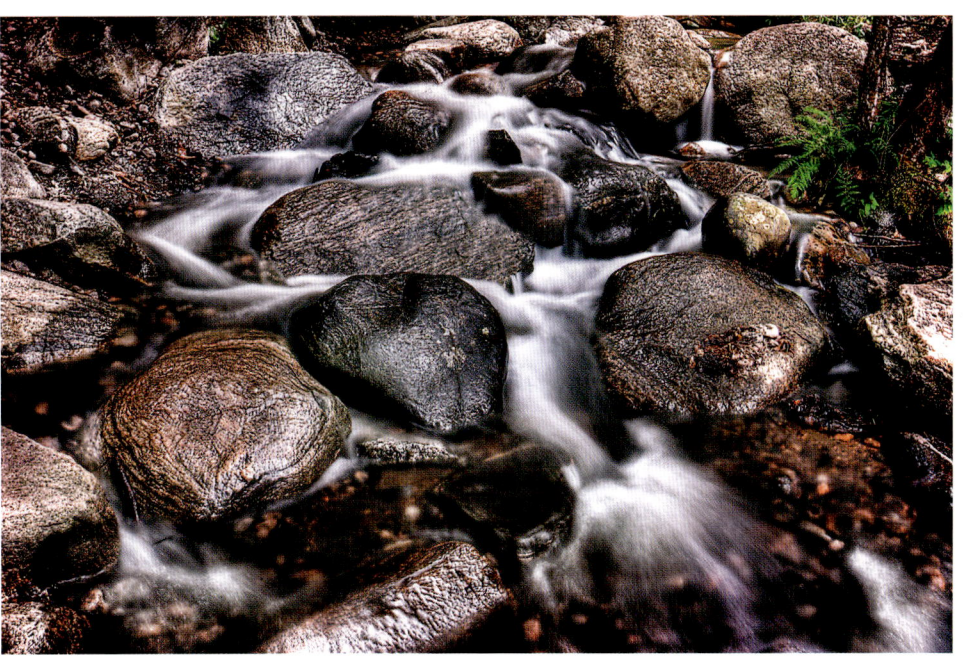

Focus is More than It Seems

The average camera user probably hasn't given much thought to focus. After all, the majority of new digital cameras come equipped with a slew of automatic functions, and focus is often a given.

Therefore, focusing seems to be an unlikely concern these days. The design of the camera has made it virtually foolproof, so the photographer no longer needs to worry about whether or not the image is sharp. And so it appears that nobody seems to think much of focus any more.

However, for photographers, focus is an art. I say "art," because a real photographer must consider all of the tools at his/her disposal and focus is an essential element in a great photograph. Out of focus is equally important, both aesthetically and compositionally.

Beyond the physical act of focusing the lens, there is also the mental focus of the photographer. This is the awareness of the subject, and an understanding of its significance, beauty, cruelty, importance, and truth. Focus is therefore a much larger slice of the photographic process than most would think. In most cases, it is focus that makes the image.

Focus as a Creative Tool

I like to think of focus as one of the more important creative tools, not unlike an artist's brush and just as significant. Focus is a way to underscore the subject. It is a way to point at the main character of the image, and as such it will make or break any subject. Focus and all of its possibilities takes center stage in the making of a great image. It frames that which we want to share with our audience and it leads us through the photograph, enhancing the details of the subject. Consequently, it is one of the primary tools at our disposal.

Early in my career as a photographer, I worked hard to make my images as sharp as possible throughout the entire scene. In part, this seemed important because I admired photographers whose own work exhibited the same characteristic. In particular, I was enamored by the work of Ansel Adams and other members of Group f/64. These masters of photography produced images using large-format cameras, with lenses stopped down to the smallest available apertures in order to maximize the depth of field.

Using small aperture settings and focusing at hyperfocal distance seemed (at the time) to be the best representation of nature. After all, everything in the real world is sharp; no objects are naturally out of focus.

It is the purpose of this book—at least in part—to demonstrate that I was wrong in this assumption. Not only was I wrong, but it also limited the creative possibilities of artistic focusing.

The eye has a particular way of seeing what is in front of it and it is important to distinguish the similarities between human vision and the variations that occur in camera vision, as well as to understand the differences between the two. At the start of this book, I will discuss some of the very basics of focus by looking at how we see as humans, and how the camera sees.

Creation as Play

The word "creative" generally implies that one is inventive, imaginative, experimental, original, and artistic. It also connotes fun, play, and pleasure. To me, it is all of these things, but it is also a discovery process.

Creativity is how I discover the world and myself. Utmost to the creative possibilities outlined in this book is the concept of fun. As an artist, I have always considered the act of creation as play. On the following pages are a few images showing some of the focusing techniques that we will cover in this book.

BELOW: *The point of focus was placed at the very front of this old fire truck; everything else is in relative sharpness.*

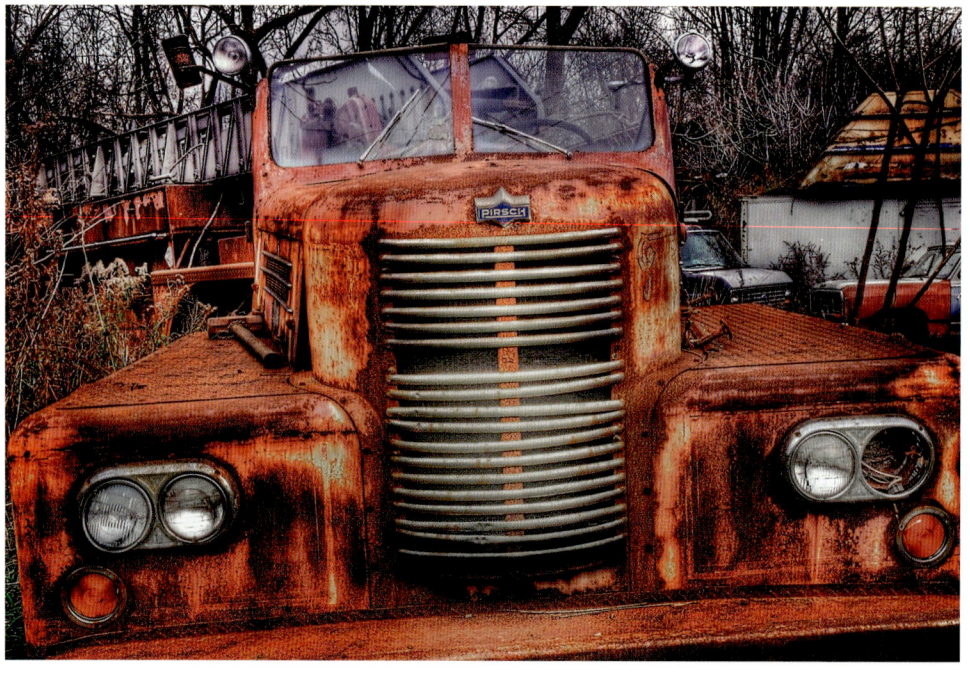

THE ZEN OF FOCUS // INTRODUCTION

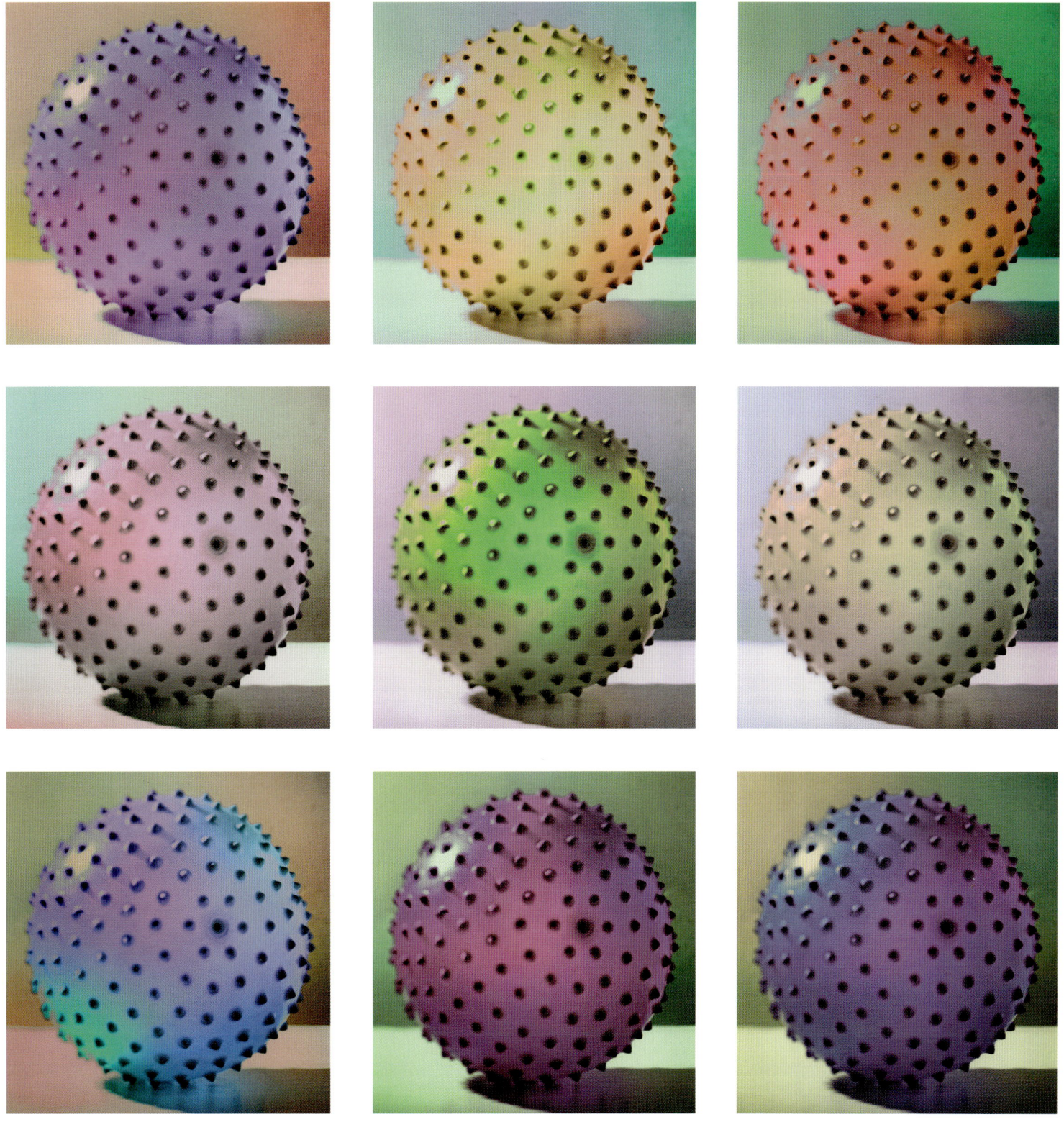

ABOVE: *The original ball was photographed using a focus stacking process, then arranged to create this composite.*

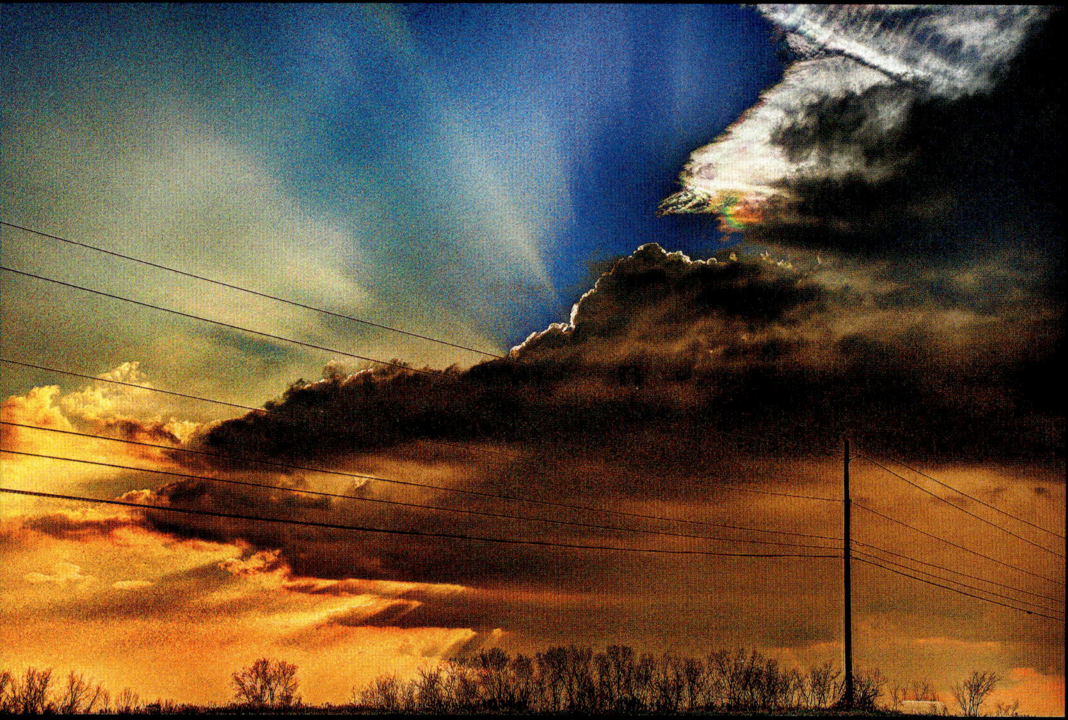

Gallery | Introduction

LEFT: *Taken shortly before sunset, this multiple-exposure HDR sky was photographed handheld at a medium aperture setting. The aperture helped to keep everything in relative sharp focus, while allowing the shutter to operate fast enough for each of the exposures.*

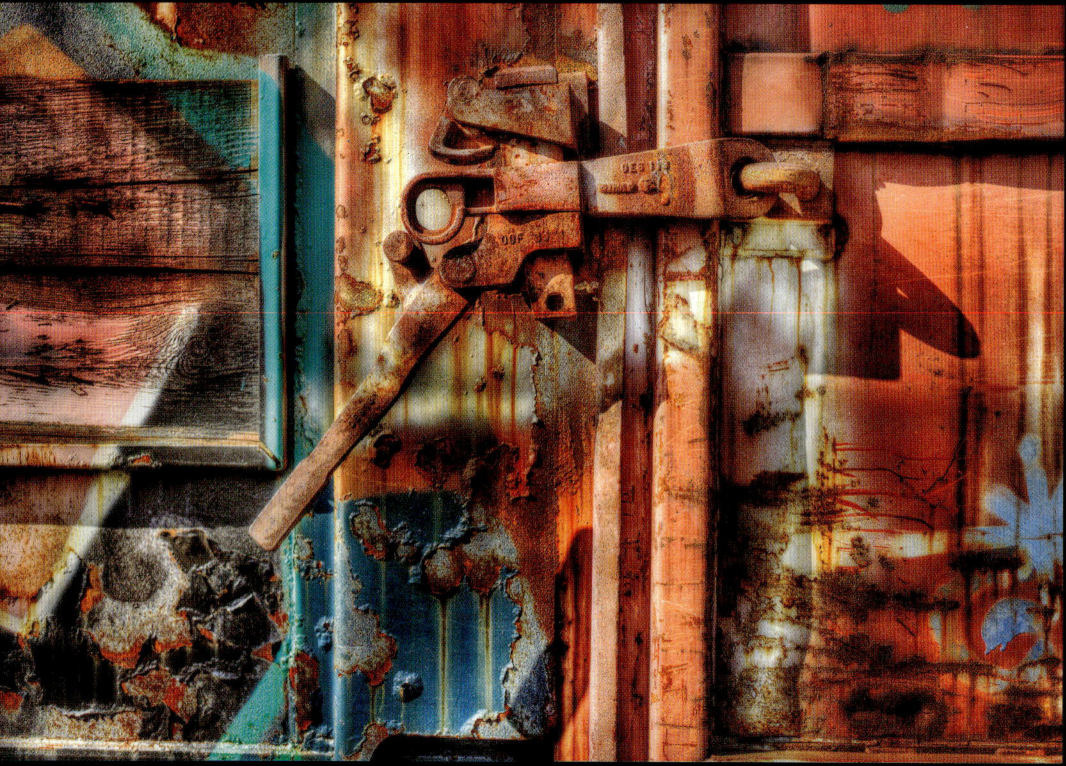

LEFT: *A stitched image requires all adjoining images to be equally sharp. This composite was created with a grid of approximately nine different photographs that were stitched together to create a very large and highly detailed mural-sized image.*

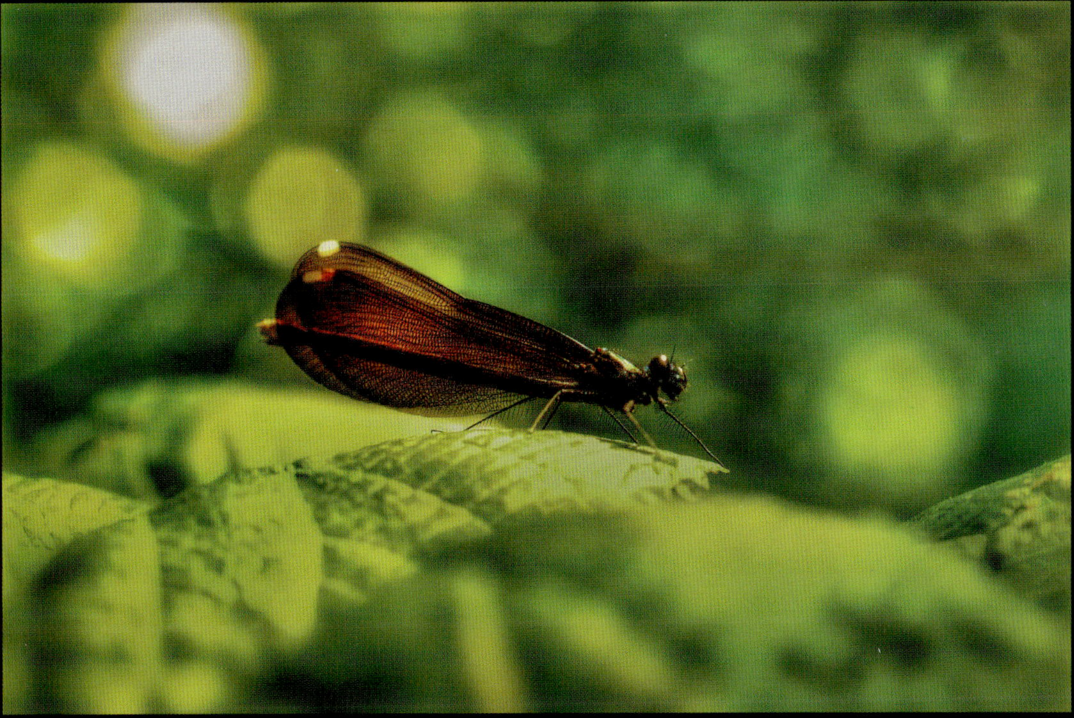

LEFT: *The out-of-focus bokeh shapes add interest to the sharply defined insect and act as a soft backdrop. The circular shapes mimic some of the details of the subject's head and wings.*

BELOW: *For this photograph, the lens was tilted away from the normal axis to alter the plane of focus. This shifts the focus as well as the depth of field.*

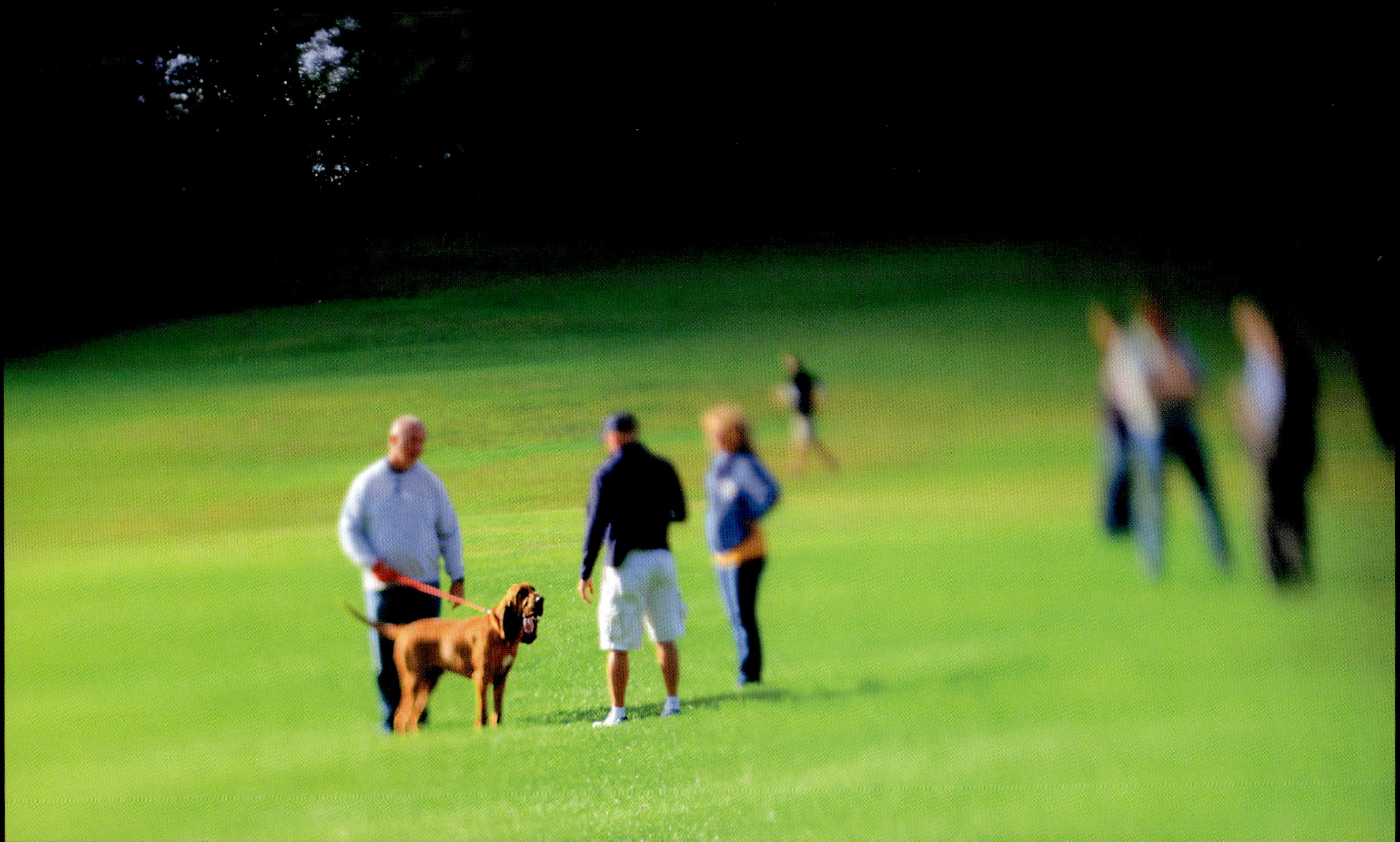

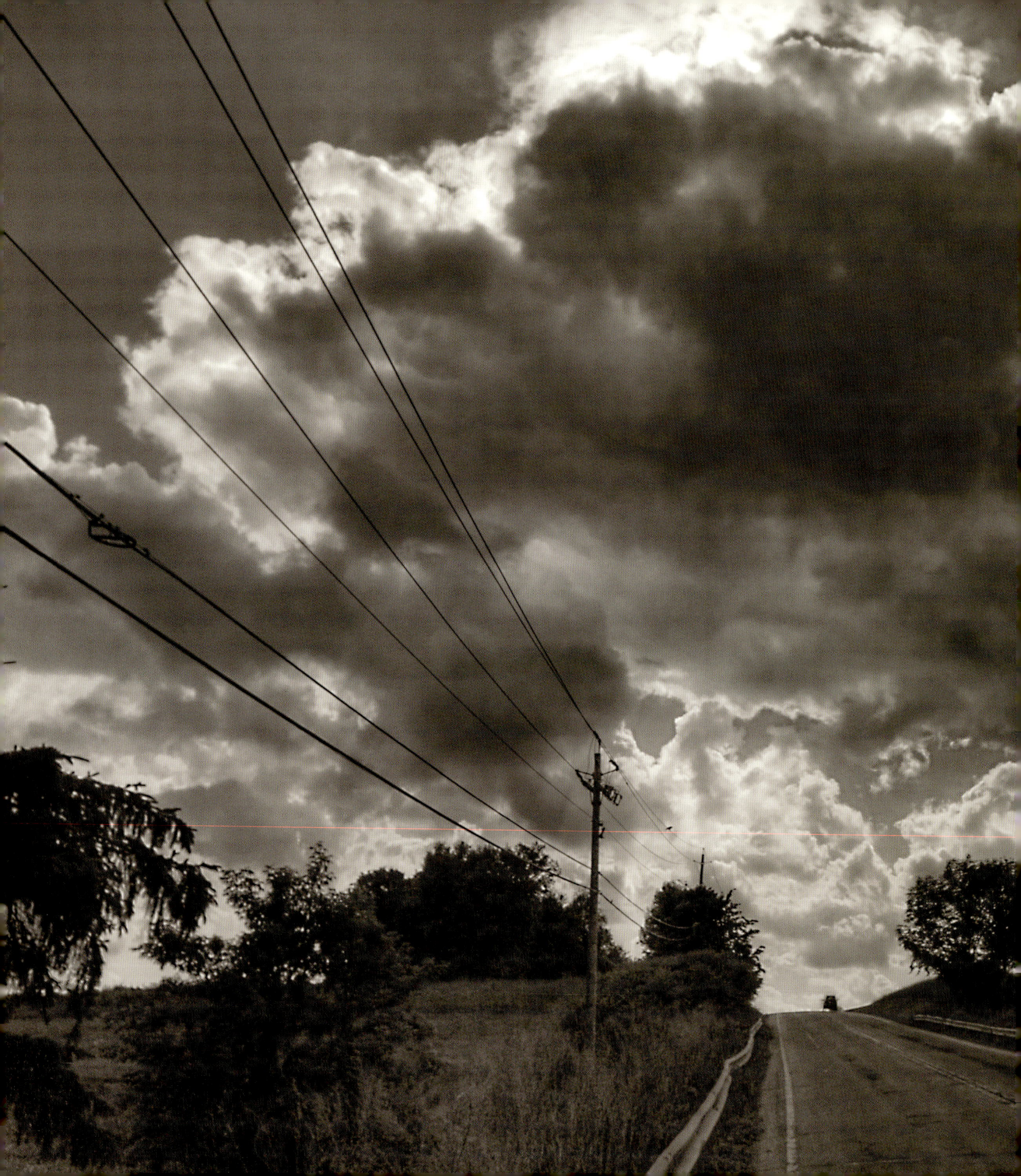

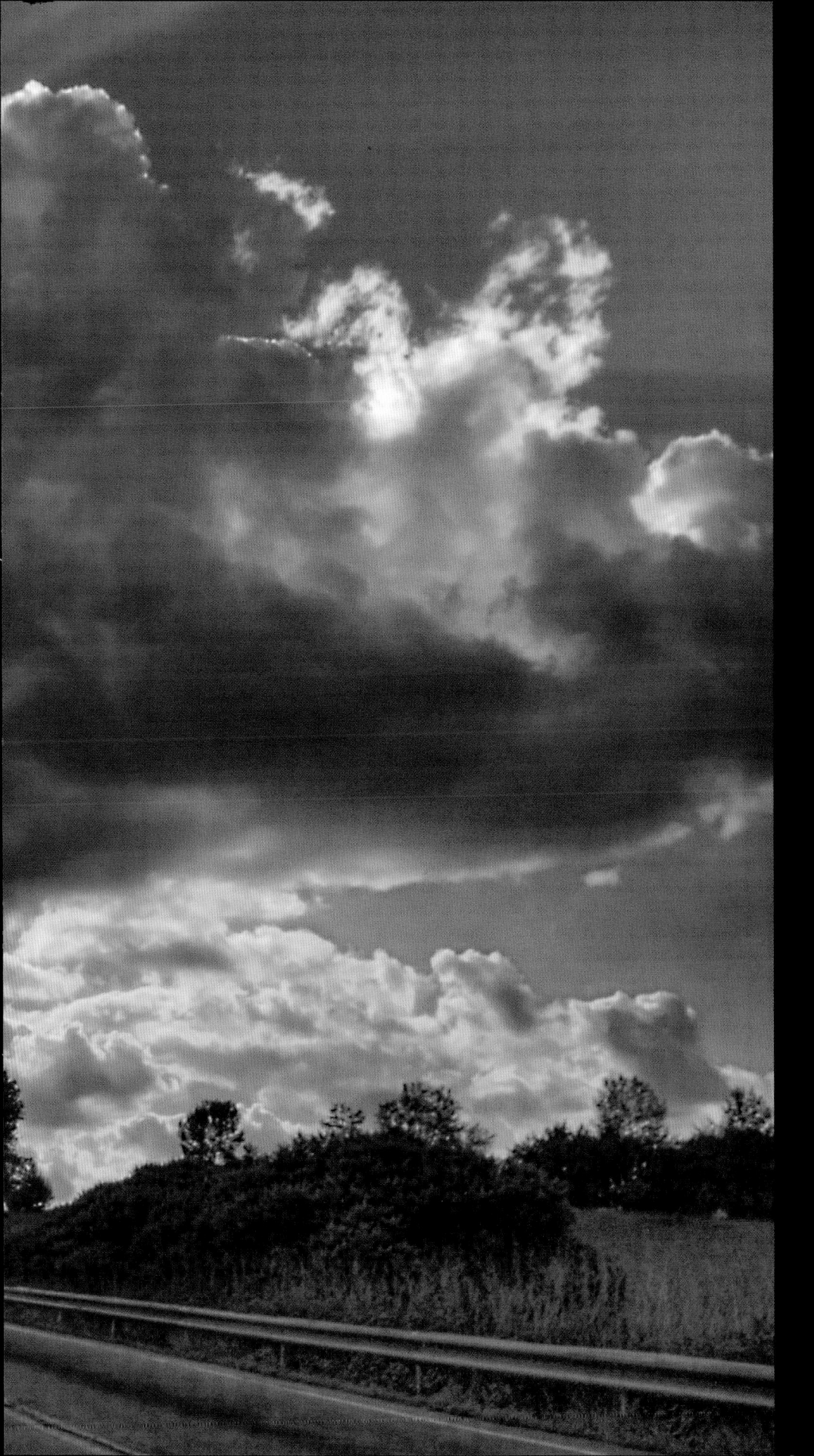

01 // LIGHT

Light is Our Palette

The one thing common to all photography is light, so before we go any further, we should spend some time looking at the basic functionality of how light and lenses work.

Properties of Light

One of the properties of light is that it travels in straight lines, until acted upon by another object, such as a surface, an edge, or object density such as glass.

Although light travels in straight lines, it does so as waves of energy. Light is a portion of a broader spectrum of electromagnetic radiation that includes, gamma rays, X-rays, ultraviolet, visible light, infrared, microwaves, and radio frequencies.

For our purpose, electromagnetic radiation refers to the wavelengths that make up the band of wave frequencies that we call "visible light." At either end of this spectrum is invisible radiation, starting with ultraviolet and infrared (ultraviolet radiation has a shorter wavelength than the visible violet light and infrared radiation has a longer wavelength than visible red light).

Color Theory of Light

Without getting too deep into the physics of light (which in itself is a subject beyond this book), it would be good to discuss some basic concepts before moving too far along.

Light is made up of various colors. The principal components of white light are red, green, and blue, which make up all of the colors in the visible spectrum. This means that all of the colors that we can see are created by mixing these three primary colors of light. White is created when all wavelengths are combined equally.

Much of what we see is either reflected illumination or light from a direct source. Light sources such as the sun produce light that is a mixture of wavelengths. However, while the sun is considered a white light source, the color we see or associate with sunlight contains an unequal mix of wavelengths, depending on the time of day.

"Of what use are lens and light to those who lack in mind and sight?"

—ANONYMOUS

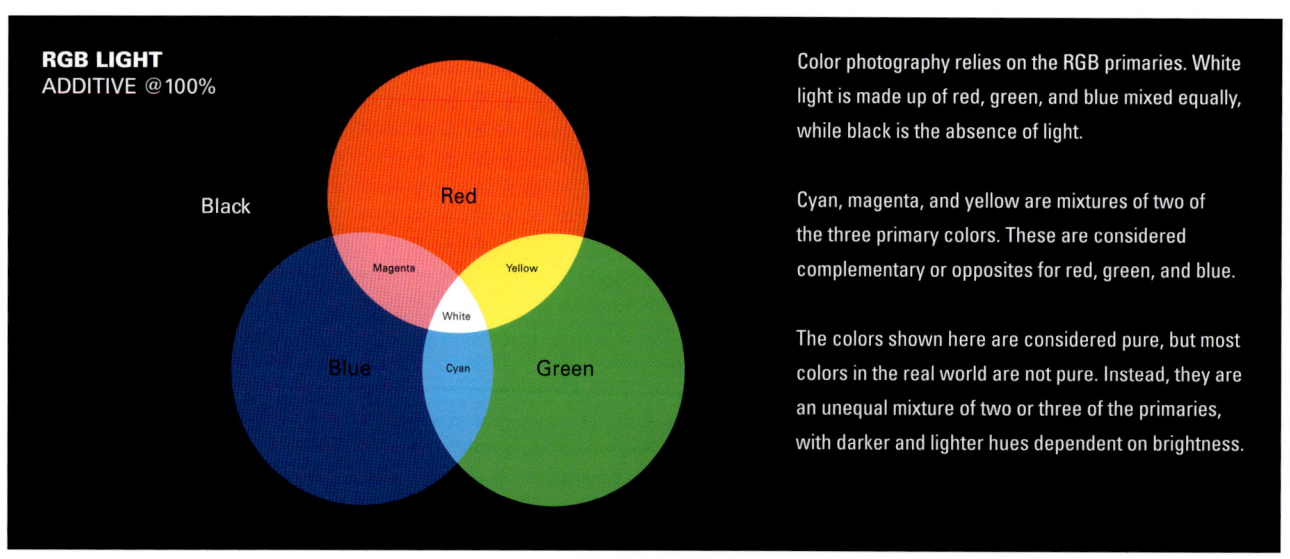

RGB LIGHT
ADDITIVE @ 100%

Color photography relies on the RGB primaries. White light is made up of red, green, and blue mixed equally, while black is the absence of light.

Cyan, magenta, and yellow are mixtures of two of the three primary colors. These are considered complementary or opposites for red, green, and blue.

The colors shown here are considered pure, but most colors in the real world are not pure. Instead, they are an unequal mixture of two or three of the primaries, with darker and lighter hues dependent on brightness.

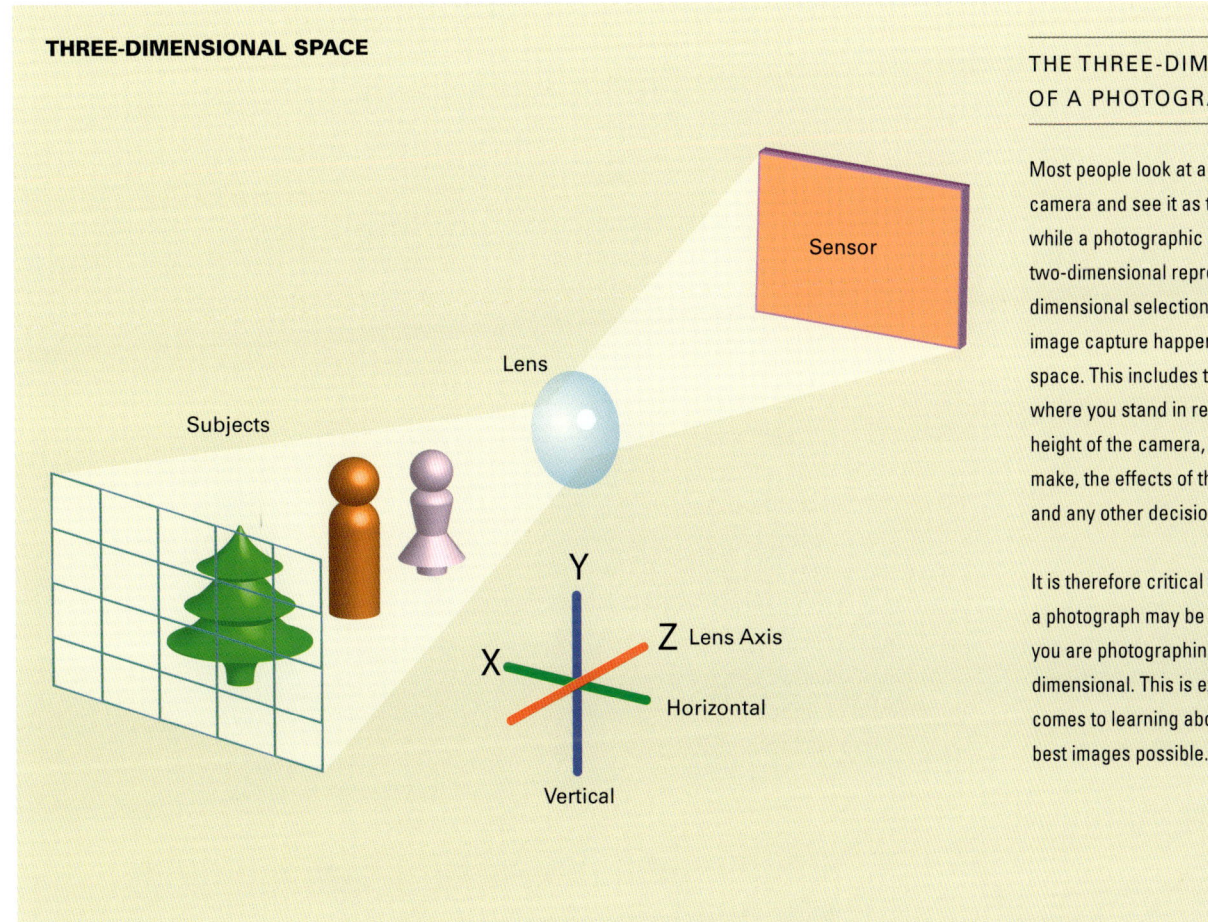

THREE-DIMENSIONAL SPACE

Sensor
Lens
Subjects
Y
X Z Lens Axis
Horizontal
Vertical

THE THREE-DIMENSIONALITY OF A PHOTOGRAPHIC VIEW

Most people look at a subject or scene on their camera and see it as two-dimensional. However, while a photographic image is indeed a bite-size, two-dimensional representation of a three-dimensional selection of reality, everything about image capture happens in three-dimensional space. This includes the angle you shoot from, where you stand in relation to your subject, the height of the camera, the focal length choices you make, the effects of the light, focus, depth of field, and any other decisions you might make.

It is therefore critical to keep this concept in mind: a photograph may be two-dimensional, but what you are photographing is almost always three-dimensional. This is extremely important when it comes to learning about focus and producing the best images possible.

Light & Lenses

The manner in which radiated light travels through a camera lens is determined by its wavelength. As light hits the front element of a lens, it enters a denser material (usually glass), which causes the light to slow down and bend inward. As the light exits the lens elements it is bent again; this bending of the light is called refraction.

The problem that lens designers face is that the longer the wavelength, the less refraction takes place, so the red end of the spectrum bends less than the blue end. Therefore, the wavelengths passing through a lens will not converge at the same point of focus. This causes the colors to produce images that do not line up exactly on top of each other. This is known as chromatic distortion or chromatic aberration, which leads to color fringing along the edges of elements within the image, and an overall loss of sharpness.

Lenses therefore need to be designed to compensate for this, so that all wavelengths are bought to focus at a single point. This is largely achieved through the use of multiple lens elements, corrective curvatures, and multiple coatings. However, the problem can still persist with certain types of lens (particularly zooms), requiring correction with image-editing software.

Why We See the Colors We See

The objects we see around us reflect and absorb different parts of the visible spectrum, and it is this that gives them their color.

Put simply, a red object appears red to our eyes because the surface of the object absorbs green and blue wavelengths from the visible spectrum and reflects the red wavelengths. Likewise, a green object absorbs the red and the blue wavelengths and reflects the green wavelengths.

However, it isn't always a single primary color that is reflected back—multiple reflected colors can combine to create a new hue. A cyan object absorbs the red wavelengths from the white light source and reflects the green and blue wavelengths, for example, while a yellow object absorbs the blue wavelengths and reflects red and green.

Of course, we also have a couple of absolutes: white objects reflect all wavelengths equally, while black objects absorb them completely.

Even more hues can be created by subtle variations in the object's absorption and reflection of the various wavelengths. Indeed, in the real world, most of the colors we see are not pure color. That is because the surfaces of real objects have different characteristics for absorption and reflection.

A red apple, for example, might reflect mostly red, but could also reflect a portion of the green and perhaps a smidgen of blue to produce a particular reddish coloration. Likewise, a green leaf reflects mostly green, but may also reflect a bit of red and some blue. Any wavelengths that are not reflected are absorbed.

ABSORPTION AND REFLECTION

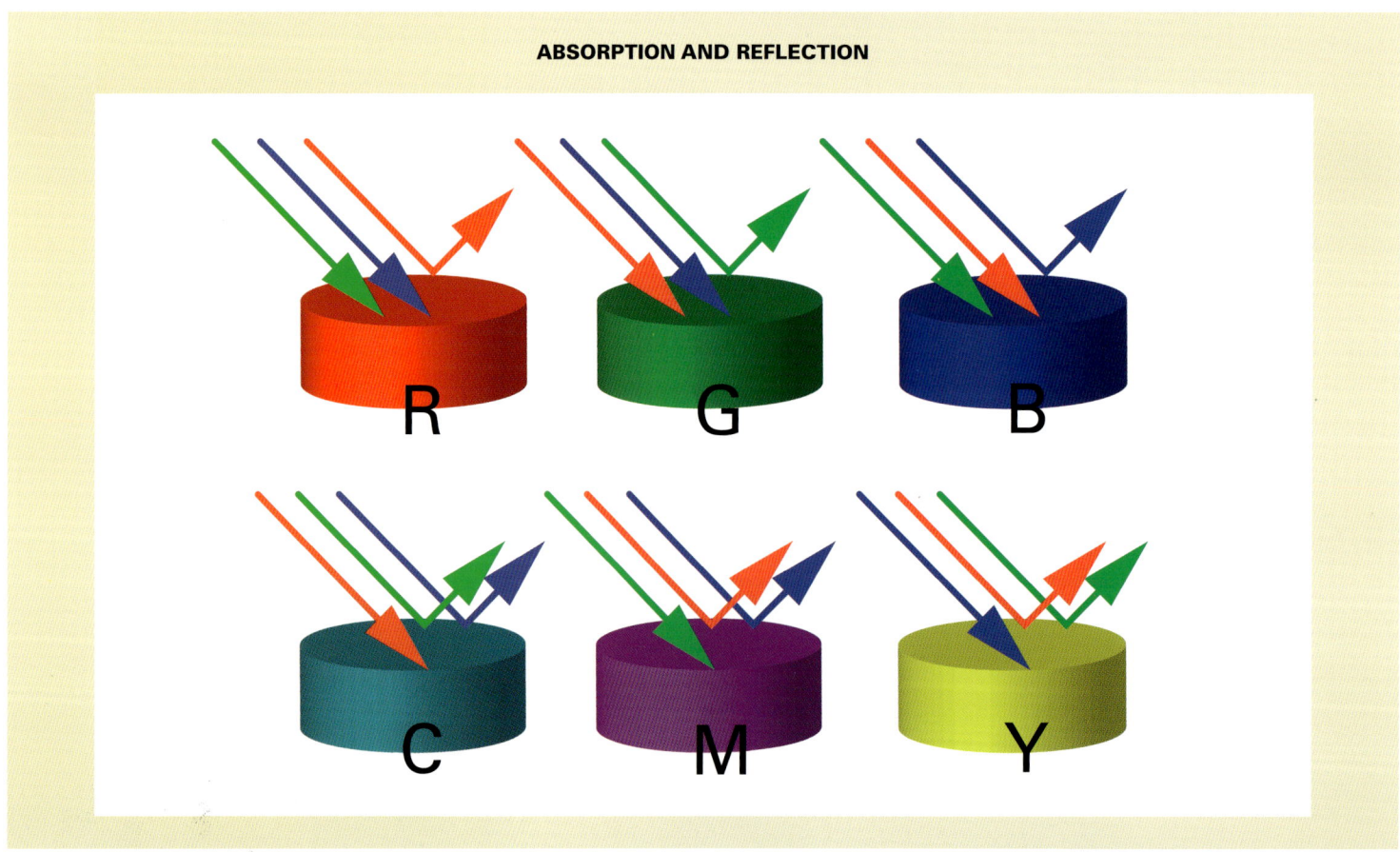

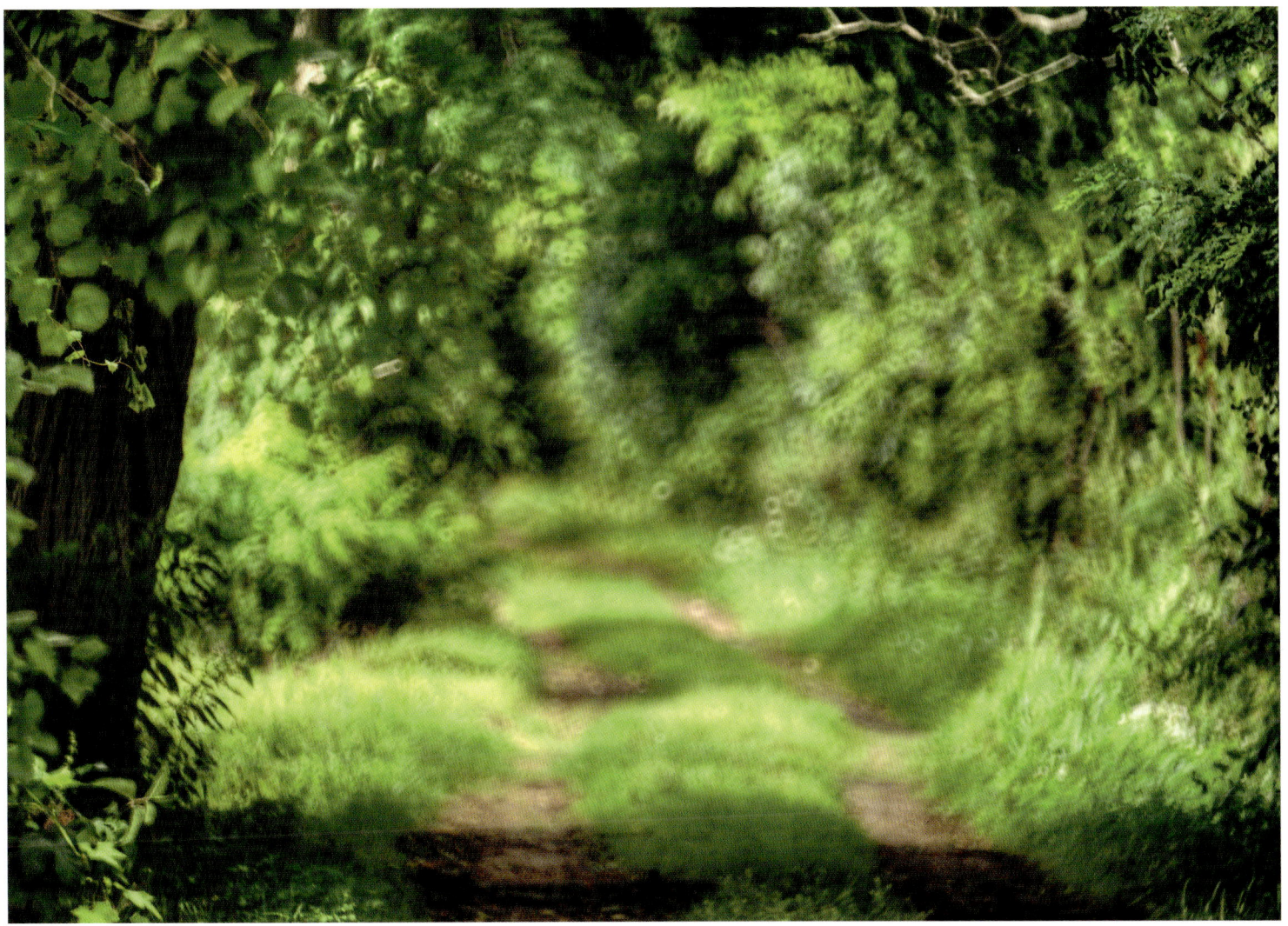

LEFT: *As explained in the text, the particular hues we perceive are the result of other wavelengths being absorbed by the surface of the reflected object.*

ABOVE: *The green in this image is a result of green wavelengths being reflected by the subject, as well as smaller portions of red and yellow. The colors in any image are determined by the wavelengths of light that are reflected and absorbed by the surface they are falling on.*

How Optical Systems Work

The simplest way to produce an image is with a pinhole. A pinhole in a box can be used to project an image of outside subjects onto the opposite interior surface.

A Pinhole & Light

Pinholes form images based on the simple law that light travels in straight lines until acted upon by another surface.

In the diagram below right, you can see how the subject reflects light back toward the camera in straight lines. Each ray of light that passes through the pinhole ends up projected upside down and reversed right and left on the opposite interior surface of the box, forming an image that represents the subject's color and brightness.

When we place a light-sensitive receiver (such as photographic film or a digital sensor) at the back of the box, the different colors and brightness values can be recorded, creating a photograph.

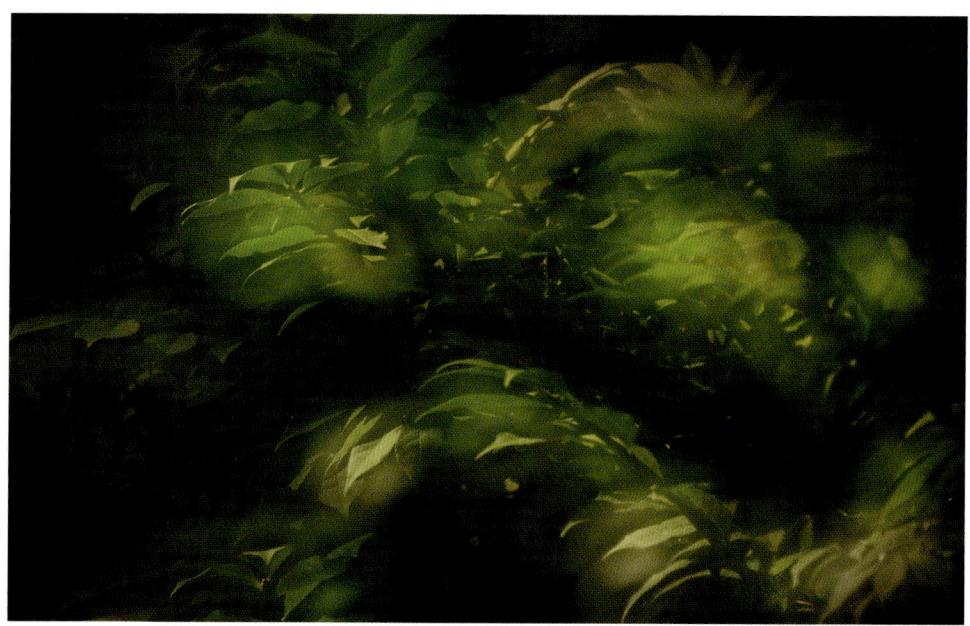

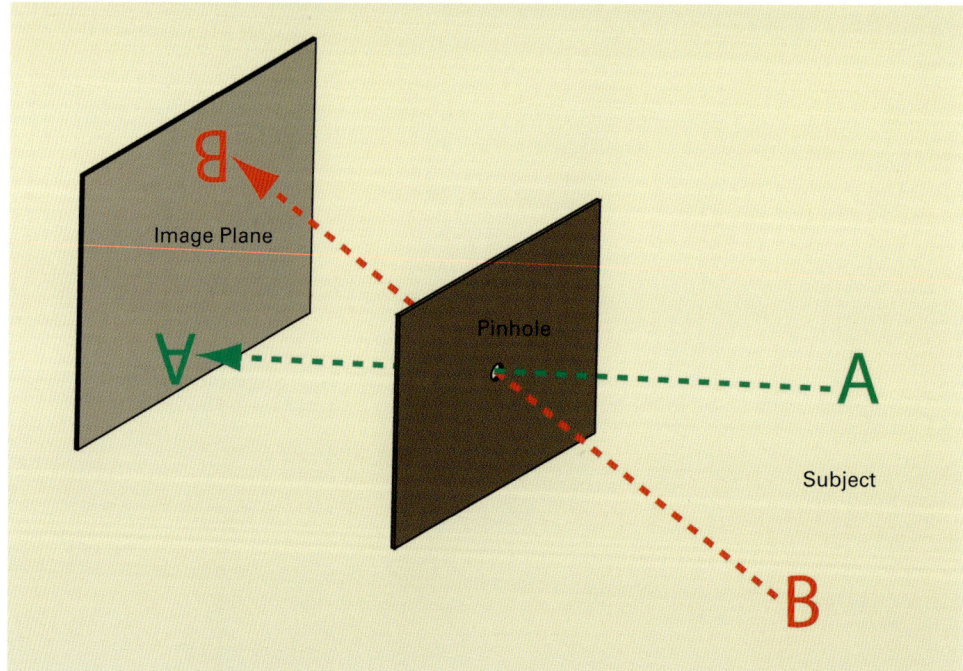

RIGHT: *Light from different parts of the scene travel in straight lines and strikes the sensor/film, forming an image that is produced from the variation in subject brightness.*

ABOVE RIGHT: *A pinhole is quite capable of producing an image. The photo was shot using a custom-made medium-format film camera with a precision pinhole as a "lens."*

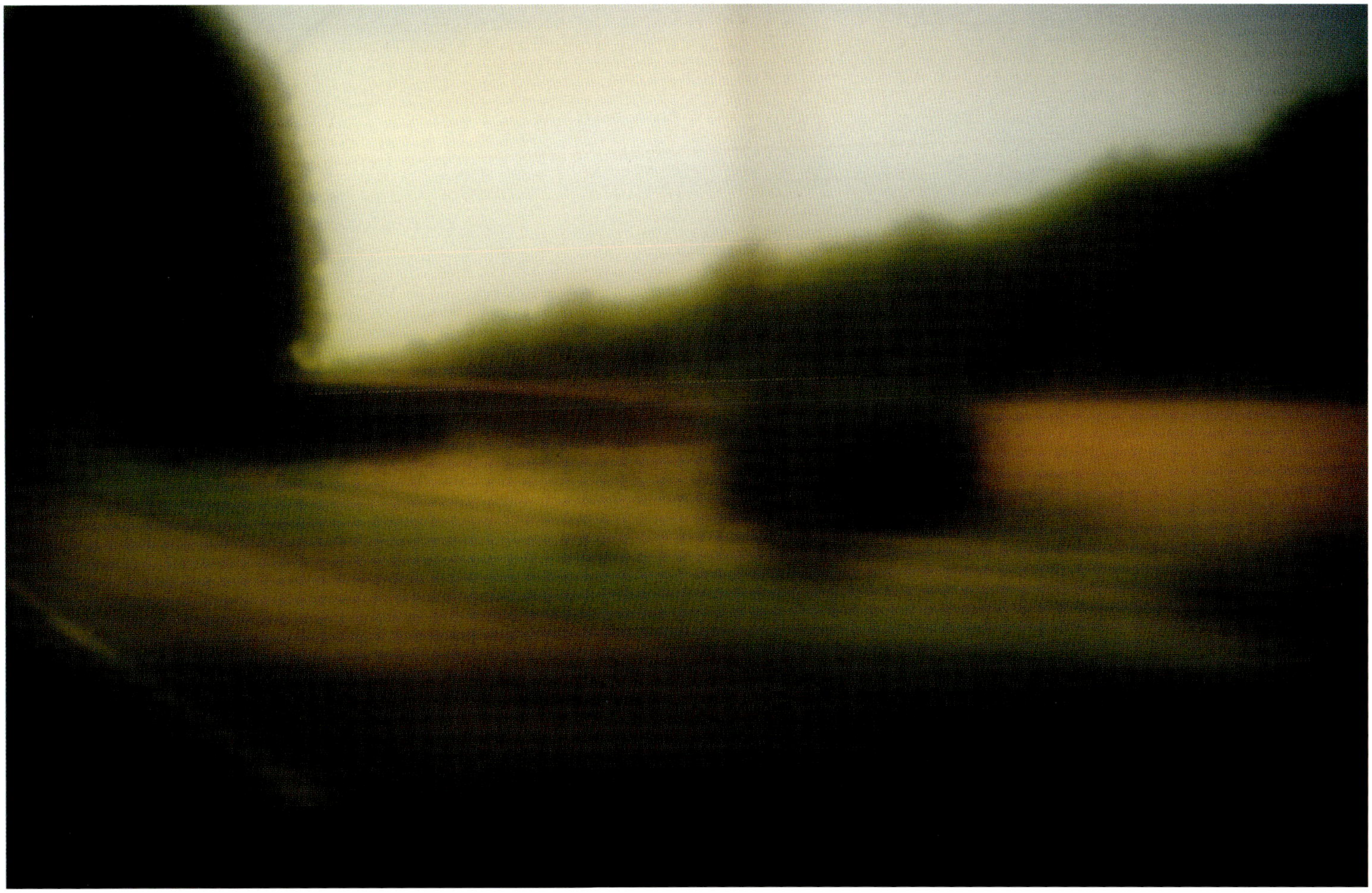

01 // HOW OPTICAL SYSTEMS WORK // LIGHT

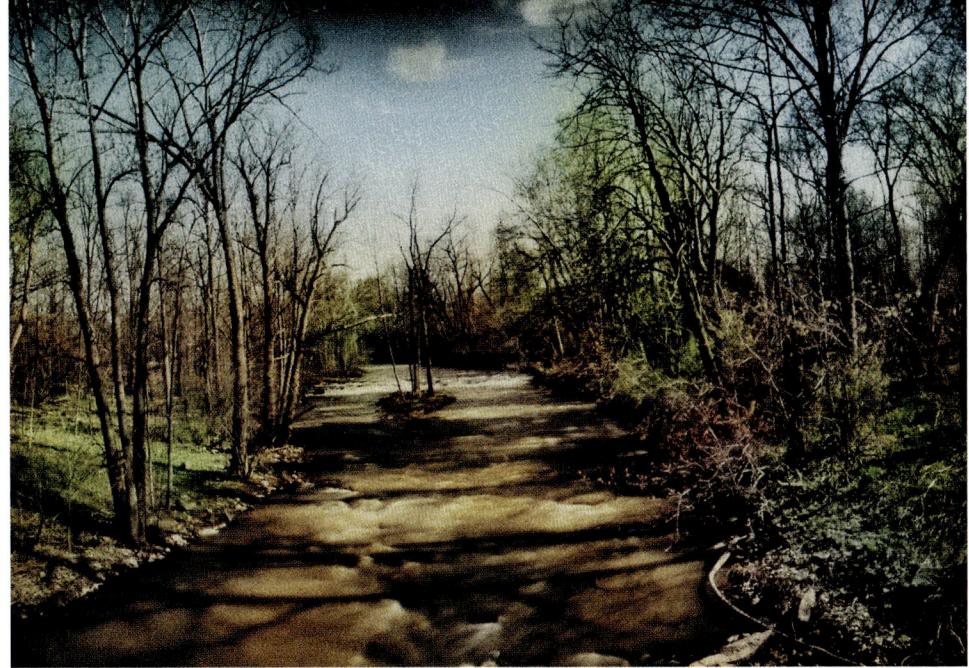

ABOVE: *Pinhole images produce some very soft renditions, which in color can start to feel like paintings. This image was taken while driving along a roadway.*

LEFT: *This image was shot with a Zone Sieve, which is similar to a Zone Plate, but made from multiple holes arranged in concentric circles. They are both considered pinhole techniques. However, unlike a pinhole, they focus a portion of the light to a focus point in a similar manner as a lens.*

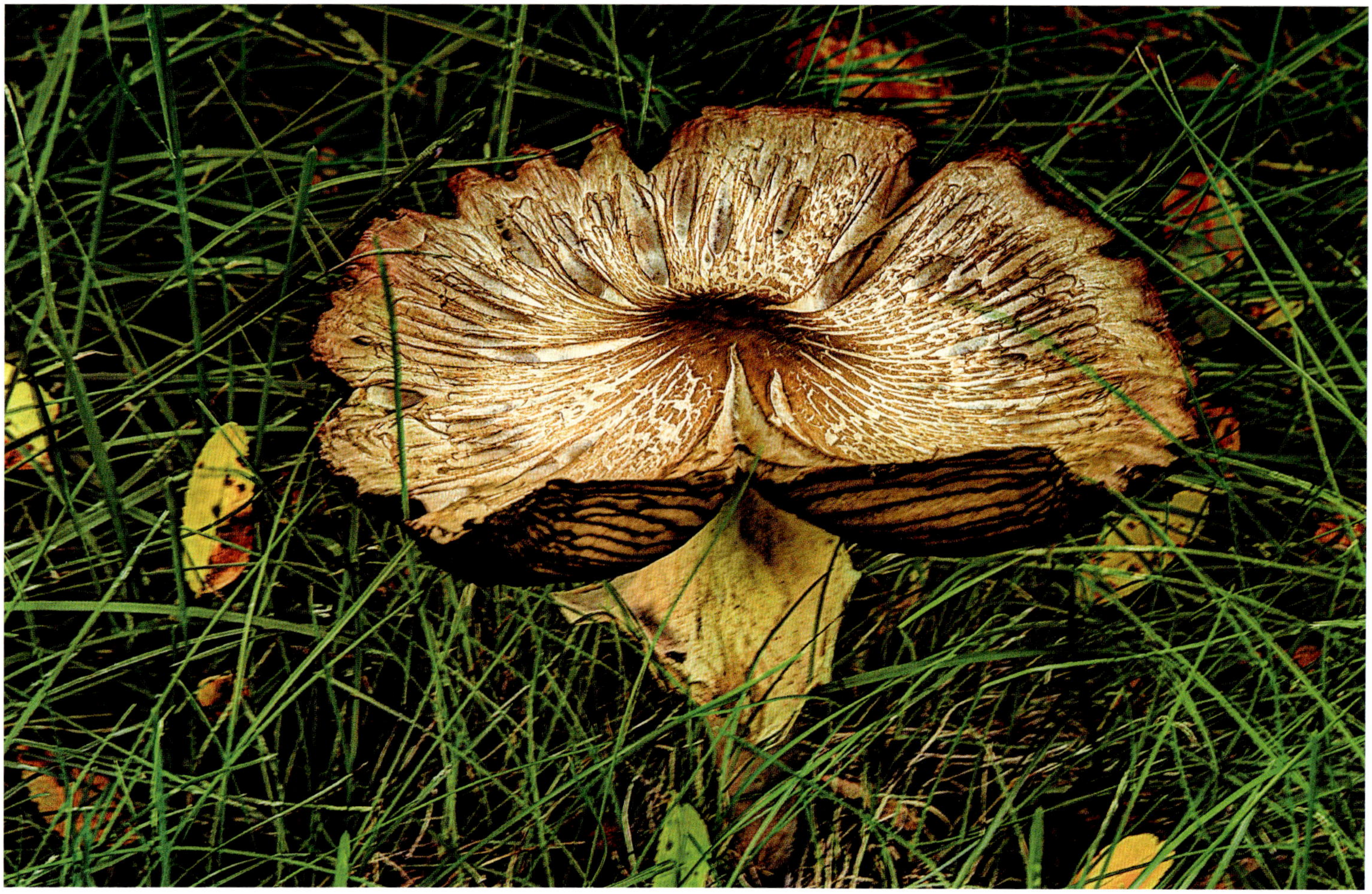

How a Lens Sees

The main difference between a pinhole and a lens is that a lens captures more of the rays of light radiating from the subject and focuses them to render an image; a pinhole simply projects the light directly.

Controlling the flow of light through a lens is the aperture, which is an opening that can (usually) be varied in size to allow more or less light to reach the sensor. The more light allowed through in a given time, the faster the lens exposes the sensor to light. I like to compare the aperture to a window shade: wide open it will allow a large quantity or volume of light to pass through, while if it is opened only partway, less light will pass through.

As well as allowing you to control how much light is transmitted, a lens is also designed to focus that light. In the simplest

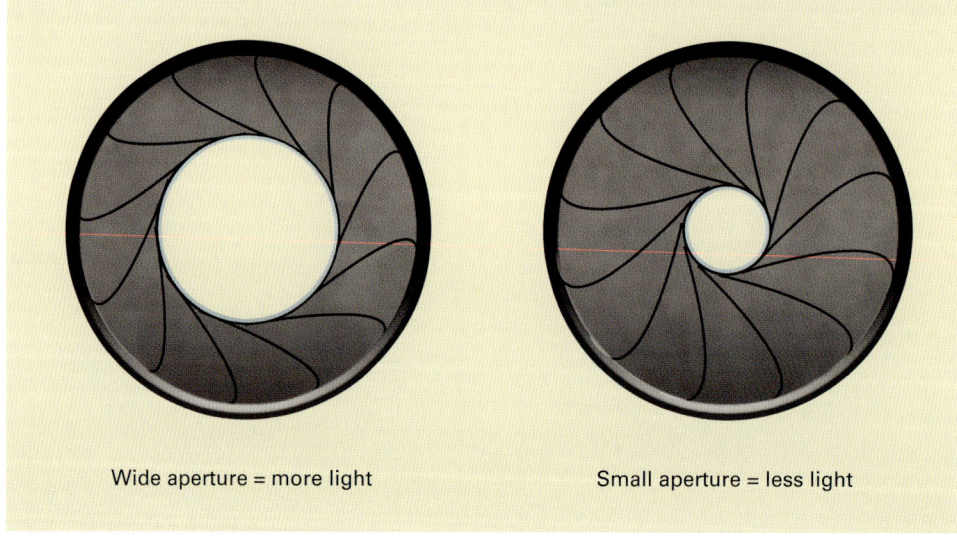

TOP: *The aperture mechanism's primary purpose of regulating light intake has numerous knock-on effects in the final state of the image.*

sense, this means that a lens focuses all of the light corresponding to a single plane in the scene onto the focus plane. A focusing mechanism in the lens will allow you to set the point of focus either automatically and/or manually.

RIGHT: *When passing through a lens, colors are separated by variations in their wavelength. As a result, they will not focus at the same point on the focal plane (the film or sensor) unless the lens is designed to reduce this effect.*

BELOW: *Close-up images like this are quite tricky—they often require more light (i.e., wider aperture), but they also need greater depth of field (i.e., narrow aperture). It's up to you to know when and how to strike the right balance.*

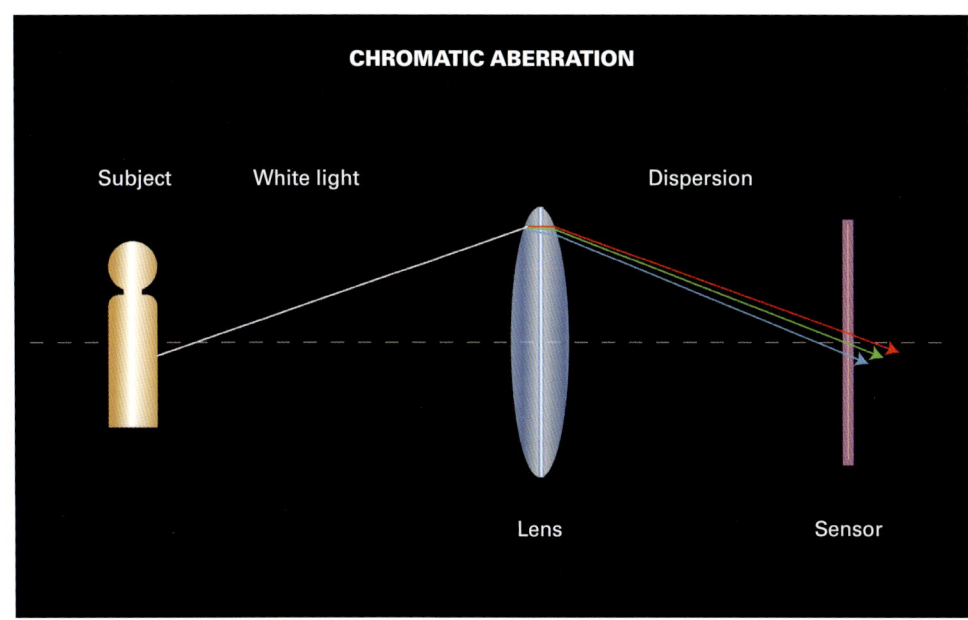

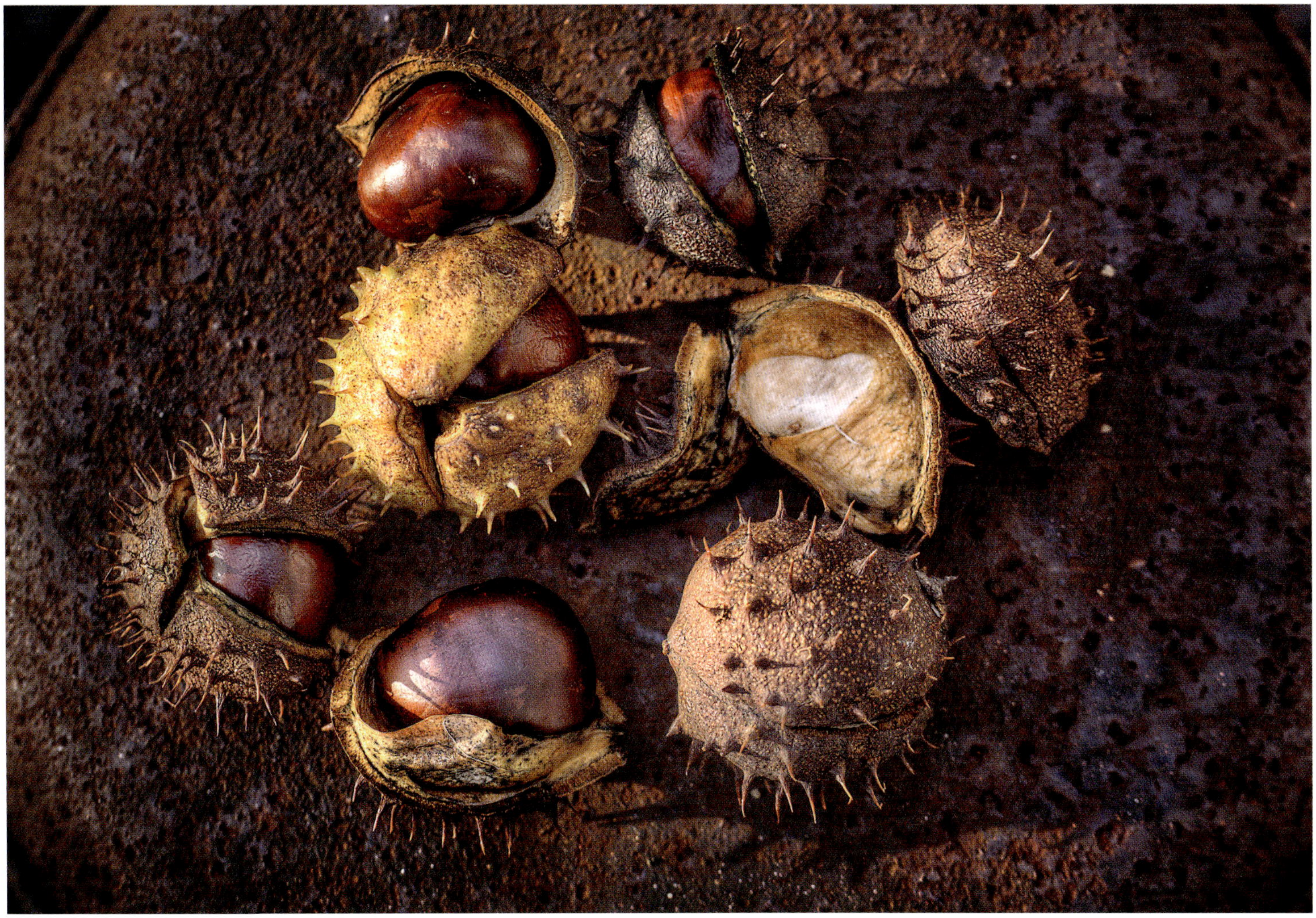

Human Vision

The human eye sees only a single point in space as "sharp"—everything else is in the periphery of that point. If we look at an object or a subject (such as the type on this page), our eyes see only a single letter or word in absolute sharpness. This allows us to scan through the rest of the sentence to read it, rather than seeing everything in equal sharpness (it would be pretty difficult to read this text if we saw everything in equal sharpness). The other words are still seen, but not as sharply.

Likewise, the eye scans elements within view when we look at a broader scene. We take in the whole scene through our peripheral vision, but sharpness is limited to the center of the view. In this way, we can concentrate (focus) on the area of most importance or interest within a scene.

The eye can also focus on things at different distances, so subjects in front and behind the point of interest will fall out of our sharp view. We could say that the eye is very focused on single points in space.

To see details sharply, the eye needs to scan a scene, and this is what happens when we look at a photograph. The eye is pulled through an image by the details, color, tones, lighting, and focus it contains, effectively leading us to the subject.

ABOVE RIGHT: *The structure of the human eye concentrates the sharpest portion of vision within the center of the view. The surrounding view produces a relative sharpness—a kind of panorama that we call the peripheral view. To see things sharply, we rely on shifting our point of view or rolling our eyes such that the sharpness falls onto the fovea, which contains the highest concentration of light-sensitive cones.*

RIGHT: *The size of the pupil in the iris determines the amount of depth that the eye can see at a given distance. The pupil opens or closes with the amount of light available.*

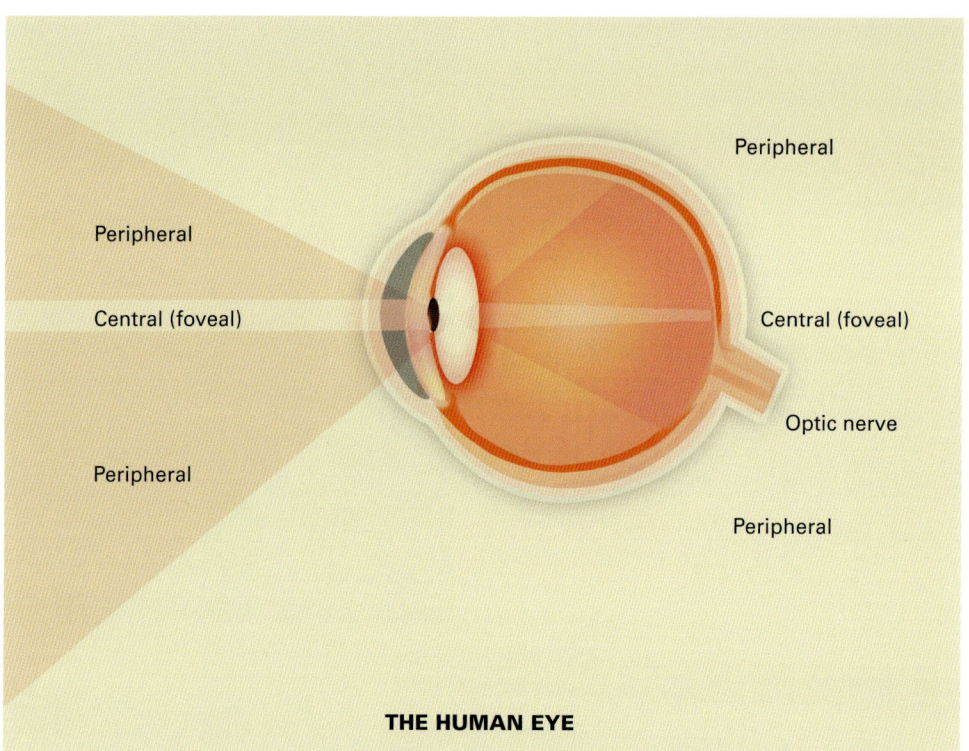

THE HUMAN EYE

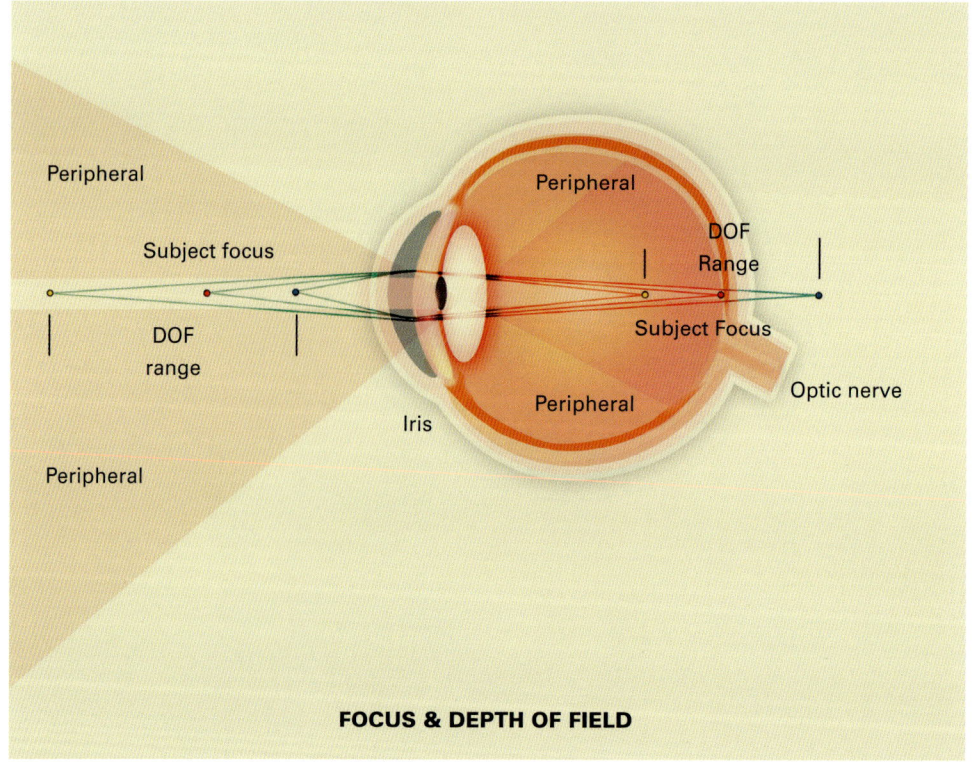

FOCUS & DEPTH OF FIELD

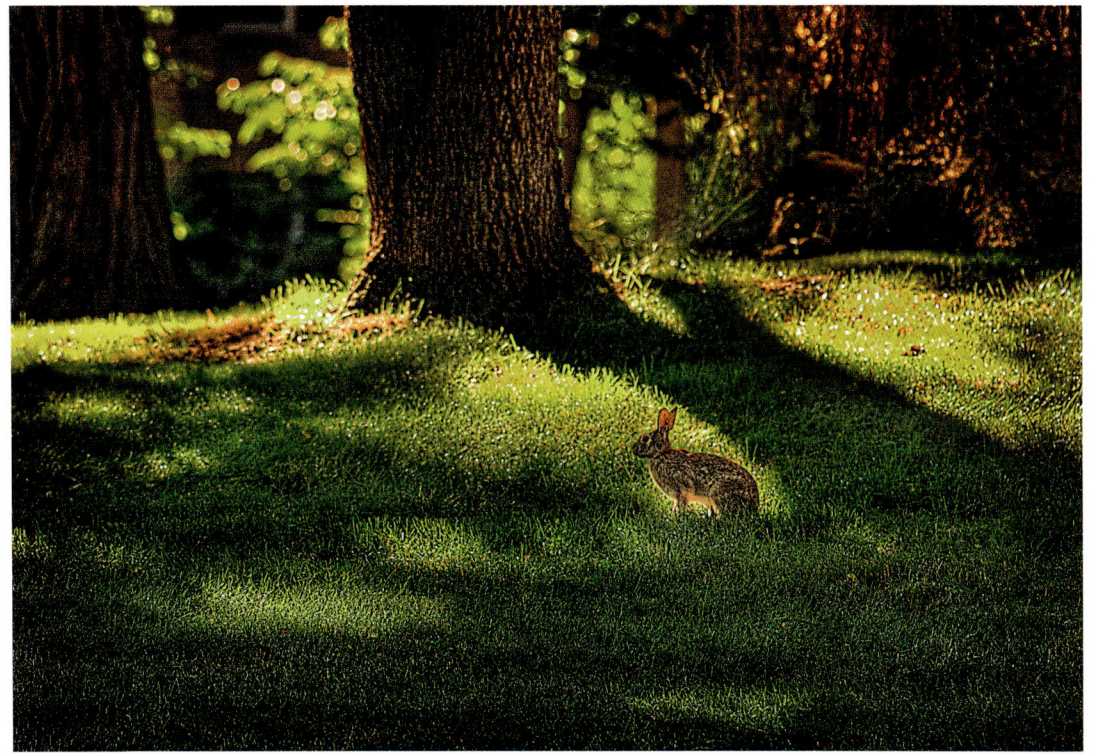

"Photography is about finding out what can happen in the frame. When you put four edges around some facts, you change those facts."

—GARRY WINOGRAND

ABOVE LEFT: *Aperture is useful for separating the main subject from the background. The human eye is attracted to the sharpest object in the image scene.*

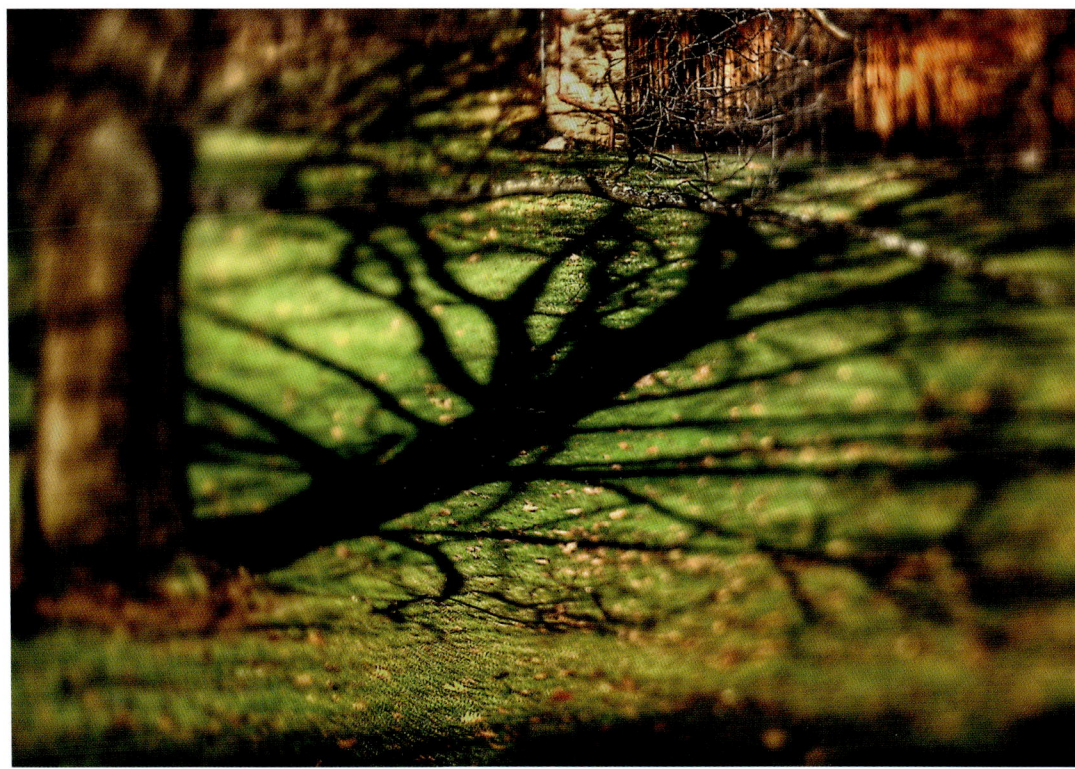

LEFT: *While most photographers try to create sharpness throughout their images, the eye actually doesn't see in the same way. This image mimics the way we see the world. Even when an image is sharply defined, we view it by scanning across the page.*

Focus is Relative

With most imaging technology, there is only one plane of sharp focus in a photograph, and that focus plane is generally parallel to the camera sensor. Everything else is in "relative sharpness" to the plane.

The photographer usually (but not always!) attempts to focus the lens on the subject of the photograph. Wherever in the scene the subject might be, the rest of the image in front of and beyond that point will be out of focus. Or, more specifically, it will be in focus only to a relative degree. This has to do with how a lens functions as a collector of light.

A general rule that most photographers use states that depth of field (the zone of "acceptable sharpness") extends a distance of approximately 1/3 in front and 2/3 beyond the point of focus. The extent of this acceptable sharpness is determined by several factors, including the aperture used.

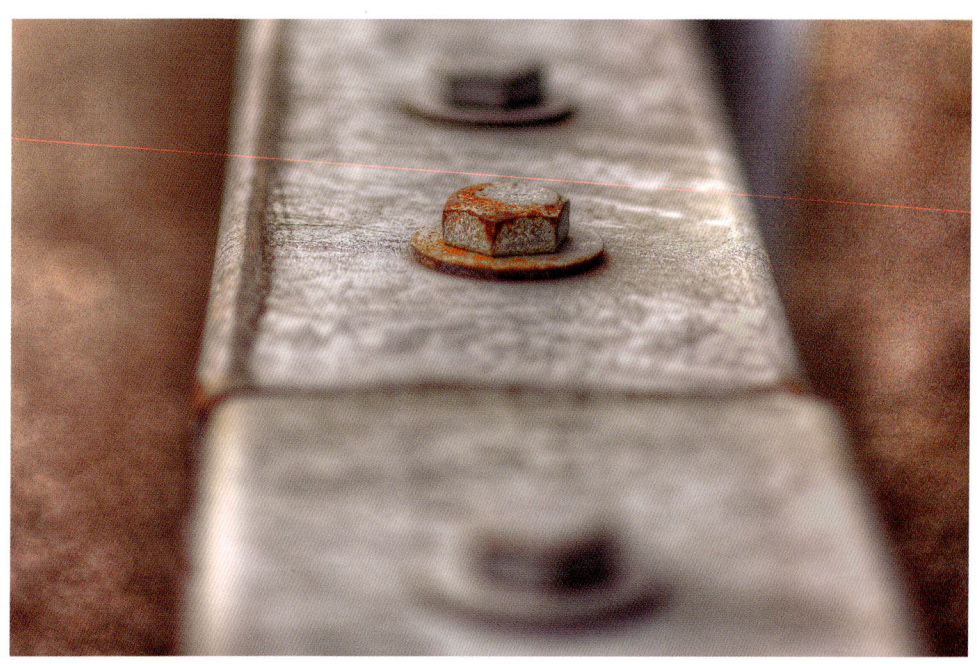

ABOVE: *The bolt shown in the foreground is less sharp that the one in the distance. The exact focus is on the center bolt.*

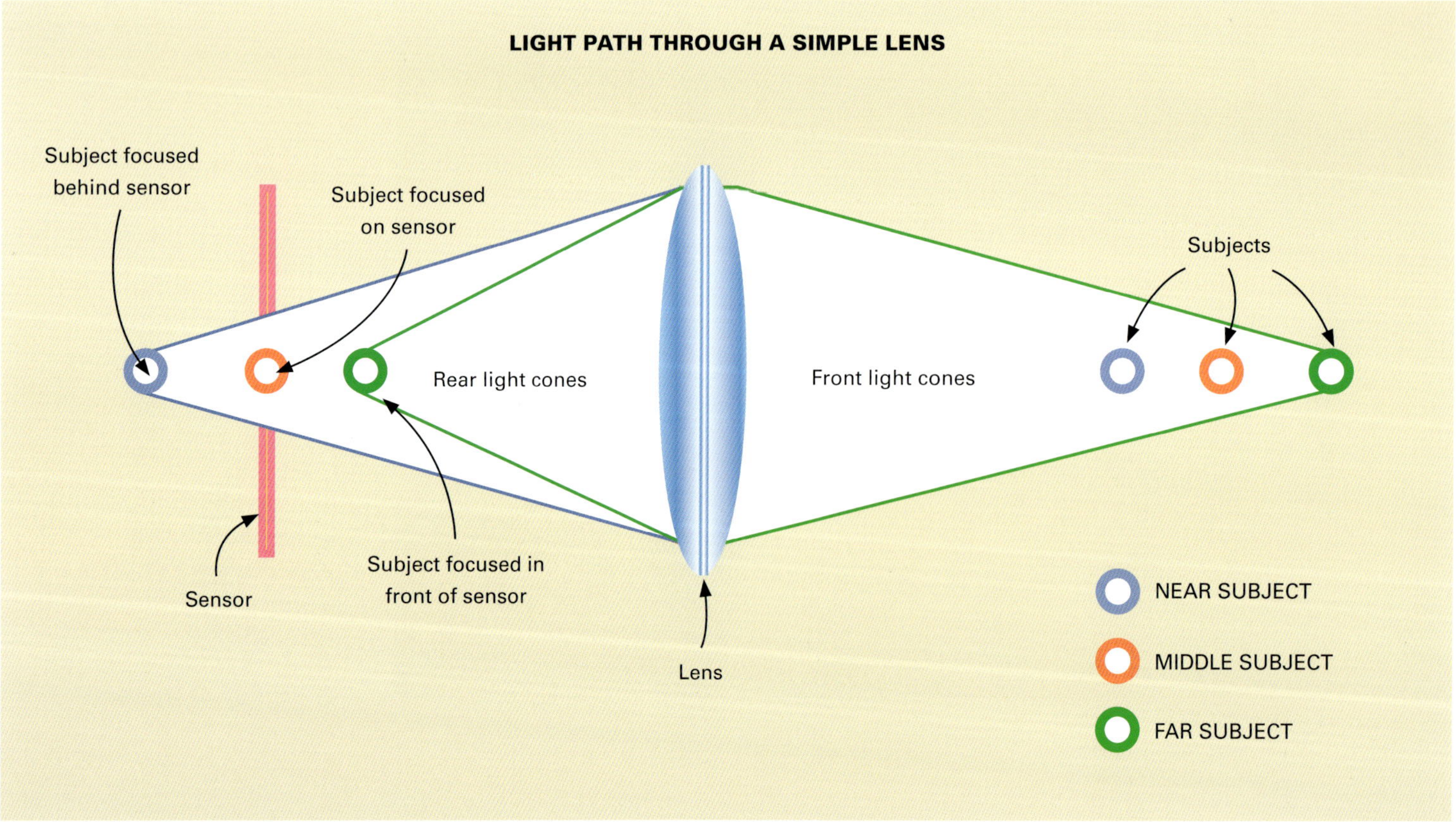

The Image Circle

All photographic lenses produce an image circle, which is a cone-shaped projection of all of the light points in the scene that travel through the lens. If you take a lens off a camera and hold it up to a white surface, you can see that the image is projected over a fairly large circular area: in most cases, the image circle is much larger than the area recorded by the sensor.

The image circle formed by a given lens is not the same as a focus cone. Rather, it is the collection of all the focus cones gathered and projected by the lens.

Image circles are much larger on longer focal length lenses than they are on short focal length lenses, although the image circle on most lenses is the same in terms of image perspective.

The main difference between any two focal lengths is the relative size of their image circles: longer lenses project their circles over a larger area. In the case of a telephoto lens, for example, the sensor captures only a tiny portion of the lens' much larger projection. A wide-angle lens has a much smaller image circle, and therefore most of the image circle is within the capture area of the sensor.

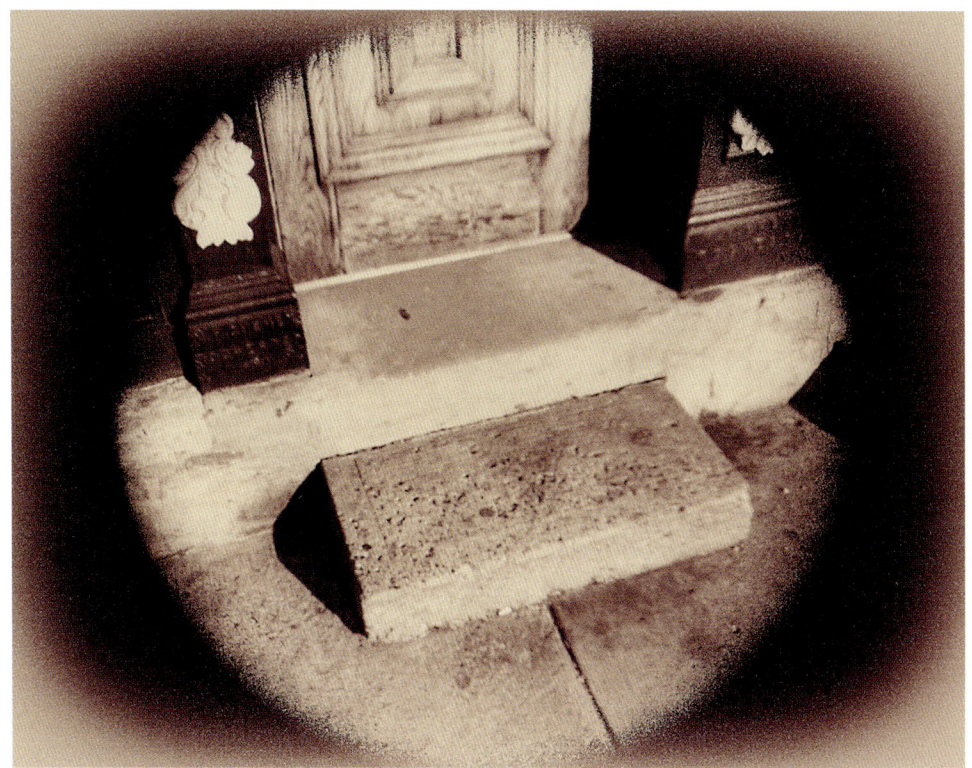

ABOVE: *All photographic lenses create image circles, which are upside down and backward when viewed from inside the camera.*

BELOW: *An old 16mm movie lens mounted to a Micro Four Thirds camera creates an image circle that is in part blocked by the barrel of the lens. This is because the lens was meant to cover a film frame that is much smaller than the camera's sensor.*

LEFT: *This illustration shows the cones created for subjects at different distances from the lens. In this example, the red circle (a middle-distance subject) is focused on the sensor plane; subjects nearer to and farther from the lens fall behind and in front of the sensor respectively.*

Collecting Light

The main purpose of a lens is to gather the light rays from any and all points within the frame of the photograph. If we think of the lens as a capture device, it will be easier to understand how it works.

Everything visible in front of the camera is either reflecting light, transmitting light, or is a light source. In most photographs, the light is generally reflected from objects, although in some cases we will also have actual light sources, such as lights in a room, vehicle lights, or the sun. In each instance, the light is usually reflecting or projecting in all directions, which causes it to disperse.

A pinhole or a lens can capture only those rays that pass through their openings. I like to use the analogy of a bucket set out in a rainstorm. The bucket acts to catch water, but is able to catch only those raindrops that happen to fall directly into it. The rest falls elsewhere and is not captured, no matter how heavy the rainfall is.

In the case of a pinhole, we are allowing

BELOW: *Each point in this scene projects light in all directions, some of which hits the camera's lens. The light falls on the lens as a projection of those light rays, which we refer to as a cone of light. As the light travels through the lens it is refracted and forms another light cone on the rear side of the lens.*

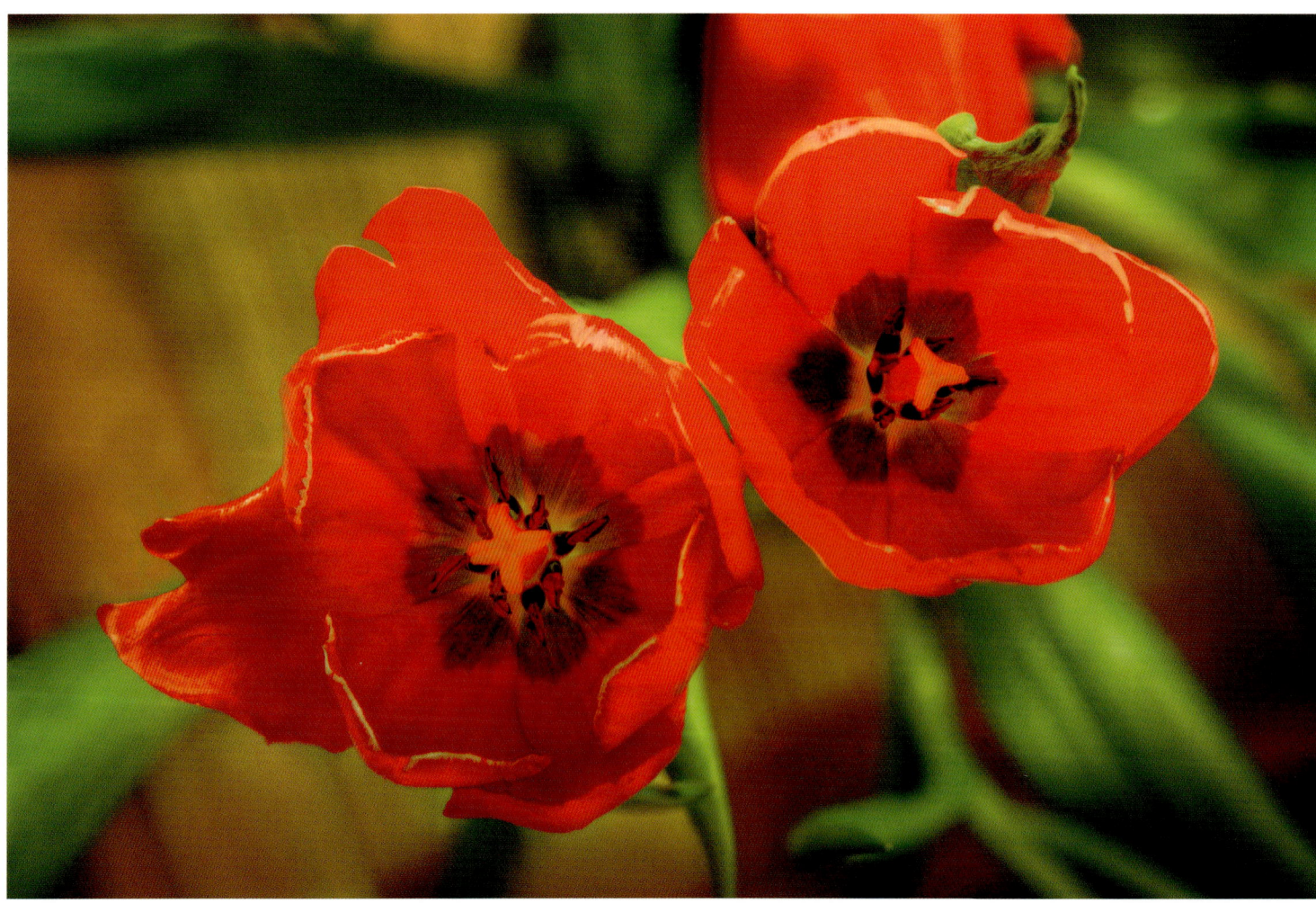

01 // COLLECTING LIGHT // LIGHT

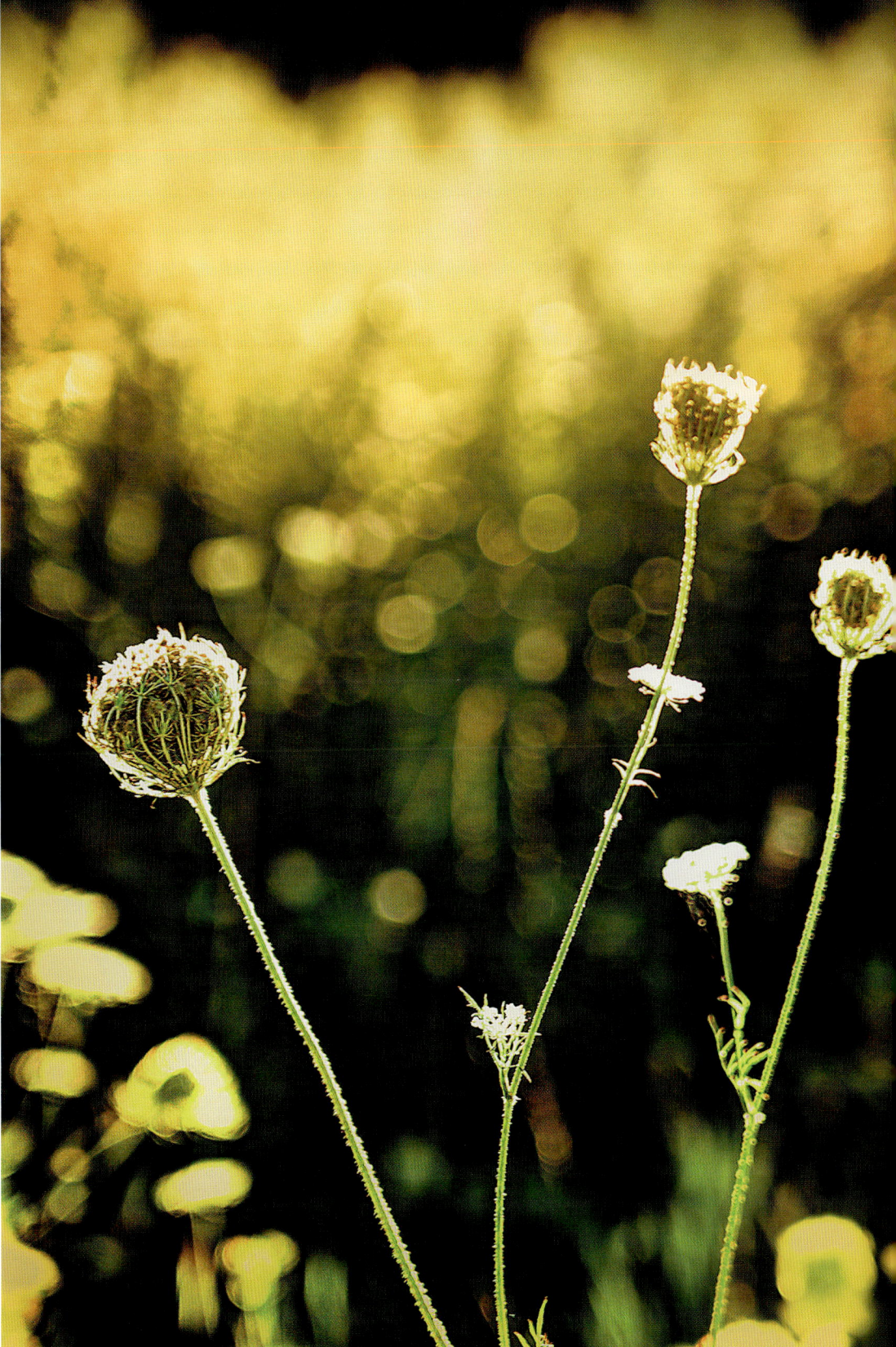

only a fraction of the light to enter the camera and expose our sensor. In simple terms, we are capturing only a few rays of light from each subject object.

A lens, however, takes all of the rays from a single point in the scene and refocuses them back to a point inside the camera. The rays that are captured form a cone of radiated light on either side of the lens. You might think of it as being like holding a bunch of uncooked spaghetti: if you hold it at one end, it fans out. Imagine this as the type of radiation that is happening at every point in the scene you are photographing.

With a camera lens, the finest focus is at the intersection of the cones, or what we call the "focal point," with everything else within the cones being out-of-focus light.

RIGHT: *A thin plane of focus is what separates the foreground plants from the background of out-of-focus details.*

Aberrations

Although modern lenses are designed to deliver the best possible results, certain compromises often need to be made. These compromises can lead to certain artifacts that can detract from (or sometimes enhance) an image.

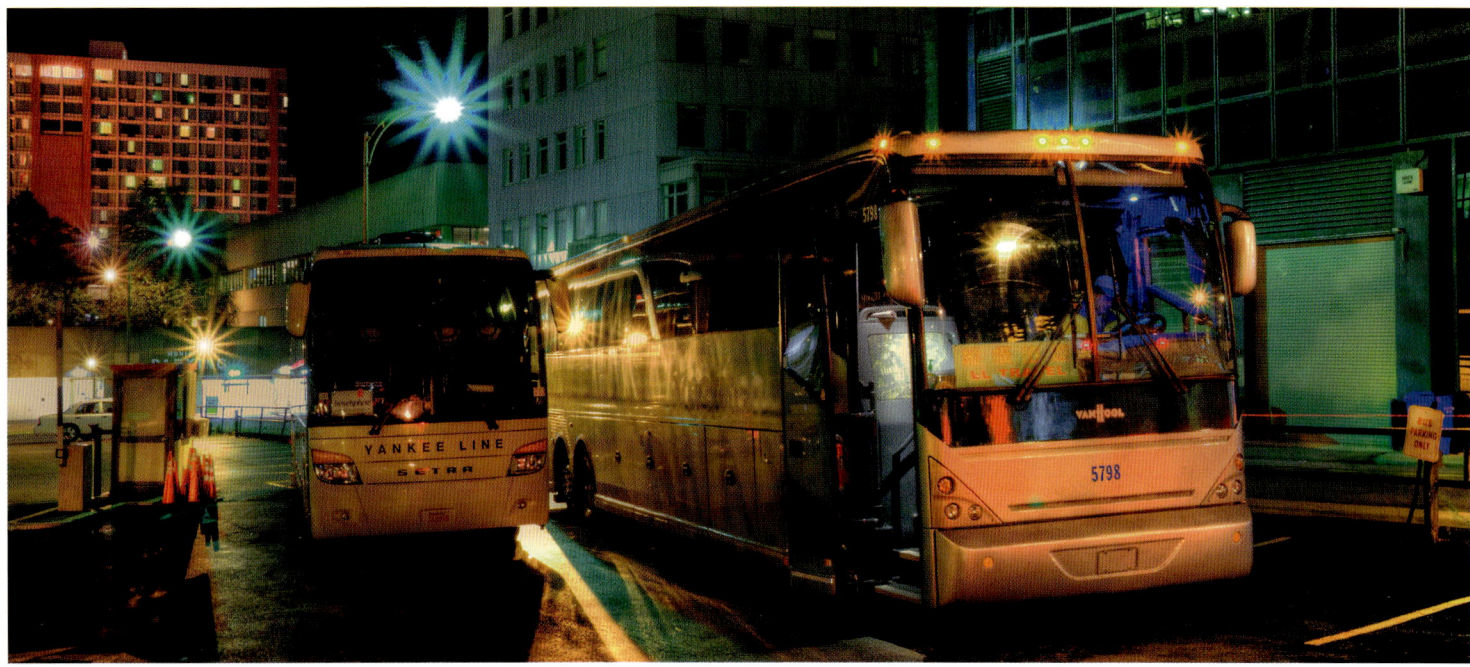

Lens Flare

In the past, it was commonly advised not to shoot into the sun. Instead, the received wisdom was that you should have the sun over your shoulder, which meant having it behind you.

One of the main reasons for this advice was to avoid lens flare, which can potentially be caused by any direct light source falling on the front of the lens.

Lens flare is normally an unwanted effect that can cause a number of irregularities to appear in a photograph. It is caused by diffraction—the reflection and scattering of non-image-forming light as it strikes the various elements in the lens.

Direct sunlight is one of the most common sources of lens flare. As the light enters the surface of the glass, it bends inward, reflecting and dispersing in many directions. Acting as a secondary exposure to the sensor, it reduces contrast and produces unwanted artifacts. The effect is compounded by a dirty lens, scratches, and not using a lens shade.

Slight movements away from the source can make a huge difference in whether the light will cause flare. Even better, it is always a good idea to use a proper lens hood, or at least to shade the front of the lens from extraneous light—I often use my hand as a light shade, making sure not to hold it in the camera view.

However, there are many times when lens flare can be used for creative effect; it can be used deliberately to emphasize the angle of the light source, or to imply motion. It can also emphasize a shape, as

ABOVE: *I actually love the effects of certain types of star-shaped flare. Using a small aperture will exaggerate the effect.*

with a solar eclipse, or indicate a transparent surface, such as looking through the window of a car.

Shooting directly into the sun with a digital camera can produce a certain kind of artifact that appears as a group of small rainbows. This is the result of internal light being diffracted by the sensor. This kind of flare is not evident through the viewfinder of a DSLR, but can show up in the image.

Chromatic Aberration

Chromatic aberration is the result of a lens that cannot bring all wavelengths of light to focus at the same point (the sensor). This has the result of color fringing along the edges of objects.

Modern lenses are usually corrected for chromatic aberration, but this is not always possible: wide-angle lenses are more prone to this problem due to the increased angles in which the lens must travel through the lens, and zoom lenses suffer more than prime lenses, due to the multiple focal lengths in their design.

Chromatic aberration can have an adverse affect on the outcome of focus, but can usually be corrected using an image-editing program.

Barrel Distortion

Many lenses exhibit an effect known as barrel distortion, where lines toward the edges of the frame appear to bow outward from the center, like the sides of a barrel (hence the name).

Barrel distortion is most noticeable when such things as straight lines of buildings or a flat horizon are close to the edges of the frame—with less rigid subjects, the effect may go unseen.

As a rule, wide-angle focal lengths are most likely to exhibit barrel distortion, and zoom lenses are more susceptible to this type of distortion than prime lenses. In the case of a fisheye lens, the image is almost entirely affected by severe barrel distortion, although this is what creates the lens' distinctive look.

Pincushion Distortion

Long telephoto lenses can produce pincushion distortion, which is the opposite effect to barrel distortion; in this instance, straight lines tend to bow inward toward the center of the image.

Most prime lenses are highly corrected for these effects, and many image-editing programs have the ability to straighten these anomalies when and if they occur. Some digital cameras also have the capability to correct certain lenses using algorithms within the camera's internal software.

BELOW: *Here you can see the effect of barrel distortion (highly exaggerated for effect).*

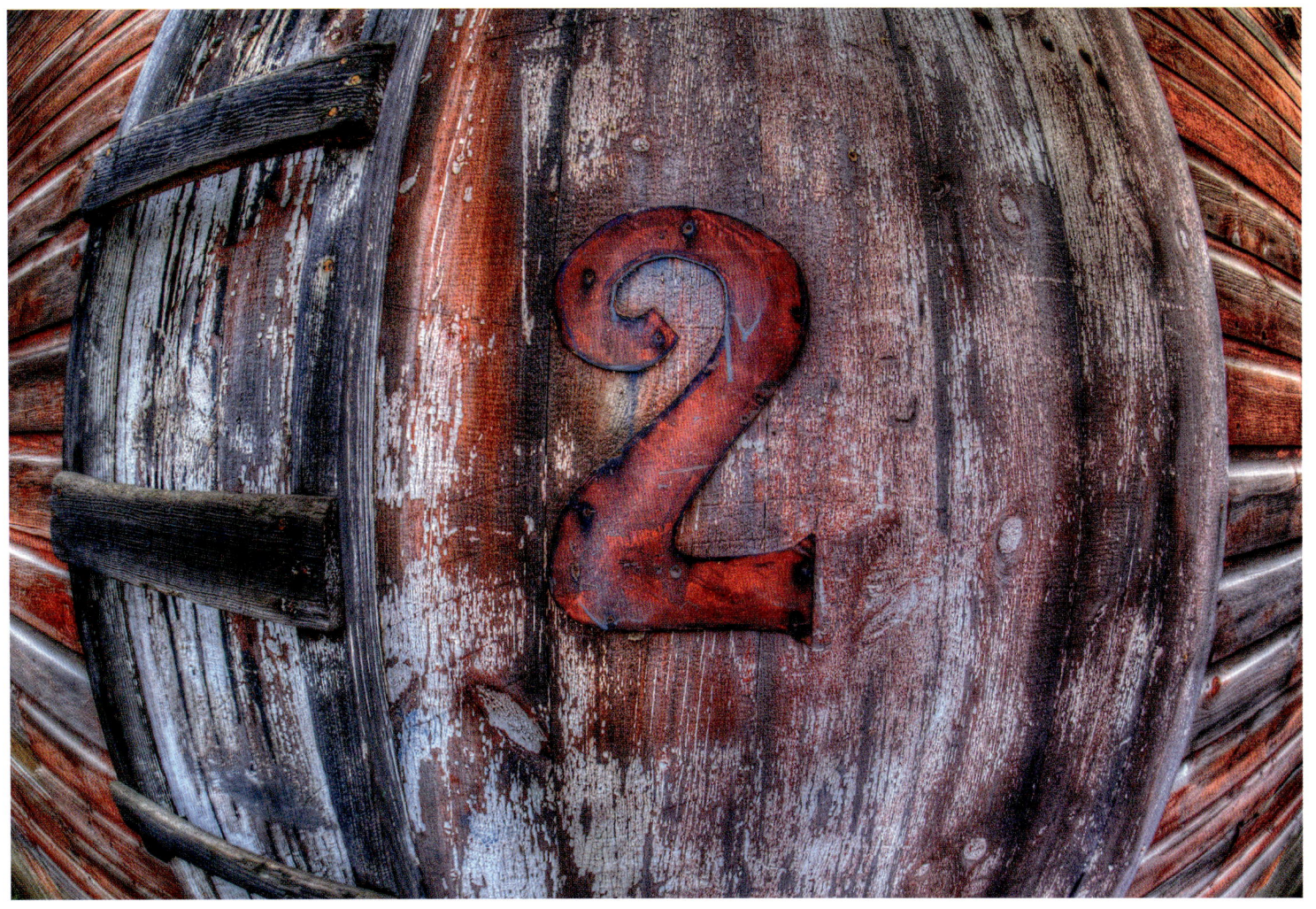

Circles of Confusion

Every point that falls on the plane of focus is light from the object radiating through the lens from exact points in the scene. However, the only part of the light cone that will be focused is the smallest point, at the tip of the cone—everything else falls into some degree of out of focus.

Any intersection of the cone through the plane of focus will appear as a circular area, which is what we refer to as a "circle of confusion." The size of a single circle of confusion depends on the point at which the cone intersects the plane of focus, with larger circles of confusion becoming what we refer to as "bokeh."

The aperture controls how circles of confusion appear in an image, and as the lens is closed down to smaller and smaller apertures, the circles of confusion become less and less visible. As we stop down the lens, we create a much thinner cone of out-of-focus light, which can cause the circles of confusion to become so small relative to the exact focus of the lens that they appear to the human eye as being sharp. This happens at greater increments in front of and behind the plane of focus as we stop down a lens.

BELOW: *Sharply focused rays fall on the image plane of the sensor while other focus points do not. The out-of-focus points are called "circles of confusion."*

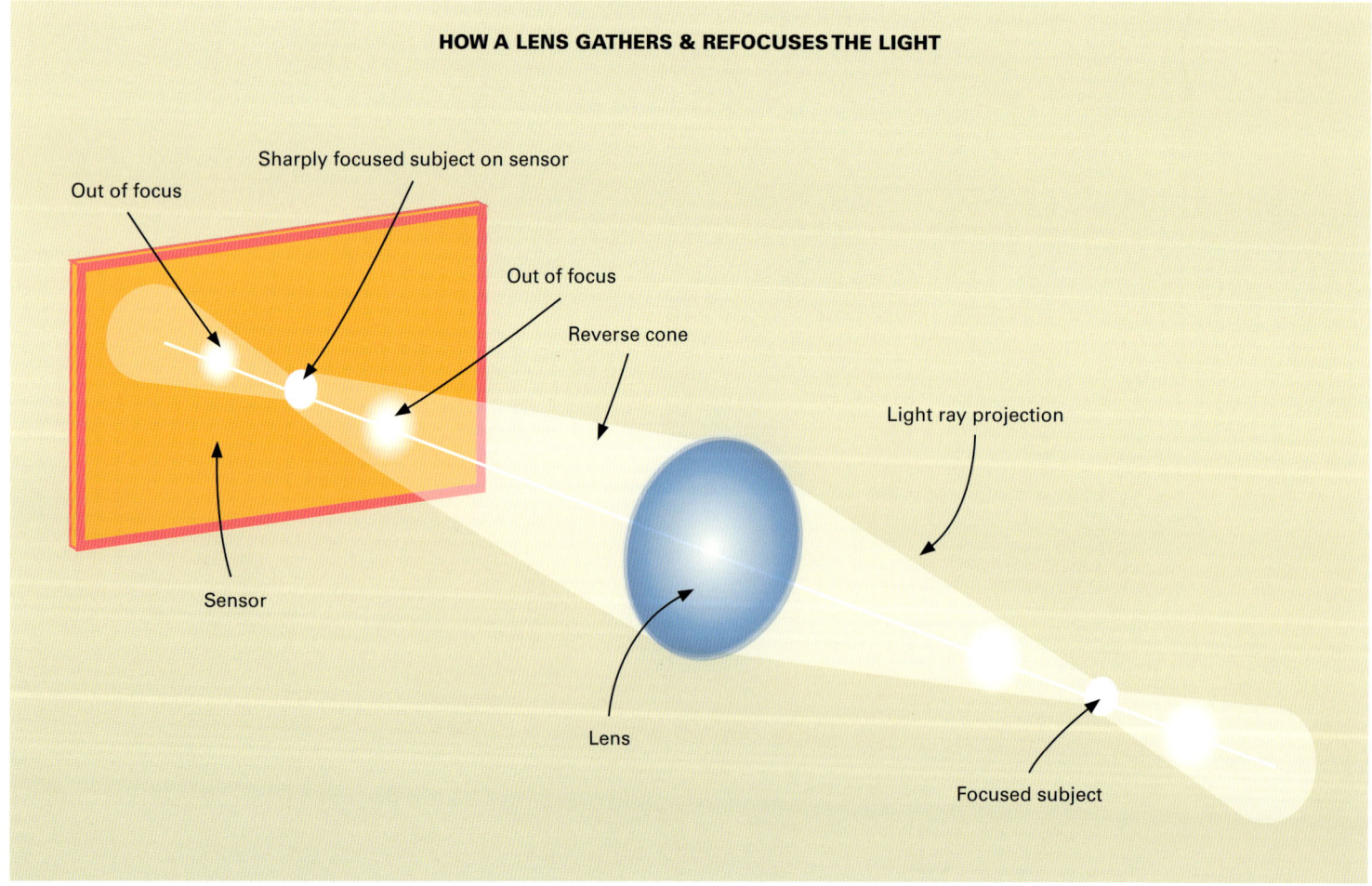

01 // CIRCLES OF CONFUSION // LIGHT

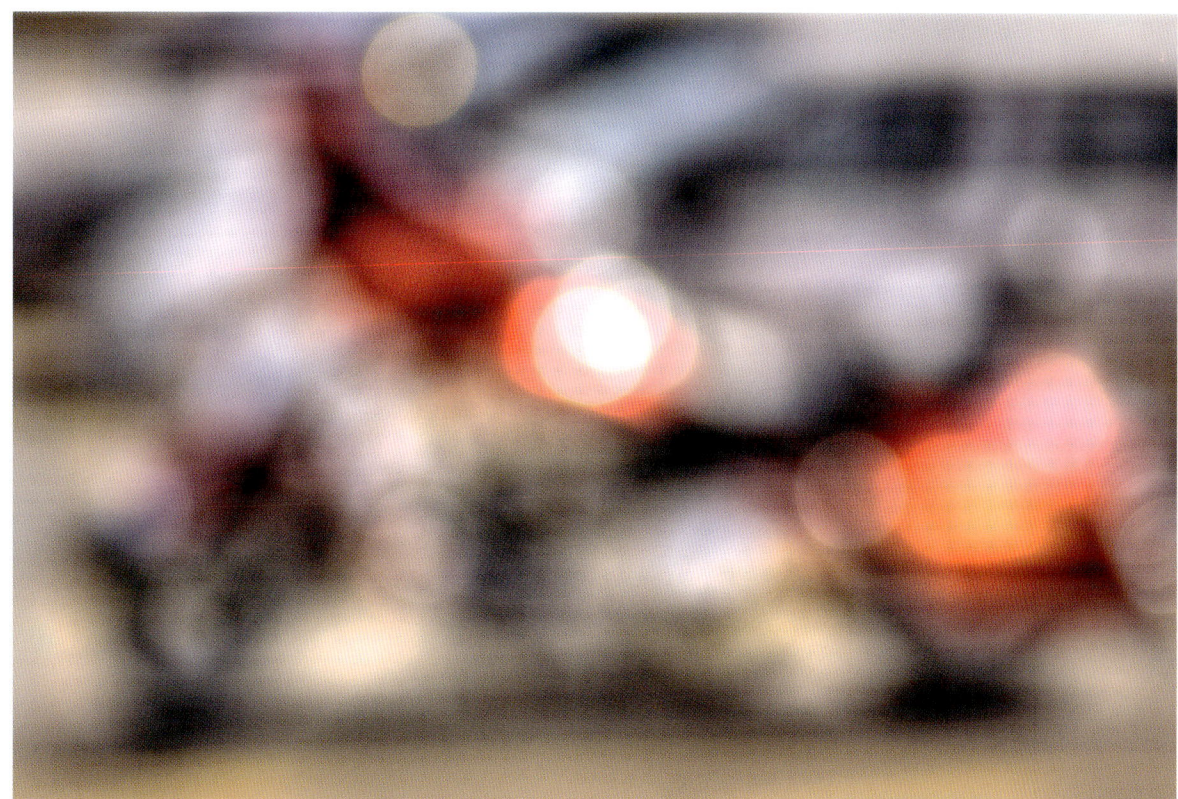

LEFT: *An image formed entirely by the out-of-focus portions of the light cones.*

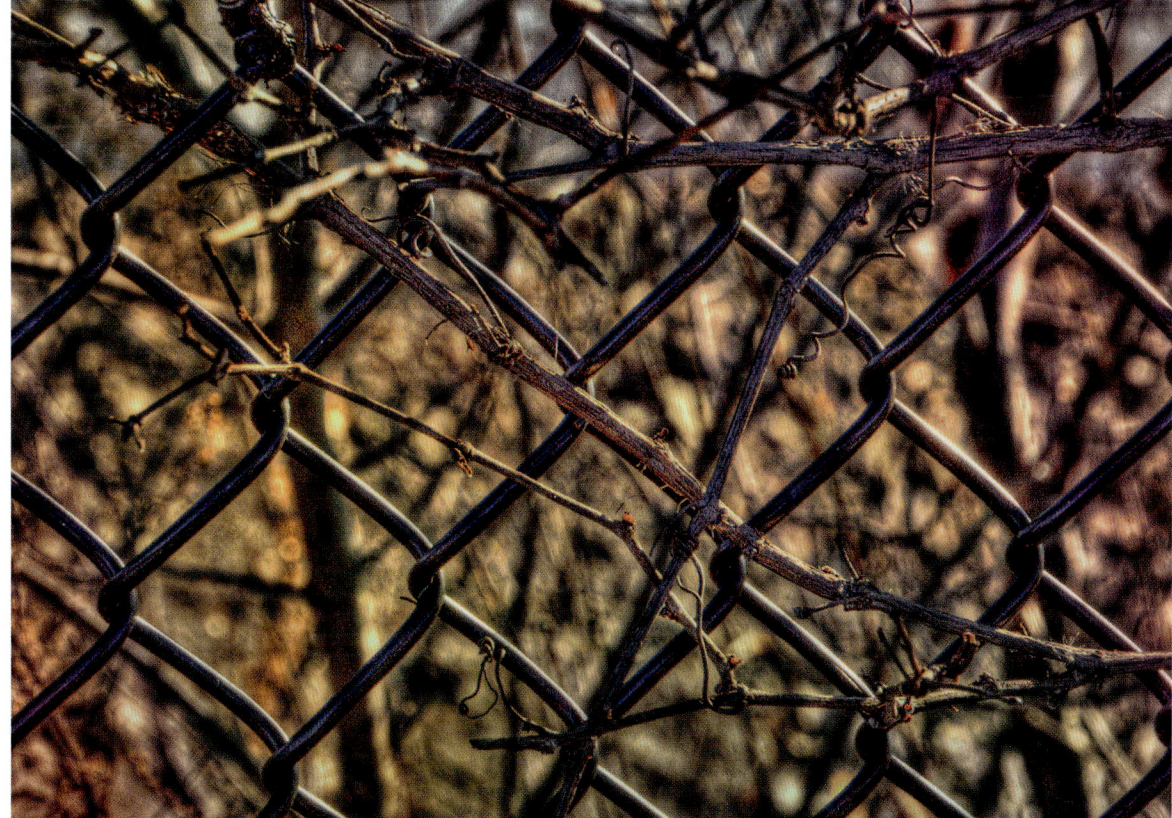

RIGHT: *The sharpness of the fence is the result of all the points of focus (cones) landing on or very close to the focal plane of the sensor. The background is made of circles of confusion, where the cones have been intersected at different points of the cone.*

Depth of Field

The lens aperture you use is the main factor in determining the extent of the depth of field; larger apertures produce a shallow depth of field, while smaller apertures create greater depth of field.

If you refer back to the discussion about cones of light, the aperture is controlling the diameter of the cones. As you stop the lens down, you create smaller cones of light (circles of confusion), which results in more and more relative sharpness in front of and behind the point of actual focus. Smaller apertures produce smaller (thinner) cones, which means the diameter of the cones' cross-sections close to the focal point are small enough to appear as sharp points in the image.

This increased focus has a lot to do with the resolving power of the human eye: when the circle of confusion is small enough, it is not perceptible as being out of focus.

However, aperture is only one element in the depth-of-field equation: DOF is also affected by the camera-to-subject distance, sensor size, and focal length. With wide-angle lenses, the depth of field can extend from near to infinity with the aperture closed down just a few stops from its widest setting, whereas longer lenses need to be stopped down further to deliver an extensive depth of field.

RIGHT: *Depth of field can exclude foreground elements from sharpness just as effectively as it can throw the background out of focus. In this case, the depth of field was quite shallow, and set farther back that some protruding twigs, but still far in front of the forest beyond.*

01 // DEPTH OF FIELD // LIGHT

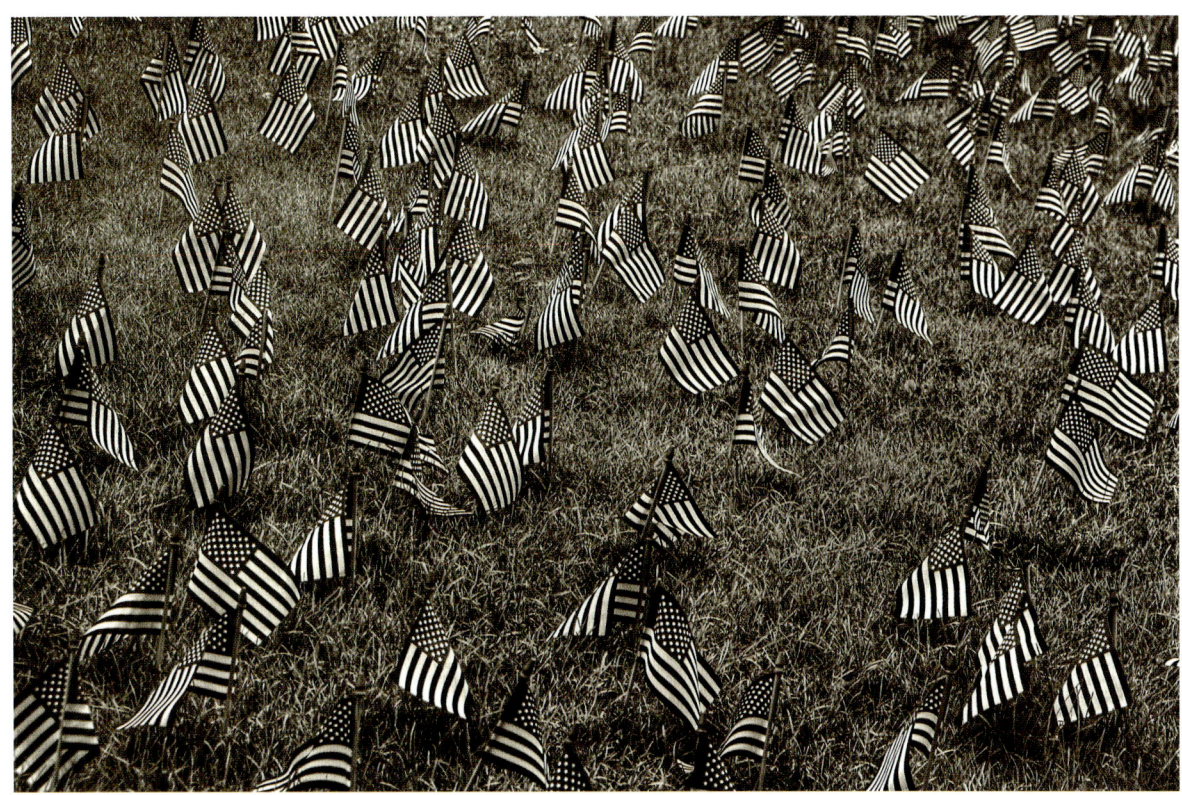

LEFT: *Maximum depth of field is a result of using the smallest apertures and focusing at the hyperfocal distance.*

BELOW: *Shallow depth of field comes from using wider apertures and longer focal lengths.*

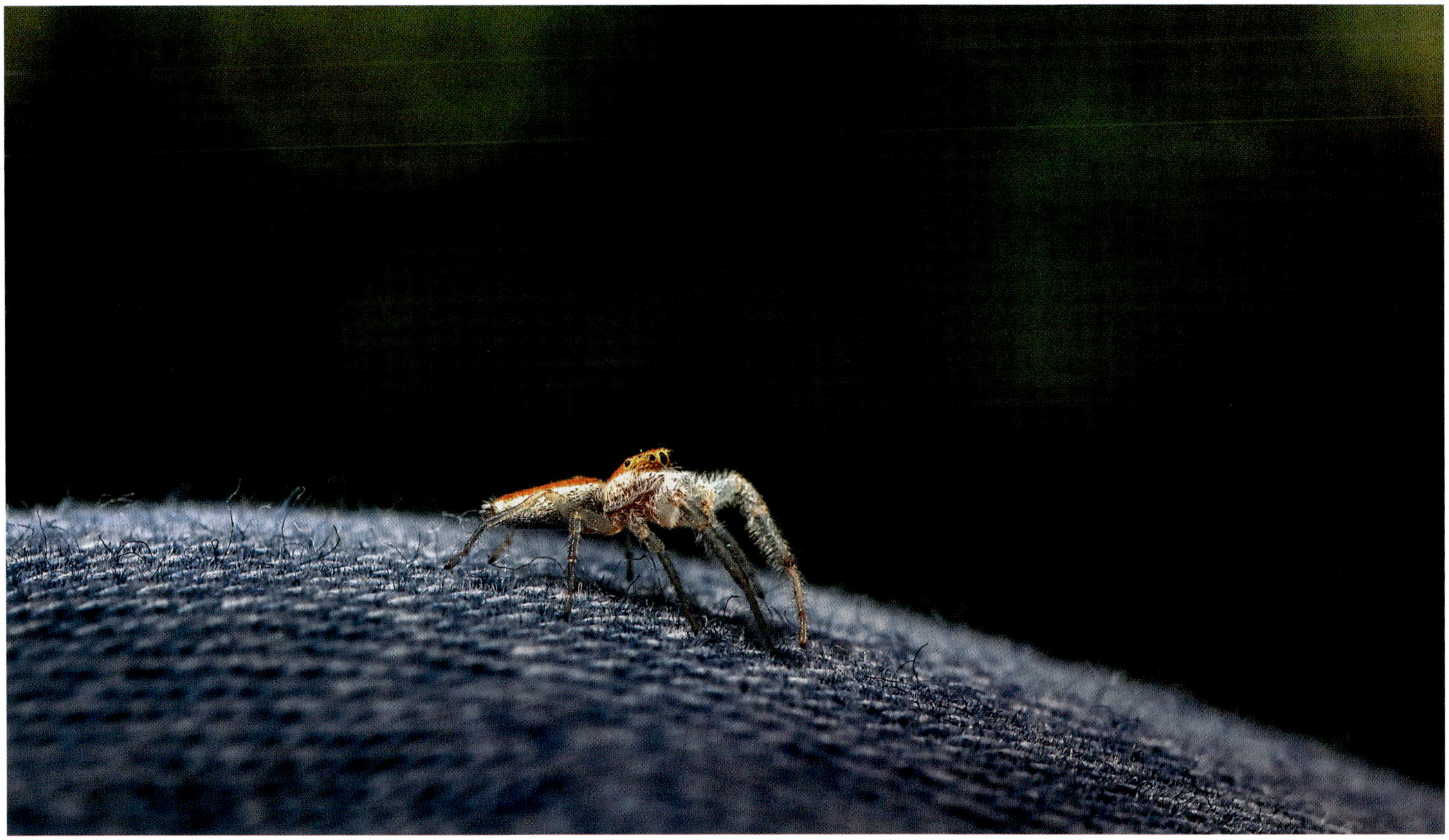

Hyperfocal Distance

The hyperfocal distance is the distance setting that produces the maximum depth of field for a lens at any given aperture. Hyperfocal focusing is a method of achieving maximum use of the apparent focus of a lens at a specific aperture and focus distance. It is used to bring into focus all of the image details you want to appear sharp in the final image while leaving the areas out of the range out of focus.

In the past, it used to be relatively simply to set the hyperfocal distance on a lens, as lenses had markings either side of the focus index or distance indicator, which indicated the depth of field at a given aperture. Depending on the aperture in use, you could simply look at the relationship between the aperture scale and the distance scale and roughly determine what parts of the scene would be in acceptable (relative) sharp focus.

However, many modern lenses (especially low-cost zoom lenses) do not offer markings for depth of field, making it much harder to focus at the hyperfocal distance and control depth of field with any great precision.

Although various depth-of-field calculators are available online, as electronic apps, and as printable charts that you can carry with you, they do rely on you being able to set the focus at a specific distance. Without a focus scale on your lens this can be challenging, although focusing manually at a guessed distance is a workable (although never accurate) solution.

BELOW: *A depth-of-field scale is used to indicate the approximate distance in front of and behind the focused subject distance when using a specific aperture. DOF is dependent on focal length, focal distance, and aperture setting.*

RIGHT: *This 23mm Fujifilm prime lens has a depth-of-field scale located adjacent to the focusing ring. This indicates the depth of field available when using a particular aperture.*

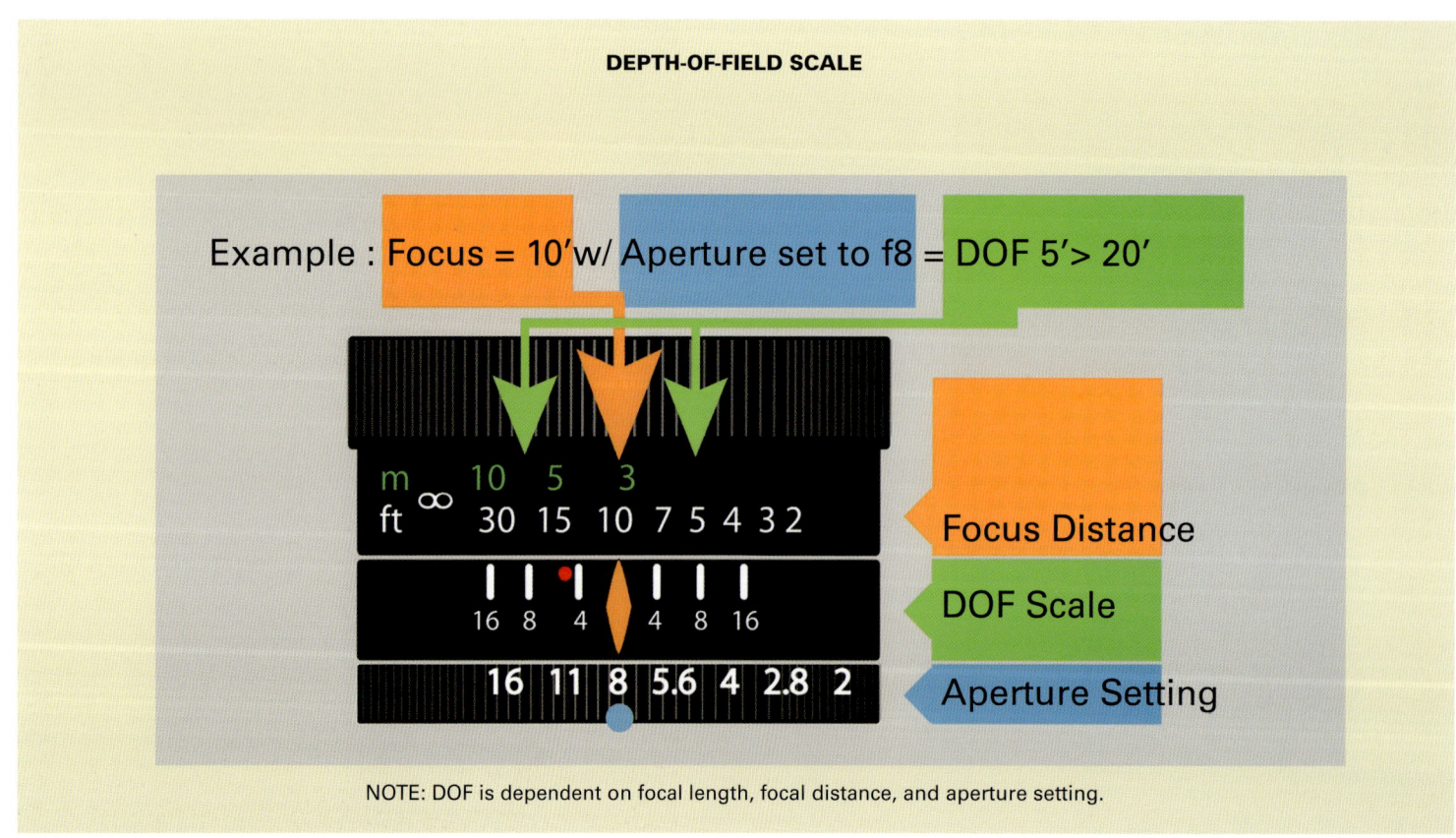

DEPTH-OF-FIELD SCALE

Example : Focus = 10' w/ Aperture set to f8 = DOF 5'> 20'

Focus Distance
DOF Scale
Aperture Setting

NOTE: DOF is dependent on focal length, focal distance, and aperture setting.

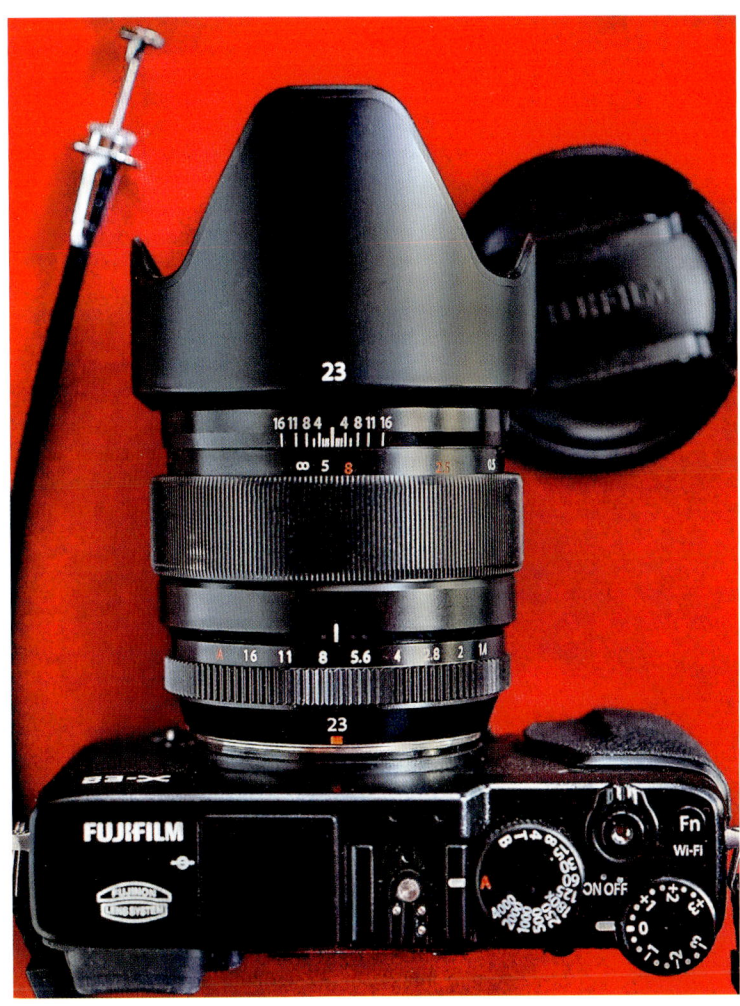

Focus Peaking

Some mirrorless cameras use "focus peaking" as a means of indicating what is "in focus" in a scene. Focus peaking overlays the preview image with a solid color to indicate where the intended subject is sharply focused.

Focus peaking can also indicate approximately how much depth of field a lens is producing: the more of the previewed image that is colored, the more of it is sharp, so the greater the depth of field. You should see that the areas in front of and beyond the sharply focused point come into focus at the rate of approximately 1/3 in front and 2/3 behind the actual point of focus.

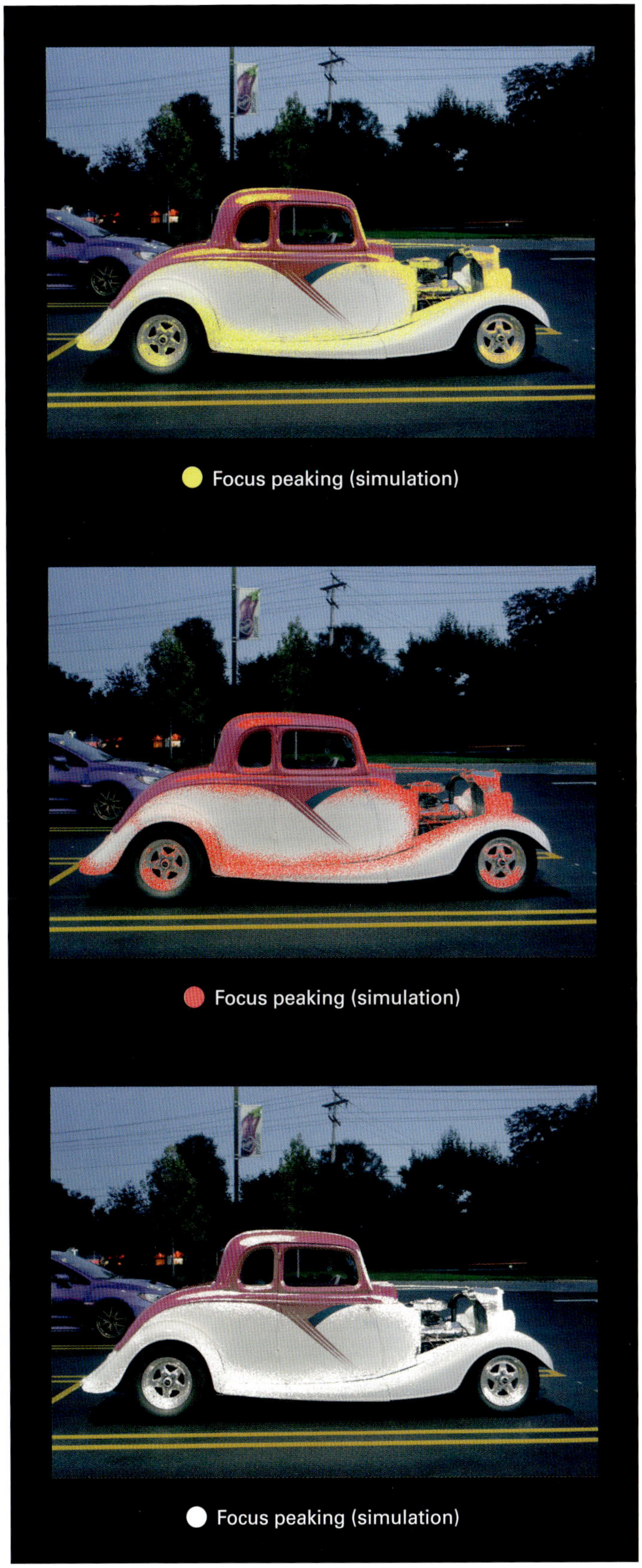

RIGHT: *Simulated views that approximate focus peaking. The choice of colors allows you to see the focus most clearly against different backgrounds.*

Filters

Most filters are used to control what light travels through the lens and what is omitted. Although many have been replaced by digital effects, certain filters still have a place in the photographer's armory.

I consider anything that alters the light between the lens and the sensor to be a filter effect, and many different effects can be achieved through filter manipulation. Filters can change the color of the light, for example, reducing the extraneous blue in daylight shadows, or they can create a soft-focus effect, modify reflections, add prismatic coloration, and create many other visual effects.

Soft Focus

Filters can be useful for creating soft-focus effects, and there are filters that are made specifically for this purpose. It is also simple (but slightly risky) to apply gel, glycerin, or petroleum jelly onto the outer surface of the filter glass. I say "risky" because there is a chance that you can accidently get some on the coated elements of your actual lens, which can damage the coatings and migrate into the body of the lens.

However, a "self-coating" method can be useful for producing a miniaturization effect. The coating can be applied to the top and bottom of a filter, which will soften those areas of the image while leaving the center of the photograph fairly sharp.

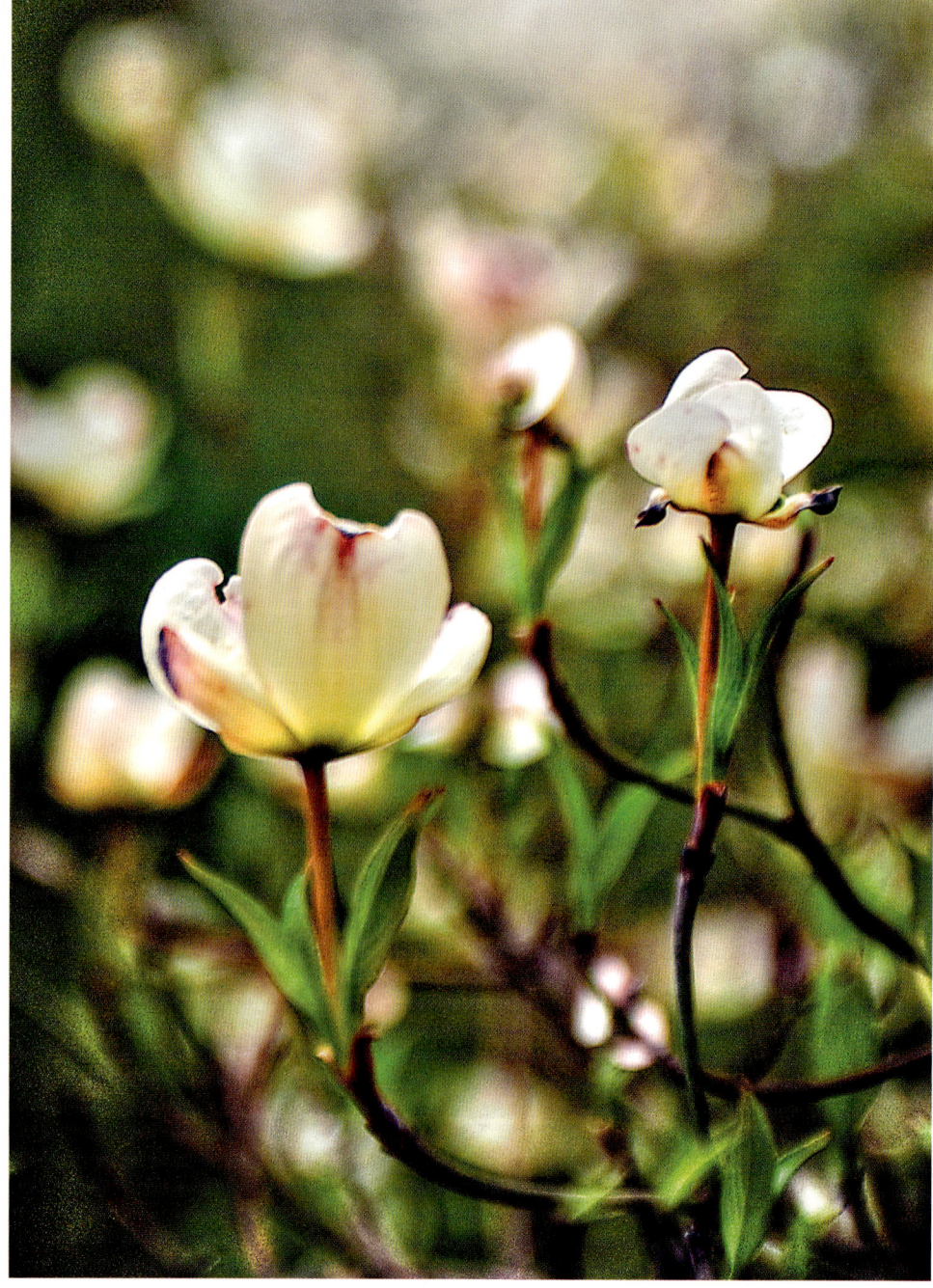

RIGHT: *If you're going to try using a soft-focus effect, it's much wiser to apply the gel to a filter, and attach the filter to the lens, rather than applying gel directly to the lens itself.*

01 // FILTERS // LIGHT

BELOW: *Polarizer filters are useful for reducing or eliminating glare from nonmetallic materials and surfaces by blocking polarized light.*

Polarizing Filters

The effects of a polarizing filter are (currently) impossible to emulate using image-editing software, as the filter has a fundamental effect on the light passing through the lens.

A polarizing filter has two main uses: to reduce reflections and glare (on glass, water, and other surfaces) and for darkening a blue sky, which will make white clouds stand out in contrast. In both instances, polarizing filters preserve color and textures.

In practice, it is important to ensure that a surface such as a glass window, a glass tabletop, or the windshield of a car retains enough reflection to maintain the feeling that there is a surface that we are looking through. When the filter is overused, it can cause the surface to disappear in the final rendition.

Similarly, it is easy to overdo the effect when photographing a blue sky, darkening it to the point that it turns an unnatural, near-black color. Uneven polarization when using a wide-angle lens is another visual trait that is best avoided.

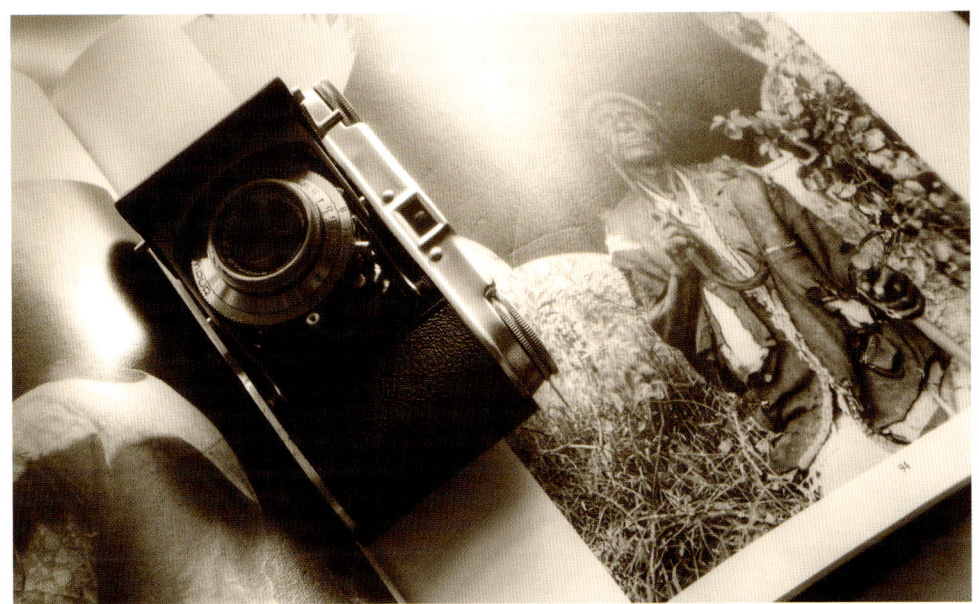

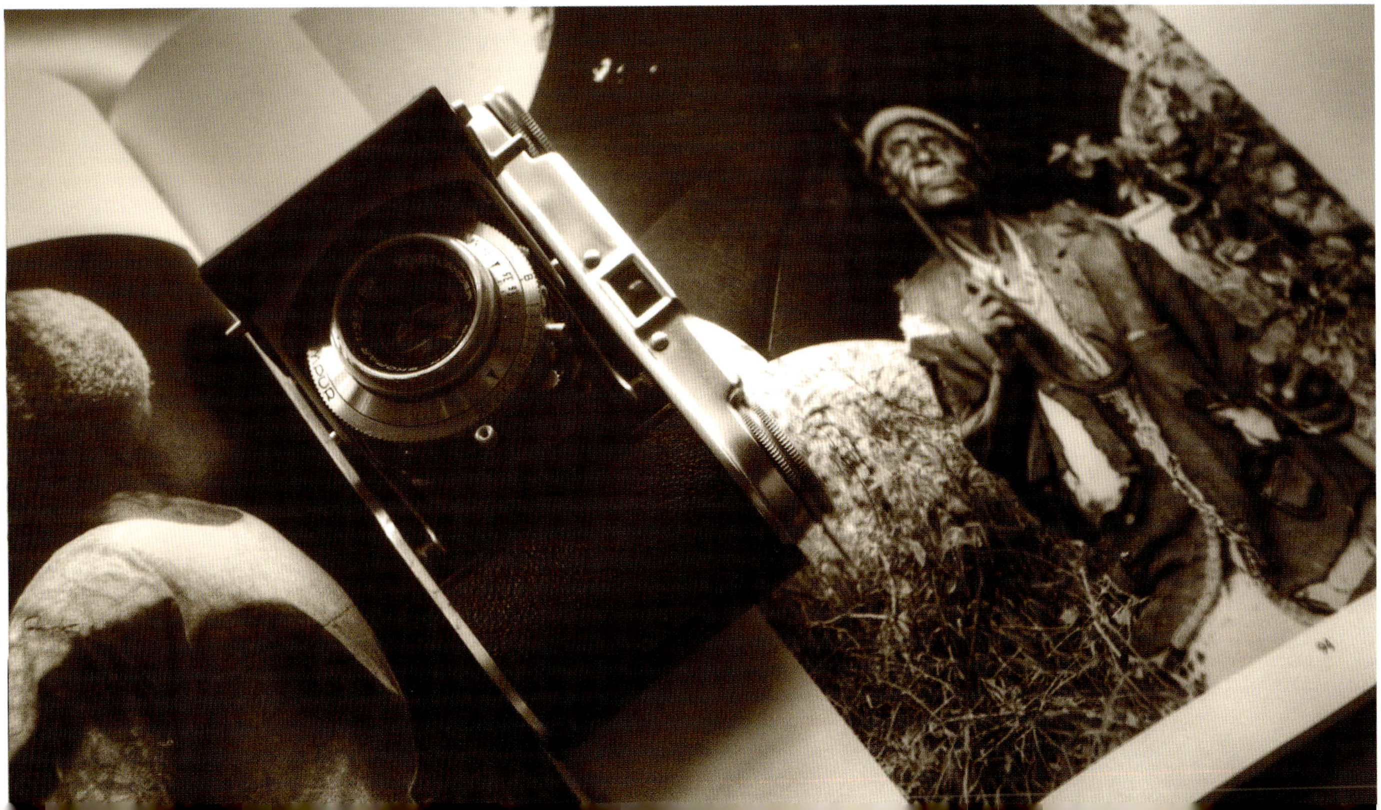

42 // 43

Neutral Density (ND) Filters

As the name suggests, a neutral density filter blocks a portion of the light from passing through it (the "density") without affecting the color (hence "neutral"). Think of it as sunglasses for your lens and you won't be too wide of the mark.

ND filters are usually produced in densities that are measured in stops of light reduction. An ND 2 filter allows half the light to pass through it (so 1-stop less light reaches the sensor); an ND 4 filter allows a quarter of the light to pass through (a 2-stop reduction); an ND 8 transmits an eighth of the light reaching it (a 3-stop reduction).

In this way, an ND filter effectively enables you to use a longer shutter speed and/or a wider aperture at any given ISO setting. You can also stack multiple filters to extend exposure times further still, although doing so can degrade image quality.

ND filters can also be used to darken the existing illumination in order to use flash as the main light source. This is an interesting way to record nearby subjects, such as a portrait shot in the bright sun. The ND filter is used to reduce the background exposure to a point that is equal in intensity to (or darker than) a flash exposure that has been calculated to produce a correct exposure with the ND filter in place. The result is a well-lit subject against a balanced—or at least controlled—background. It is also possible to adjust the output of the flash to give a similar rendition without a filter.

BELOW: *A 10-stop ND filter was used to capture this tiny waterfall. The water flow was very slow, but the filter allowed the camera to expose for several minutes. The final result captured much more volume than was actually present.*

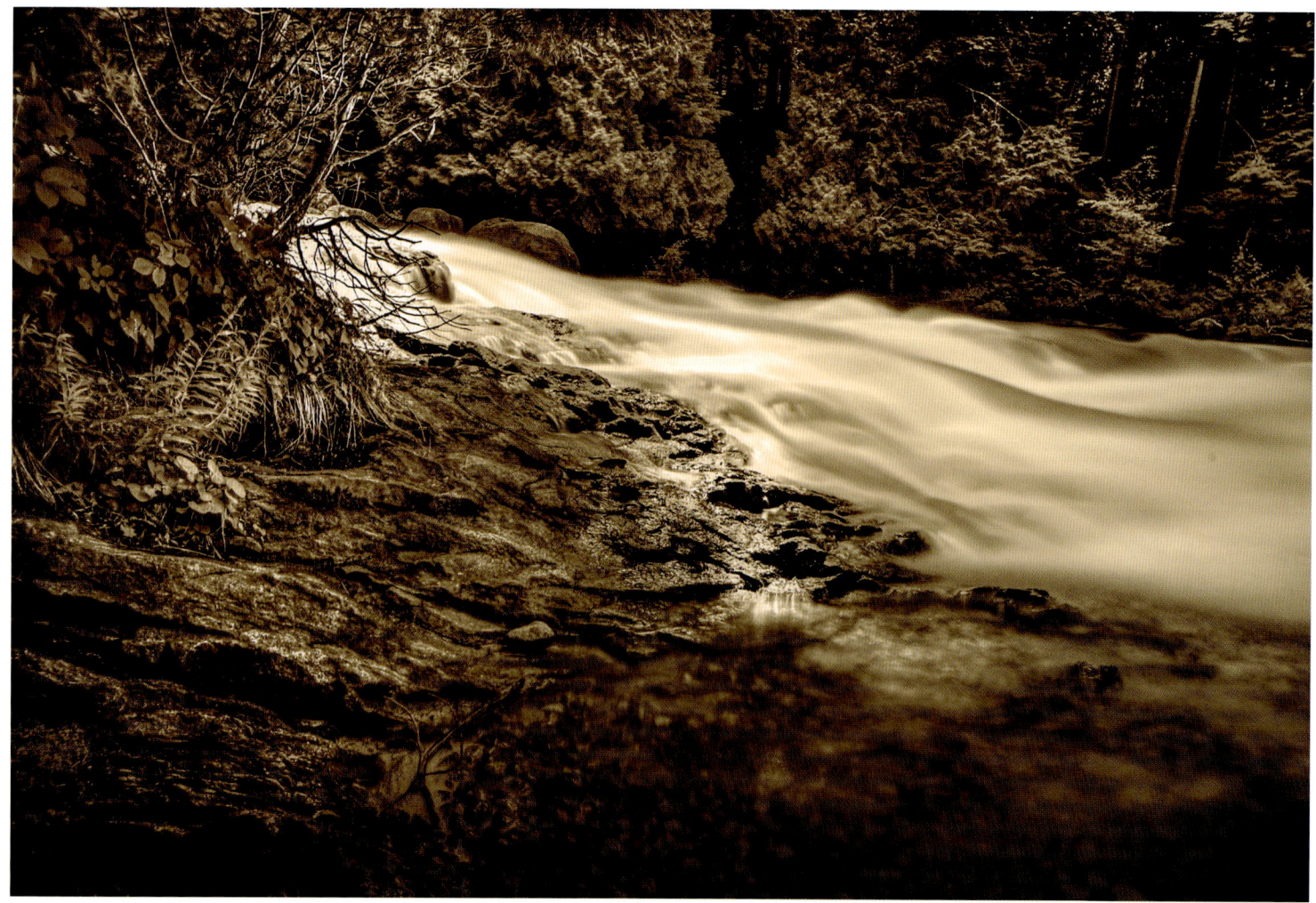

Variable ND (VND) Filters

Recently, variable ND filters (VND) have become available from companies such as Heliopan, Kenko-Tokina, and Singh-Ray. These filters allow you to "dial in" a density by using a rotating ring, so rather than having to change out the filter, it is adjusted to an appropriate density marked on the outer ring. These filters are also called fader ND or adjustable ND

A variable ND filter helps you to obtain the optimal shutter speed for images where precise control is needed over the movement of a subject such as flowing water or moving clouds. It also enables control of the aperture if you need to set a specific depth of field. Although these hybrid types of ND filter are not cheap, the advantage is that one filter can replace half a dozen fixed densities, meaning that you avoid stacking multiple filters.

However, you will need to purchase one filter for each lens of a different filter diameter, or buy filter stepping rings that will adapt the filter to fit several lenses. In doing this, you might find that the lens' shade will no longer be usable.

As with all filters, it is good practice to purchase high-quality filters, and treat them as the optical devices that they are—dust, scratches, and fingerprints on the filter can easily degrade the final image.

EXTREME ND FILTERS

There is an increasing number of "extreme" ND filters available, which will increase your exposure by 6-, 10- or even 12-stops. This type of filter is so dense that it will allow very long exposures in bright daylight; depending on the ISO and aperture settings, exposures can be timed in minutes, rather than fractions of a second.

This allows for extreme blurring of many types of subjects. Depending on the motion, some subjects may move so fast through the scene that they will not be recorded at all. This can be useful when there are objects such as people that you do not want to record.

However, this technique takes some planning and a bit of practice, not least because it is usually not possible to frame your shot or use autofocus with the filter in place. Instead, composing and framing need to be performed before the filter is fitted, which obviously makes this a more time-consuming way of shooting.

BELOW: *Sometimes you know exactly what strength ND filter is needed for a particular exposure, but I find more often it's a matter of trial and error. Variable ND filters are a great help in this regard, as you can dial in exactly the right strength for the effect.*

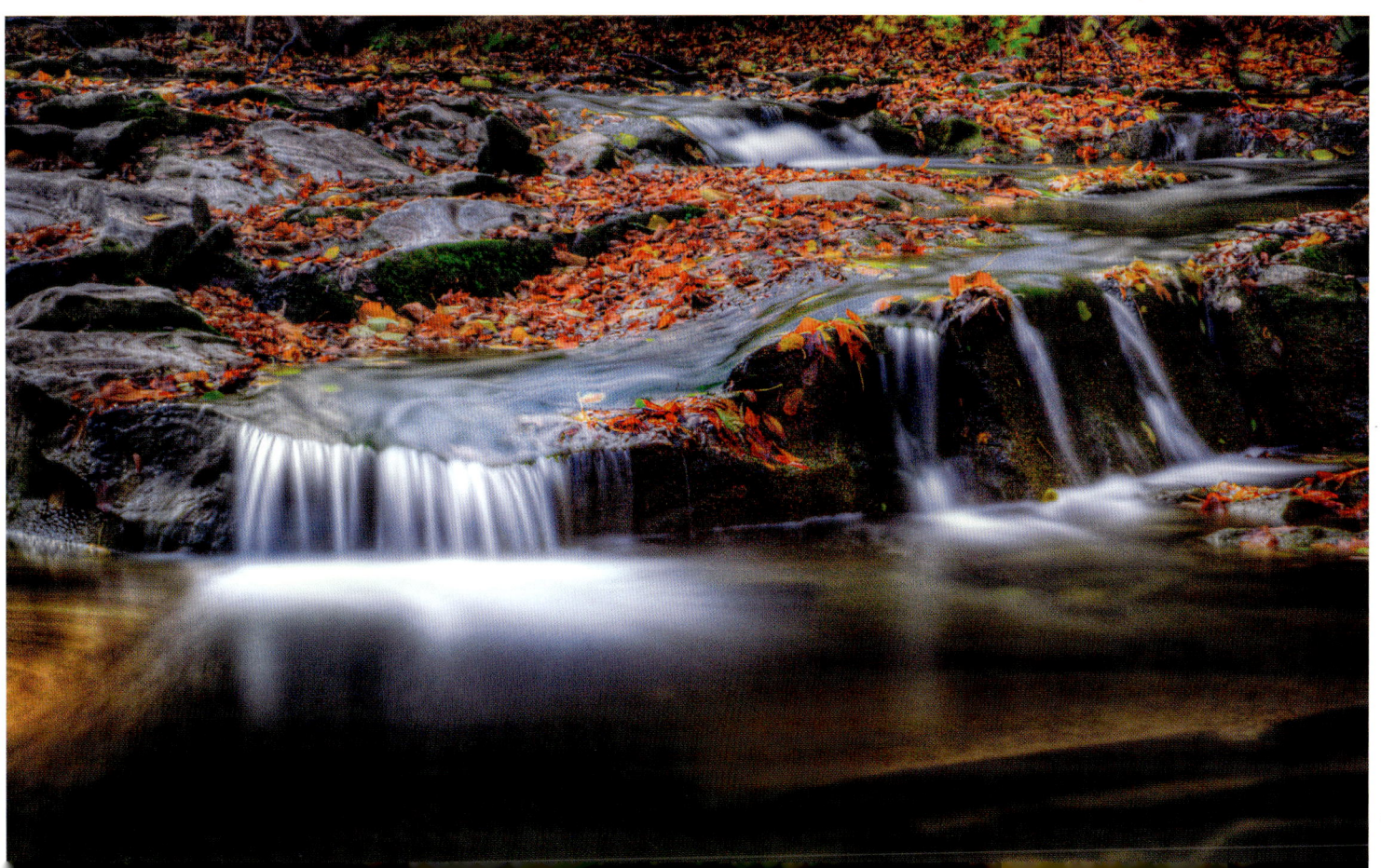

Graduated ND Filters

Graduated ND filters are most commonly used by landscape photographers to balance the exposure for a bright sky with a darker foreground. Half of the filter is clear, while the other half has a graduated neutral density coating. The filters are invariably used in a slot-in filter holder, which enables them to be positioned precisely in front of the lens.

Graduated ND filters are available in a range of strengths (typically offering a 1-, 2-, and 3-stop reduction in the exposure for the coated area of the filter), with either a soft, hard, or "razor" (extremely hard) transition from the coated to uncoated parts of the filter. In some instances, a softer transition is preferable (when the horizon line is not perfectly level, for example), while at other times it is better if the filter has a more pronounced difference.

While the effect of a graduated ND filter can be created using image-editing software, it is usually more rewarding (and often more convincing) to balance the exposure in-camera. This also prevents you increasing noise in the digitally darkened areas.

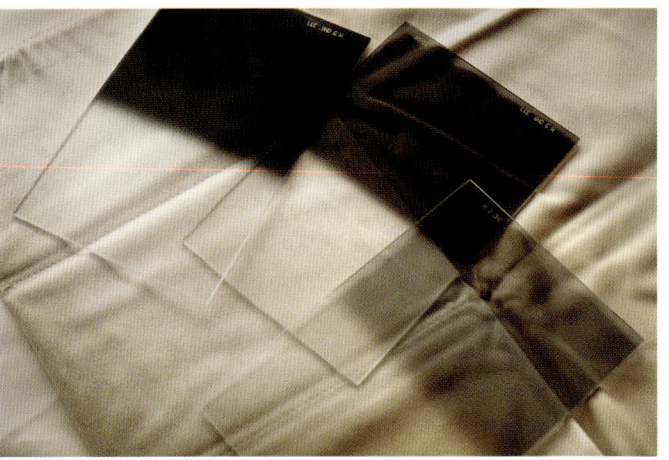

LEFT: *Graduated ND filters allow a partial darkening or slowing down of the exposure. Here are three different densities and graduations offered by Lee Filters. Note that the filter in the center has a much sharper transition between the coated and uncoated areas than the other two.*

BELOW: *The top of the frame is quite different in the before and after shots, but you can see that gradually tapers off until the exposure matches at the bottom of the frame.*

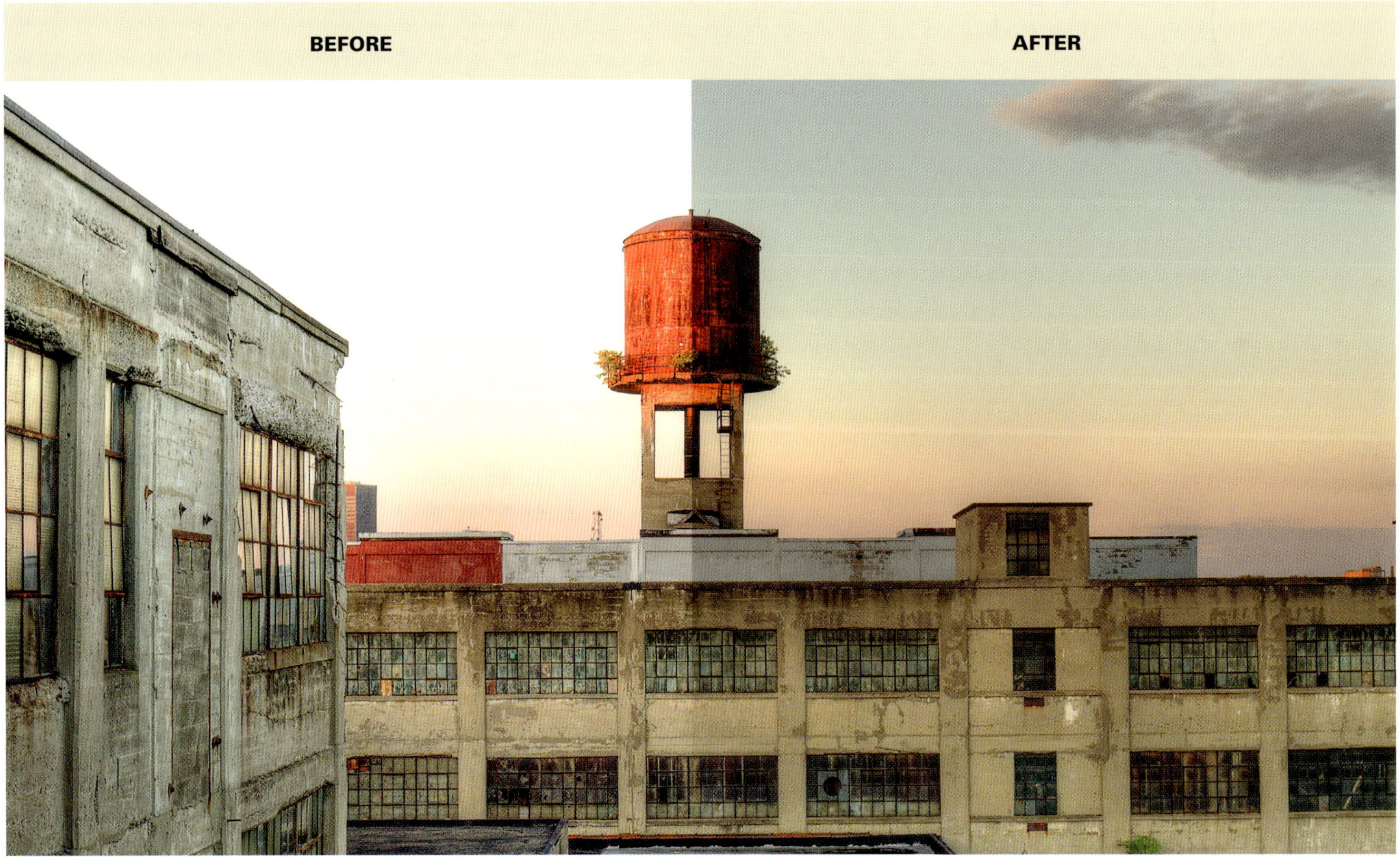

BEFORE **AFTER**

Color Gradient Filters

While graduated ND filters can be used to balance exposures, color gradient filters can be used to alter or enhance the colors of a scene. Typically, they would be used to make the sky in a landscape more interesting by adding more yellow or red (for sunsets, this can make the images more dramatic), or they might be used to make part of a scene warmer or colder.

Two filters can also be used to create color alterations to two portions of the image—the sky can be altered separately from the foreground, for example.

Colored Filters

Although using plain-colored filters in front of the lens is less common today, they were once essential for separating tones when producing black-and-white photographs on film. Indeed, the basic principle is the same when you convert a color image to monochrome during post-production.

The illustration on the right demonstrates the effect that a colored filter has on an image. A red filter, for example, will absorb the green and the blue wavelengths from the white light source, but transmit the red portion. Green and blue filters work on a similar principle. Other filters commonly used for black-and-white photography are yellow and orange. A yellow filter absorbs the blue wavelengths from the white light source and transmits the red and the green portions. An orange filter absorbs the blue wavelengths as well as a portion of the green from the white light source. All of the red light along with a portion of the green is transmitted.

In black-and-white photography, a colored filter (or its digital equivalent) will lighten elements in the scene that are the same color as, or similar color to, the filter, and darken elements that are similar to the wavelengths that are absorbed. If you use a red filter for a landscape, it will darken a blue sky, while a green filter would lighten foliage. In digital imaging, multiple filters can now be applied to a single image.

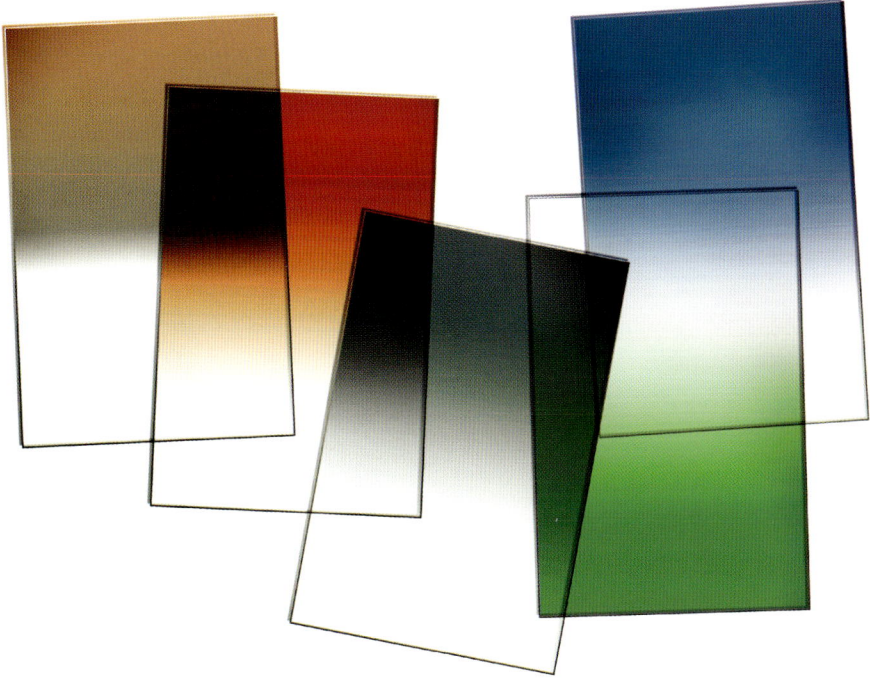

ABOVE: *Color gradient filters like these often come in packs, and are worth experimenting with to see their respective effects on different scenes.*

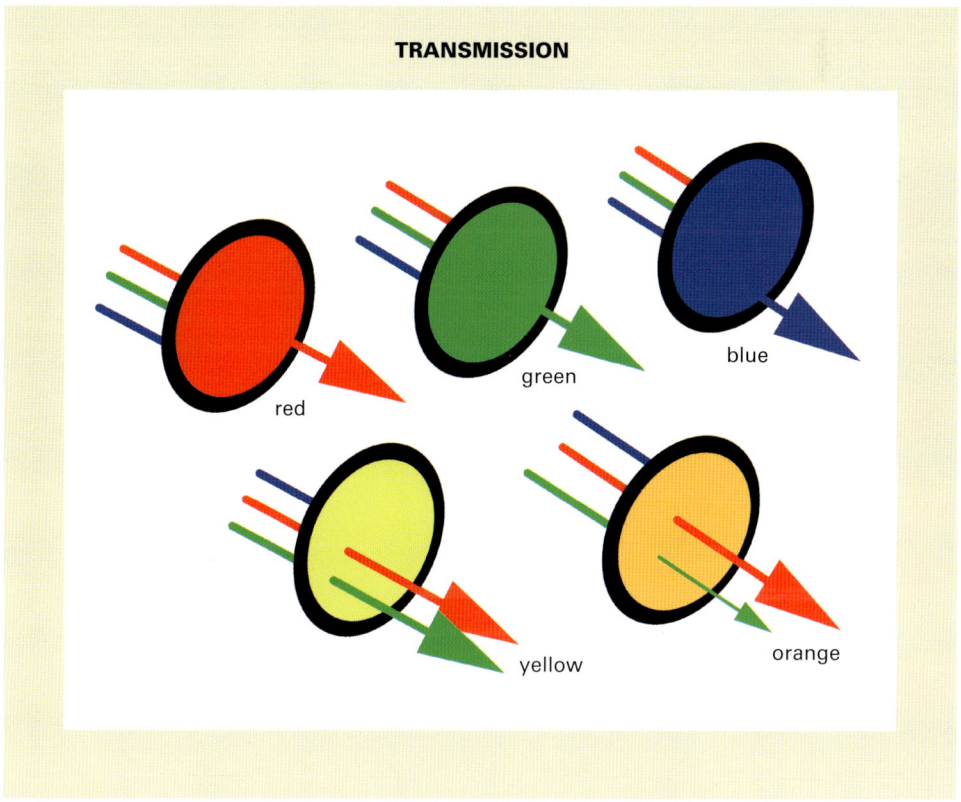

Gallery | Light

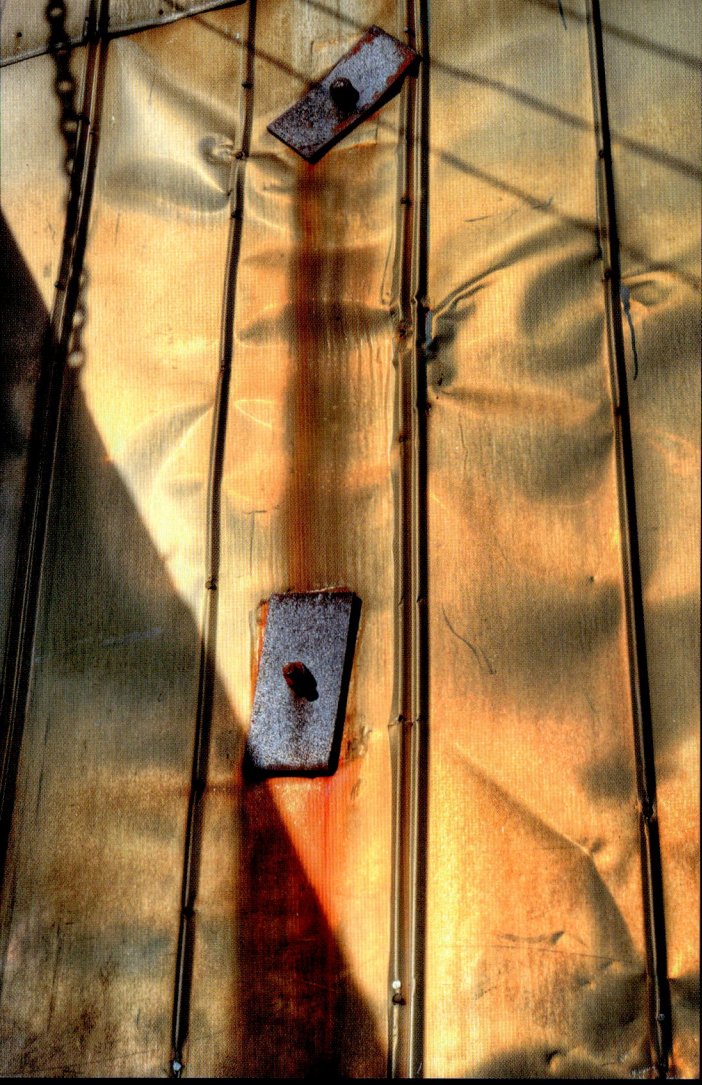
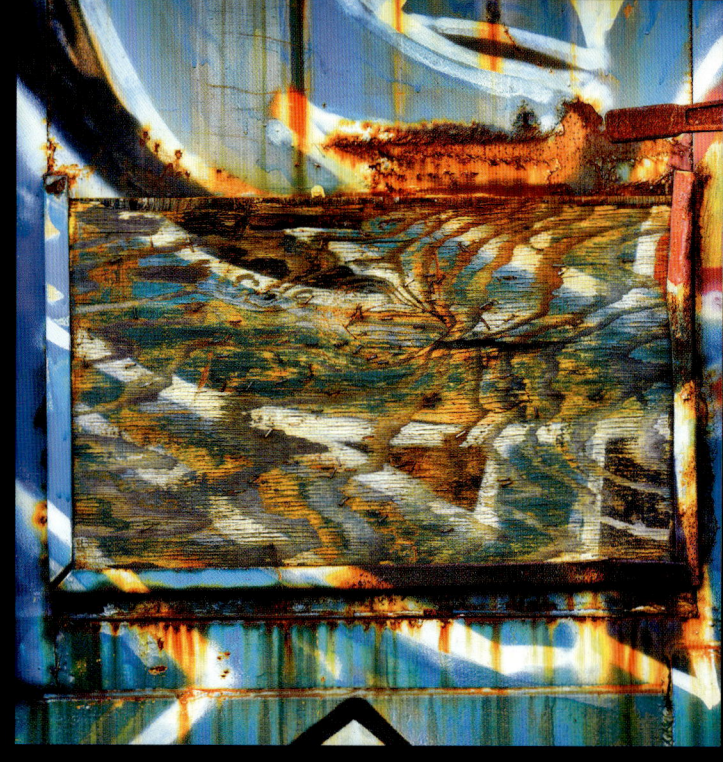
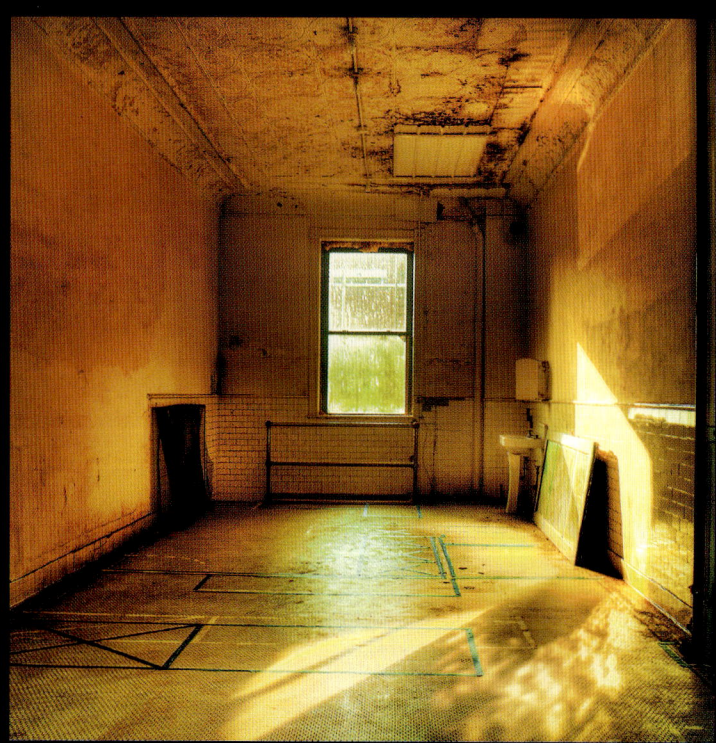

THIS PAGE: *The light in all these images, which started as pure white sunlight, takes on rich tones due to the material in the subjects off of which it reflects.*

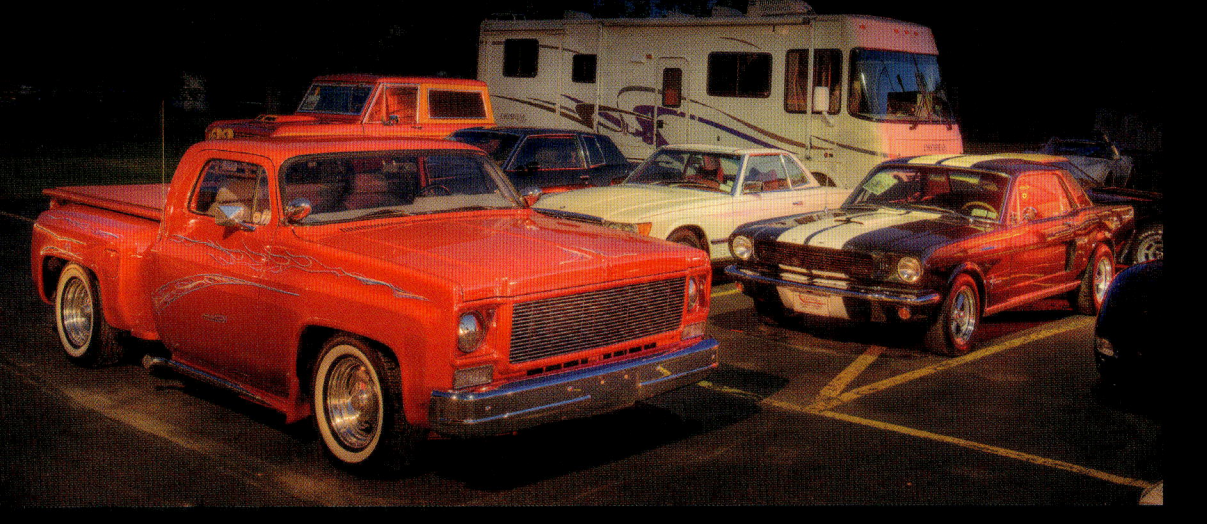

effect can be used toward creative ends as well, with hypersaturated, unreal-looking colors making up the bulk of the frame.

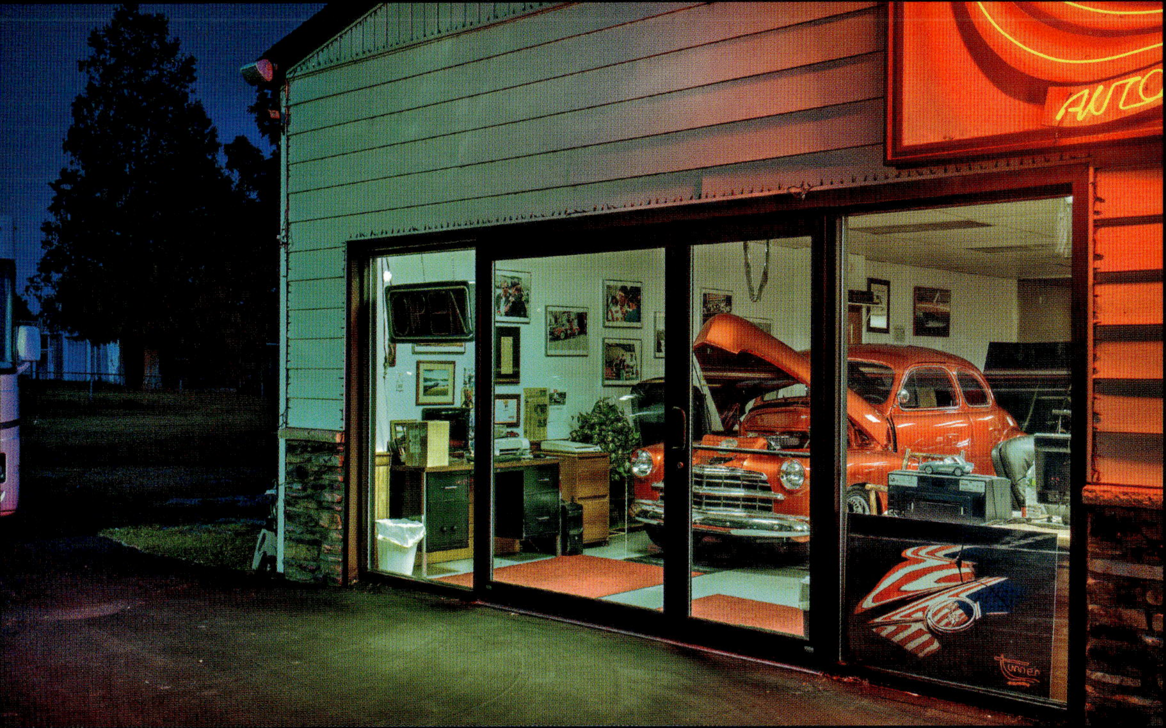

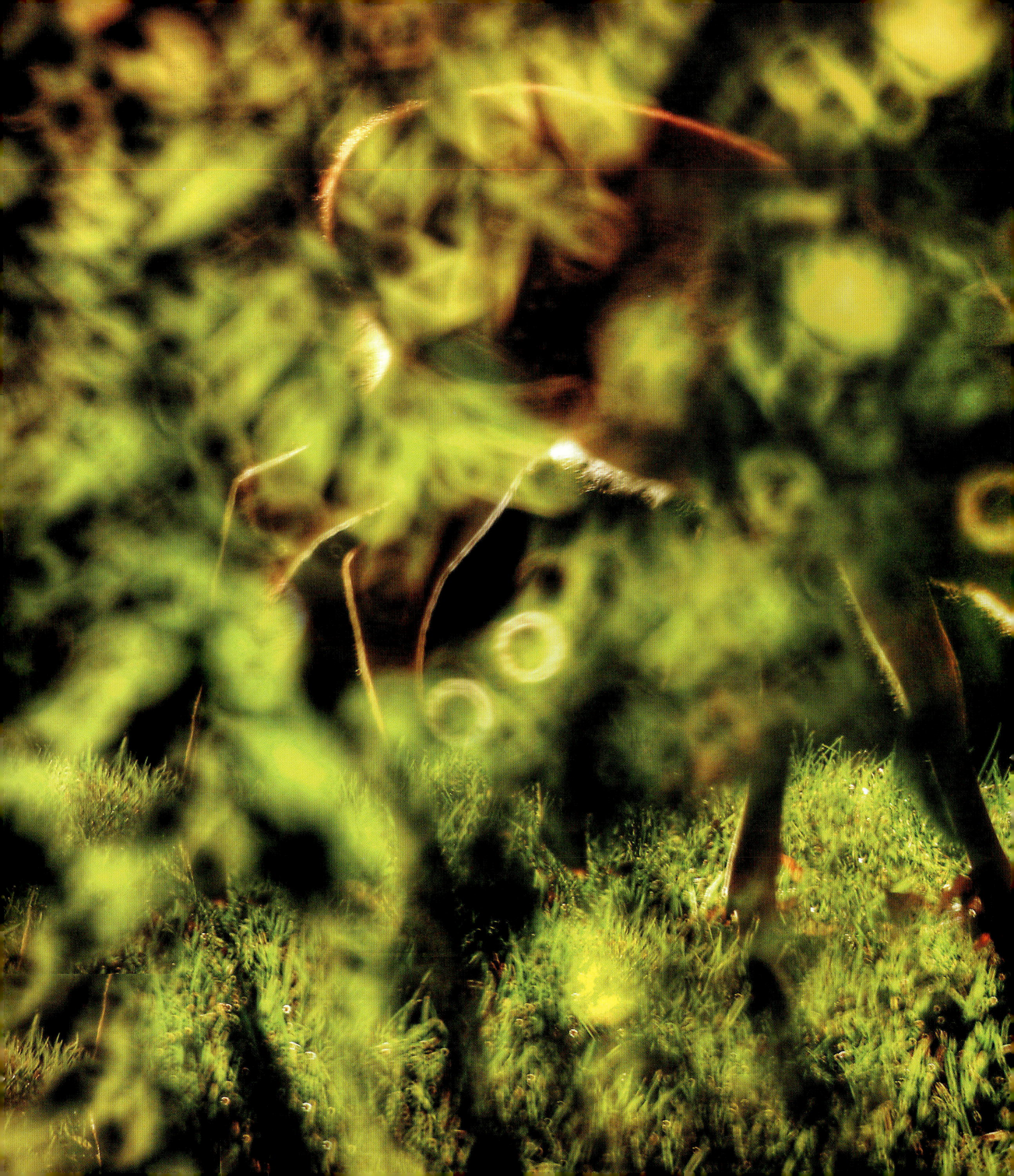

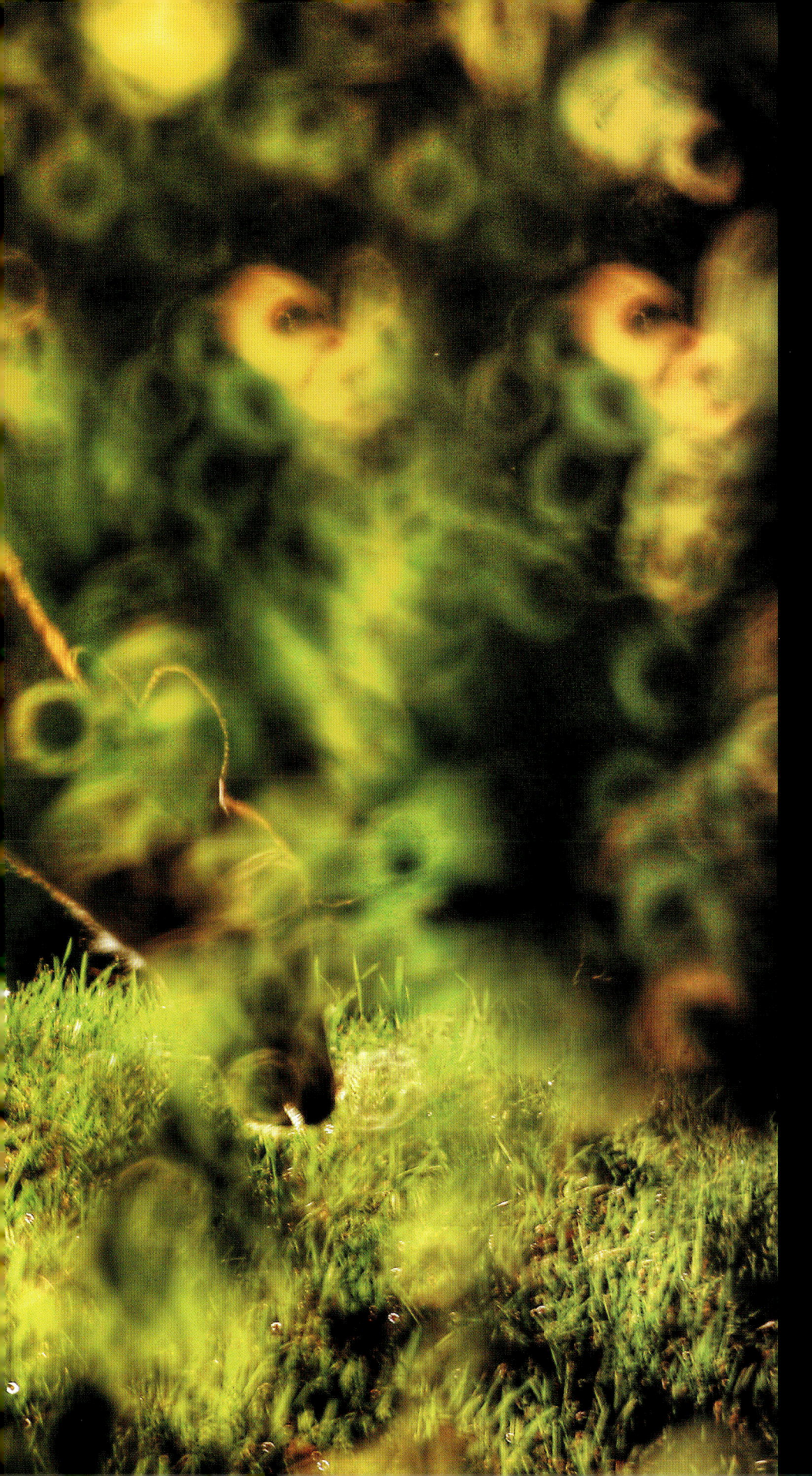

02 // BOKEH

What is Bokeh?

Bokeh comes from the Japanese word *boke*, which means "blur" or "haze." In photography, the term has been coined to describe a particular type of out-of-focus effect produced by particular lens designs.

Although bokeh can mean any out-of-focus or unsharp area of an image, most photographers accept it as the blur that happens in the areas of the image beyond the area of apparent point of sharp focus (beyond the subject).

Bokeh is usually associated with small highlights in the background, such as reflections and light sources. However, while bokeh is most noticeable in the highlights, it is produced in all out-of-focus areas; the out-of-focus light also blurs dark areas of the image.

Bokeh disks are formed by circles of confusion that are completely out of focus; they are a larger cross-section of the cones of light discussed in the previous chapter that happen to be on the sensor's image plane.

As bokeh is a product of the lens you are using, bokeh can be rendered with noticeable differences depending on the make and model. Some lenses produce what is considered a "pleasing" bokeh effect, while others produce a less desirable look—we will explore what makes a "good" bokeh lens later in this chapter.

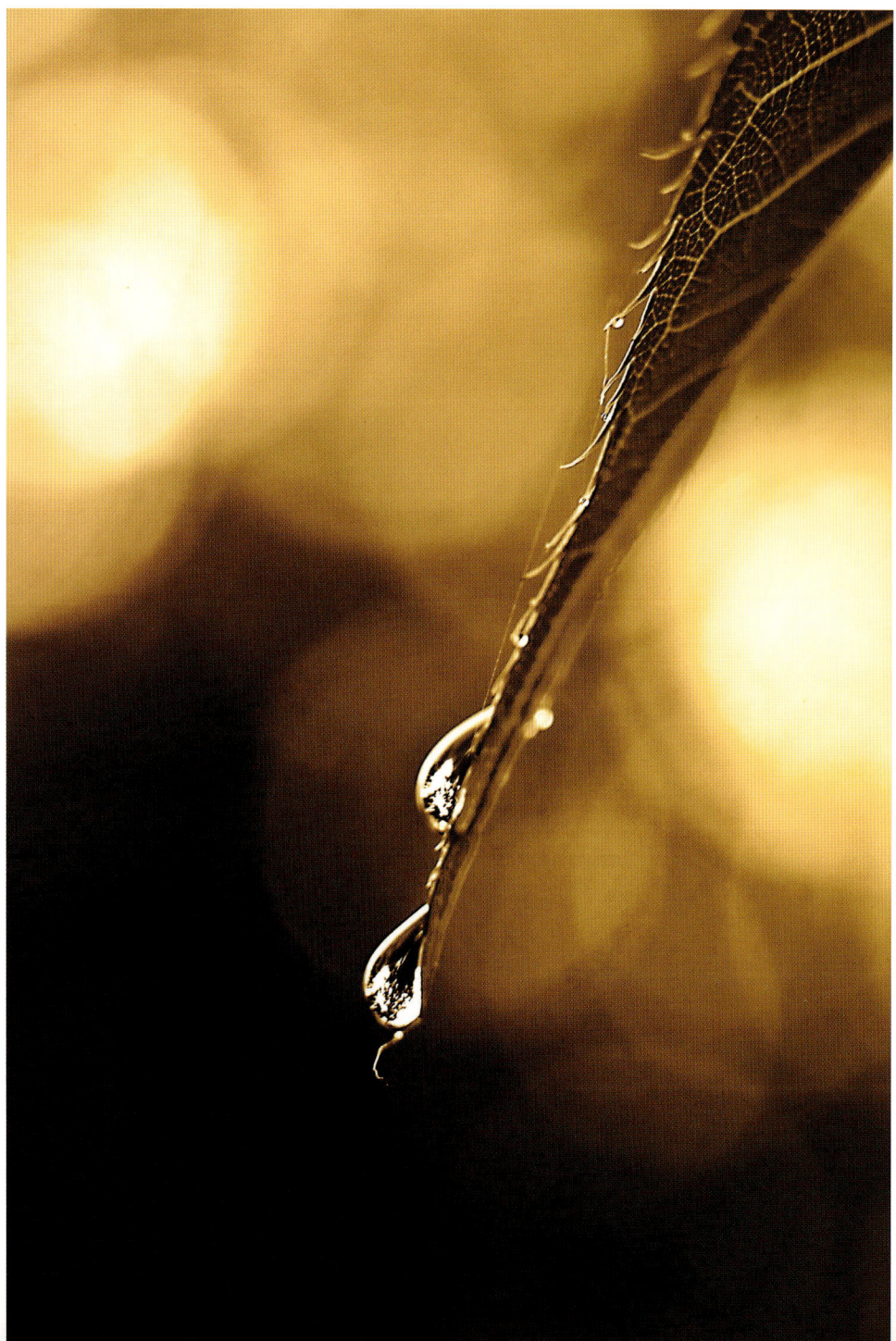

RIGHT: *Close-up shots like this often result in bokeh that is made up of far fewer, but much larger and more noticeable circles in the background.*

Bokeh Size & Detail

Depending on the lens used, the lens-to-subject distance, and the subject-to-background detail, it is possible to control the size of the bokeh. This has to do with the point along the cone axis that falls on the image plane (sensor).

If you imagine the plane of the sensor cutting through a portion of a cone, you can see that it can be almost any dimension relative to the diameter of the cone intersecting the sensor. Bokeh size is dependent on the cross section of the light cones that fall onto the image plane.

Fast lenses with wider apertures usually produce the greatest bokeh effect at any given focal length; as the aperture is stopped down, the bokeh becomes smaller and sharper. This means that the bokeh can also be controlled using the aperture setting.

Shallow depth of field usually creates the most evident bokeh, and bokeh is inversely proportionate to the subject's distance. Therefore, to produce the maximum bokeh effect, try to minimize the distance between the camera and the subject and set a wide aperture. This will increase the size and prominence of both foreground and background OOF areas. Longer lenses and macro distances will help to increase the size of the bokeh effect.

BELOW: *Bokeh is created by light cones that focus off the sensor. The rings shown at the stop of the illustration show the size of the cone intersecting the plane of focus on the sensor. The focus for each distance is shown on the left. Notice that the green cone is shown reversing itself after the focus point. That is because light continues in a straight path. The same is true for all the light traveling inside the cones.*

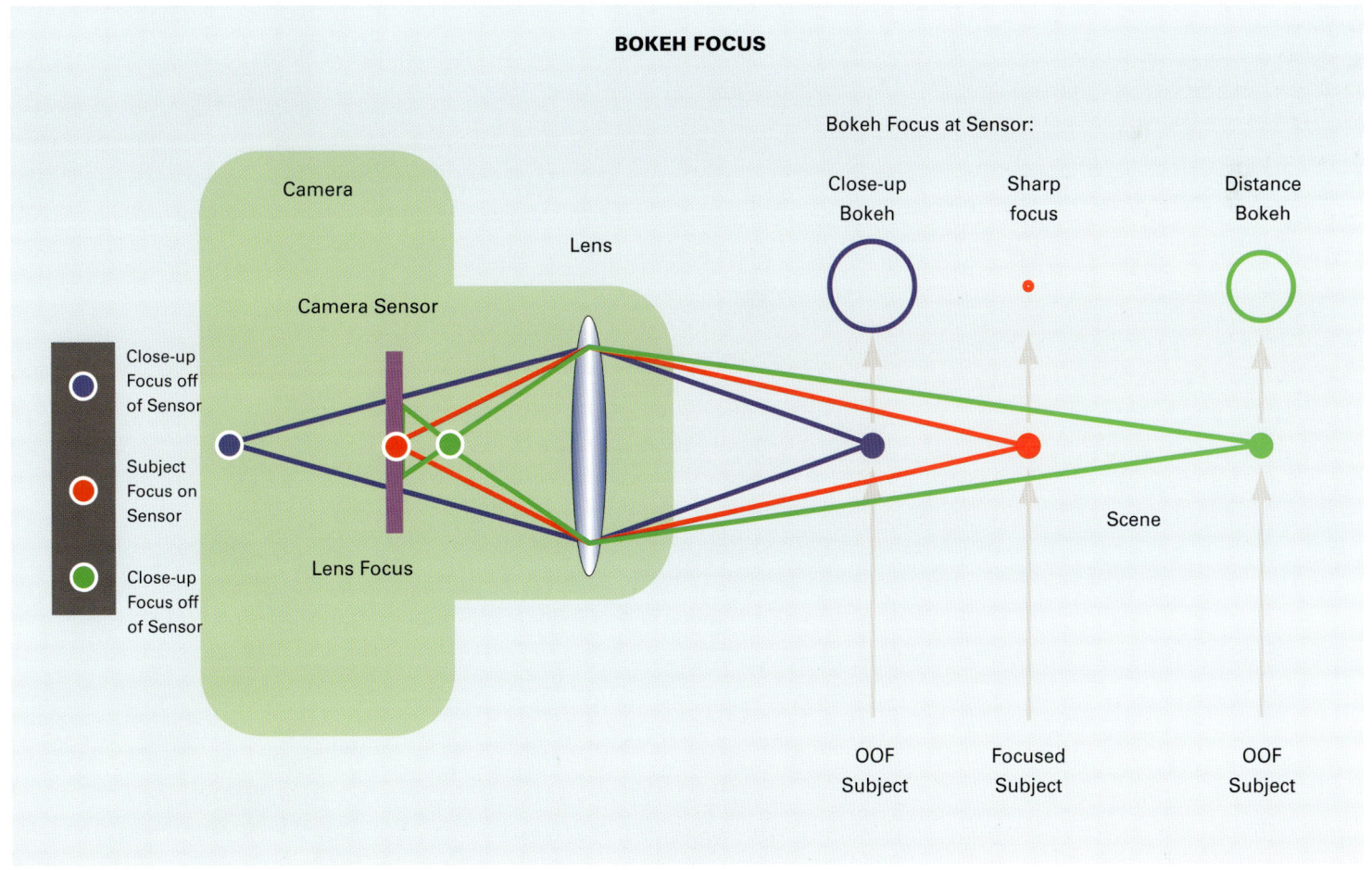

Characteristics of Bokeh

Bokeh can be created with almost any light source, but the bright lights from signs and vehicles at night are some of the easiest to use.

I sometimes shoot night scenes just for the bokeh effects, occasionally going as far as shooting almost entirely out of focus, leaving only small details sharp. The only thing required is to shoot from a distance that will allow the background to be thrown out of sharpness.

It is also possible to add your own light sources for creating bokeh. Any bright light thrown out of focus will create a bokeh circle, so you can use small LED lights (such as Christmas lights) to create bokeh shapes behind a person when shooting a portrait, for example.

COMMON BOKEH SHAPES

There is a variety of bokeh shapes, but here is a selection of the most common types.

A – Hard-edged
B – Sliced
C – Soft-edged
D – Double line
E – Onion
F – Cat's-eye
G – Spiral
H – Five-bladed aperture
I – Eight-bladed aperture

Bokeh blur is defined by the portion of the image cone at its point of intersection with the image plane. The size of the bokeh disk depends on the point of intersection of the light cone, while the blade contour of the working aperture usually creates the shape.

The distribution of light across the bokeh plane is created by a number of factors such as the curvature of the lens, lens speed, lens aberrations, and the number (as well as the design and placement) of lens elements. All of these factors contribute to the bokeh outcome, as does the subject and background distance.

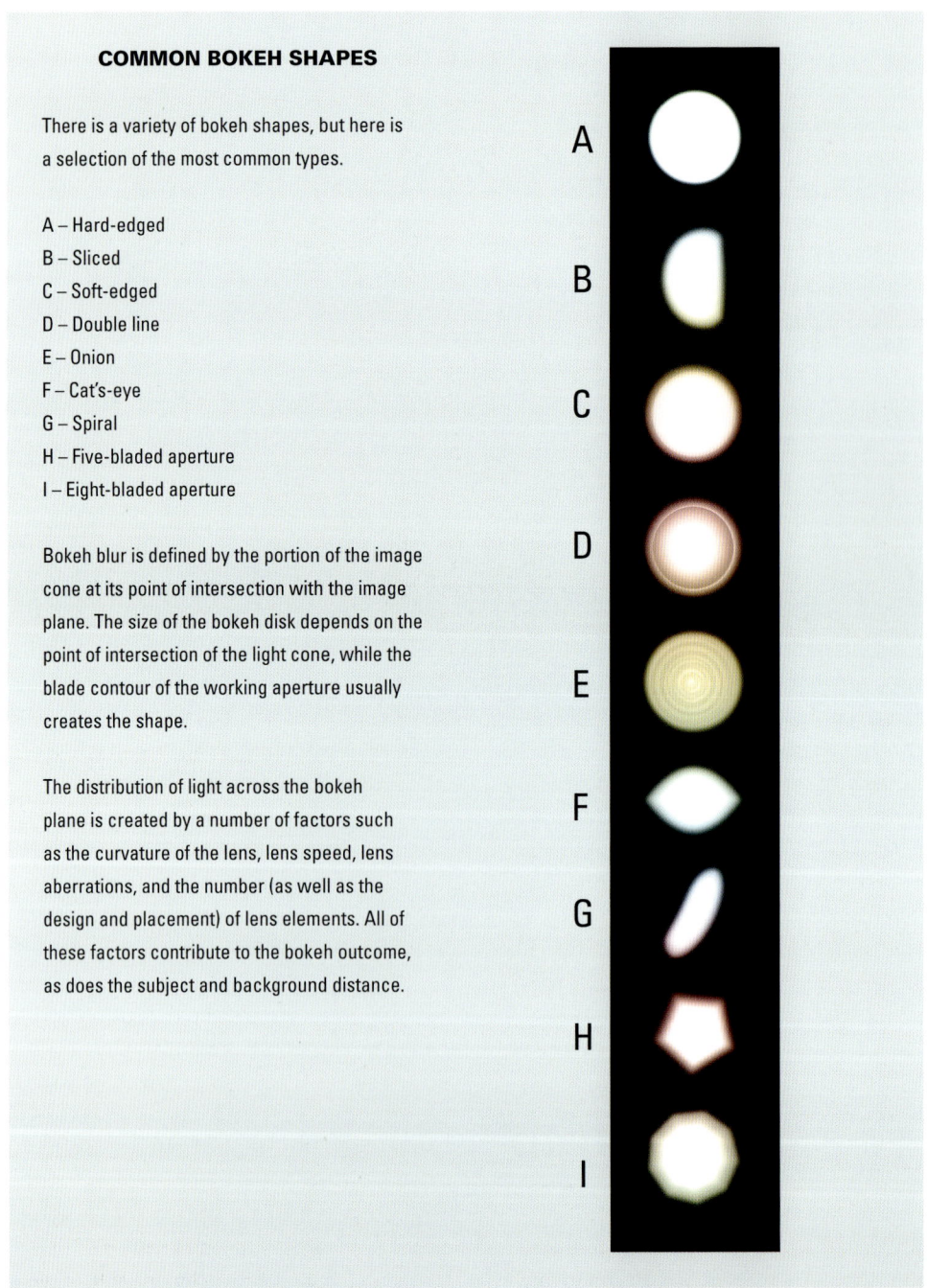

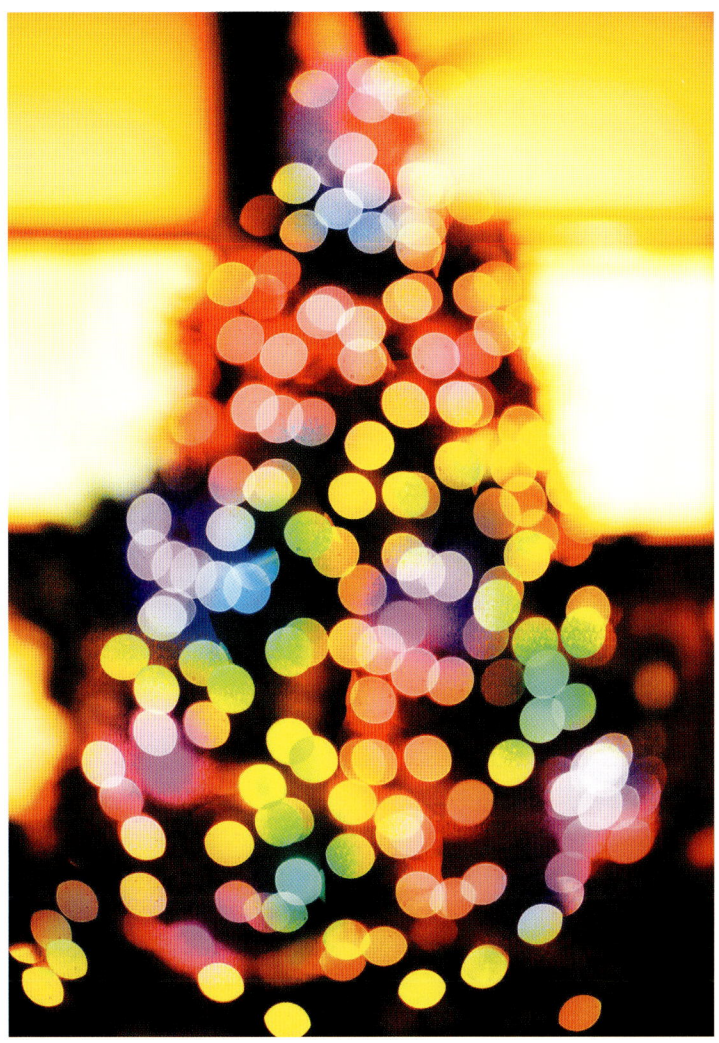 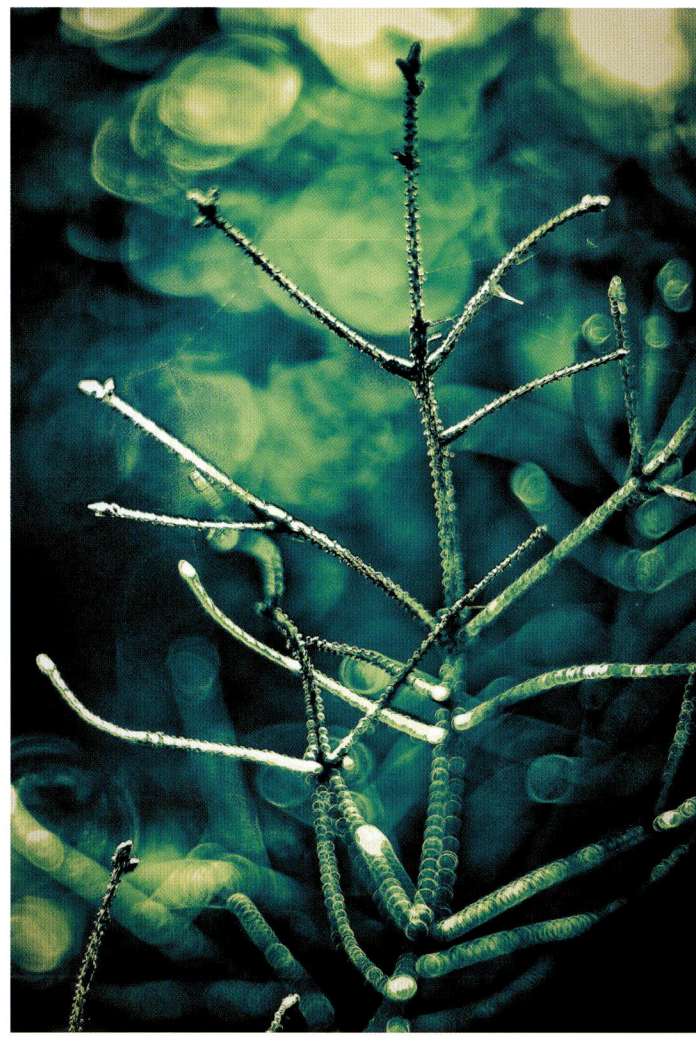

Oval Bokeh

One of the more interesting aspects of using freelensing and other off-axis techniques (see Chapter 3) is the type of bokeh that is possible. Often, the effect is oval shaped or bright on one side and soft on the other. This can be altered by the angle at which a lens is held, offset, or skewed from the axis.

Oval-shaped bokeh can also happen within the lens axis. It is a sought-after effect by some contemporary users and was a prominent characteristic of many older lenses, especially those used in collodion wet-plate photography. Many old portrait lenses exhibited this type of bokeh effect.

Usually associated with standard and wide-angle lenses used at wide apertures, the effect is due to the relationship of image cones entering the lens from extreme angles as they pass through a wide aperture, which is elongated by the shape of the aperture circle from a sharp angle.

Cat's-eye Bokeh

Cat's eye bokeh is a variant of oval bokeh that happens when light subjects are rendered toward the edges of an image. This is a result of optical vignetting; the bokeh effect narrows from the center of the image toward the corners. Consequently, the bokeh seems to swirl in a rotational pattern around the edges of the frame, as flattened disks of light.

A slightly different cat's eye bokeh effect can also happen if the inside edges of the mirror/sensor chamber clip one side of the bokeh disk. This can occur when the lens is not matched to the camera, so the lens aperture is too big (too fast) for the size of the mirror/sensor chamber. The edges of the smaller chamber cut off the edges of the light exiting the lens before it hits the sensor. This generally affects only the bokeh closer to the edges of the frame.

ABOVE LEFT: *These lights were shot with the lens out of focus, in order to produce bokeh. Notice the variation of the effect that can occur with shape and size.*

ABOVE RIGHT: *What's interesting here is how the droplets of water along the branches each produce their own bokeh circle as the branch recedes out of focus.*

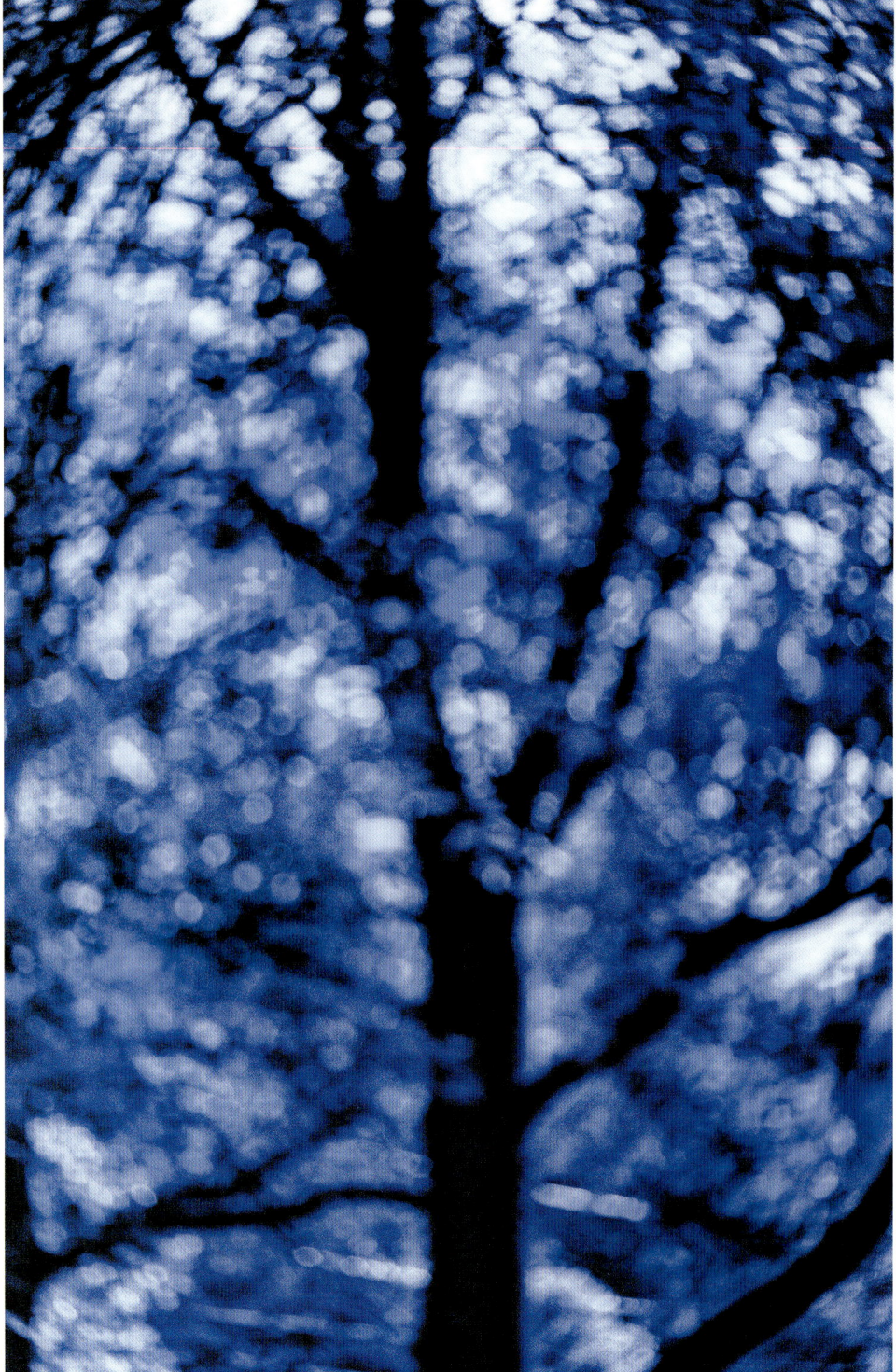

ABOVE: *Many older lenses are famous for their spiral bokeh quality. It can be quite distracting in the wrong scanerios, which is why it isn't present in modern lenses. But for expressive or artistic shots, it can be quite breathtaking.*

Spiral Bokeh

Many older lenses produce what is referred to as spiral bokeh. If you look closely, you will notice that the center bokeh appears normal, but as you get closer to the outer edges of the image circle, the bokeh disks appear flattened.

This is due to the curvature of the lens. As the outer edge light rays hit the first surface of the lens, they strike at an angle and, as they pass through the glass, the light is flattened into an oval shape.

Rays closer to the center are less affected. They are rounder in shape due to their closer proximity to the axis of the lens, which allows them to travel in a more or less straight line through the aperture.

DESCRIBING BOKEH

The characteristics of bokeh can be described in a number of ways, outlined in the grid below.

CHARACTERISTIC	OPTIONS
Edge	Slight bright line Bright line Double line Soft Graduated Hard
Double line	Yes No
Aperture shape	Round 8-sided 5-sided 4-sided Custom
Overall effect	Pleasing Distracting Neutral

BOKEH & FLASH

Unwanted bokeh can be created in various ways while using a flash. The light from the flash can bounce off reflective surfaces within the subject scene and cause both bokeh and flare.

At times, this is difficult to anticipate prior to shooting, but it can be useful in certain situations, such as when there is an interesting pattern of reflective objects. While this may seem like a rare occurrence, it is something to be aware of when you shoot with an artificial light source such as a flash.

LINEAR BOKEH

With certain linear subjects, bokeh can take on a unique appearance, with the lines of certain subjects seeming to create a distinctive type of "linear" bokeh. In reality, the look is simply a repeating pattern of circular bokeh that has similar image density along a linear subject.

The truth is that every object in the out-of-focus areas of an image is actually made of circular shapes that overlap.

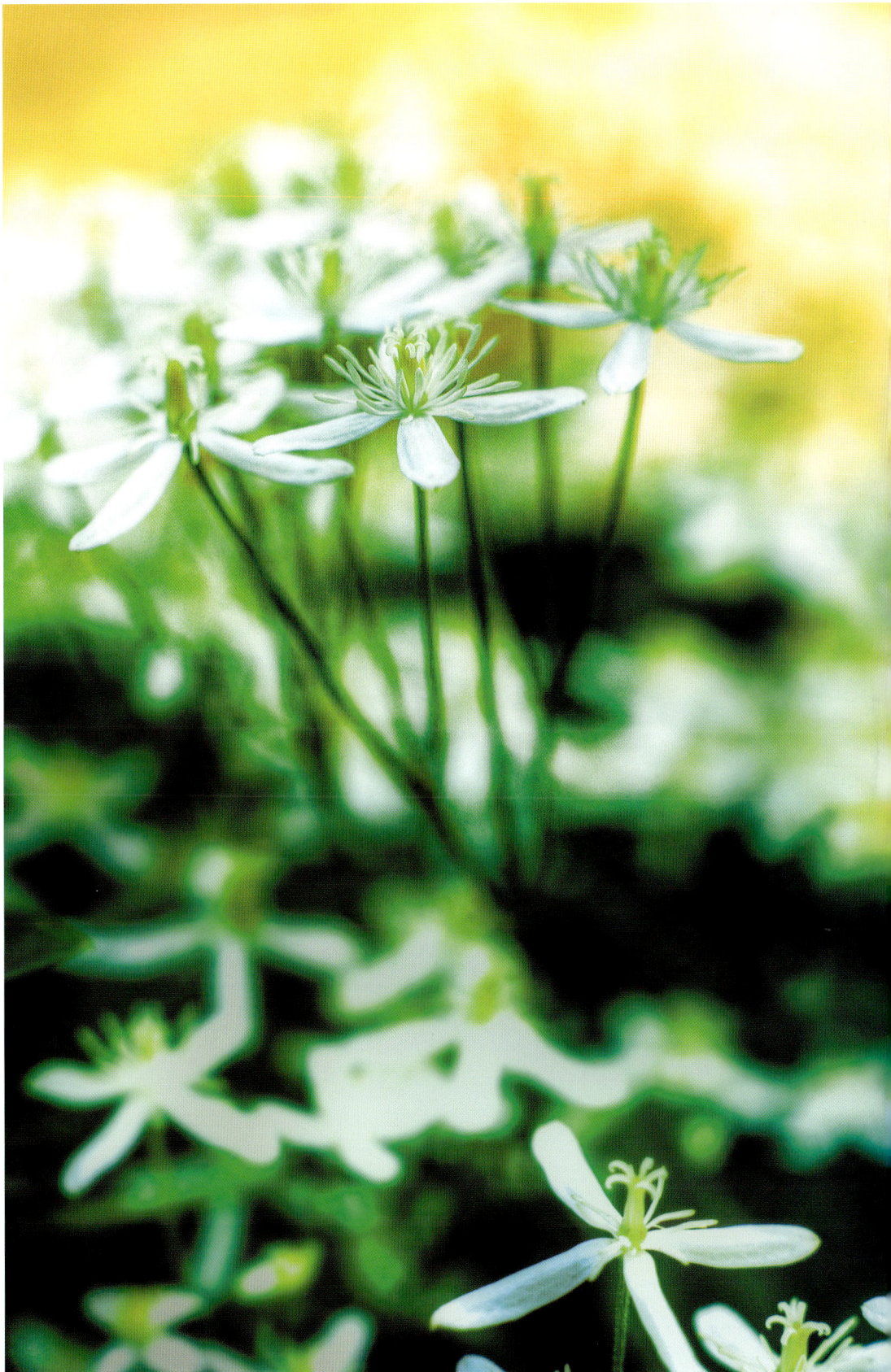

RIGHT: *Here you have a variety of bokeh combined in a single shot—some result from the lens used, others from the subject, still more from the dappled light in the background.*

How Lens Design Affects Bokeh

Different lenses produce different bokeh effects, so you may want to check what kind of bokeh a particular lens might produce before you purchase a lens.

Fast-Aperture Bokeh

Lenses with a wide maximum aperture produce the most dramatic bokeh effects and are especially effective when the subject is very close to the camera. Bokeh is not judged so much by how out of focus the background appears, though. Rather, it is how smoothly the out-of-focus area is blurred and how good it looks.

Although bokeh is usually associated with longer lenses, it is a trait of all photographic lenses. The quality of the effect can vary between different lenses, different manufacturers, and cameras used.

Some photographers prefer to use a more technical or limited definition of bokeh; they use it only to describe how the lens renders the out-of-focus points of light, and will argue that bokeh refers only to the quality or fuzziness of the circular light sources and reflections in these areas.

Other photographers believe that it is really more about the quality of the entire out-of-focus area, and not just the highlights. I tend to think of it as the latter, and do not think that there is such a thing as "bad" bokeh. To me, the bokeh is perfect when it works with the image.

Sharp bokeh can support hard-edged subjects compositionally, and the same can be said about soft-edge bokeh and soft subject matter. There are also times when a contrasting bokeh effect will work to enhance the subject. Bad bokeh is perhaps produced due to poor exposure, contrast, saturation, or lens quality.

Amazing focus results can be accomplished by simply photographing with your lens defocused: in this case, the whole image is produced from bokeh.

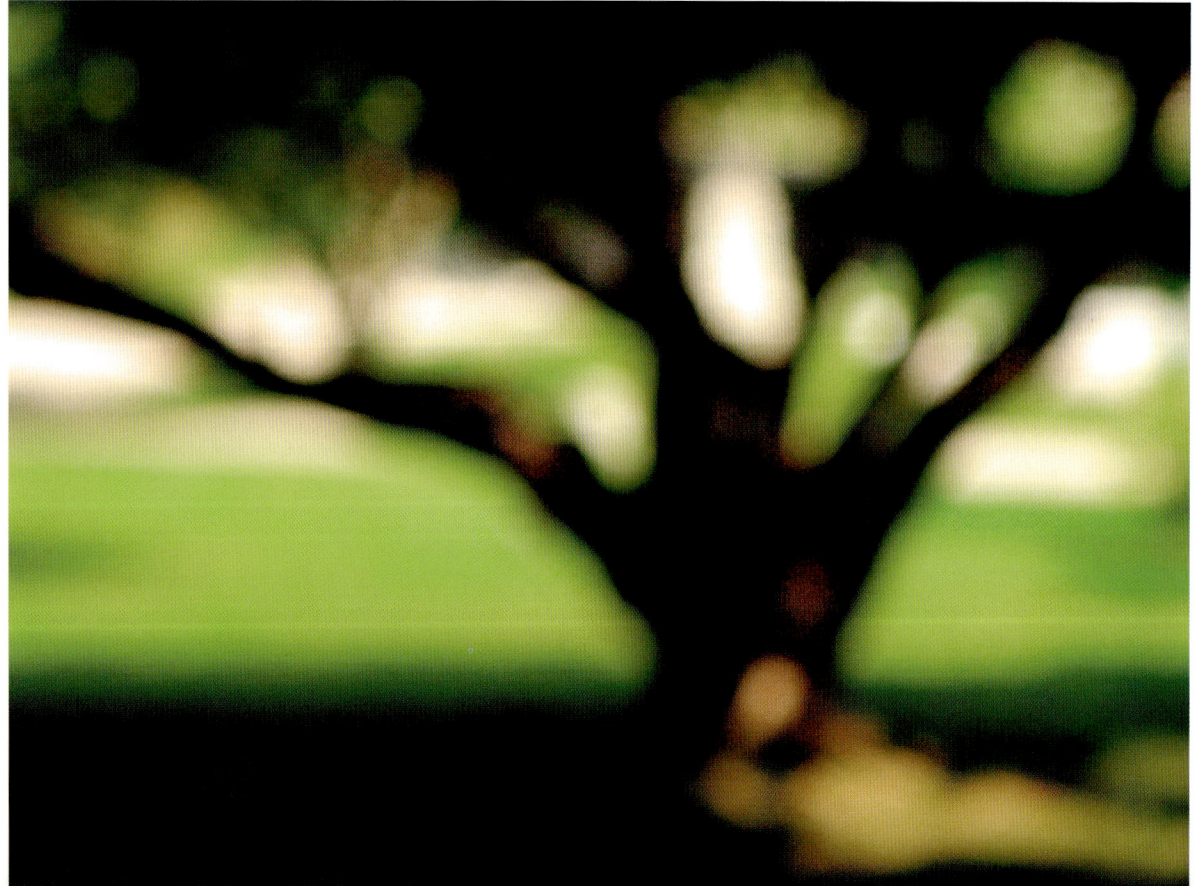

LEFT: *Throwing the lens out-of-focus results in an image that is made entirely from the bokeh effect.*

02 // HOW LENS DESIGN AFFECTS BOKEH // BOKEH

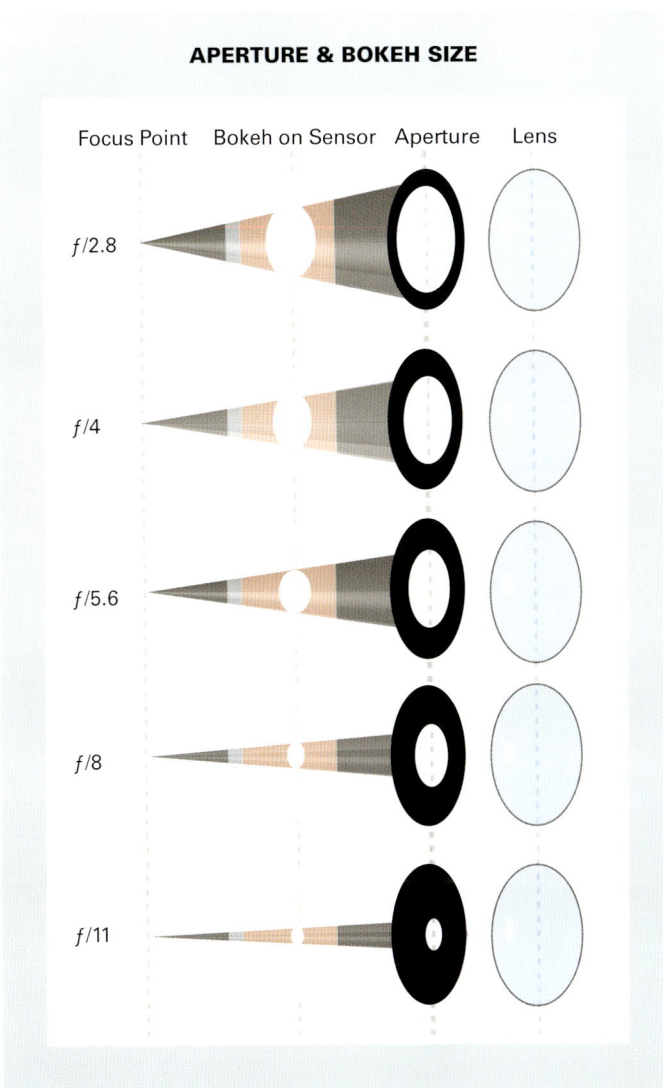

APERTURE & BOKEH SIZE

ABOVE: *Although focal length is the primary cause of bokeh, the aperture selected and the relative focus govern the scale at which it occurs on the sensor. It is the point at which the light cone intersects the sensor plane that ultimately matters. A larger cross section of the cone will render larger bokeh on the sensor. Larger-aperture openings produce larger bokeh, while smaller apertures lessen the effect, producing more depth of field, which tends to make the bokeh less pronounced and the focus field appear sharper. The longer the focal length, the more pronounced the bokeh effect.*

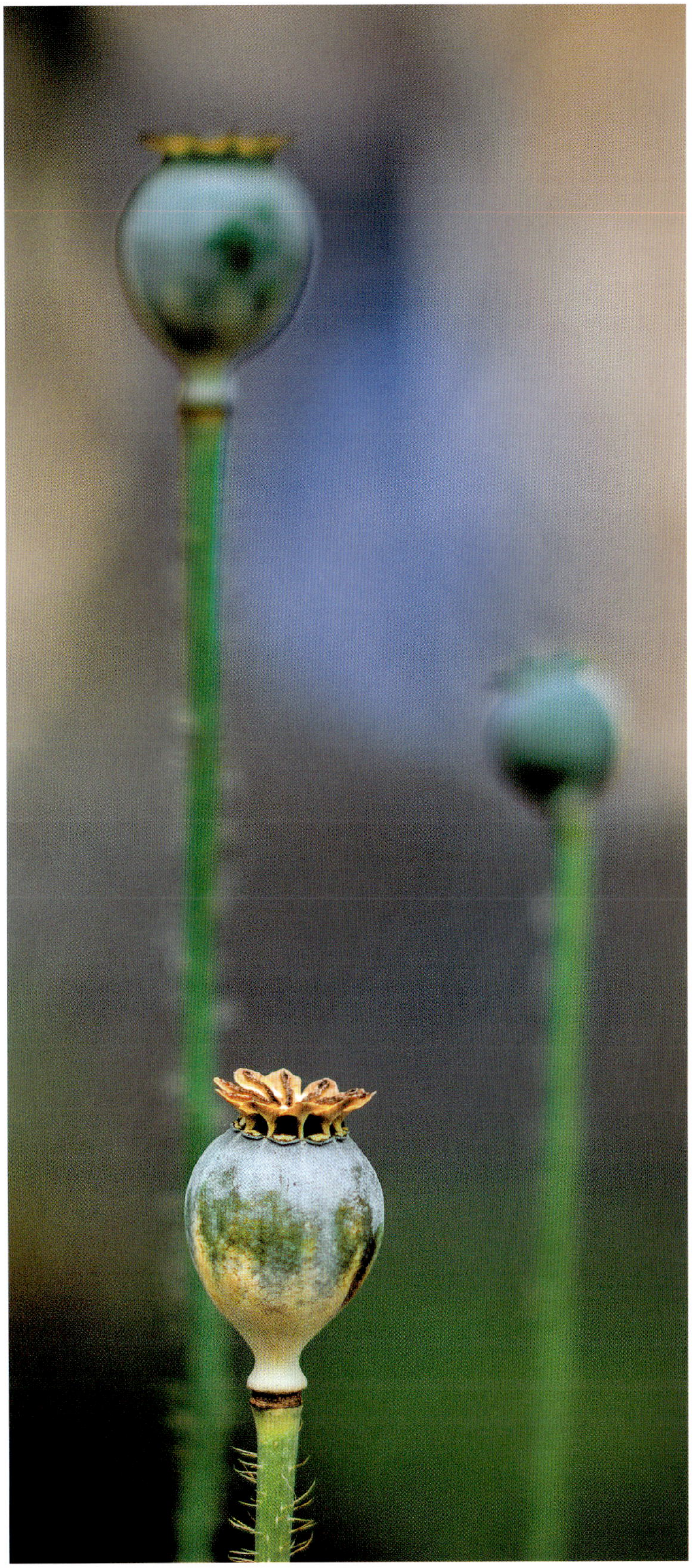

RIGHT: *Here the particular bokeh characteristics of this fast lens are apparent in the way the three flower buds are rendered: extremely sharp (in focus), outlined (just out of focus), and fully soft (farthest out of focus).*

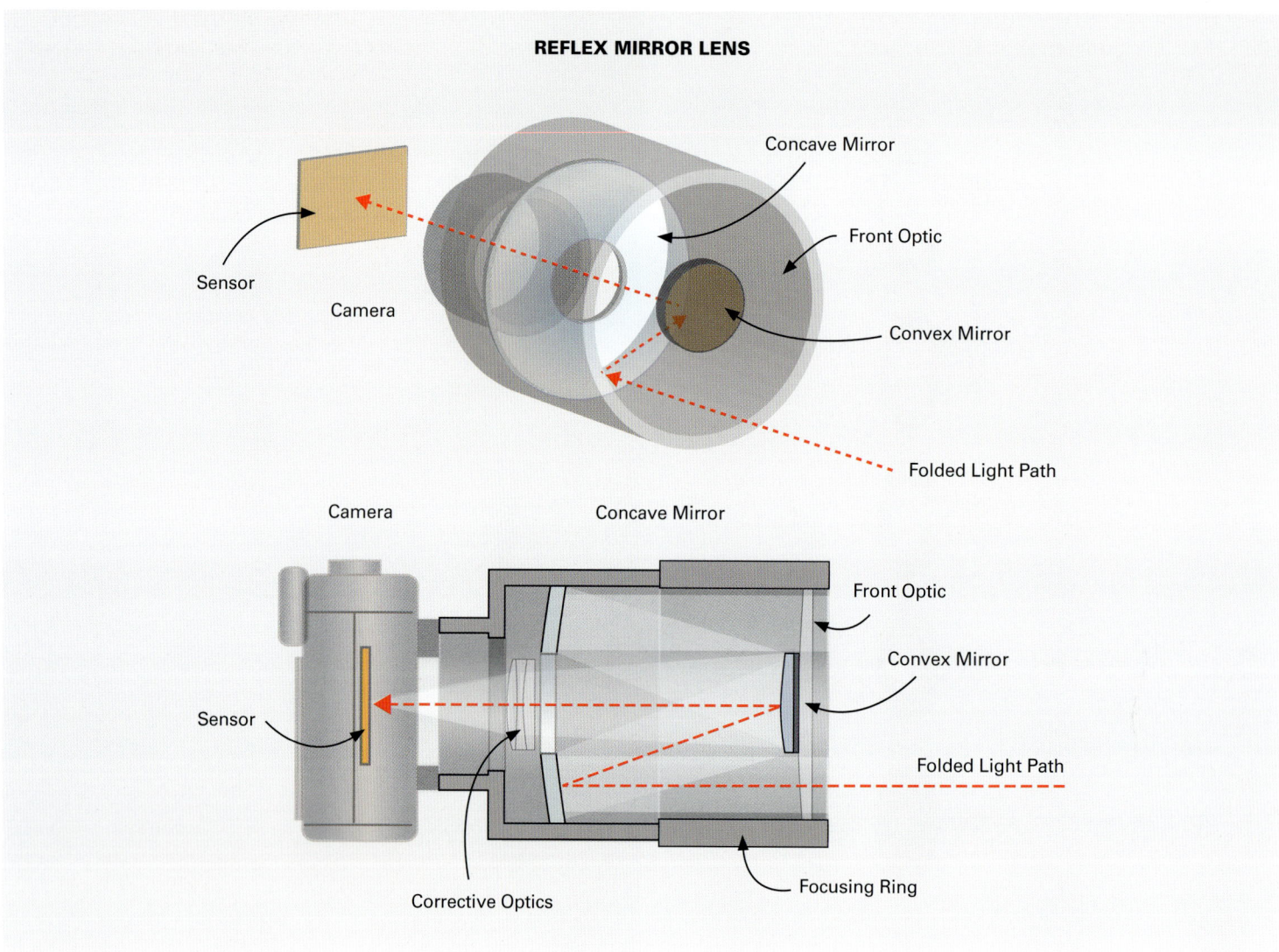

Catadioptric Bokeh

Better known as a mirror lens, a catadioptric lens produces a unique type of bokeh that some find objectionable: bokeh known as "the donuts."

Mirror lenses can use both refractive glass and reflective mirror optics in their design, with most lenses usually combining both refraction and reflection.

This means that a mirror lens is not a lens in the conventional sense. Rather, it is a series of convex and concave mirrors that reflect the light through the lens housing and focus it onto the sensor. The outer ring of the lens is a concave mirror that reflects light toward the surface of a second smaller convex mirror, which in turn reflects the light rays directly onto the camera sensor. As a result, the light is bounced through an optical path, rather than traveling directly through the lens. This enables a mirror lens to have a very long focal length in a relatively short and light lens.

However, there are side-effects to designing a lens in this way. Firstly, a mirror lens does not have an adjustable aperture; depending on the focal length of the lens, the aperture is typically fixed at $f/8$ or $f/11$. Second, the design produces a very distinctive, donut-shaped bokeh pattern that can prove to be incredibly distracting in a photograph.

ABOVE: *A mirror lens is a special lens that uses a series of convex and concave mirrors as well as a few corrective lenses in order to fold the light path, which in turn allows a "long" telephoto lens to be quite compact in size.*

02 // HOW LENS DESIGN AFFECTS BOKEH // BOKEH

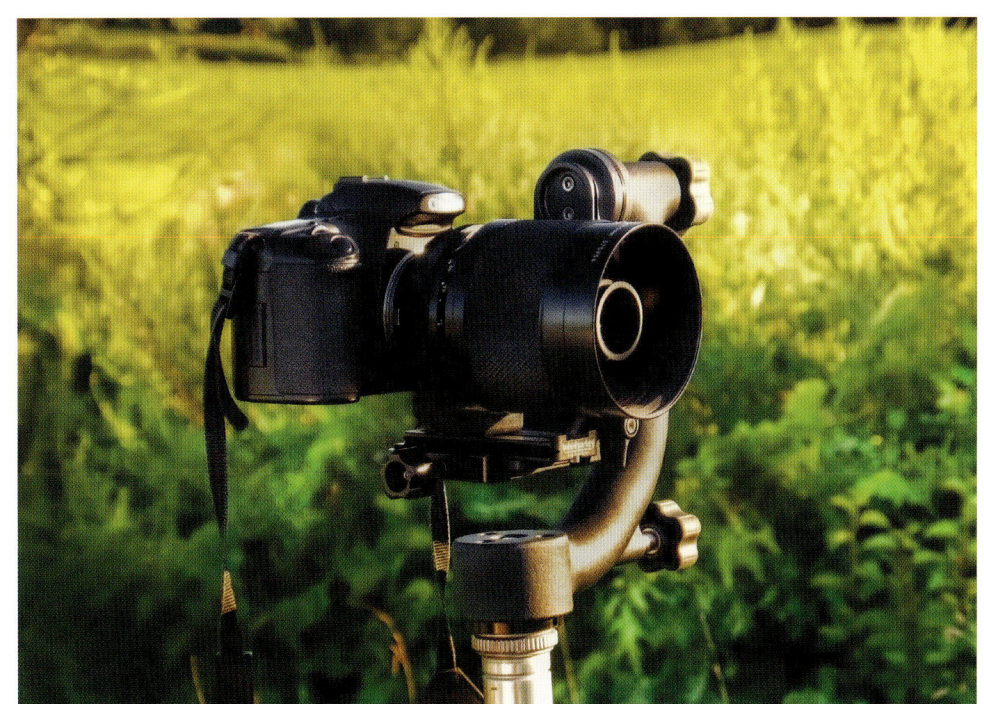

LEFT: *The Nikkor 500mm lens shown here is a catadioptric/mirror design that shows how compact the lens can be. While this makes the lens more convenient to carry, it comes with some restrictions. Most mirror designs allow only a single aperture. Also, the doughnut-shaped second mirror creates a doughnut-shaped bokeh, which some photographers find visually annoying. However, many of us find it to be interesting.*

BELOW LEFT: *The donut-shaped bokeh produced by a mirror lens can be either very interesting or very disturbing, depending on the subject and nature of the image.*

BELOW: *Mirror lenses do not use variable apertures; instead the aperture is usually fixed at f/8 or f/11. Because of their long focal length, the depth of field is very shallow, especially when used while working at close distances.*

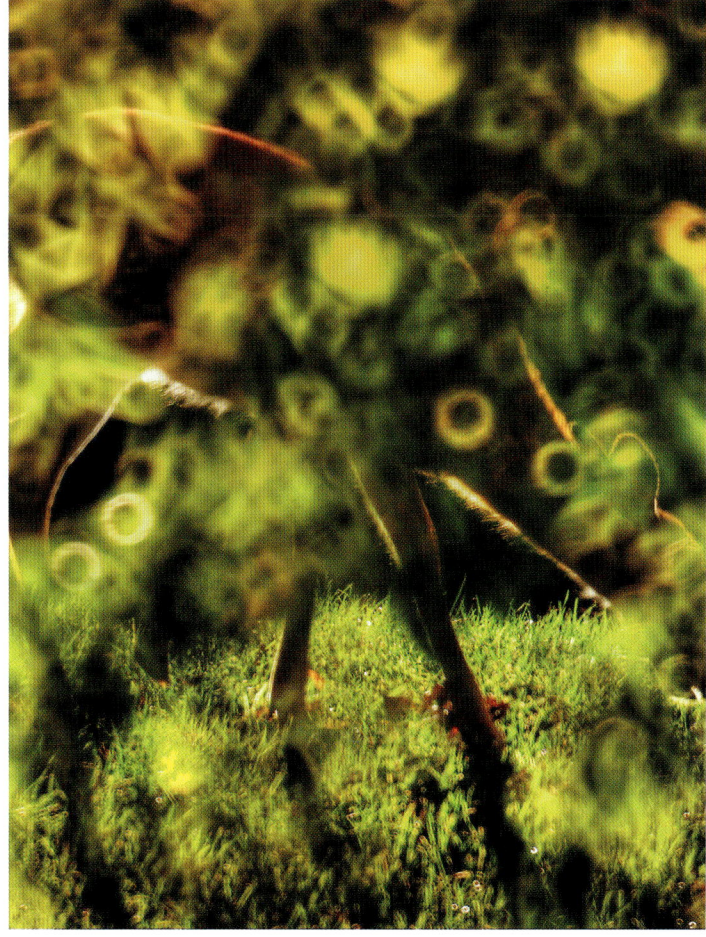

Blade Shape & Bokeh

The aperture can affect the shape of the bokeh that is rendered: octagonal bokeh is produced by apertures that uses eight blades, a lens with a six-bladed aperture produces hexagonal bokeh, and a five-bladed aperture will produce pentagonal bokeh.

In most cases, a rounder bokeh shape is considered most pleasing. As a general rule, the more blades that are used to create the aperture opening in the lens, the rounder the bokeh shape will be. However, some lenses are designed with curved aperture blades, so the roundness of the aperture comes not from the number of blades, but from their shape.

Many old lenses—especially those used for wet-plate photography—used waterhouse stops, instead of a variable aperture. A waterhouse stop is a metal (or card) plate with a single, circular aperture in it, which would be inserted into a slot in the lens to control the flow of light. To change the aperture, you simply changed the waterhouse stop for one with a larger or smaller hole in it. Because waterhouse stops are perfectly round in shape, they produce very round bokeh—modern lenses may need to include 12–16 aperture blades to achieve a similar effect.

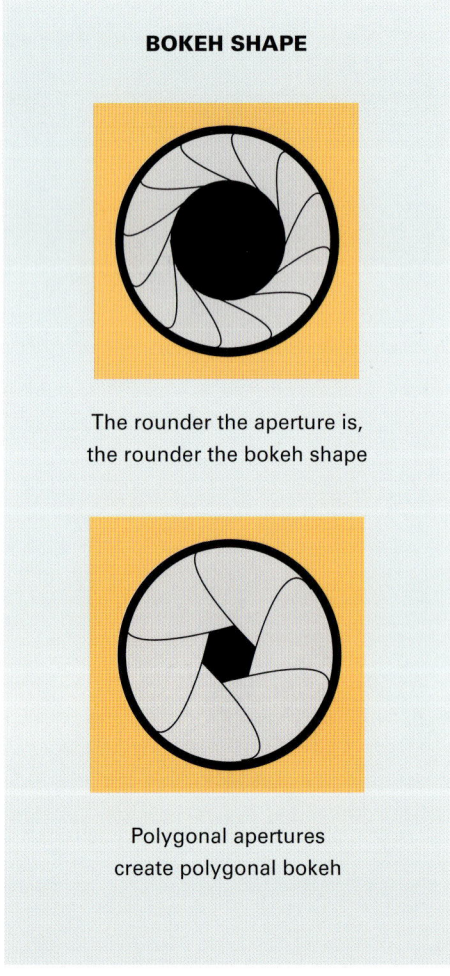

BOKEH SHAPE

The rounder the aperture is, the rounder the bokeh shape

Polygonal apertures create polygonal bokeh

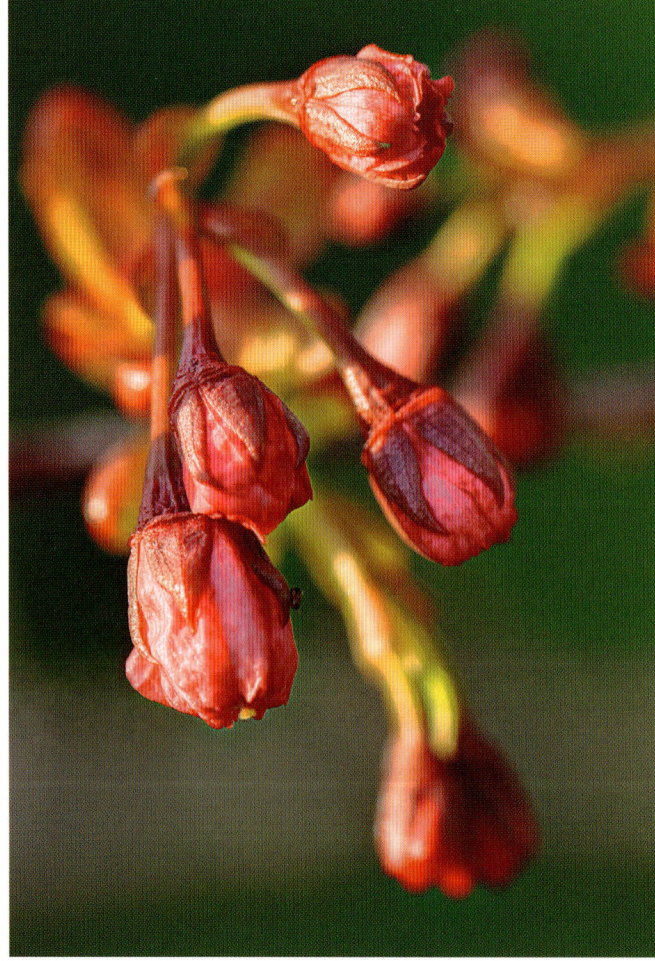

LEFT: *Bokeh is not always defined as a shape. To create the bokeh effect, we need to have background details that will take on the shape of the aperture when defocused. An out-of-focus area without detail can render a nice soft background.*

02 // BLADE SHAPE AND BOKEH // BOKEH

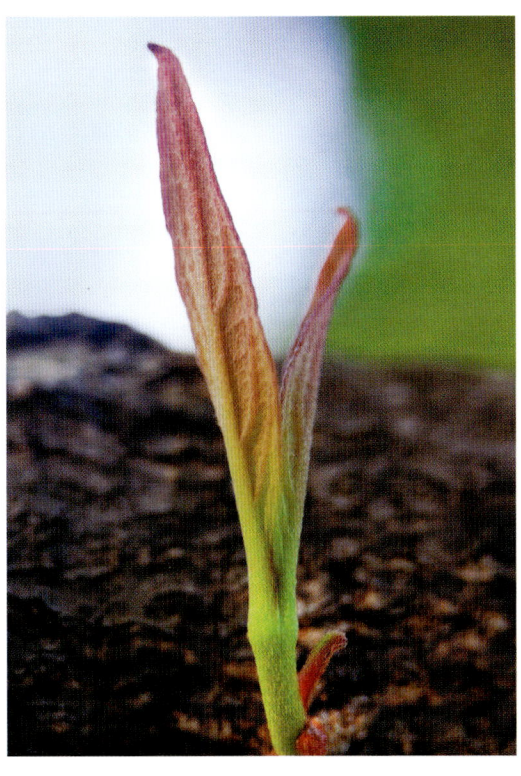

LEFT: *The bokeh here was produced using a plastic lens taken from a single-use camera and mounting it on a digital camera. The lens has fixed focus, which restricts its use to macro photography. The aperture is also fixed to a wide opening.*

BELOW: *The light shapes found under a tree in bright light are actually multiple pinhole images of the sun. Each spot is a distorted image of the sun.*

Natural bokeh

Bokeh by itself doesn't seem to exist in nature: the real world that we see is generally made up of solid, "sharp" objects, whereas our camera lens can see things in degrees of out-of-focus.

However, bokeh-like shapes can occur, such as when the sun shines through the leaves of a tree on a bright sunny day. This effect is similar to the way in which a pinhole camera functions, with each leaf opening effectively acting as a giant pinhole.

If we could look at a single instance of this phenomenon, we would see an image of the sky and the sun. However, the aperture shapes created by the leaves are softened by the scale of the opening, and obscured by the shear number of "pinhole" apertures.

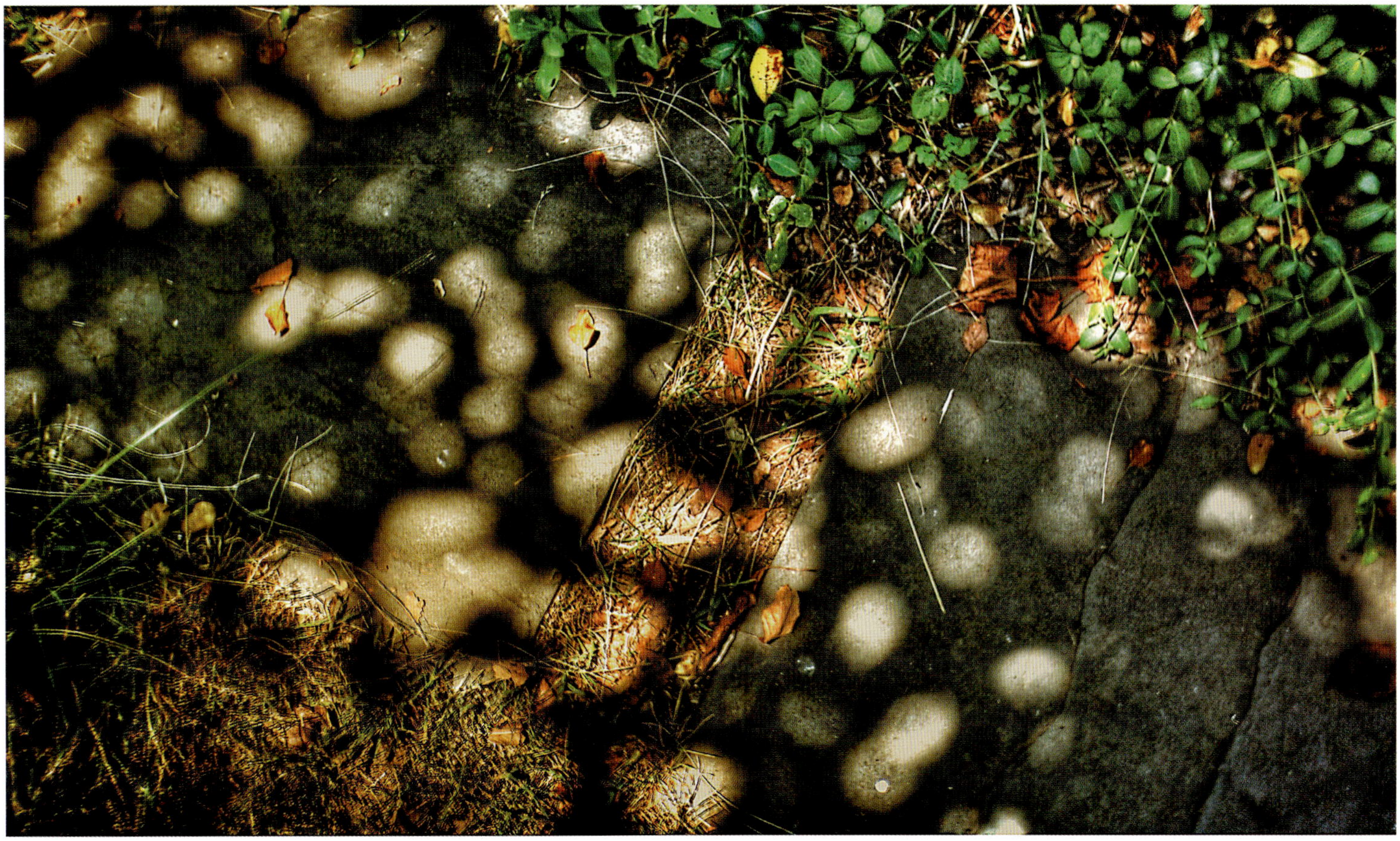

Utilizing Bokeh

Bokeh usually becomes unattractive when it fights with the subject, so many bokeh lovers like what is called "soft and creamy" bokeh, which refers to the edges and the body of the bokeh structure.

Soft and creamy bokeh is seen as soft gradations of color, which creates an eye-pleasing separation between sharp foreground subjects and background softness. However, I find that there are numerous bokeh types that can work their magic in different ways.

For instance, a hard-edged bokeh might help to reinforce a certain composition that deals with a hard-edged subject, or it might be used to contrast a soft-edged subject. There are also many opportunities that can produce what I call "bokeh patterning."

In any composition, the eye moves naturally to any element that is "different," and while bokeh can be used to lead the eye through a composition, it can also become a distraction.

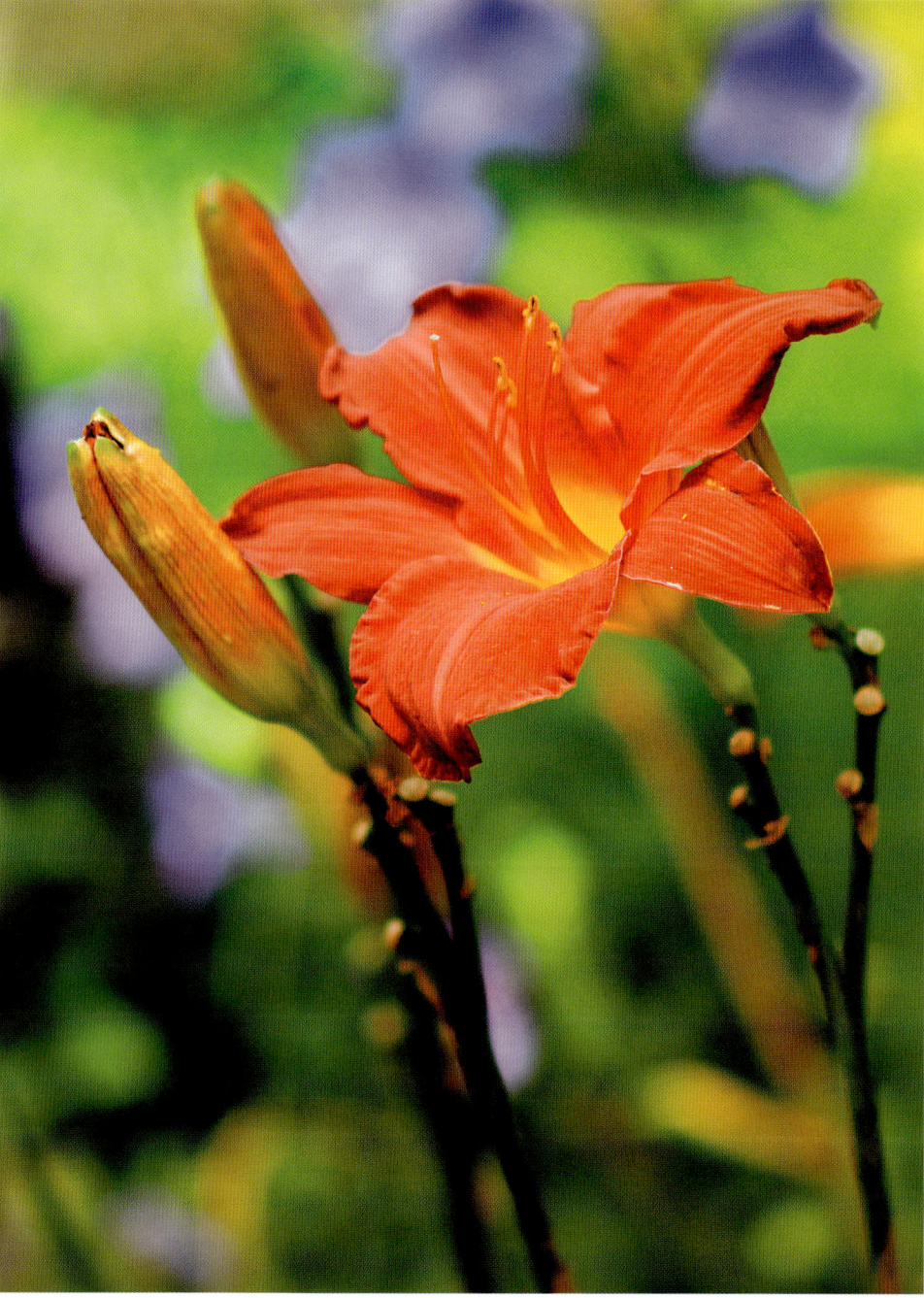

RIGHT: *Various kinds of bokeh can occur with different lenses and with variations in focus and light. Color and the degree of sharpness are important to consider for compositional reasons.*

Anything that takes the eye away from the main subject should be considered carefully—it is OK to have the eye move around an image, but eventually you want it to come back to the actual subject. The common consensus is that everything else in the photograph should support the theme and the main subject, and not fight with it.

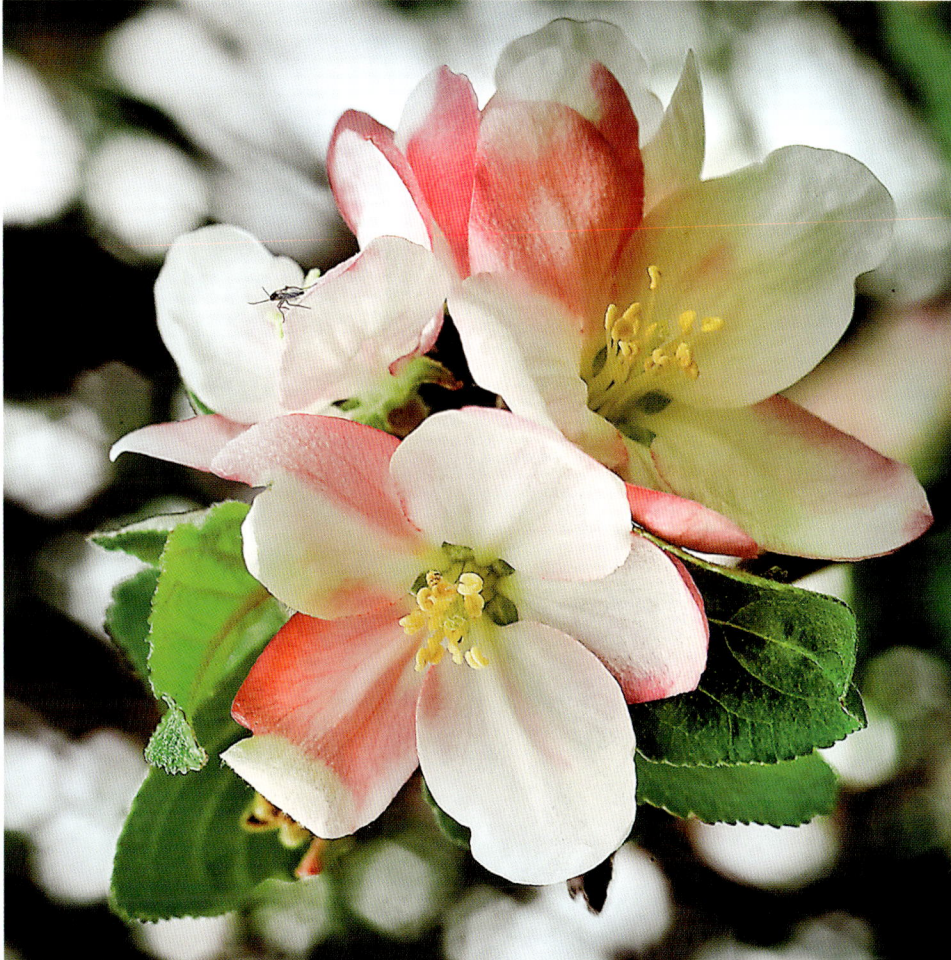

RIGHT: *Shooting close to your subject with a wide aperture makes bigger bokeh.*

BELOW RIGHT: *Bokeh can be useful to separate a sharp subject from its background. It is intentional that the only thing sharp in this image is the blade of the knife; the thin focus places emphasis on the blade.*

BELOW: *The soft bokeh background helps to separate these sharply contrasted flowers.*

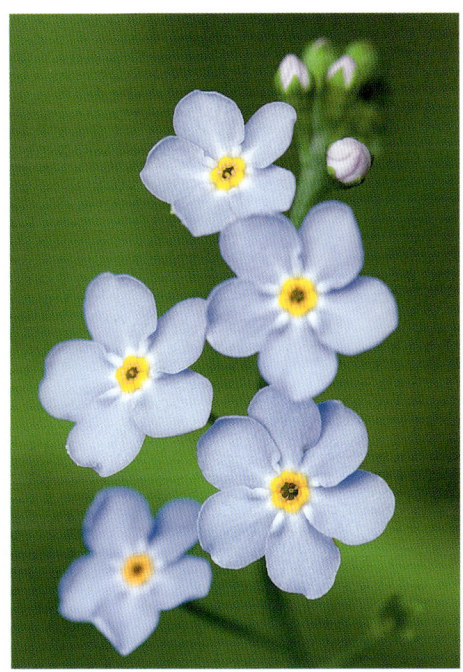
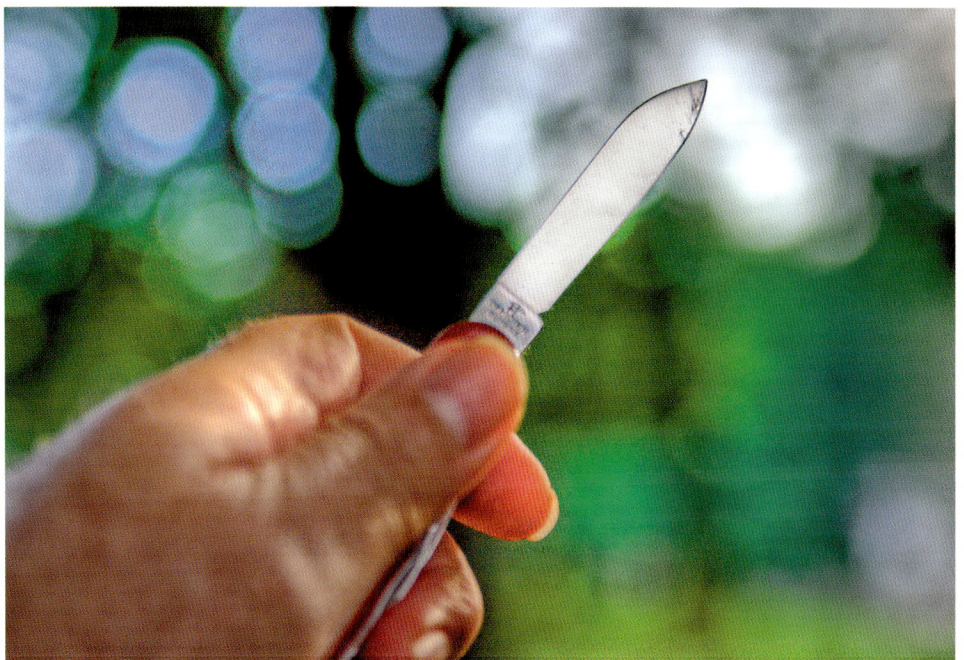

Shaped Bokeh

Although bokeh shape is usually a result of the shape formed by the lens aperture, it can also be created by using a shape as an aperture.

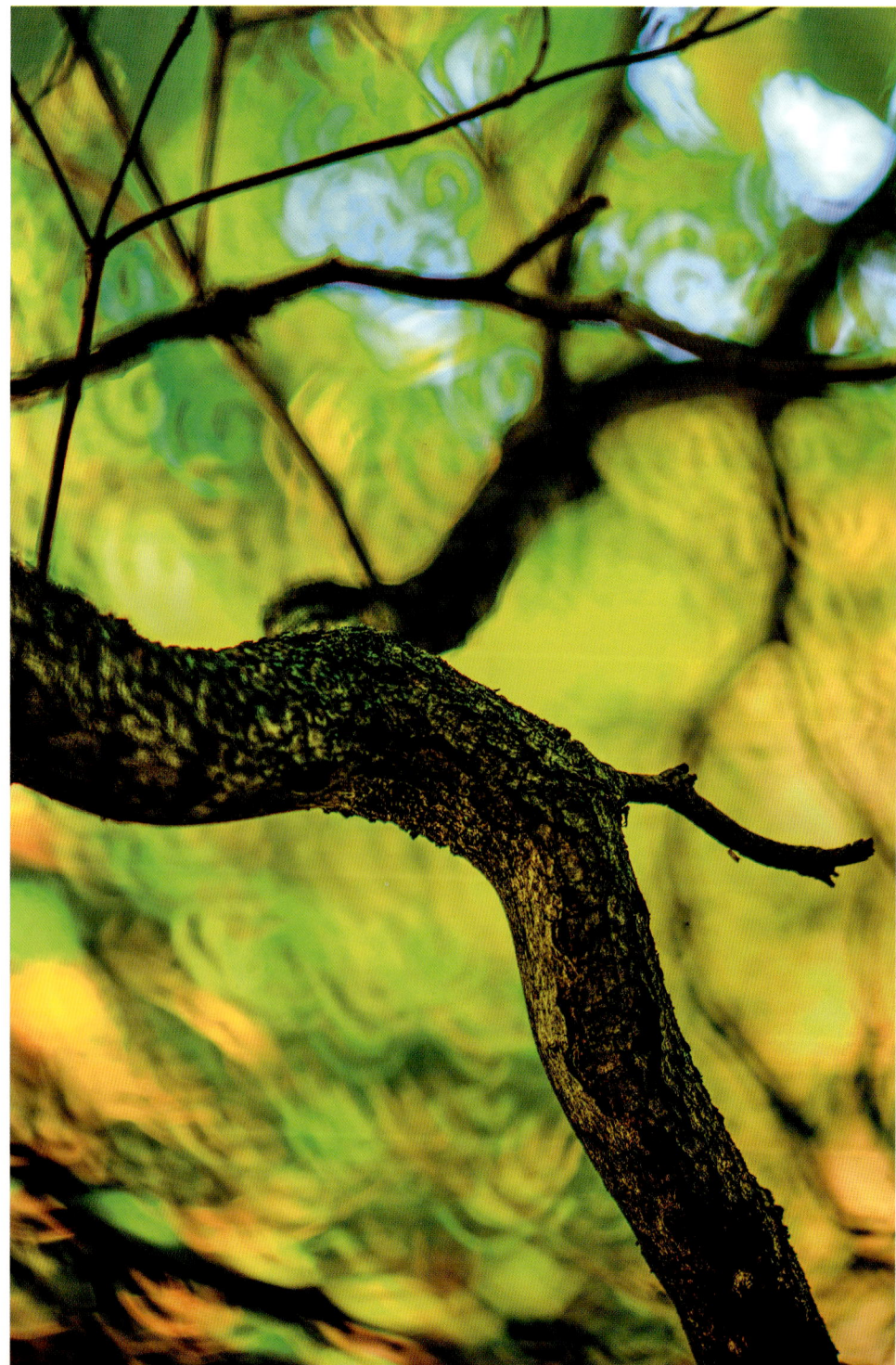

Shaped bokeh can be created in any one of a number of ways: by cutting a shape from a piece of black material, such as paper or card; by purchasing premade shaped filters; or by finding items with odd-shaped holes. The images on these two pages were all produced using homemade cutouts or "found hole" objects.

Ideally, your homemade aperture should be located between the elements of the lens, as this will place it at the lens' nodal point. However, this is generally not possible unless you are using an old lens with waterhouse stops. Instead, the shaped aperture can be mounted in front of the lens in the filter position (a filter ring or a filter adapter can be used to hold the bokeh filter in place).

Once in place, the out-of-focus highlights will take on the shape of the cutout opening, and this also becomes the working aperture for the exposure.

One of the best things about this technique is that it allows the main subject to remain perfectly sharp, while the aperture softly shapes the rest of the image. The longer the lens, and the closer the subject, the more pronounced your results will be.

RIGHT: *Cutting shapes from black paper disks can produce shaped bokeh effects.*

02 // SHAPED BOKEH // BOKEH

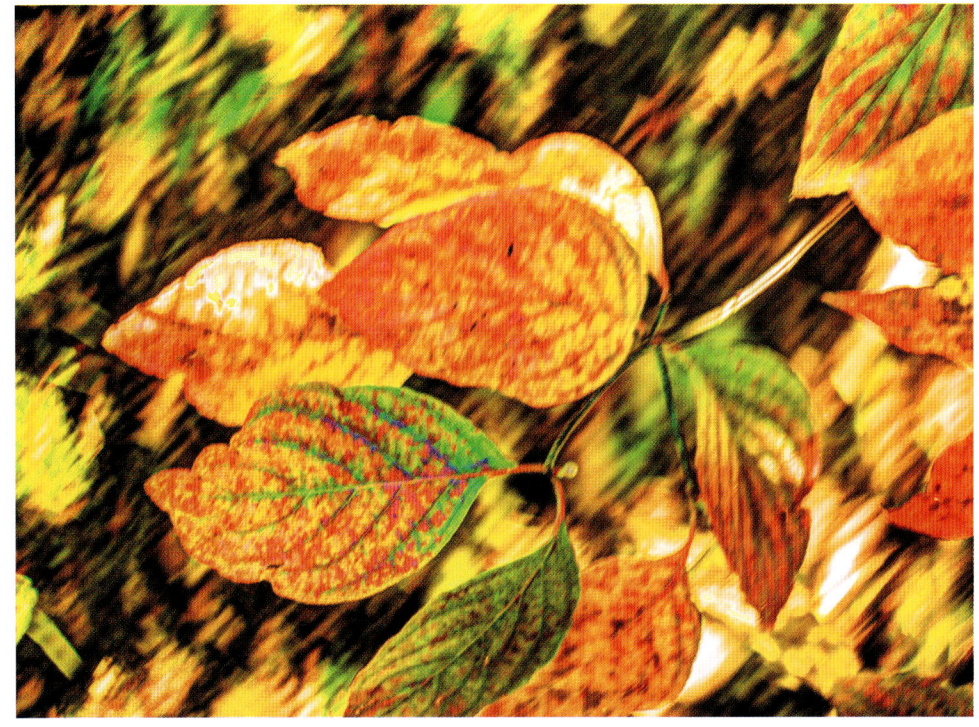

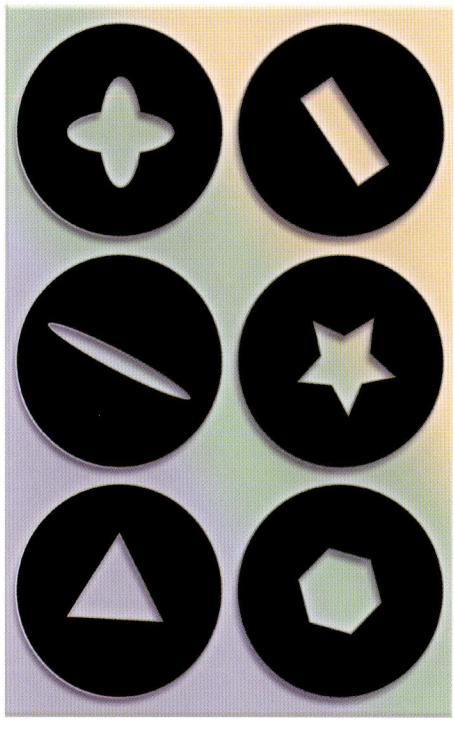

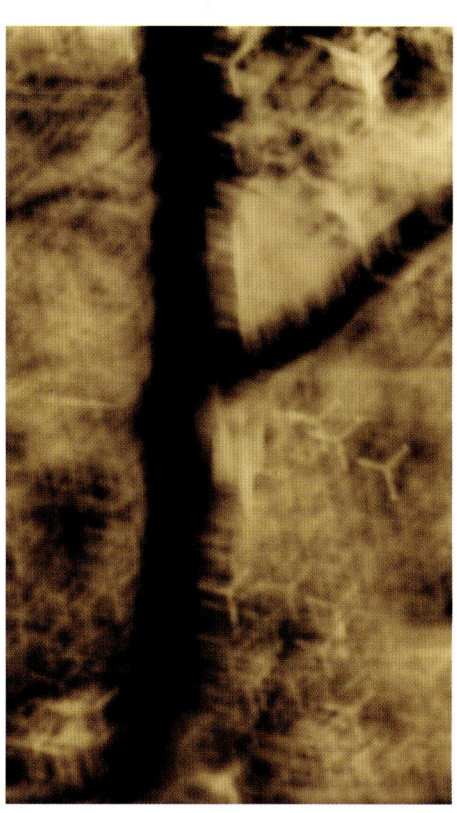

Cutout Bokeh

Unfortunately, this technique has created a plethora of images featuring heart-shaped and star-shaped highlights, which has turned it into something of a visual cliché. Therefore, I would use this technique sparingly and only when it might be useful to do so. Unique shapes also do not need to be recognizable shapes—the shape used should be one that controls the bokeh rather than making it distracting or trite.

To use this technique, it is best to open the actual lens aperture to its maximum setting (the new cutout will act as the "working" aperture for the exposure). In order to maximize the effect, it is useful to move close to your subject, and position it with brighter, more specular highlights in the background.

ABOVE: *Result of a bokeh shape added to the front of a lens.*

ABOVE RIGHT: *Just a small sample of the kinds of bokeh discs you can create yourself.*

RIGHT: *Found objects with interesting openings can be used to produce bokeh effects. A found metal disk with a Y-shaped opening created the interesting effect in this tree study.*

Faking Bokeh

Faked bokeh cannot be accomplished fully using simple blurring techniques in your image-editing program, but there are some more specialist software algorithms that can produce convincing bokeh-like results.

I hesitate to credit an artificial technique with the ability to deliver bokeh because nothing is as good as the real phenomenon of lens-created bokeh. However, Alien Skin makes a software plugin that is capable of producing very interesting results that can be used to blend a soft, bokeh-like background into an image.

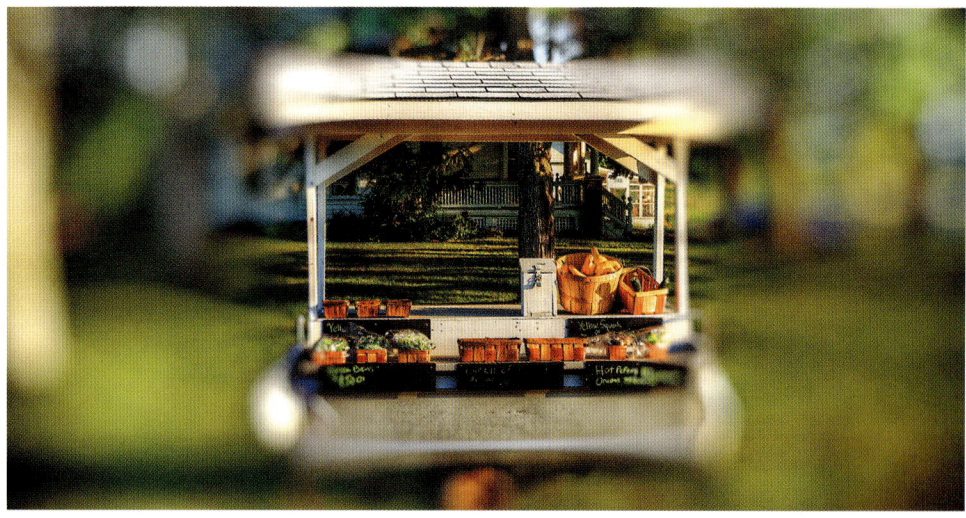

RIGHT: *Bokeh effects can be produced using software such as Alien Skin's Bokeh plugin.*

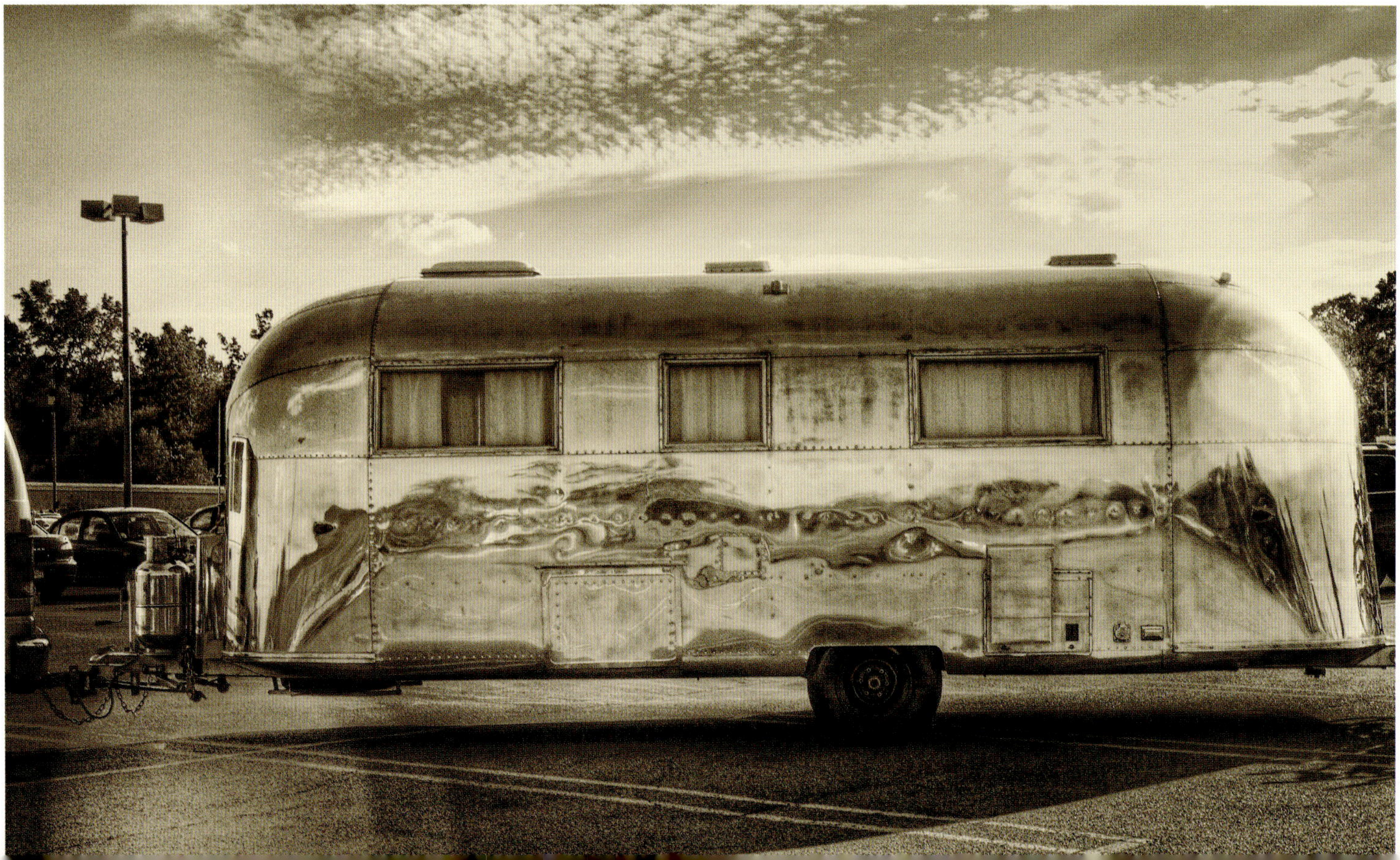

Bokeh Brushes

Post-production can allow you to simulate bokeh through the use of carefully created brushes in your image-editing program. Generally, I use a self-made brush that has a density and gradient similar to the kind of bokeh effects I like. These brushes can then be used to airbrush spots of varying density or opacity into the background of an image. However, care must be taken if you want to produce a natural-looking effect.

As well as creating bokeh, you can also improve dull or ugly bokeh by carefully adding color or brightness. Again, this needs to work with the image, rather than fight for attention—in digital photography, there are few things that are worse than a poorly done digital effect.

Layering Bokeh

Most good image-editing programs allow you to use layers, and these can be used to create a number of blending effects that can simulate bokeh. Layers can also allow a bokeh image to be combined with an image that does not exhibit the effect you want. All these techniques are discussed in depth in the software chapter (pages 148–167).

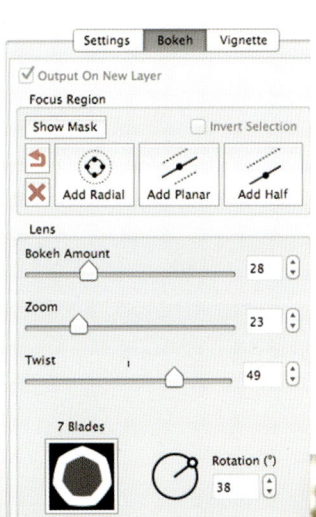

ABOVE: *Shaped brushes can be made fairly easy in programs such as Adobe Illustrator and Photoshop. You can also find preset Photoshop brushes online that are meant for this purpose.*

BELOW: *Bokeh shapes were artificially added to the right side of this street scene using Alien Skin's Bokeh software.*

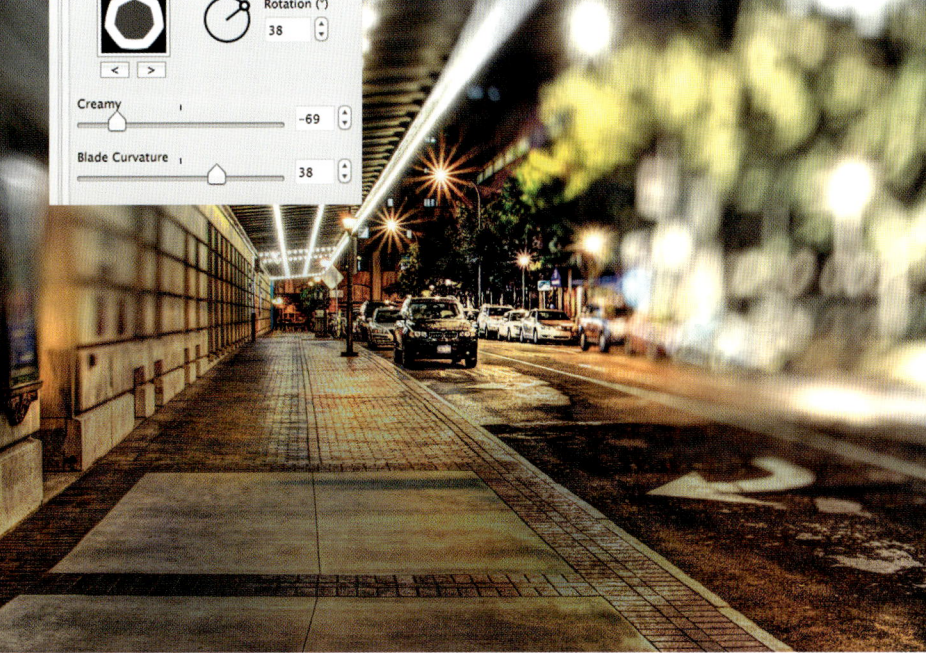

LEFT: *The bokeh-shaped flare on the back end of this trailer was created artificially in Photoshop. I wanted to place emphasis on the brightness of the sun and the reflective surface of the subject.*

Pinhole Bokeh

Bokeh is usually not associated with pinhole photography. This is because light travels in straight lines and therefore there should not be any apparent blurring with a pinhole that would cause bokeh in the same way that a lens might render it.

There is a good reason that a pinhole is not as sharp as a lensed image: the whole image is made up of nothing but bokeh circles. Normally, the effects of pinhole bokeh are hard to see, because they are usually miniscule details within a pinhole image.

A tiny pinhole creates a very small cone of light, so the image formed is not going to produce a pinpoint accurate rendition. Instead, the image is made up of soft circular projections of all the light points in the scene. Each tiny circular spot is blended into the adjacent circles to create a slightly blurred likeness of the scene being imaged.

The size of the opening or pinhole determines the size of the projected cones, while the distance from the camera will also produce proportionally smaller or larger image circles relative to the size of the opening.

BELOW: *Although very small, the pinhole produces a conical shaped projection on the film plane or sensor, which is the size of the pinhole relative to the radiating light that passes through the opening from any single point in front of the camera. As the distance increases from the subject, fewer rays are allowed to pass and the cone becomes a bit thinner (red projection) therefore the circles of confusion are slightly smaller than from subject points that are closer to the camera (blue projection). Because the light is a conical projection the effect at the sensor is similar to what happens with a lens the light points are made up of slightly different sizes of circles of confusion. The conical shape of the light that is projected from the opening is why pinhole images are not as sharp as what a lens can produce.*

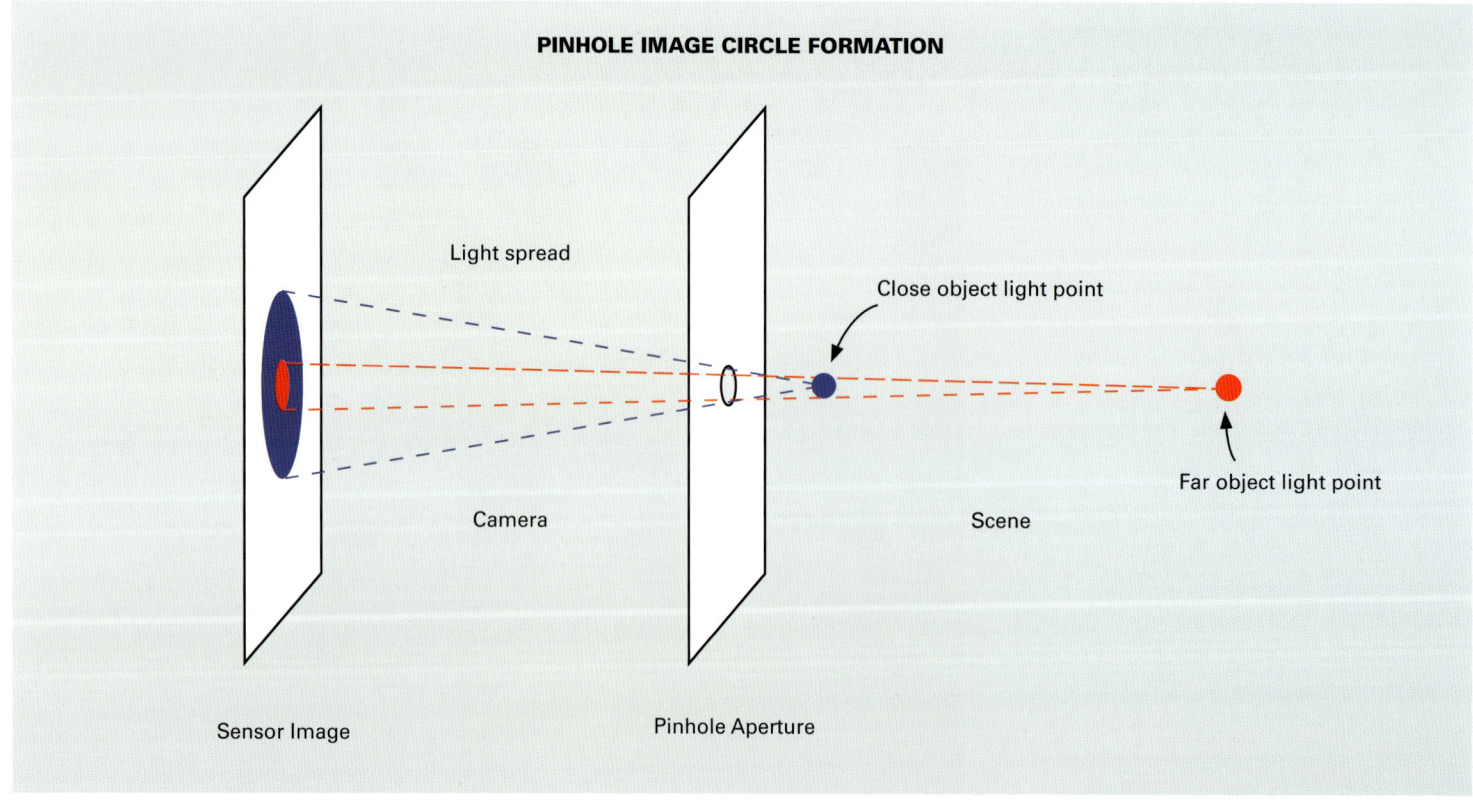

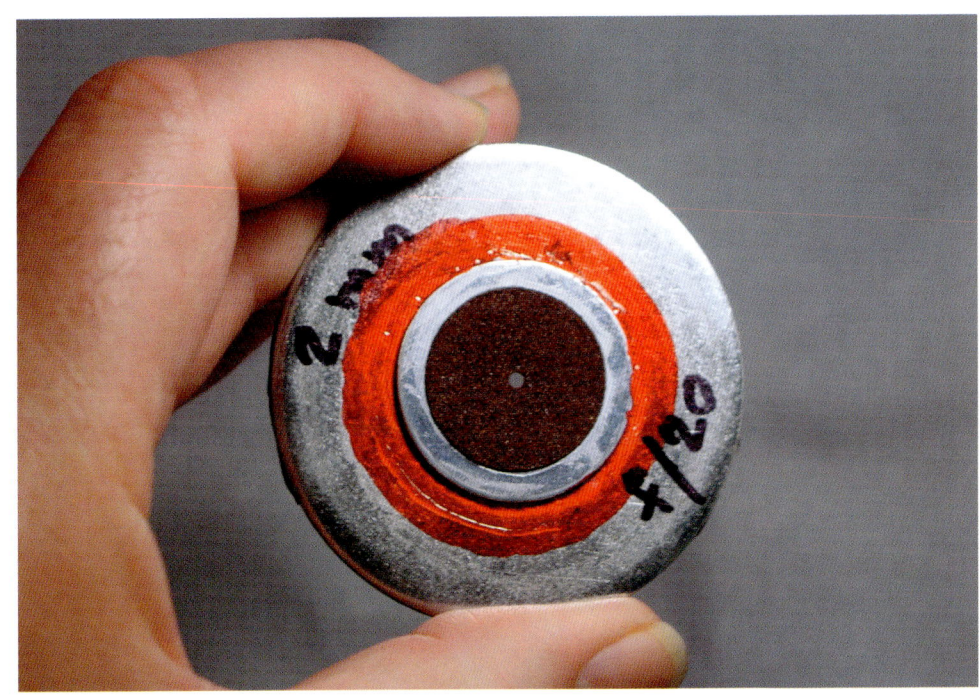

To illustrate that there is plenty of great bokeh concealed in a pinhole image, I used an opening that I will call a "mega pinhole." The diameter of the opening used to create the image below is approximately 2mm in diameter—the effect it gives is like blowing up a small portion of an image created with a much smaller pinhole.

LEFT & BELOW: *A 2mm-sized Mega Pinhole mounted to the front of a DSLR was used to create the image below.*

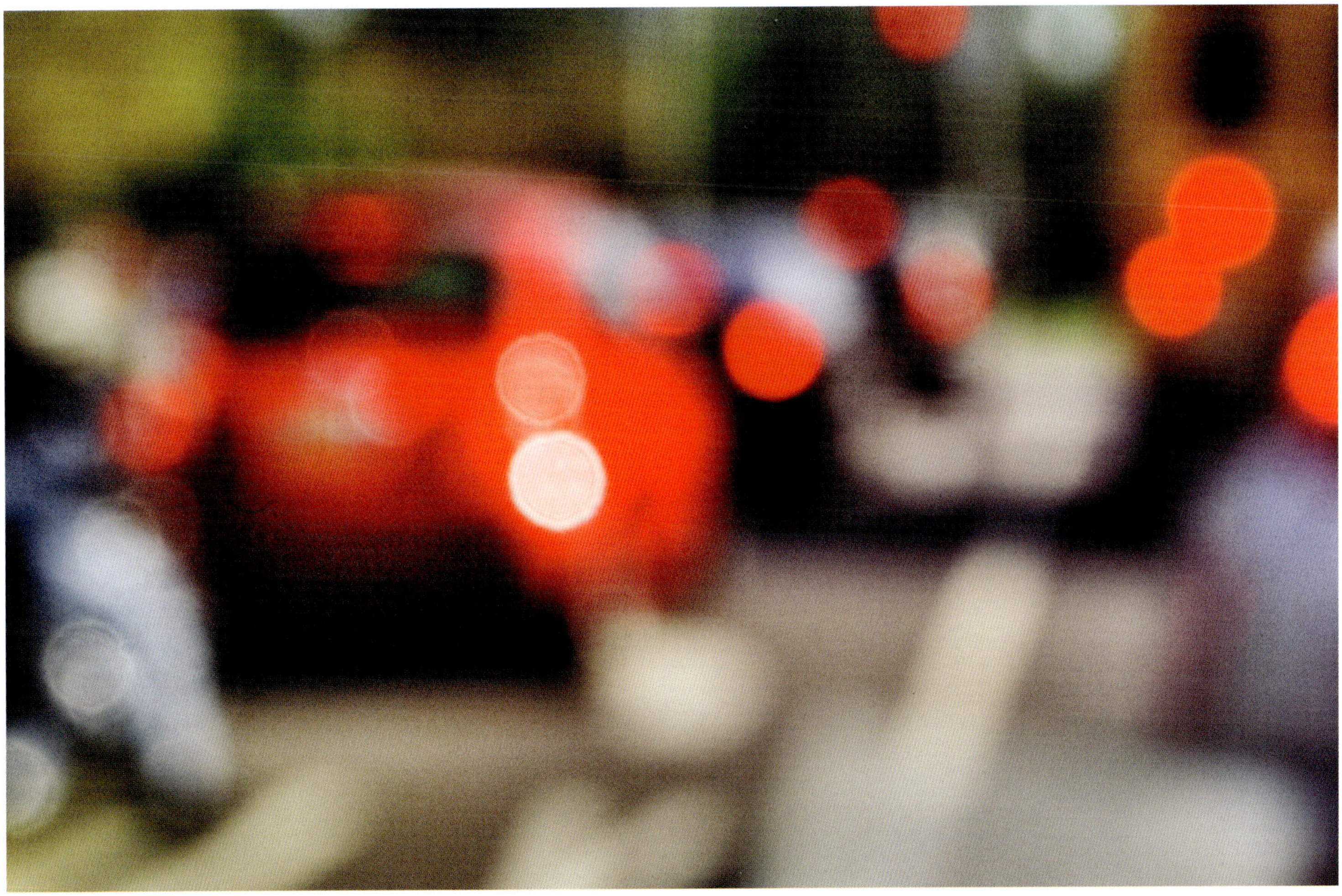

Gallery | Bokeh

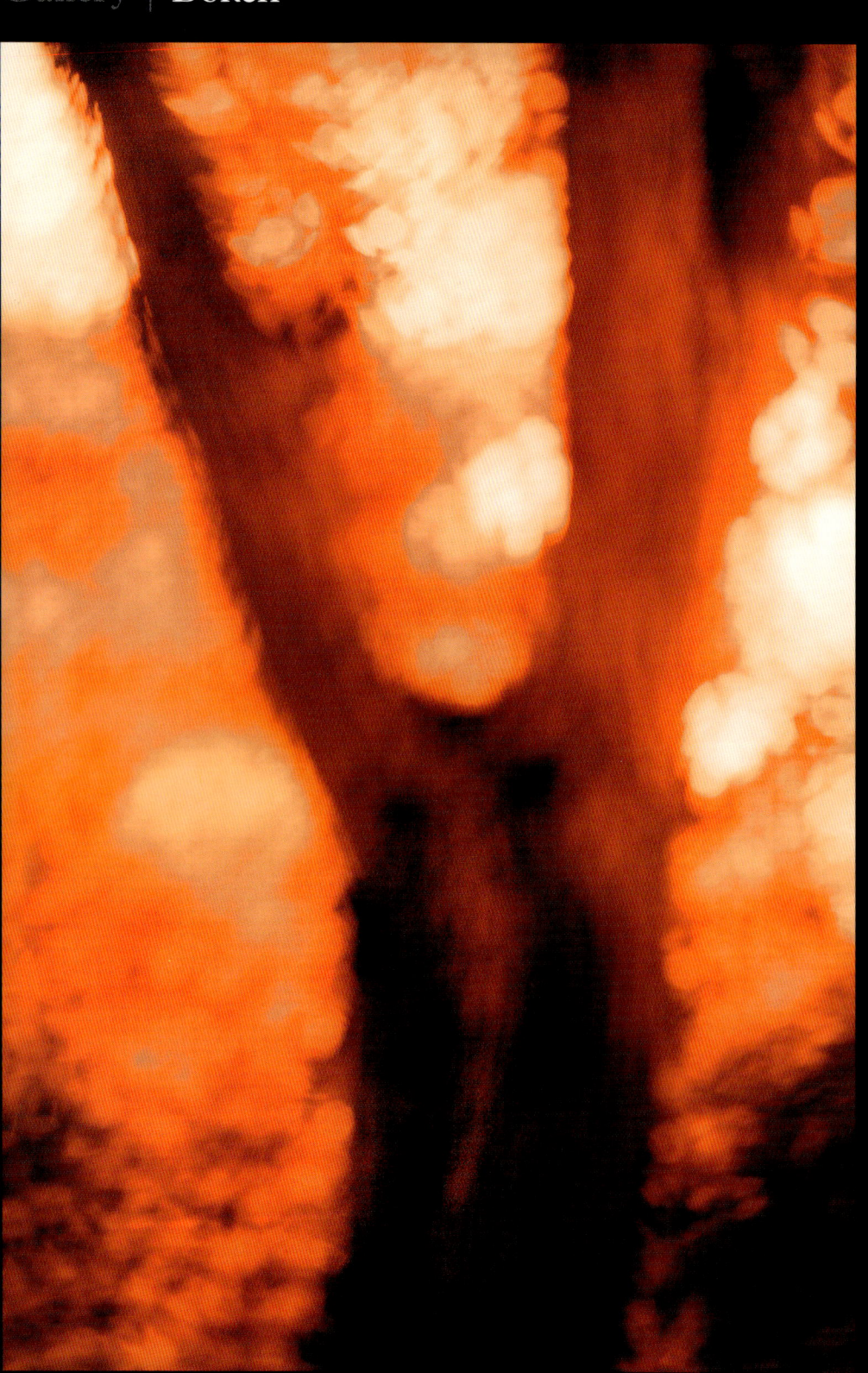

LEFT: *Bokeh patterns can be created using nothing but OOF and bokeh. This image was created using a multiple-aperture technique.*

ABOVE RIGHT: *Interesting bokeh can be created with very simple lenses. The image of this dogwood bud was produced with a plastic lens adapted from a single-use camera.*

ABOVE FAR RIGHT: *Found lenses can produce very nice bokeh. The image was produced with a plastic lens from a single-use camera.*

RIGHT: *Macro imaging produces very thin depth of field, which usually leaves the background completely defocused. In order to get more sharply defined information along the Z-axis, a smaller aperture is needed. However, thin depth of field can be very interesting.*

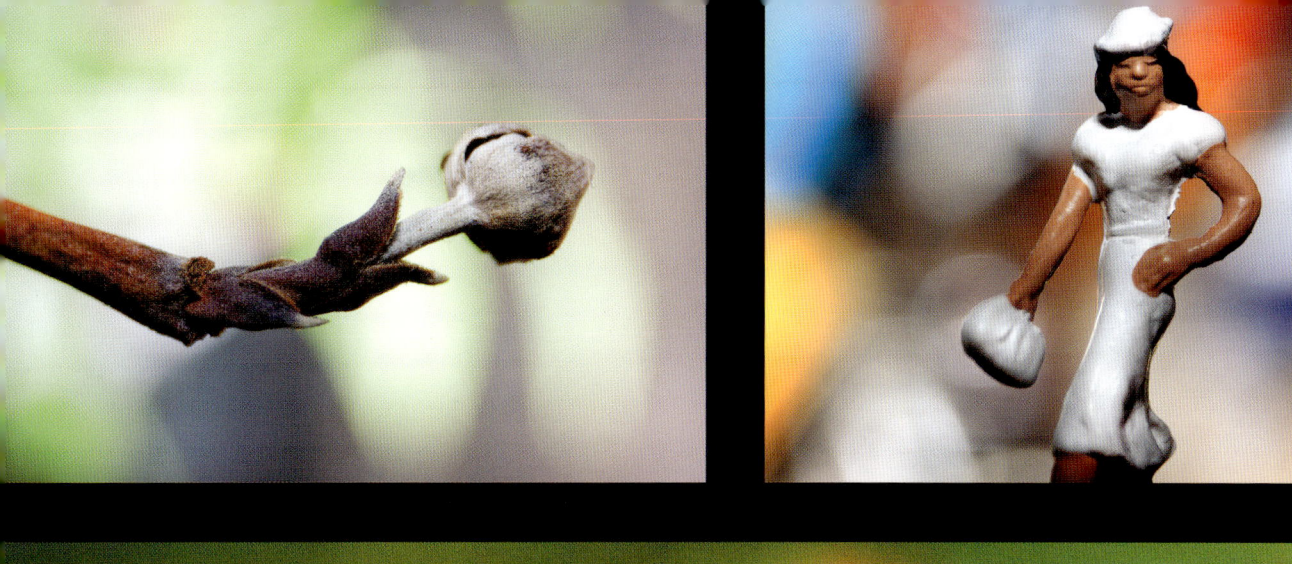

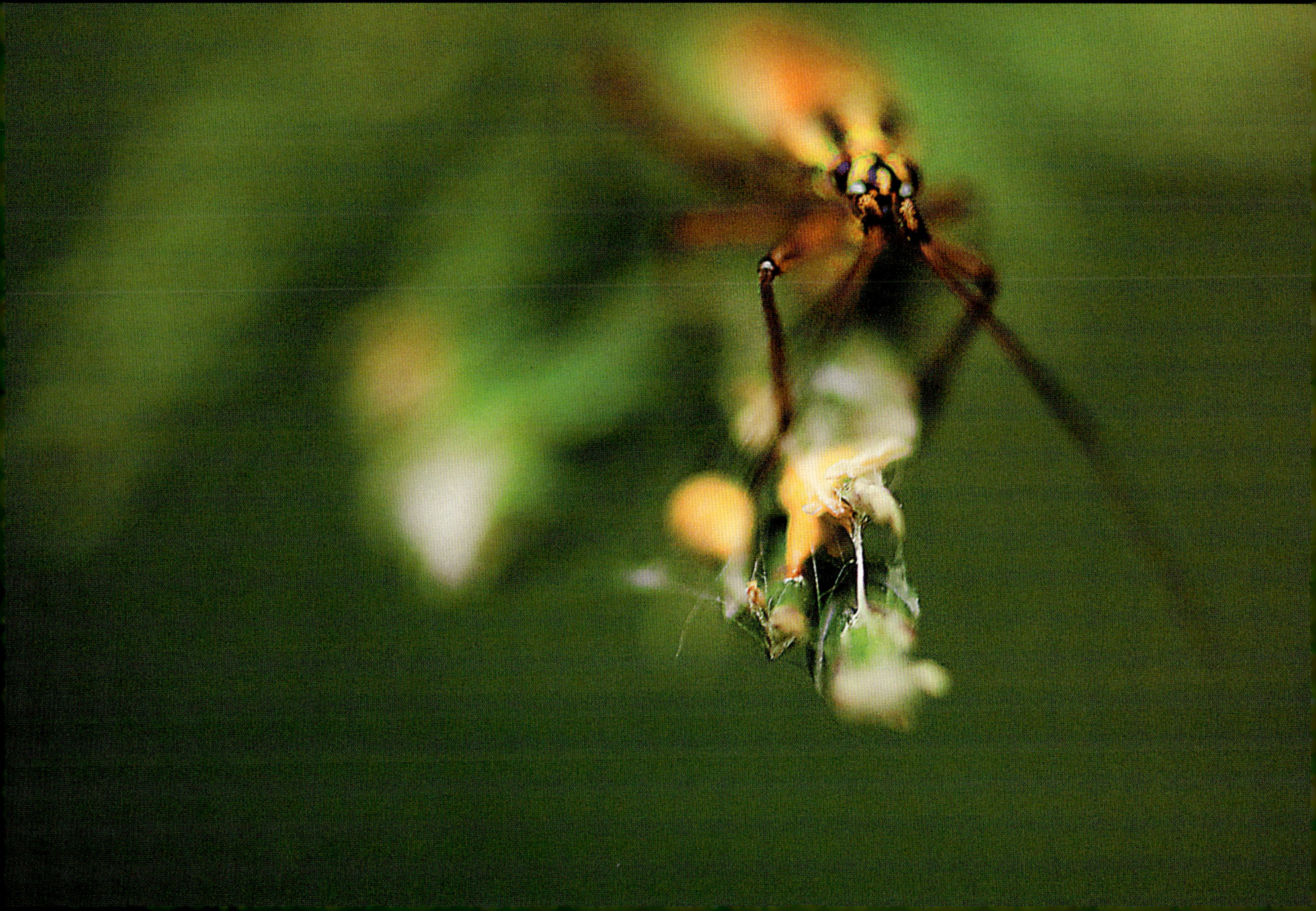

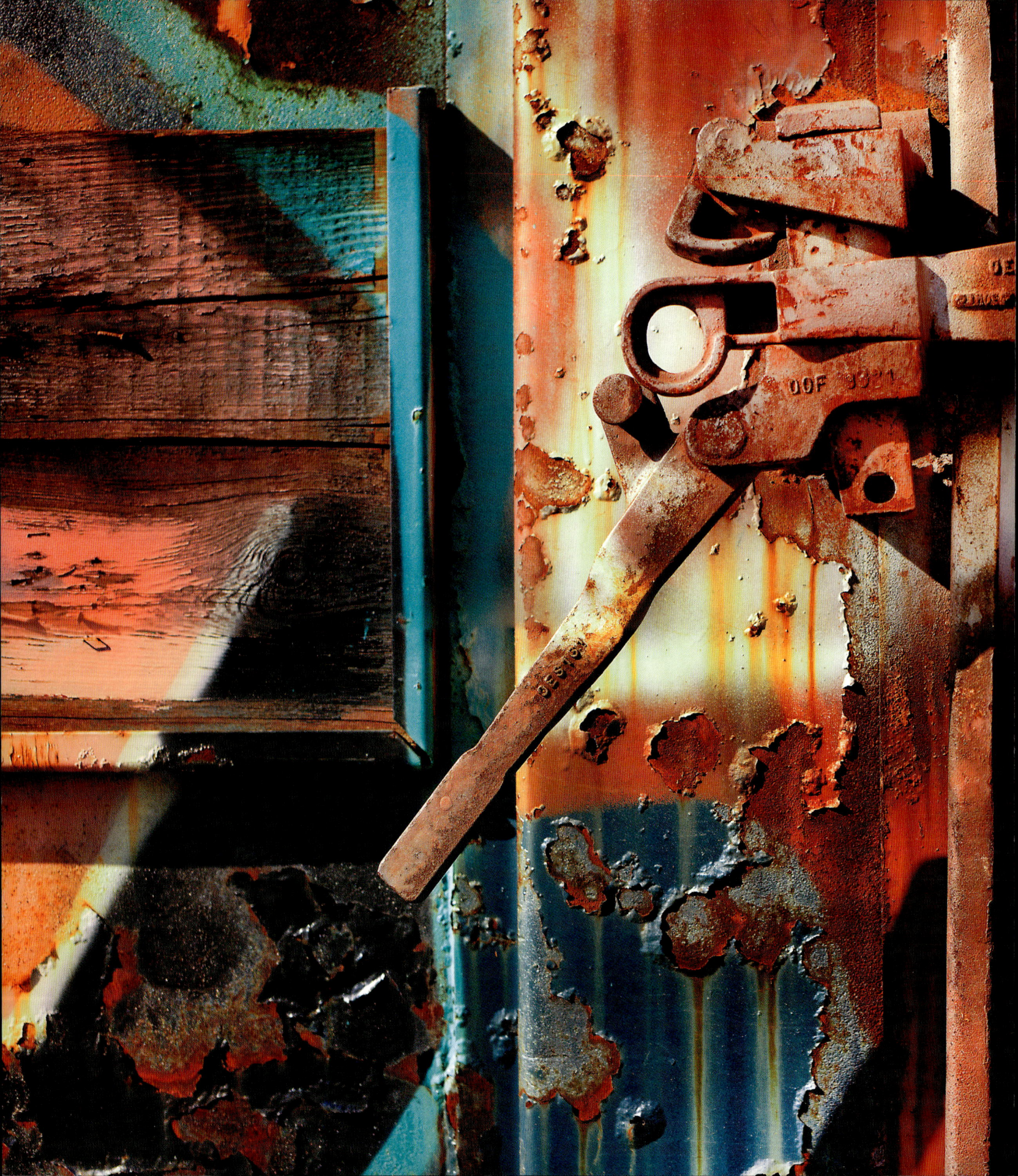

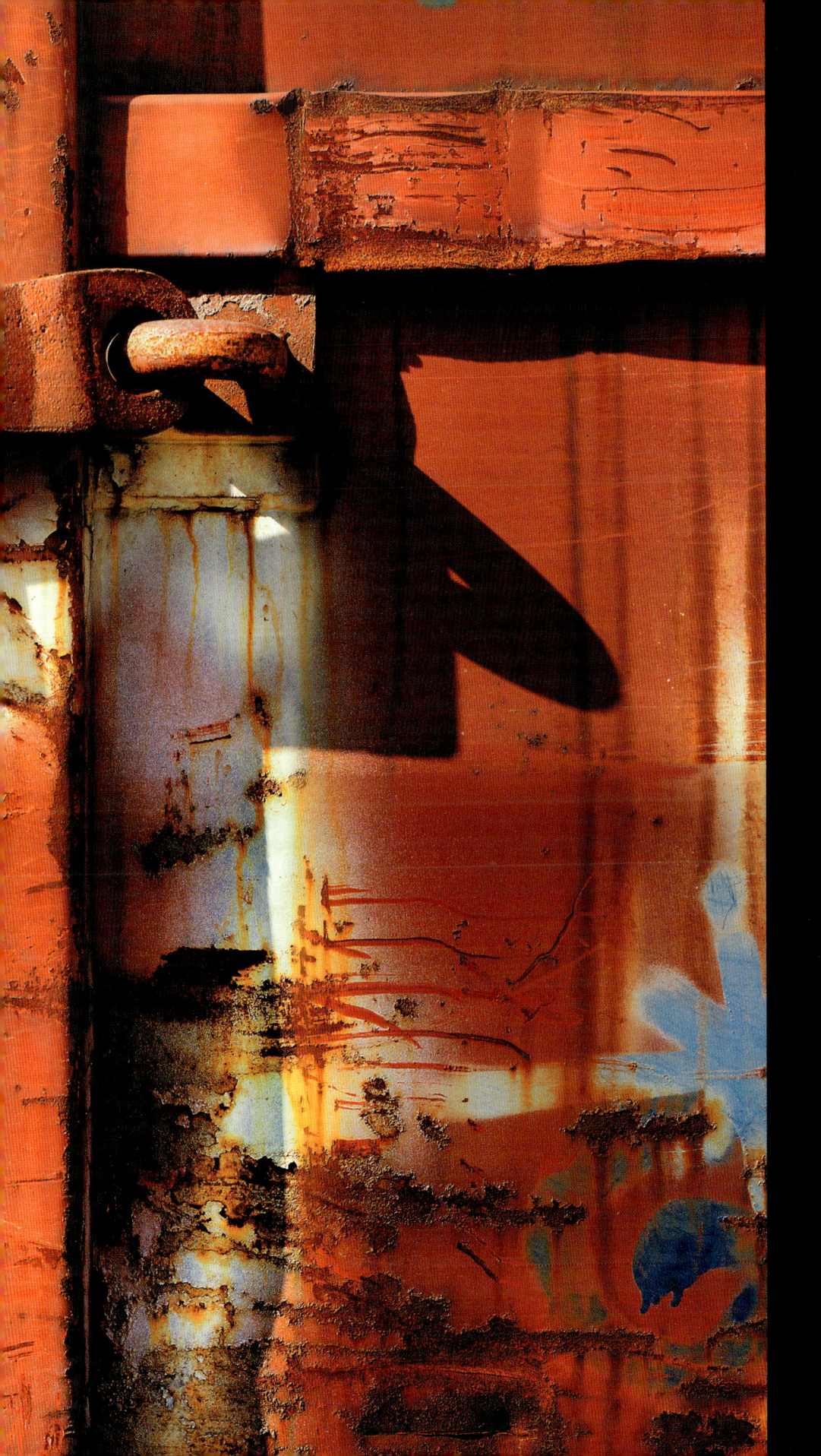

03 // OPTICS & EQUIPMENT

Placing Sharpness

Selective focus would seem to be a no-brainer; you either choose a point in the scene to place your focus, or you let the camera do it for you. But, as simple as that may seem, there are many things to consider when choosing what to focus on and how to make the best of the focusing options.

There are many ways to make focusing work for the subjects you shoot. In fact, each and every image can offer new opportunities for making creative decisions about the focusing techniques you might use.

Leaving it up to your camera is not a very creative way to achieve the best focus for the image you are trying to produce; shooting using your camera's Auto mode is not very creative and doesn't really count as a skill. Understanding what the camera is capable of and using that capability is much more proficient and allows for almost endless possibilities for making great images.

However, remember that sharp focus is not always the answer. There may be many reasons to make things sharp, but there are many other arguments for making things out of focus instead.

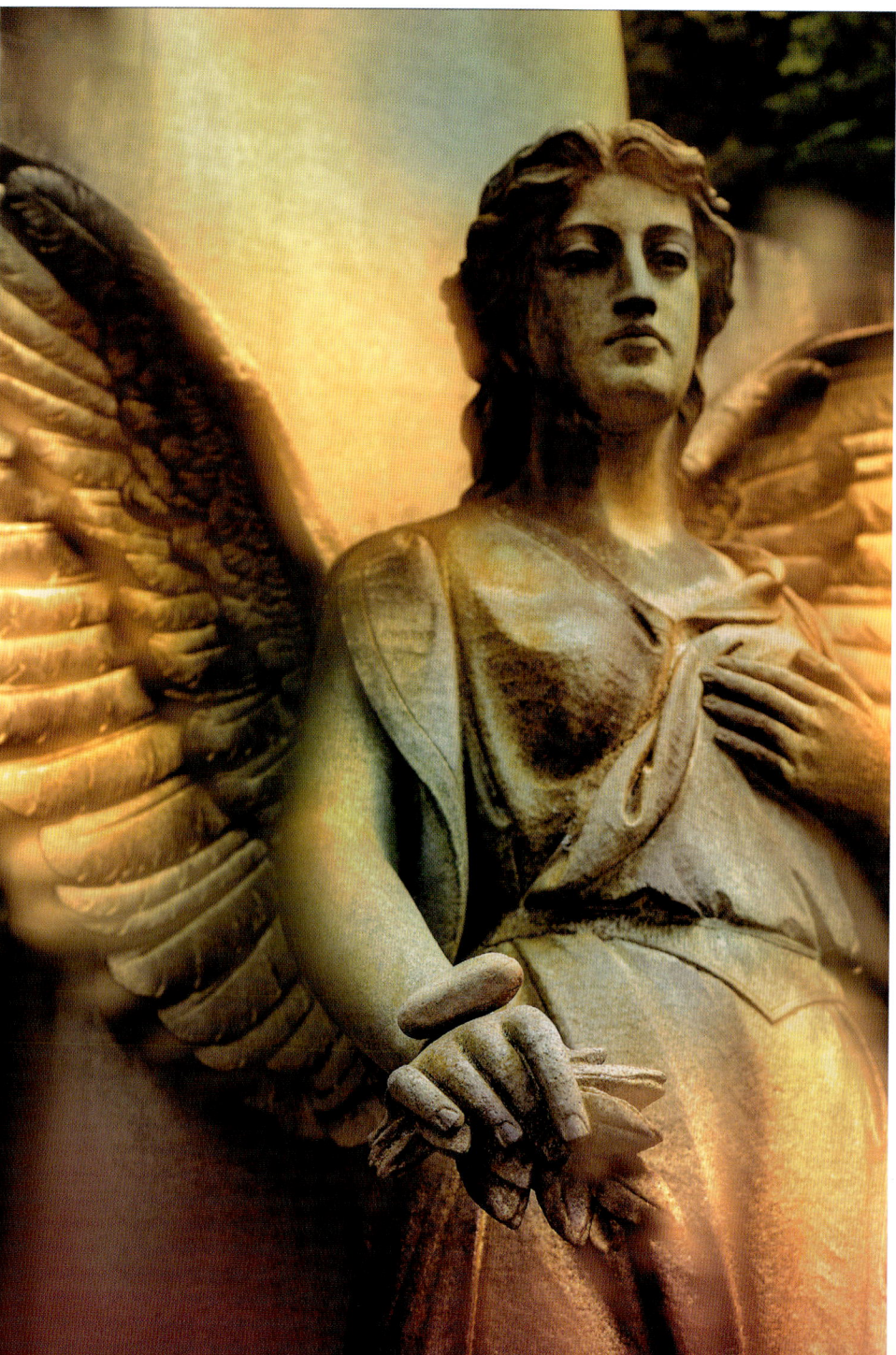

RIGHT: *Lenses can produce a variety of effects based on what is made sharp and what appears out of focus.*

The Art of Defocusing

Every part of a scene has a part to play in the production of an image, and the out-of-focus areas are just as important as the in-focus elements. Generally, out-of-focus areas should support the overall composition and serve with other compositional elements to direct attention toward the main subject.

The art of focusing also has its opposite—the art of defocusing. One of the most useful tools we have in photography is the ability to choose what we want to be sharp, what we want to be out of focus, and how much of the scene is somewhere in between perfect sharpness and blur.

BELOW: *The usual method for making sure things are sharp in an image is to stop down the aperture. However, it is not as simple as that if you want the best result: a skillful image-maker will look at the scene and determine what exactly needs to be sharp before shooting.*

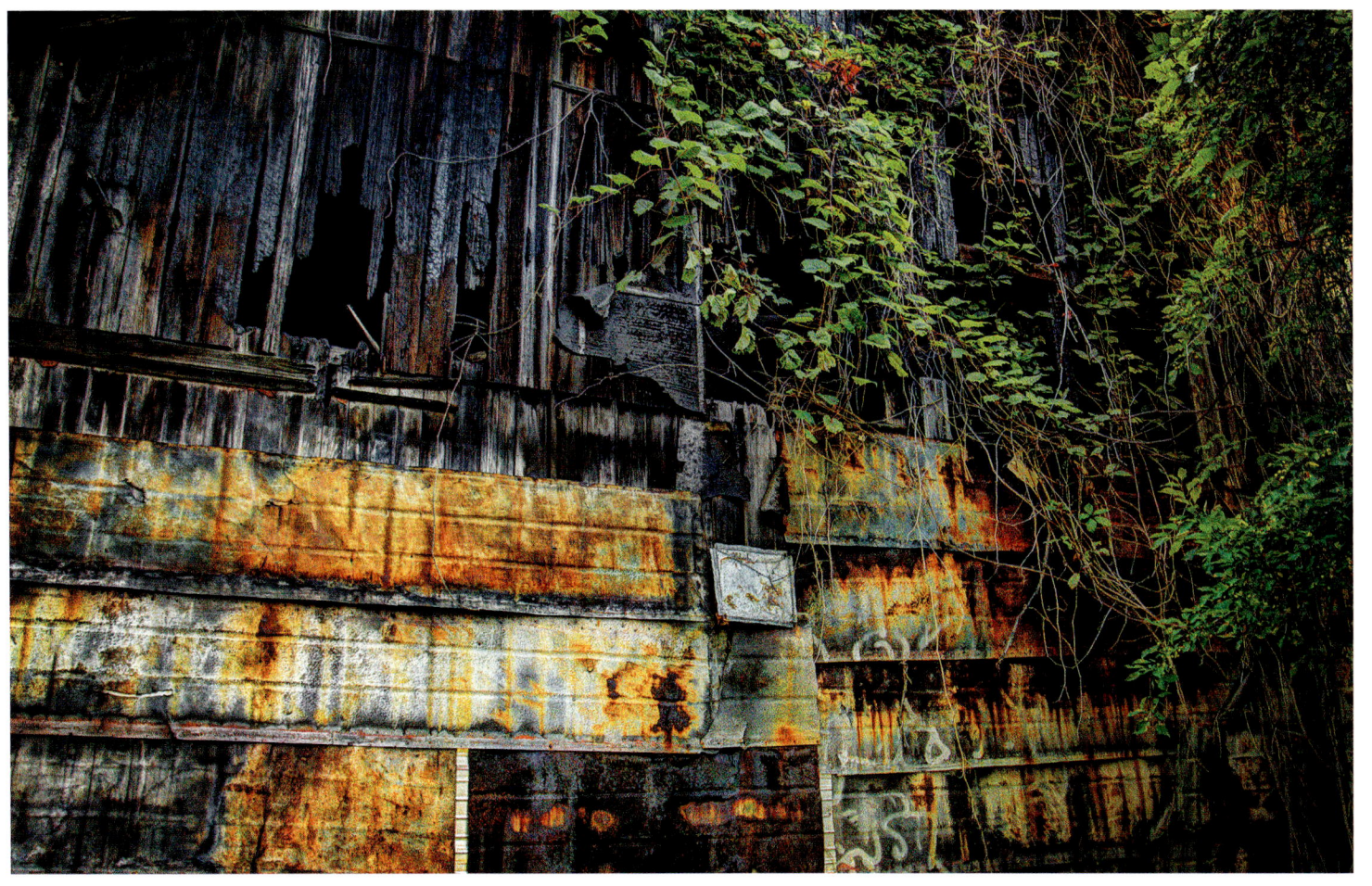

Focal Length

Today, there seems to be an endless variety of fixed focal length and zoom lenses, ranging from extreme wide angle to extreme telephoto.

If we look at all of the great images in the history of photography, the majority have been produced with what is referred to as a "standard" or "normal" lens. This is a lens that reproduces the world as close as possible to the way we perceive it through normal sight. Elements in the foreground, middle ground, and distance are displaced visually in proportion to our real-world perception, so objects and perspective appear to be at the correct distances and angles to our experience of them. Basically, a subject 10 feet away in "real life" will appear to be 10 feet away in the image.

While some will argue that the world is seen as more of a wide-angle view, the facts of perspective dictate otherwise. This may be because we see with two offset

BELOW: *A tripod was used to capture a series of long HDR exposures. This statue was caught late at night using a vintage 55mm Nikon Micro lens on a full-frame Sony mirrorless camera.*

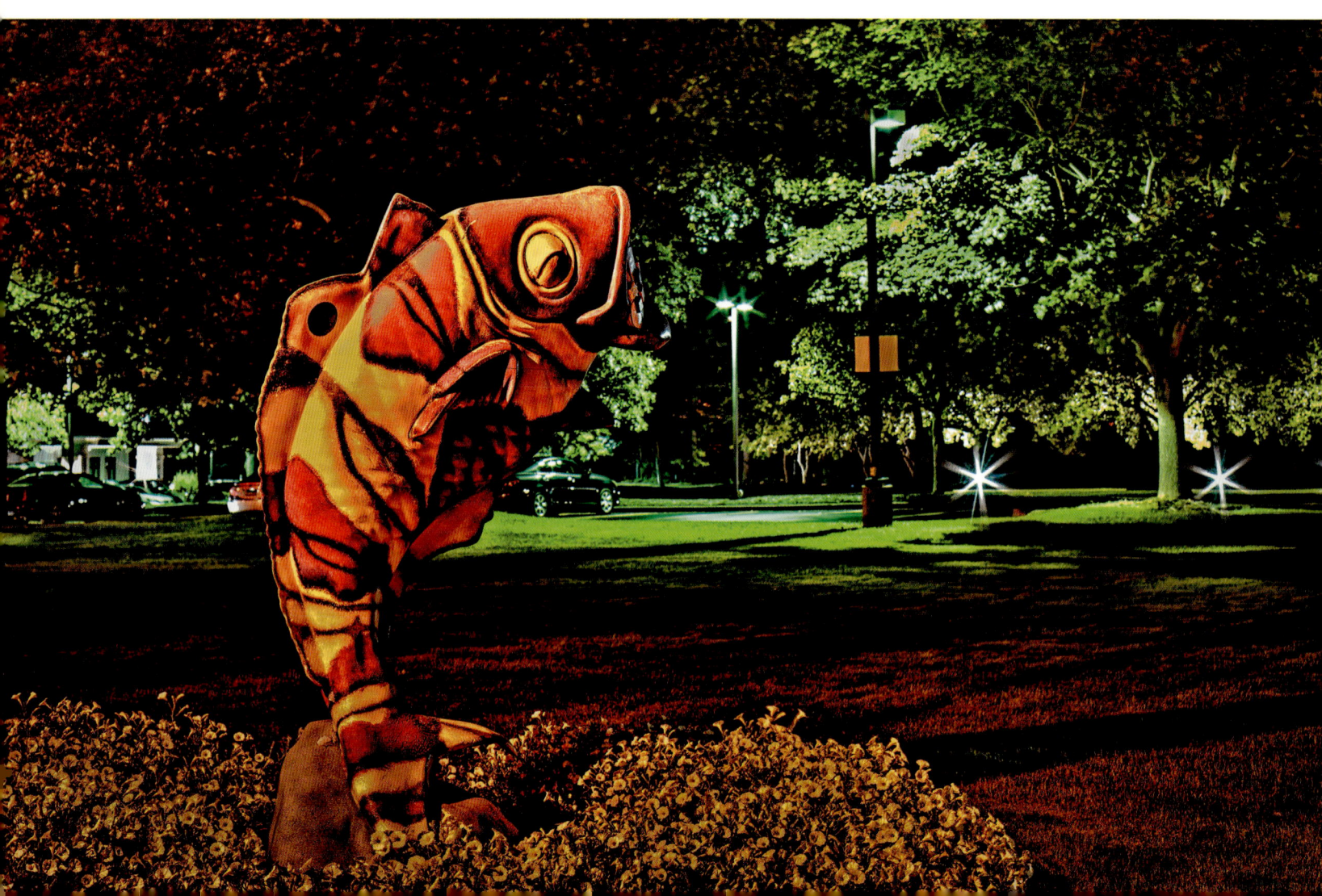

lenses (our eyes), which widens our overall view of the world. However, the camera is a one-eyed entity and the standard lens is considered the lens that best duplicates the real perspective of our world.

The standard focal length varies depending on the format of the camera, but it is essentially a focal length that matches the diagonal measurement of the image area. Therefore, the standard focal length for a full-frame camera (or 35mm film) is 43mm, although 50mm is more commonly used.

Although a standard lens might not deliver the immediately striking results that a wide-angle or extreme telephoto lens can, it has advantages that many photographers do not appreciate. First and foremost is brightness. A 50mm prime lens can be designed with the widest apertures—many manufacturers have produced very fast lenses in the range of $f/1.4$, $f/1.2$, or even $f/1.0$. This is great for shooting in very low lighting situations, but it will also enable you to use a faster shutter speed, shallower depth of field, and create bigger bokeh.

The ability to see your world through a normal lens in a unique way can be a difficult but attainable goal. To many, it may seem easier to exploit the distortion of a wide-angle lens or to play with the compression effects of a long focal length. Consequently, many photographers now rarely use the "normal" range of their zoom lenses, but tend to use either the wide or the telephoto extreme instead.

However, forcing yourself to see the world through a standard view can help you to become a better photographer. You have to work harder to create your shots, rather than simply zooming for creative effect, and this will immediately make you look harder at the world around you. In turn, opportunities you never noticed before can become apparent.

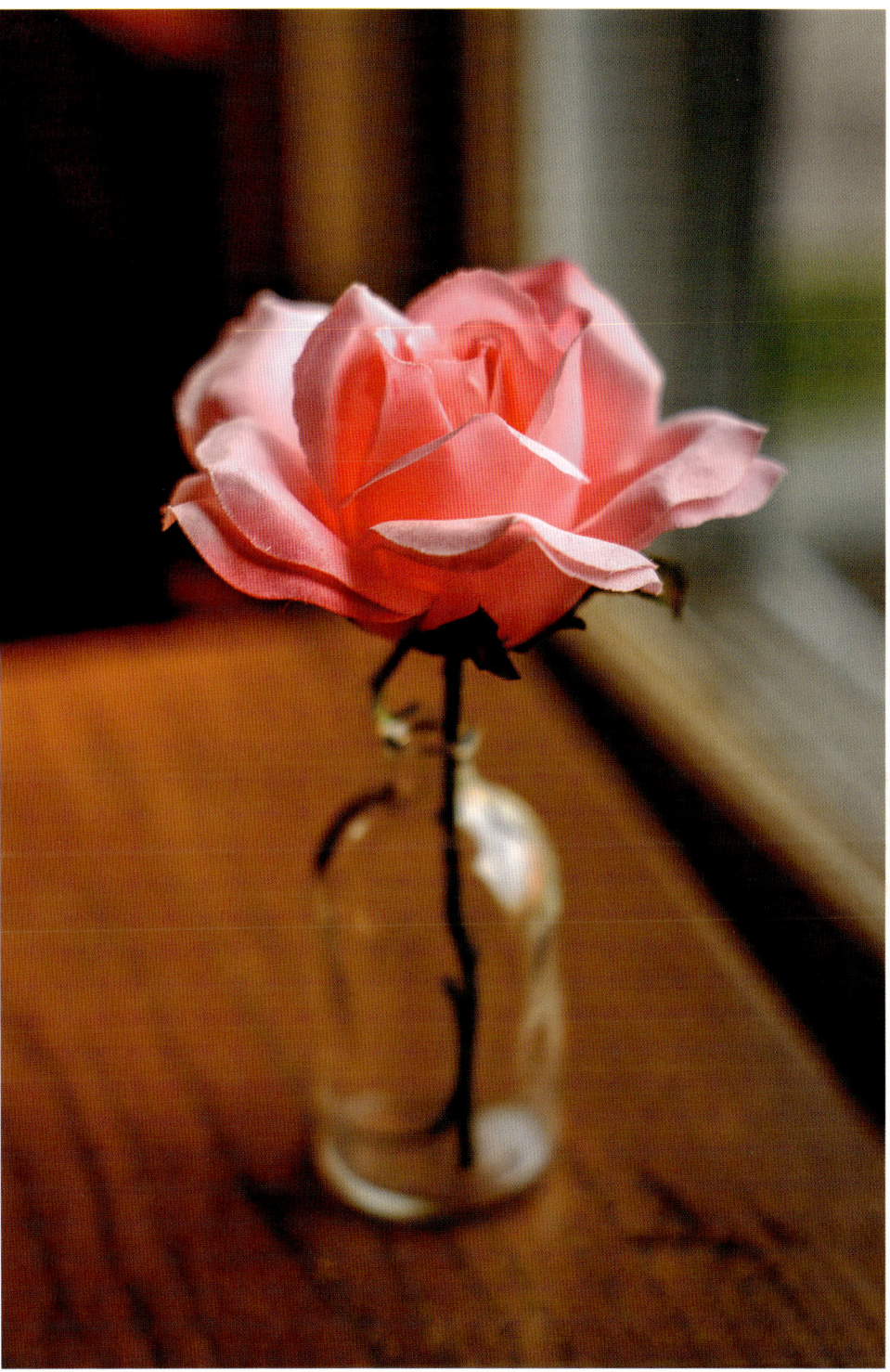

ABOVE: *A normal lens presents the subject in a very natural way. It produces a view where everything seems to be at a natural distance from the viewer. In this example, the wide-open aperture creates a shallow depth of field that is parallel to the focal plane of the sensor. The effect is one where the main subject looks relatively sharp, while the areas outside that plane are thrown into relative out-of-focus, which nicely mimics the way we see the world.*

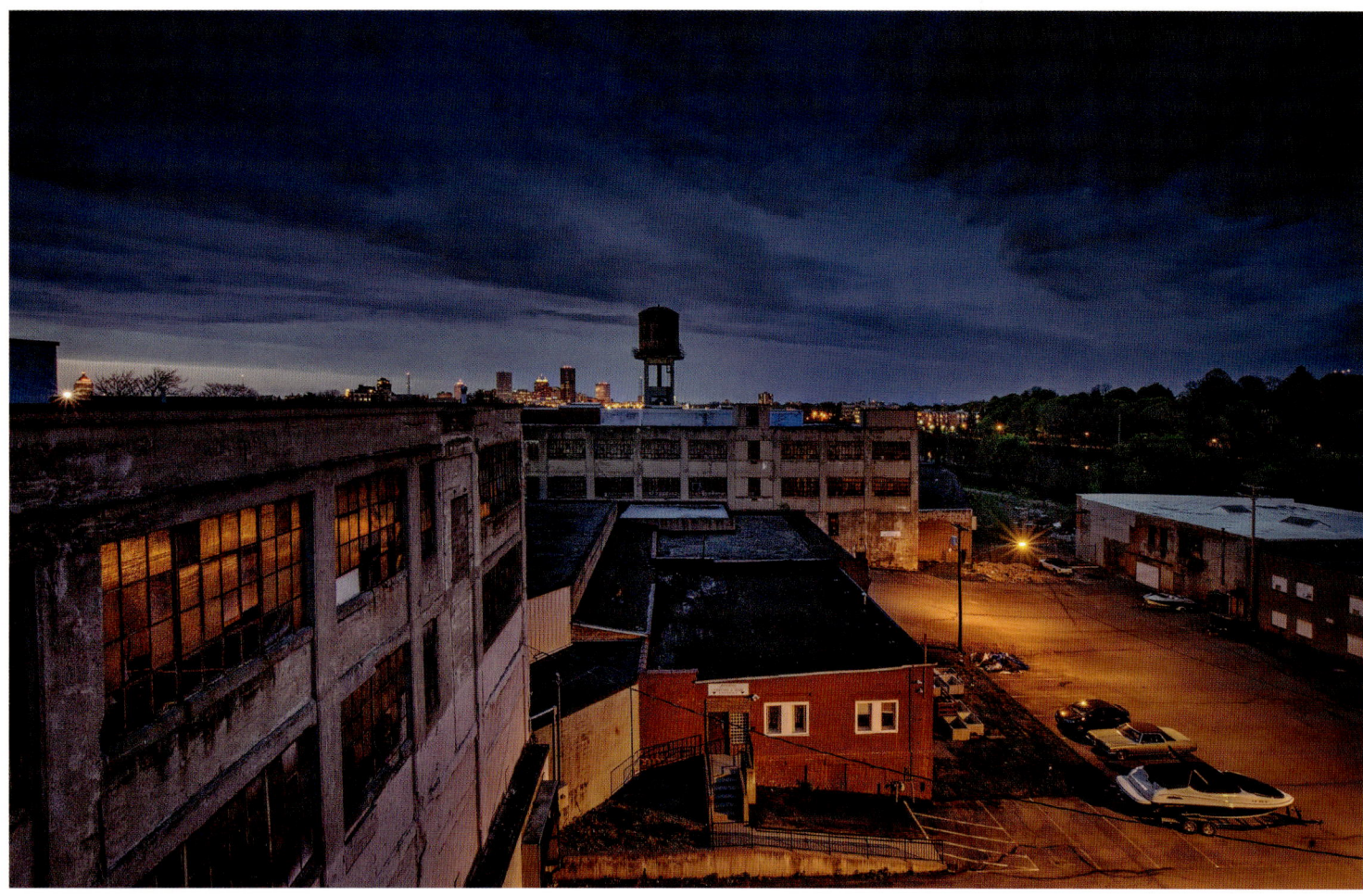

Wide-Angle Lenses

Wide-angle lenses are those with a focal length wider than "standard." One of their main advantages is that, as well as capturing a wider angle of view, they provide great depth of field when shooting at moderate apertures and shooting from the hip.

Mild wide-angle lenses are useful for capturing street shots of people, interiors, or anything else where you want to "fit more in" without it becoming overly distorted, while more extreme wide-angle lenses can be used to create a dramatic sense of space in a landscape.

Both fisheye and extreme wide-angle lenses are great fun to use and can produce very dramatic results when used correctly and with the right kinds of subjects and lighting. However, as with anything else, moderate use of these lenses is recommended to avoid your shots becoming repetitious, and even then it should be used only if it works for your subject.

Telephoto Lenses

While this book covers many different lenses, the basic principles are the same for all. Telephoto lenses simply have much larger image circles that are cropped by the size of the sensor. Due to the relative magnification of the focused image, the relative sharpness of the depth of field is reduced at any give aperture. This means that the reduction of DOF becomes more obvious at longer and longer focal lengths. As the focal length increases, so does the relative close-up distance. This means that telephoto lenses produce much narrow depth-of-field sharpness and their closest focus is farther away from the sensor.

ABOVE: *It's quite easy to get things in focus from near to far when using a wide-angle lens.*

RIGHT: *Telephoto lenses are useful for stripping out the context and isolating small details against an out-of-focus background.*

CROP FACTOR

If you own a camera with a cropped-format sensor (APS-C or Micro Four Thirds), then your lenses will have a "crop factor" applied to them. This is because focal lengths are given in relation to their angle of view on a full-frame (35mm film) camera. A smaller format sensor does not record as much of the image circle projected by the lens, so you get a narrower angle of view (effectively like using a longer focal length lens). Depending on the camera's sensor size, the crop factor could effectively extend the focal length by 1.5–2x, so a 20mm wide-angle lens behaves more like a less extreme 30–40mm lens instead.

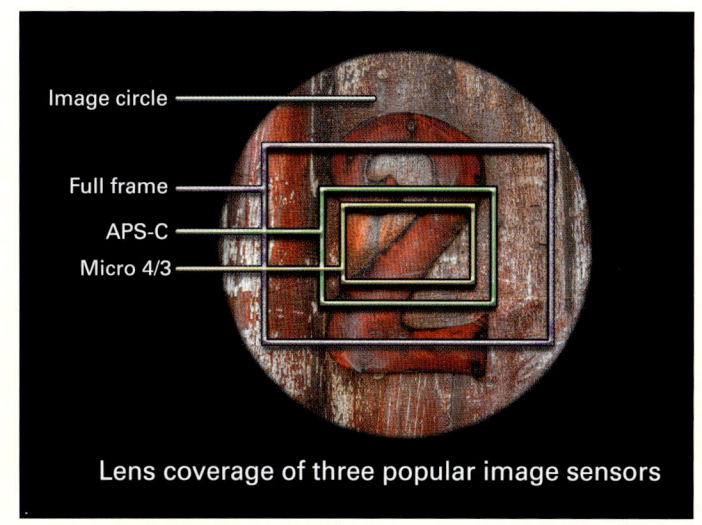

Lens coverage of three popular image sensors

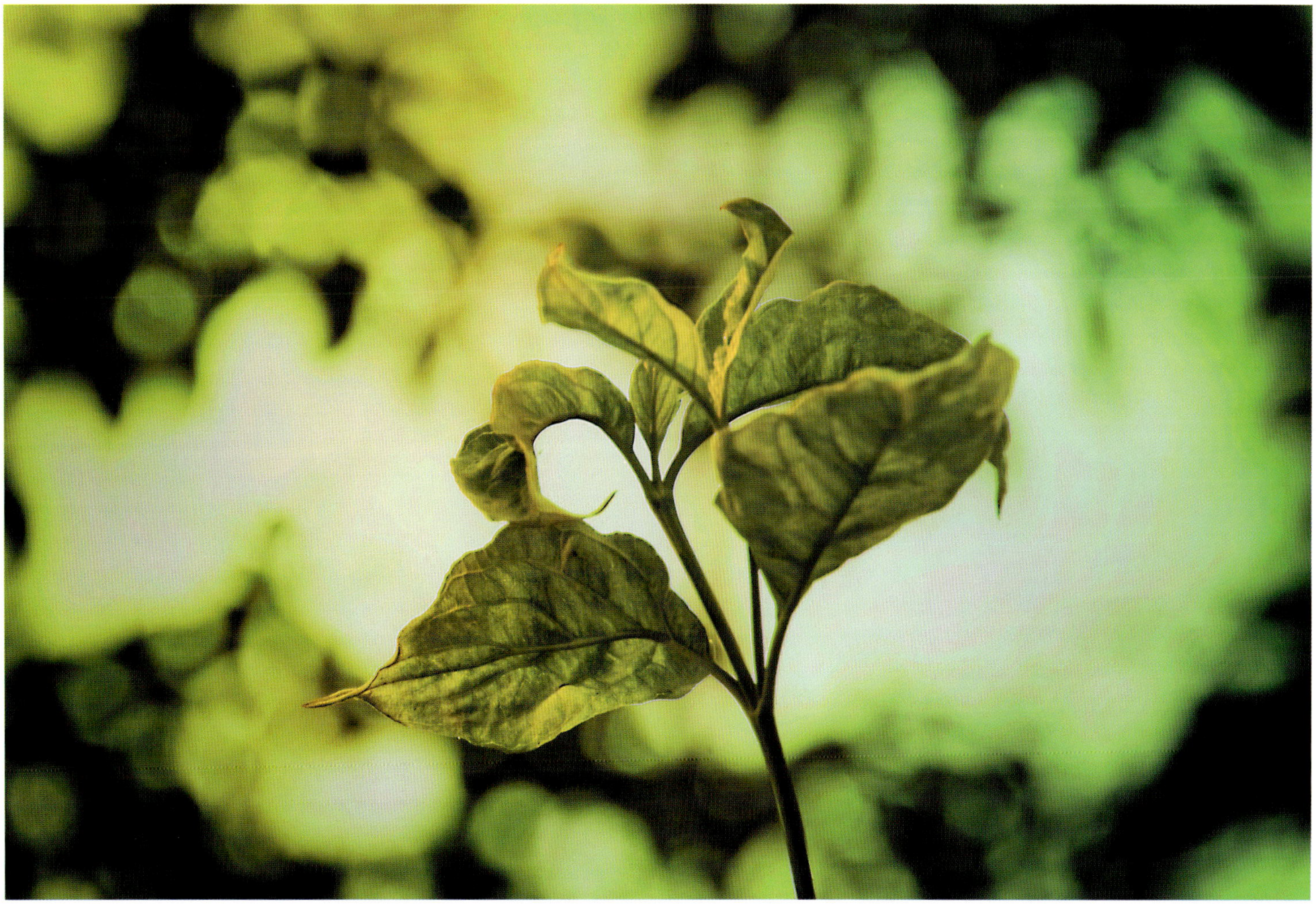

Mirrorless Cameras

The combination of smaller sensors and interchangeable lenses allows mirrorless cameras to open up a world of opportunity when it comes to using older (but still very usable) lenses in the digital age.

Mirrorless cameras have a much smaller physical size than a DSLR, yet retain most of the excellent features that come with a larger camera. They are great for shooting High Dynamic Range (HDR) images and are capable of high-quality video—some of the latest models can shoot 4K video.

The popularity, quality, and adaptability of the Micro Four Thirds system championed by Olympus and Panasonic have led to the introduction of similarly adaptable camera systems from other manufacturers—Sony's Alpha range, for example, and Fujifilm's X-series.

The advantage with this type of camera is the elimination of the retractable mirror, which takes up space inside a traditional SLR camera between the lens and the sensor. This reduces the distance from the lens mount to the sensor, which allows a greater range of lens possibilities.

Consequently, there are many different types of adaptor available to photographers using mirrorless cameras, enabling them to use lenses from cameras such as Contax, Hasselblad, Mamiya, Voigtländer, as well as the more "mainstream" camera brands. This means that nearly any interchangeable lens produced over the past 50–60 years can be adapted to a mirrorless camera, enabling older, "legacy" lenses to find new homes.

Mirrorless cameras are very capable and fun to use, and can adapt to almost every shooting situation. I love the mirrorless format because of its versatility, and because the cameras have a feel that is reminiscent of my old Leica. In most cases, the image quality is also comparable to any DSLR.

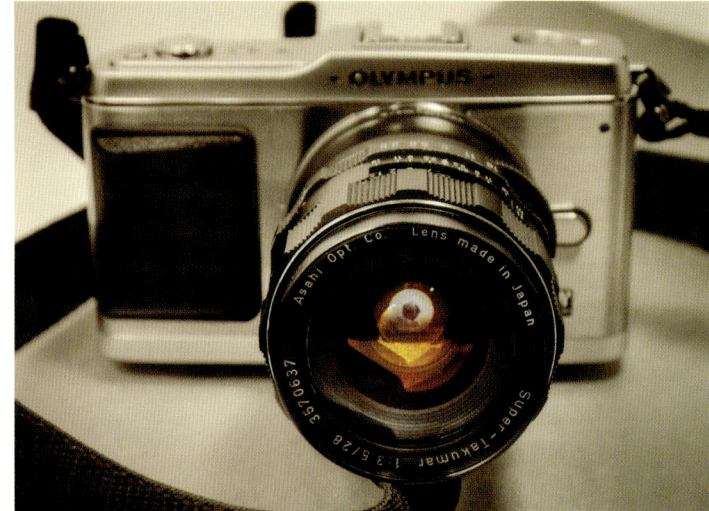

LEFT: *This Olympus Micro Four Thirds camera is hosting a beautiful Pentax M42 screw-thread lens from the 1970s. Because of the camera's sensor size, the lens' 28mm focal length behaves like a "standard" lens. This camera has the honor of (largely) bringing the mirrorless genre to fruition.*

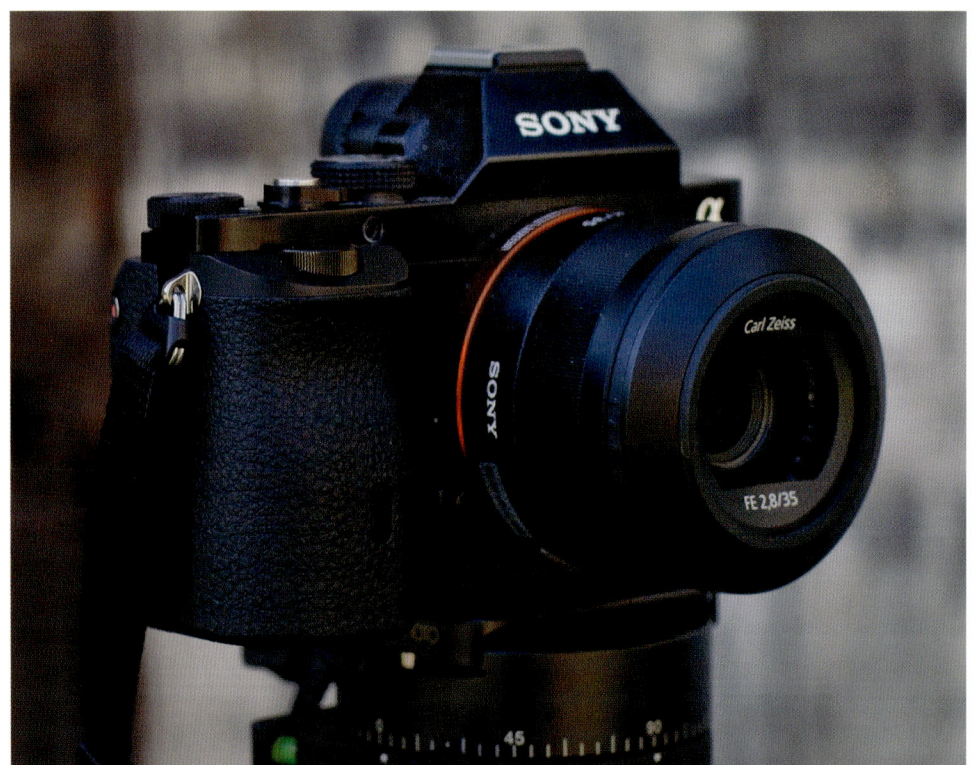

03 // MIRRORLESS CAMERAS // OPTICS & EQUIPMENT

RIGHT: *A Fujifilm X-series mirrorless camera is easily carried into the open stairways and winding paths of picturesque places such as New York State's Watkins Glen.*

LEFT: *The Sony A7 and its siblings, the A7r and the A7s, have some of the highest-resolution full-frame digital sensors on the market. The combination of a large sensor and small, mirrorless body created a camera that set a new standard in digital imaging. As a result, cameras with larger sensors in smaller bodies are becoming the norm.*

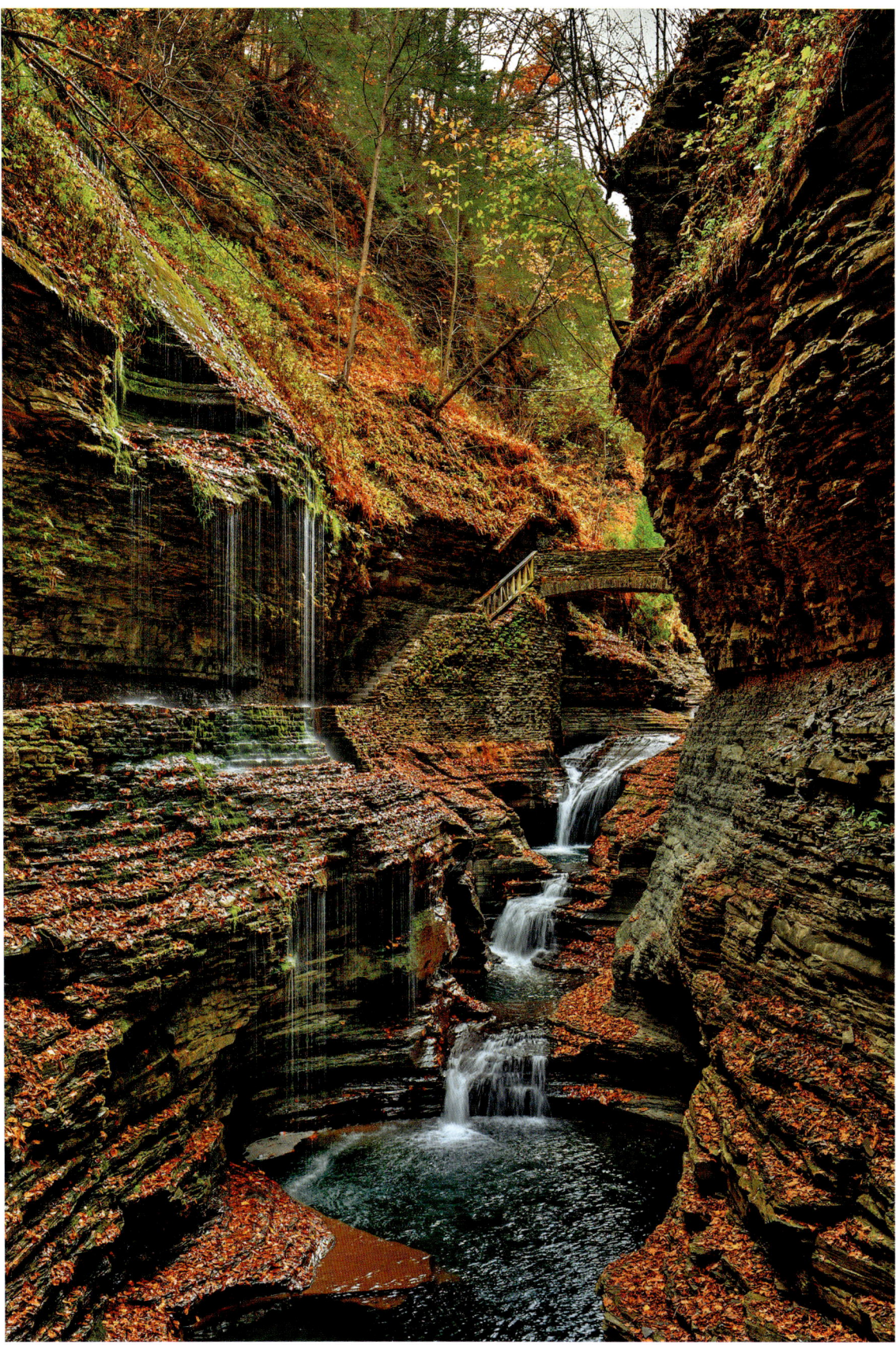

Large-Format Cameras

In a regular camera, such as a mirrorless camera or a DSLR, the lens and the focal plane are perpendicular, so the lens, the subject, and the back of the camera are all parallel to each other.

Most cameras and lenses are engineered to ensure that the sharpest focus is entirely on the focal plane (either the camera's sensor or film). When a lens is focused on a point, anything at the same distance as that point will be rendered as sharply as possible across the entire sensor.

Effectively, there are two parallel image planes: one is the plane of focus in front of the camera and the other is its projection on the sensor. One way to think of it is as having a sheet of glass extending across the scene horizontally and vertically at the distance at which the lens is focused. Everything pressed against that glass will be in equal focus in your photograph.

With a large-format (or "view") camera, tilt, shift, rise, and fall movements allow the lens to be rotated so that it is positioned at a different angle to the image plane. This allows the plane of focus (your sheet of glass) to be manipulated so that it is not necessarily parallel to the film (or sensor), allowing even greater versatility when it

BELOW LEFT & RIGHT: *This beautiful Deardorff large-format film camera was built with a number of movements that are useful in many types of photography. The photograph right shows a few of the camera movements that are possible: a front tilt, a front rise, a front swing to the left, plus a back swing to the right.*

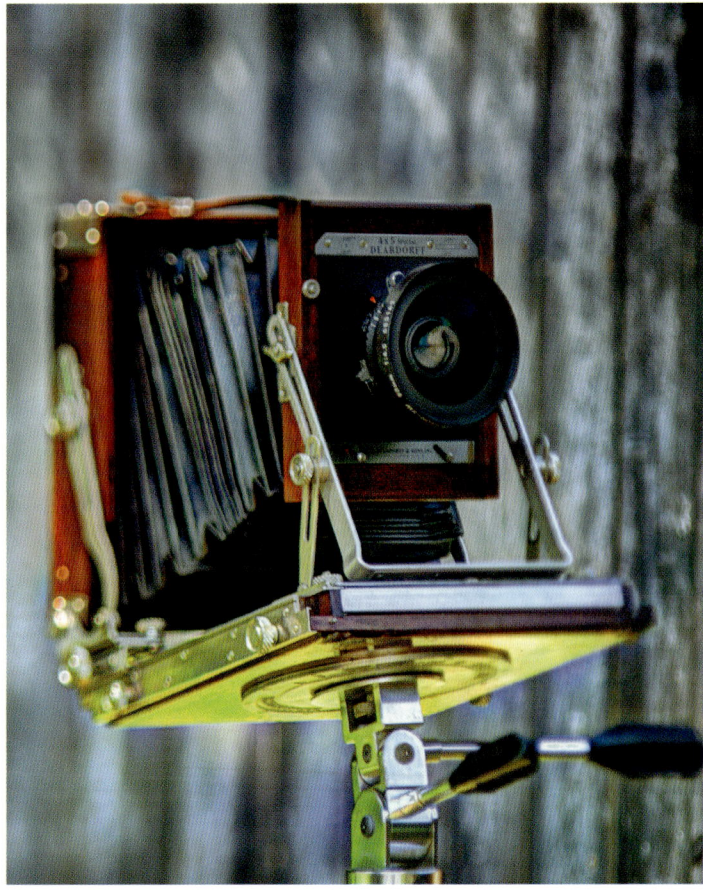
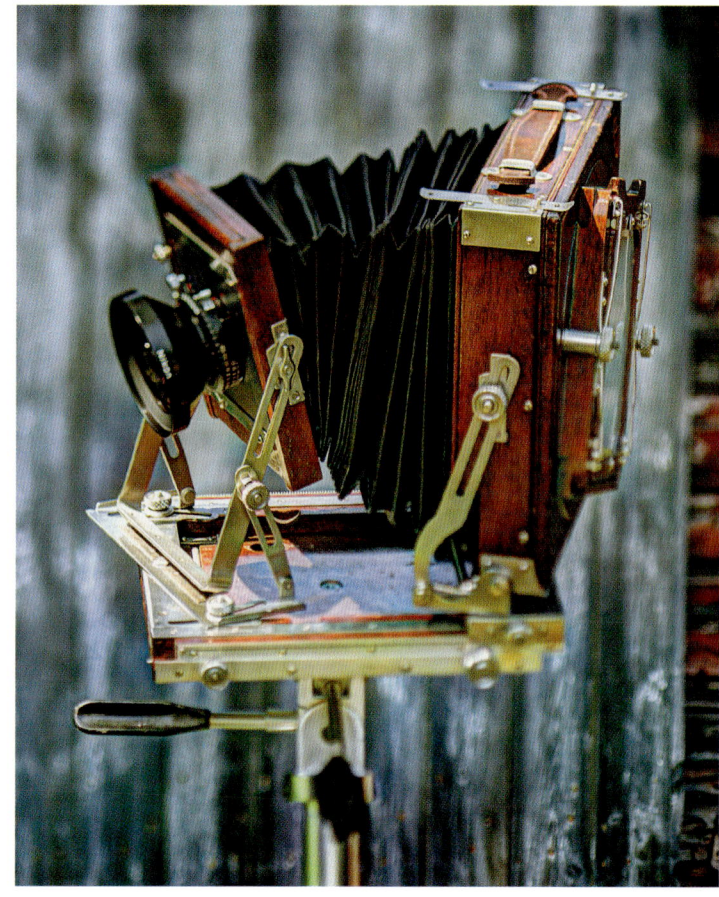

comes to choosing precisely what in the photograph is in focus.

The movements of a large-format camera can be used for numerous technical and creative purposes, including correcting perspective, controlling depth of field, and enabling selective focus. The two most common uses of camera movements are for controlling what appears in focus and for correcting the convergence of parallel lines in a scene.

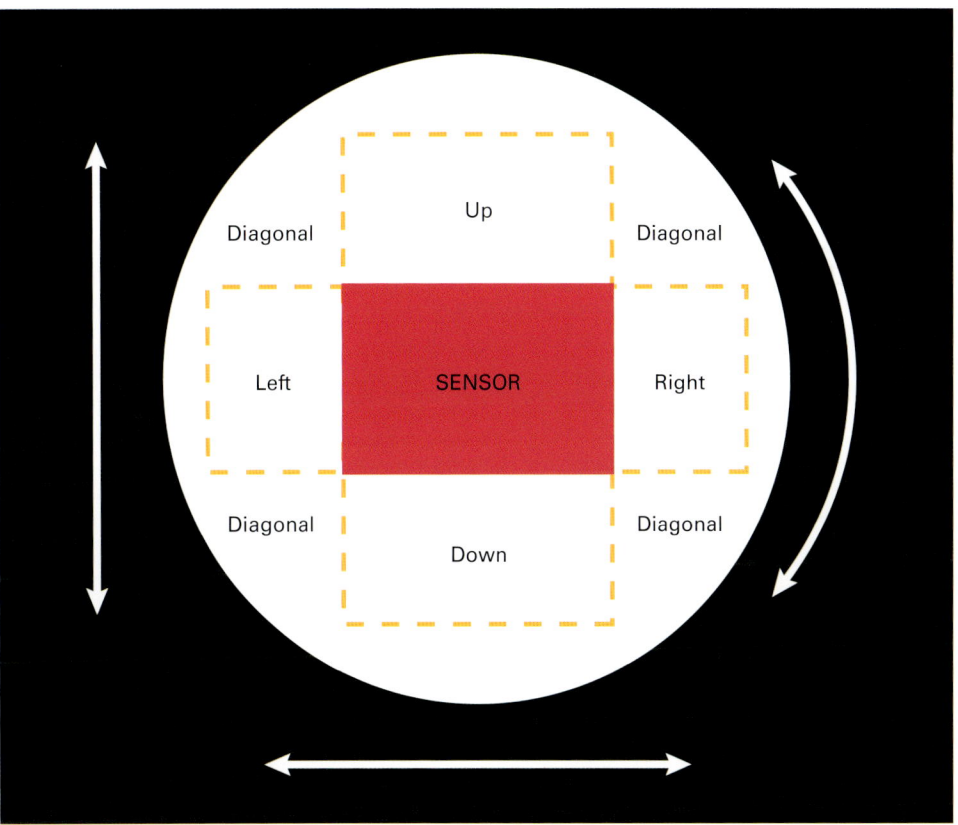

ABOVE: *As with any camera, a large-format camera captures a small portion of the image circle projected by the lens. Cameras that have movements can allow the lens to move to another point within the projected circle.*

Lens Movements

There are four common camera movements. *Shift* describes lateral movements to either the left or right, while *rise* and *fall* refer to upward and downward shift movements respectively. In each instance, the lens remains parallel to the film (or sensor), unless a *tilt* movement is also applied.

Tilt allows the lens to be turned to the left or right, or up or down, so that it is no longer parallel to the image plane. This is typically used for one of two purposes: to create selective focus effects, where a narrow, well-defined section of the image appears in focus, or to maximize depth of field at a given aperture.

Large-format cameras are typically used for architectural, industrial, and product photography where the movements can be used for technical purposes, to correct perspective and focus. However, there are also times when a landscape photographer of a still-life photographer might use one or more lens movements for creative effect.

Although it is primarily the design of the camera that determines how far a lens can be shifted or tilted, the image circle produced by the lens is equally important.

The larger the image circle, the greater the range of possible movements becomes, as—without moving the camera—the lens can be shifted in almost any vertical or lateral direction to reveal a new portion of the projected image.

When using tilt or shift movements, it is usually best to work with slightly longer lenses, as these allow for more movement due to their larger image circles. Wide-angle lenses have comparatively smaller image circles, which can limit the scope of any camera movements.

CAMERA TILTED UPWARD
Building appears to fall backward.

BELOW: *Simply tilting the camera produces the distorting effect of the building falling backward. At the same time, the straight verticals are also keystoned from the bottom to the top of the image.*

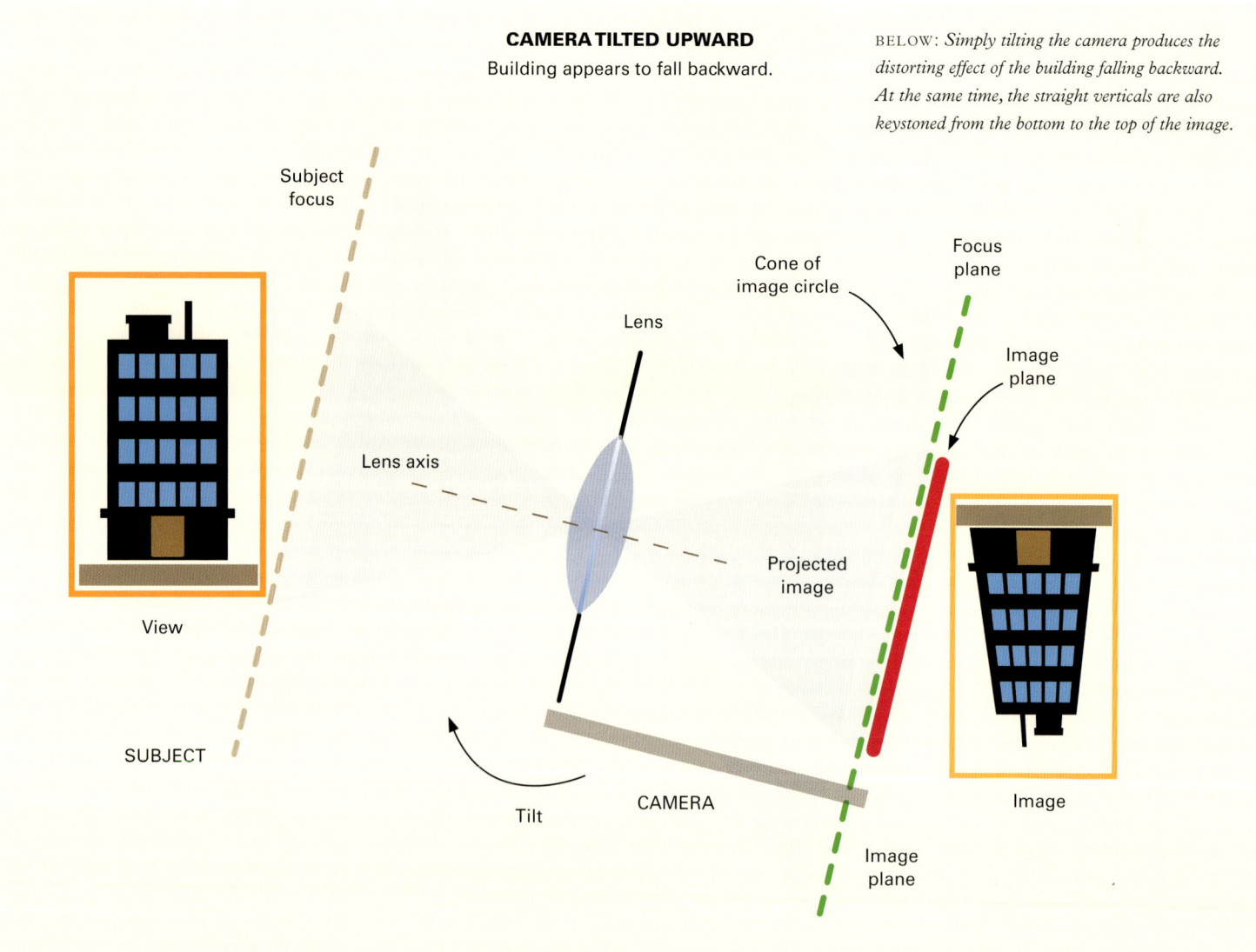

03 // LARGE-FORMAT CAMERAS // OPTICS & EQUIPMENT

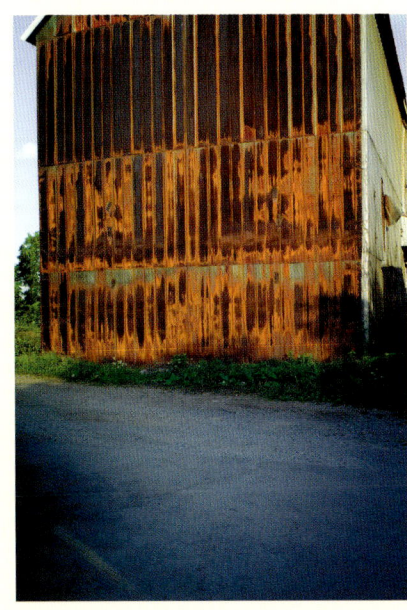

ABOVE: *Photographing tall buildings is problematic. Shooting them to maintain parallel sides often leaves the top of the building out of the frame and shows more foreground than necessary.*

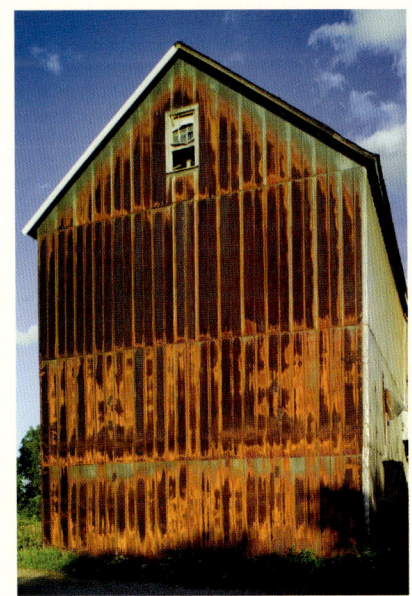

ABOVE: *With a large-format camera, the lens can be shifted upward to place the building on the sensor. This changes the projection on the focus plane needed to see the top of the building, while maintaining vertical lines.*

NORMAL CAMERA VIEW
Building is cut off at the top, plus too much foreground.

CAMERA LENS RISE
Subject is parallel to focus plane—lines stay straight.

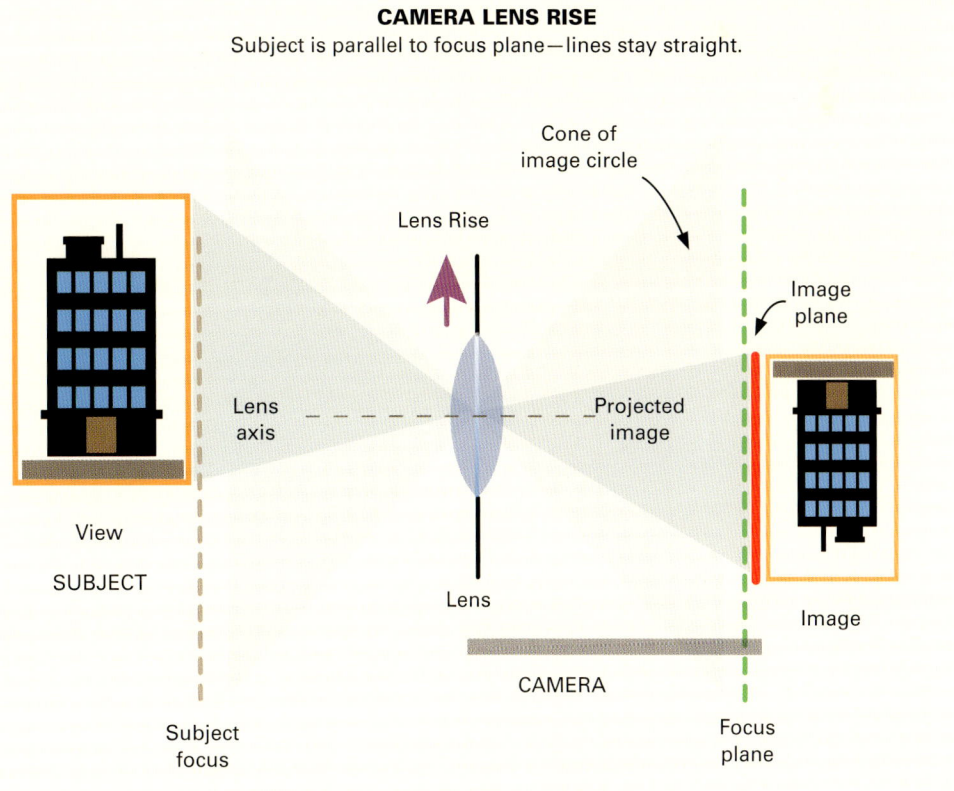

Rising Front

A commonly used movement on a large-format camera is a "rising front" when photographing a tall building. It is usually difficult to include the top of the building and keep the sides parallel to one another: as soon as the camera is pointed upward to take in the top of the building, the sides will appear to start to converge, creating a "keystone" effect where the building seems to be leaning backward.

In order to keep the sides straight, we need to keep the camera's film plane (or sensor) perpendicular to the front of the building. With most cameras, this means being far enough away to see the building in its entirety, or being higher up in an adjacent building so the camera doesn't need to be tilted upward.

However, with a large-format camera, the back of the camera can be set perpendicular to the building, while a "rising front" movement shifts the lens upward to take in the building in its entirety.

BELOW & RIGHT: *To produce an image of an angled subject such as a building (right) that shows everything along the surface as sharply as possible, the back and front of the camera are rotated to place the wall focus onto the image plane. A fence, as shown below, would be another example.*

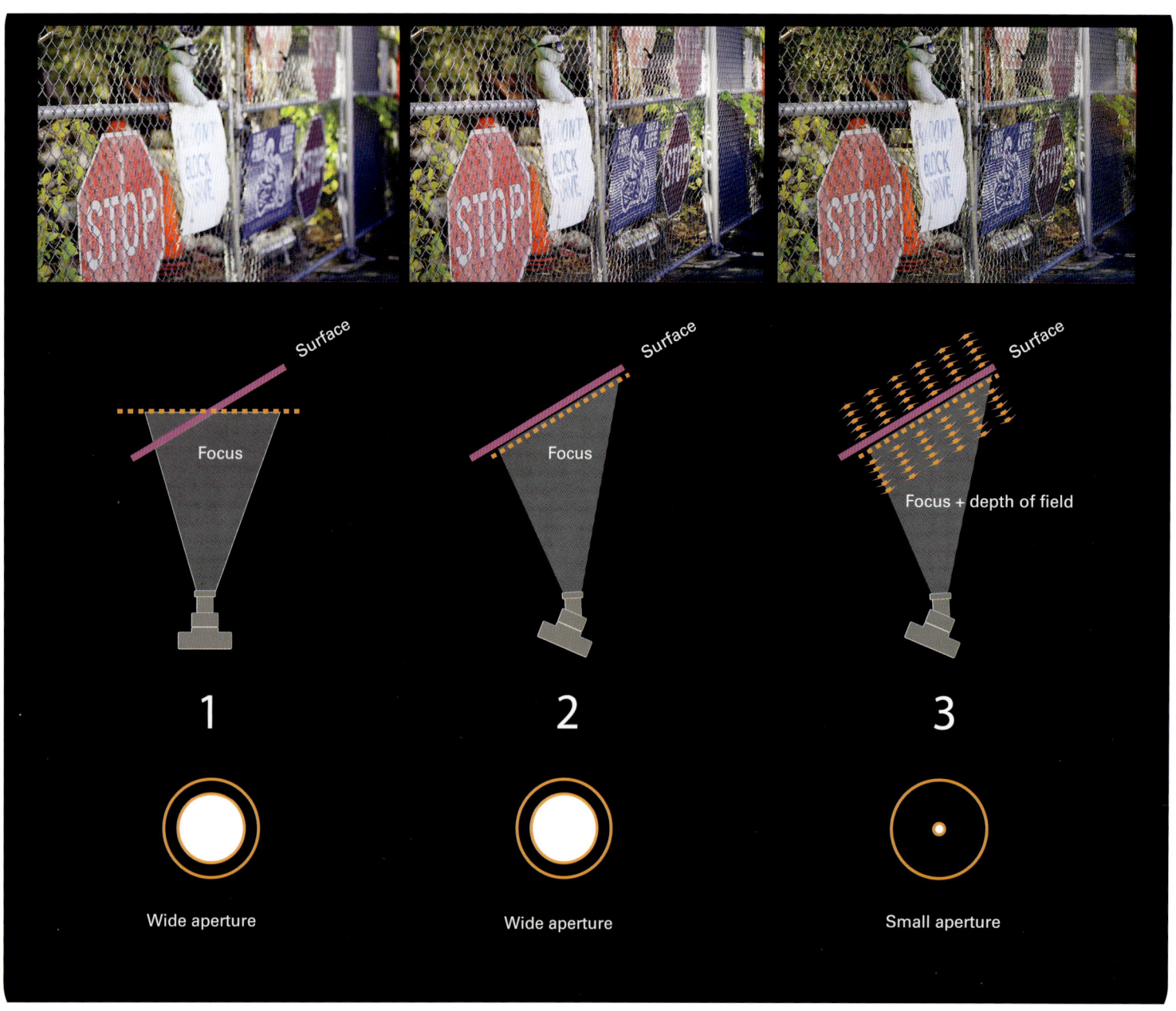

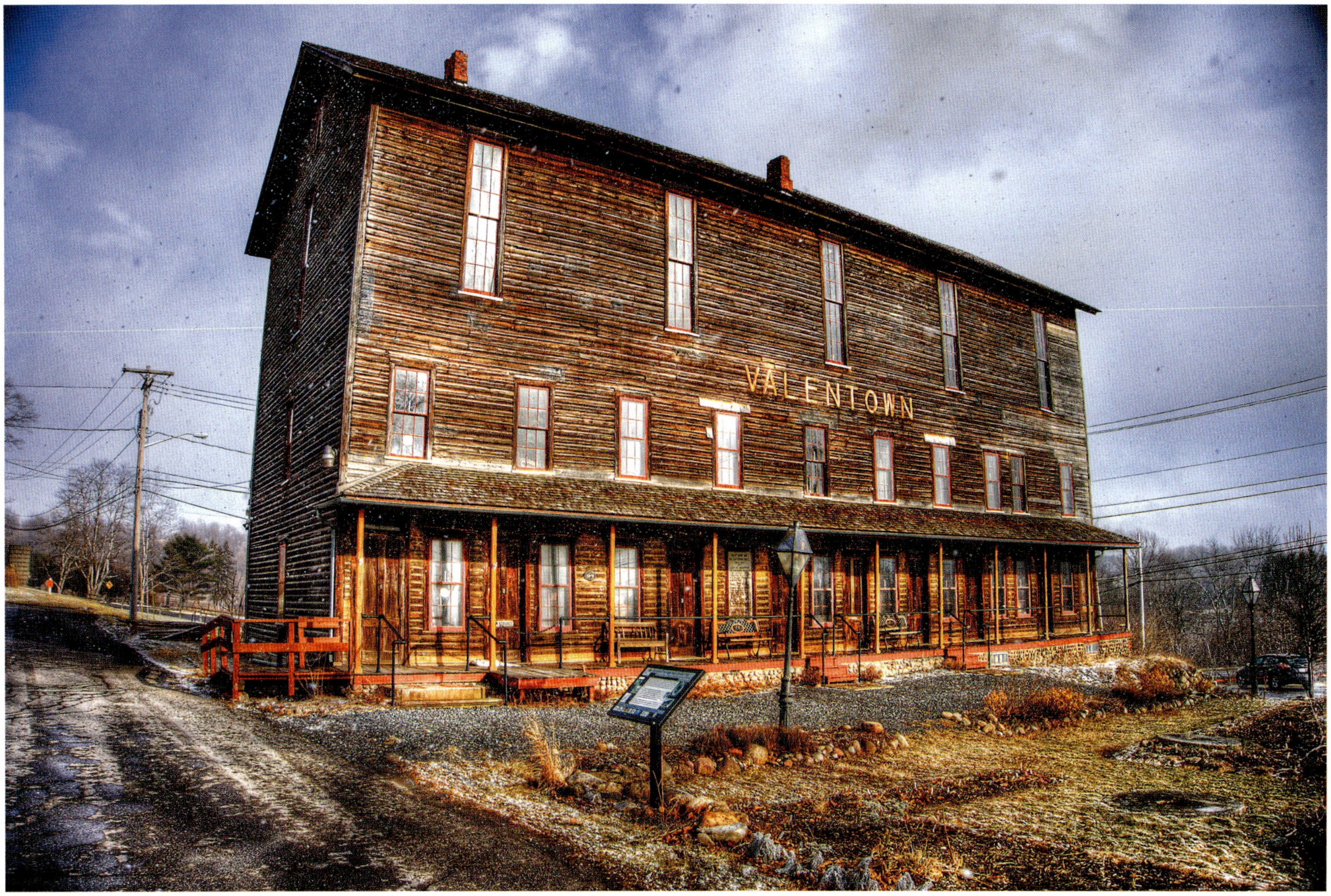

Scheimpflug Principle

The Scheimpflug principle shown here essentially adjusts the focus of the near end of a plane to be focused on one side of the image plane and the far end to be focused on the other. The result is a perfectly sharp plane of focus on subjects such as tabletops, looking down the side of a building, or a flock of ducks swimming on a pond. There are many other times where the Scheimpflug principle can be used to obtain focus on a plane.

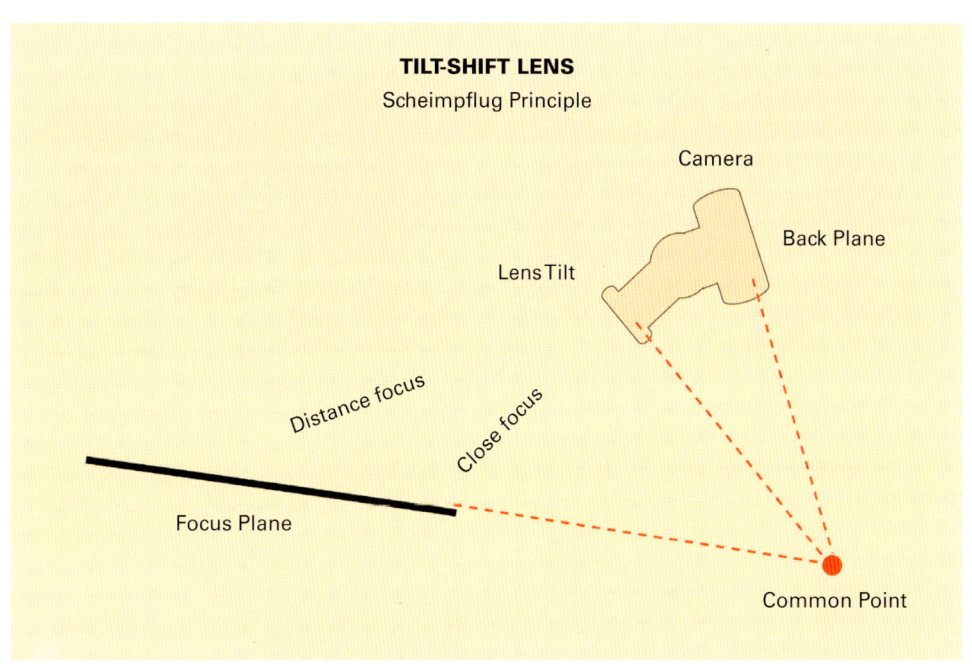

Tilt-Shift Lenses

Tilt-shift (or Perspective Control) lenses are built to replicate many of the movements of a large format camera, but in a lens that can be used on a mirrorless camera or DSLR.

Like the movements on a large-format camera, a tilt-shift lens allows you to manipulate the plane of focus (your glass sheet), so you can control what is and isn't in focus.

To achieve this, the lens needs to be designed so that it projects a larger image circle, and also needs to accommodate the various mechanisms needed to adjust the lens. Consequently, tilt-shift lenses tend to be heavy, slow to use (manual focus and exposure are common), and expensive, with only a select few manufacturers currently producing them.

It is also possible to use one of the growing number of tilt-shift lens adaptors with a conventional lens to achieve similar results. However, the movements may be rather limited when compared with a real tilt-shift lens and you may not be able to focus at infinity, depending on the camera/lens combination.

As a very general rule, using the lenses from a larger camera format is usually the best option if you want the greatest range of movements, as the larger the format, the larger the image circle needs to be. Using medium-format lenses on a full-frame DSLR, or full-frame lenses on a Micro Four Thirds camera would be a good start point.

Zörk makes two adaptors that can be used in conjunction to provide a considerable amount of shift (the Zörk Pro Shift Adaptor), as well as a sizeable degree of tilt (the Zörk Multi Focus System). This is made possible in part through the use of medium-format enlarging lenses, which have large image circles.

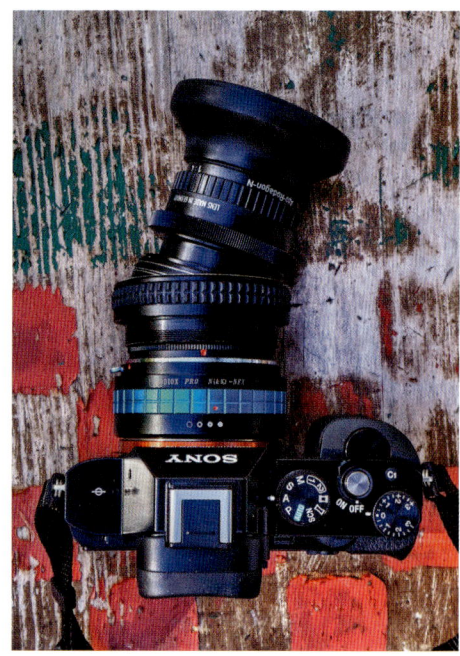

ABOVE: *The Zörk MFS uses medium-format enlarger lenses to create a versatile tilt lens. Here it is shown mounted to a Sony mirrorless body using a Nikon–Sony adaptor (with the blue band).*

LEFT: *Tilt and shift movements are usually controlled by micro-adjustment knobs built into the lens. In most cases, one controls the rise and fall (shift) and another rotates the lens to alter the lens angle (tilt) relative to the image plane. Most movements can be positioned at different rotations around the lens axis as well.*

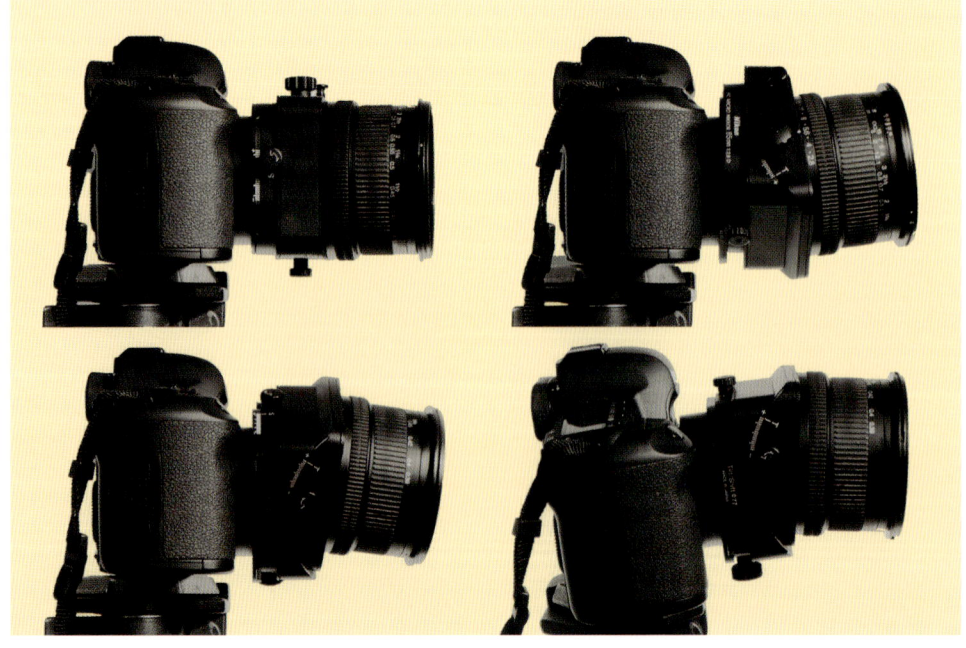

03 // TILT-SHIFT LENSES // OPTICS & EQUIPMENT

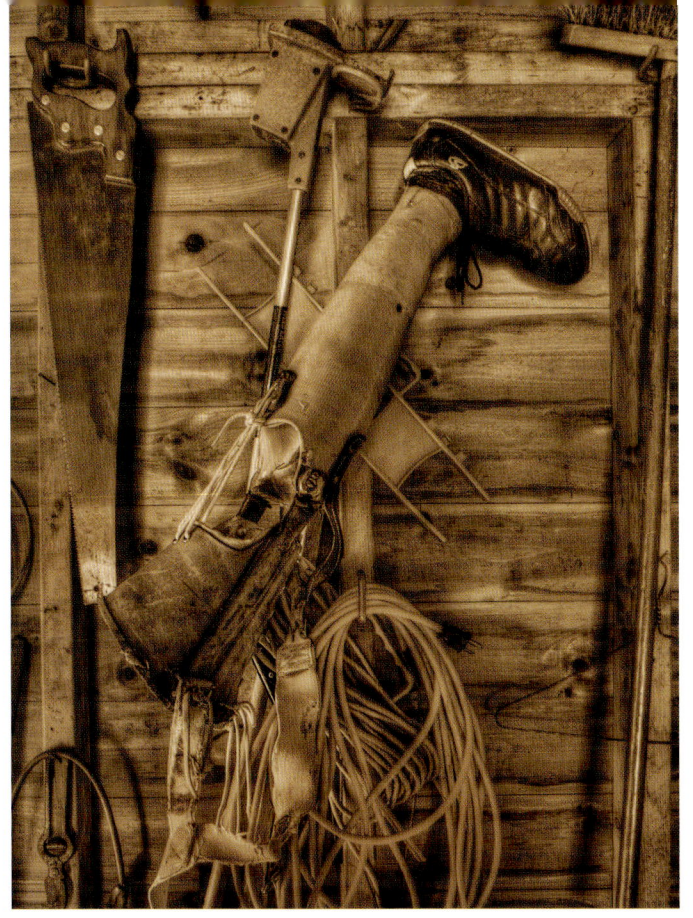

LEFT: *Using a tripod and a Nikkor 28mm Perspective Control lens mounted to a Sony A7 mirrorless camera, I shifted the lens vertically to "lower the view," enabling me to keep the vertical lines of the structure straight.*

BELOW: *In order to maintain sharpness across the tops of these headstones, I used the Zörk's tilting capability to place the focus plane on the tops of the grave markers. The aperture was set to allow enough depth of field to make the ground sharp as well.*

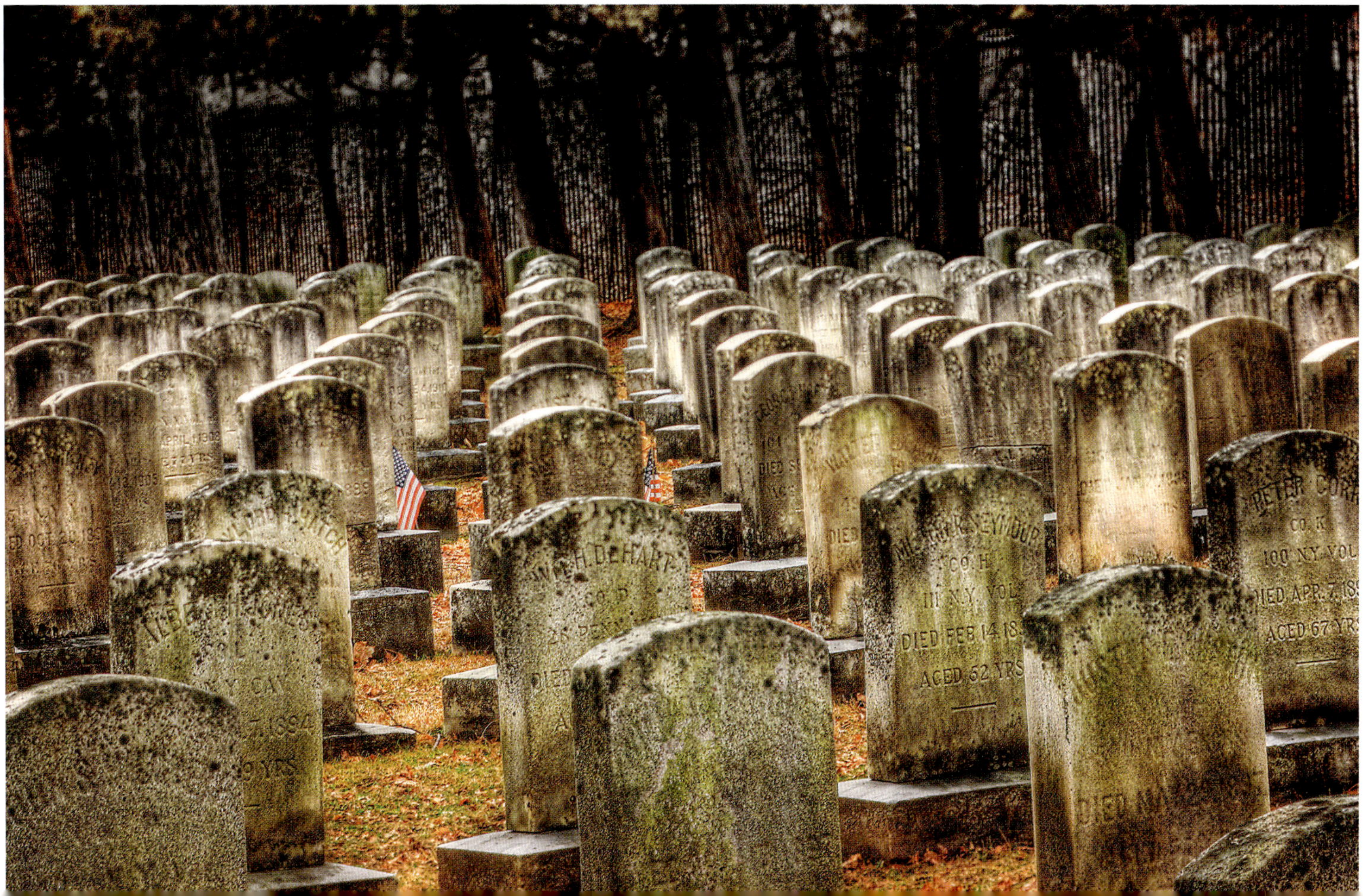

Miniaturization

A popular use for tilt-shift lenses is to create images that give the world around us the look of a small-scale model, so people look like ants, cars appear toy-sized, and lakes look like puddles.

The effect is an illusion, based on the way in which we see the world around us. Our sense of scale has at least some dependence on the areas that we read as out of focus relative to those that are in focus. If we see shallow depth of field, and the subject is already small in the frame, then we tend to think of the subject as being very close to us. And if the scale is small, then we tend to read the image as being of something very tiny. Put simply, we are "tricked" into reading the scene as being part of a miniature world.

In order to produce this transformation, you need an interchangeable lens digital camera, a tripod, and a lens that can tilt away from the normal lens axis. The lens could be a tilt-shift lens, a conventional lens on a tilt adaptor, or even a DIY lens, as outlined on the following pages.

For the purpose of miniaturization, you need to tilt the lens so that it creates a thin sliver of focus on the focal plane, with the rest of the image made up of out-of-focus light. This creates a very defined "sweet spot" of selective focus that can be used to pick out the subject, and it is this shallow focus that creates the miniaturization effect: our eyes tell our brain that we are much closer to the subject than we actually are, so we naturally assume that means the subject is small in scale.

BELOW: *This miniaturized view of a mall at night was shot using a Zörk MFS adaptor fitted with a medium-format enlarging lens.*

RIGHT: *These cars have a miniaturized appearance due to the defocused foreground and background details created by a Zörk MFS adaptor.*

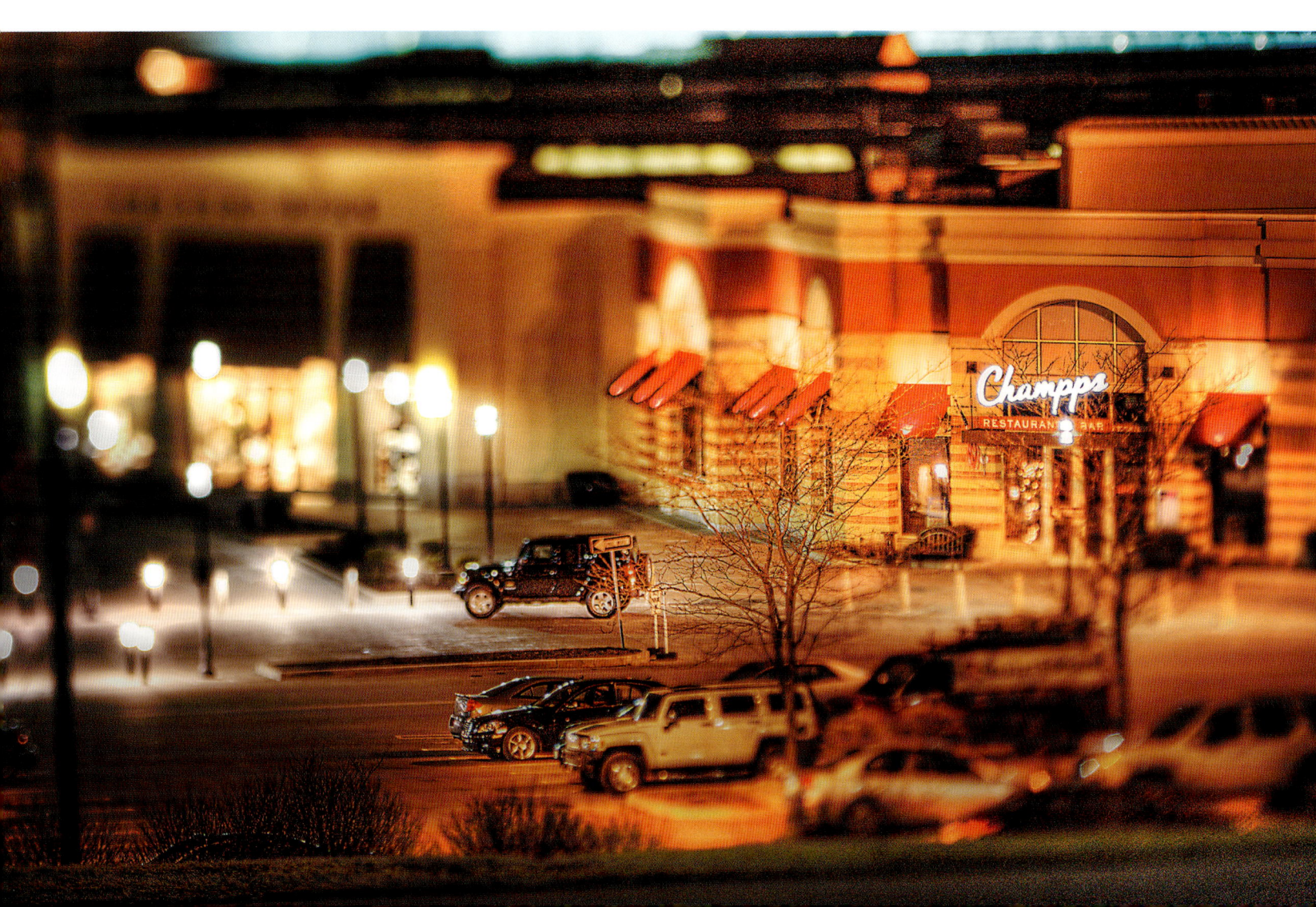

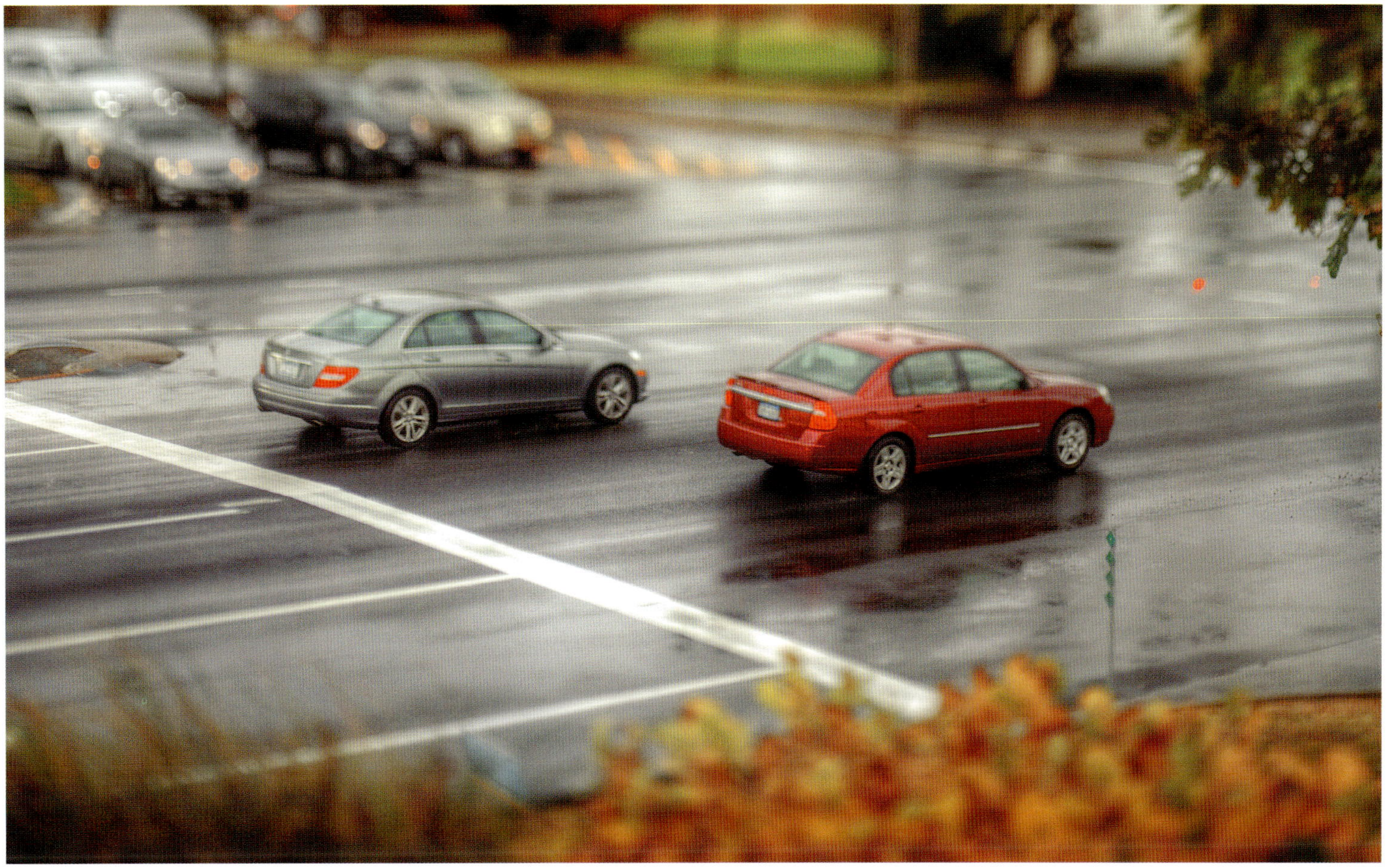

03 // TILT-SHIFT LENSES // OPTICS & EQUIPMENT

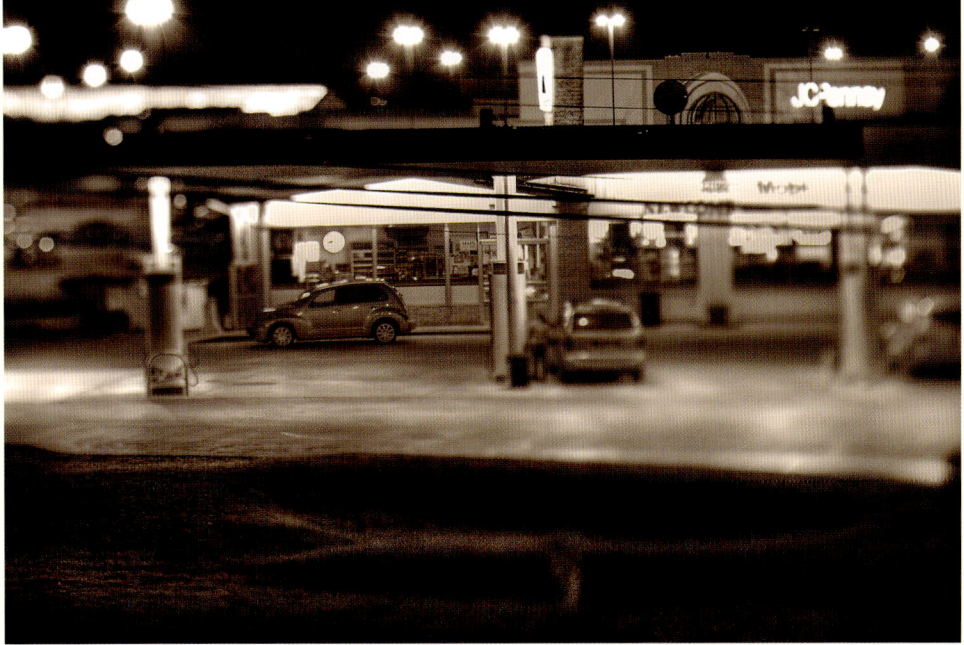

VIDEO & MINIATURIZATION

Most DSLR and mirrorless camera users will find that their cameras can shoot video as well as still images. If so, it is easy to create miniaturized worlds that are in motion. The effects can be pretty amazing and incredibly convincing—it's easy to think that what you are seeing in the video is a tiny toylike playground of miniature objects.

While it is fun to create miniature videos of cars on a freeway, boats moving around in a harbor, or people in a busy street, the effect seems even more playful when using stop-motion photography to speed up the action. In either instance, the secret is to shoot from above with the focus sharply on the moving objects.

DIY Lenses

Although buying a tilt-shift lens or lens adaptor is an easy option, it is not necessarily an inexpensive one. However, with a little ingenuity it is entirely possible to construct your own tilt lens.

Using a DIY lens on a digital camera is great fun—basically, you have absolute freedom to push and pull on the lens, swinging it back and forth, up or down, until you get the focus the way you want.

A number of years ago, I created my first homemade tilt lens by fitting an enlarger lens to a car CV boot. This was simply held in front of the camera body while pushing, pulling, and twisting it to get the desired focus. The idea behind this contraption was to create images where the plane of the lens focus cut through the image plane at an angle, so that only selective areas would be sharply focused. The idea was to create a soft focus on either side of the subject, just like using the tilt movement on a large format camera or tilt-shift lens.

After several prototypes, I found that a black rubber shock absorber boot taped to a drilled-out body cap of my SLR was a better choice. The lens had to be held in place with rubber bands and would dangle in a suggestive manner in front of the camera, but these were minor inconveniences compared to the image I could create.

Over the past ten years, I have built a number of variations of this lens and consider them among my favorite lenses for both digital and analog photography. I find that the images produced with a DIY lens tend to provide more satisfaction than anything produced commercially. This is not only because of cost saving, but also because they work well and are easy to build—there is a lot of pleasure in making the lens that you use to create your images.

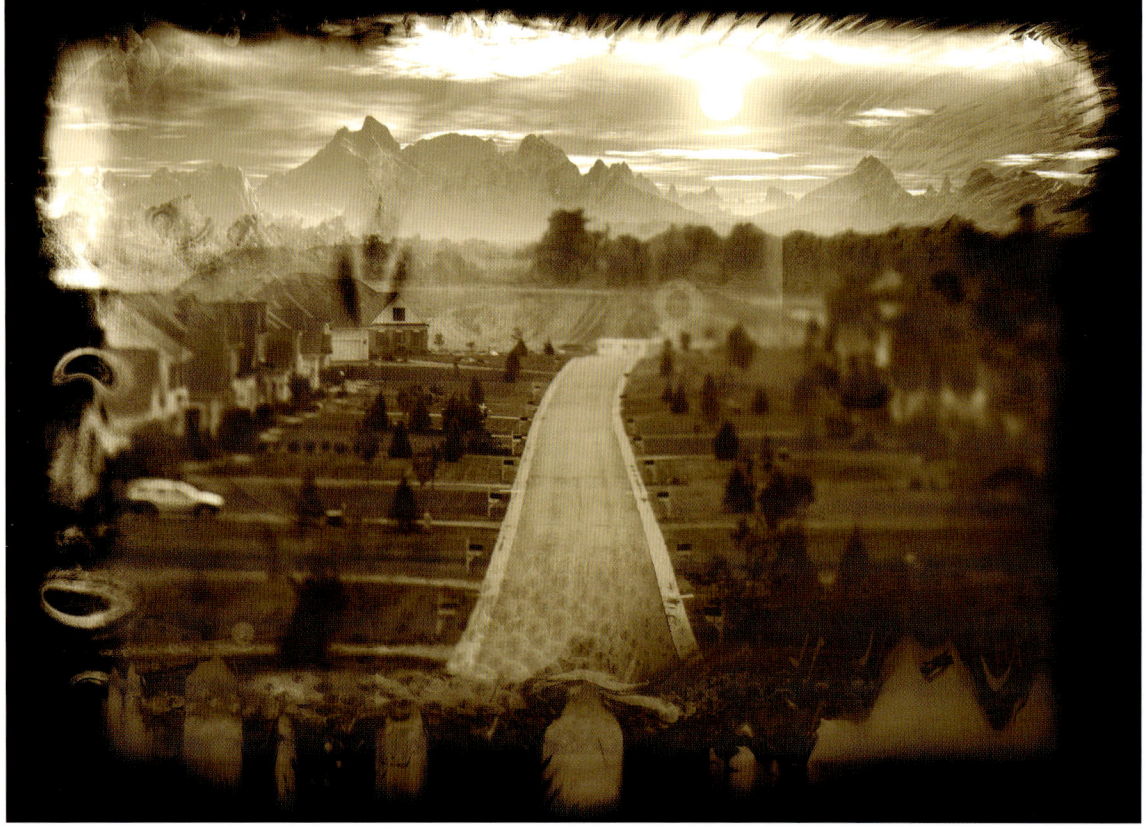

LEFT: *This combined image was shot with a homemade lens that was tilted heavily to the side so that the focus plane ran down the street. The background is a computer-created 3D scene that was layered in using Photoshop.*

RIGHT: *Two of many different homemade DIY tilt-shift lenses that I use regularly. These are both built using a Nikon body cap as a mounting system.*

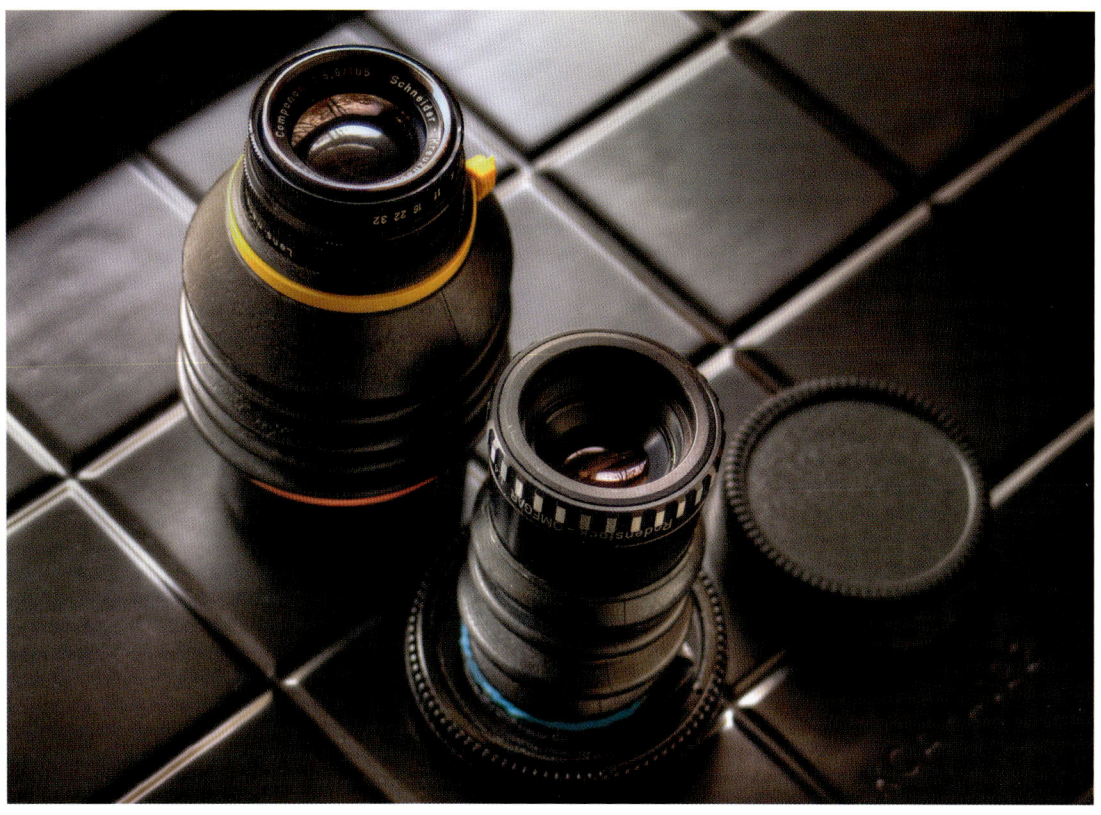

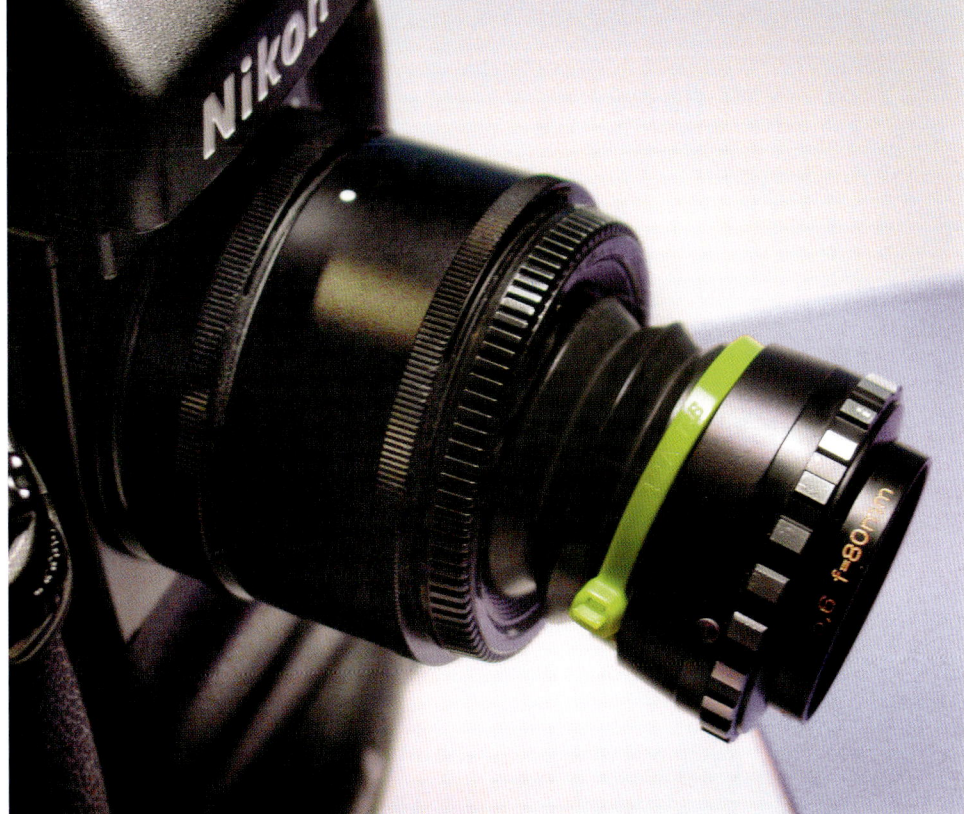

LEFT: *This lens was made from an enlarger lens and extension tubes.*

Freelensing

Over the past decade, I have experimented with a number of unorthodox methods for making images. One of my favorites is a technique that can produce some amazing imagery, provided you take certain precautions.

Freelensing is accomplished by holding a lens in front of the camera, rather than mounting it to the camera in the usual way (hence the term "freelens"). The main principle is that the lens can then be moved around, swiveled, and shifted with one hand, while your other hand controls the camera. The act of swiveling and shifting the lens gives you the opportunity to control the focus and create tilt and/or shift effects.

One of the main benefits of this technique is that you can simply remove your lens and hold it in front of the camera to see if it will work. Often, you will find that it is impossible to focus at infinity, due to the flange-to-sensor distance. You can still focus the lens, but only on subjects that are closer to it (this is essentially the same principle as fitting an extension tube between the camera and lens).

BELOW: *The images produced by freelensing can be dreamy and almost otherworldly in appearance.*

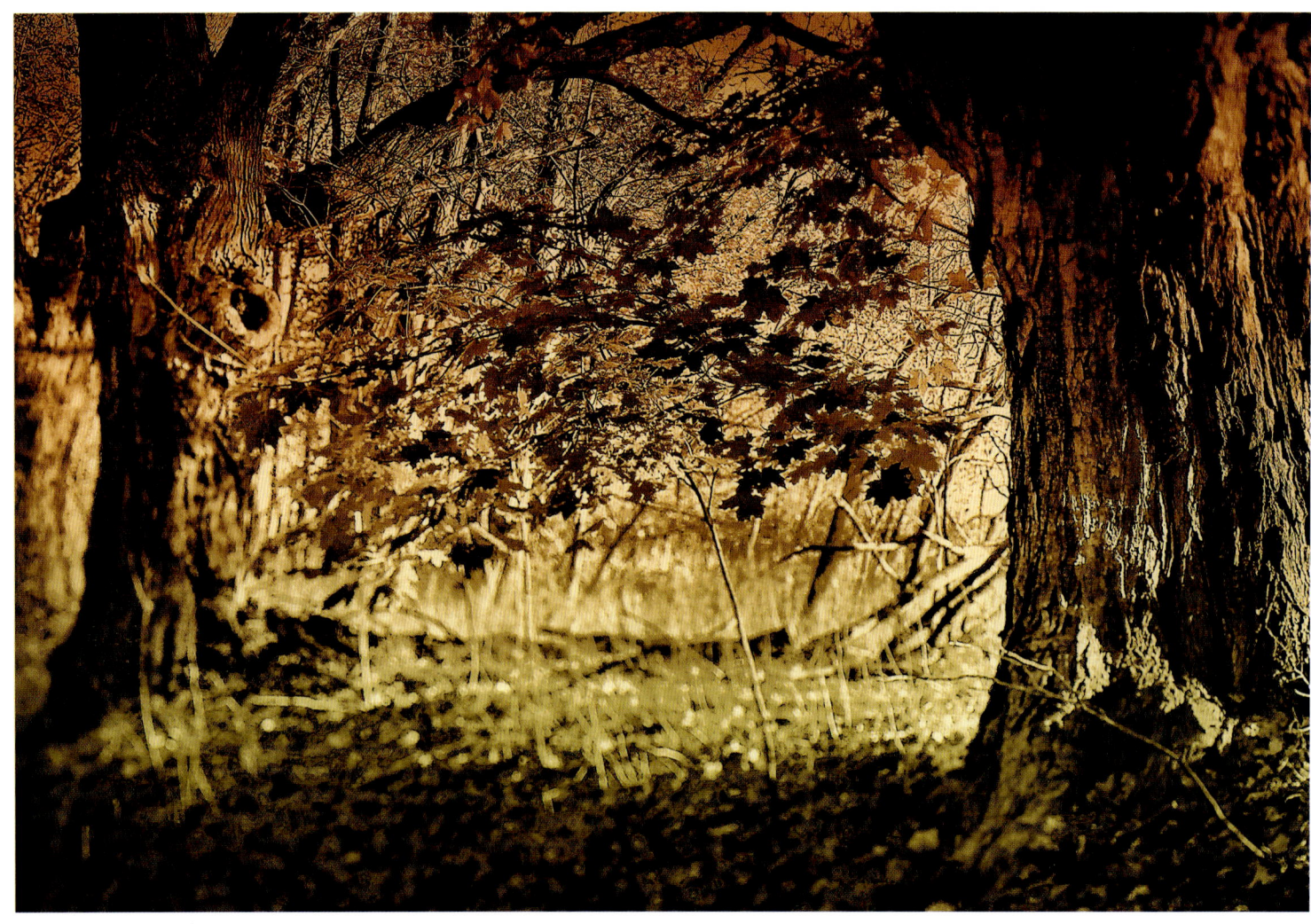

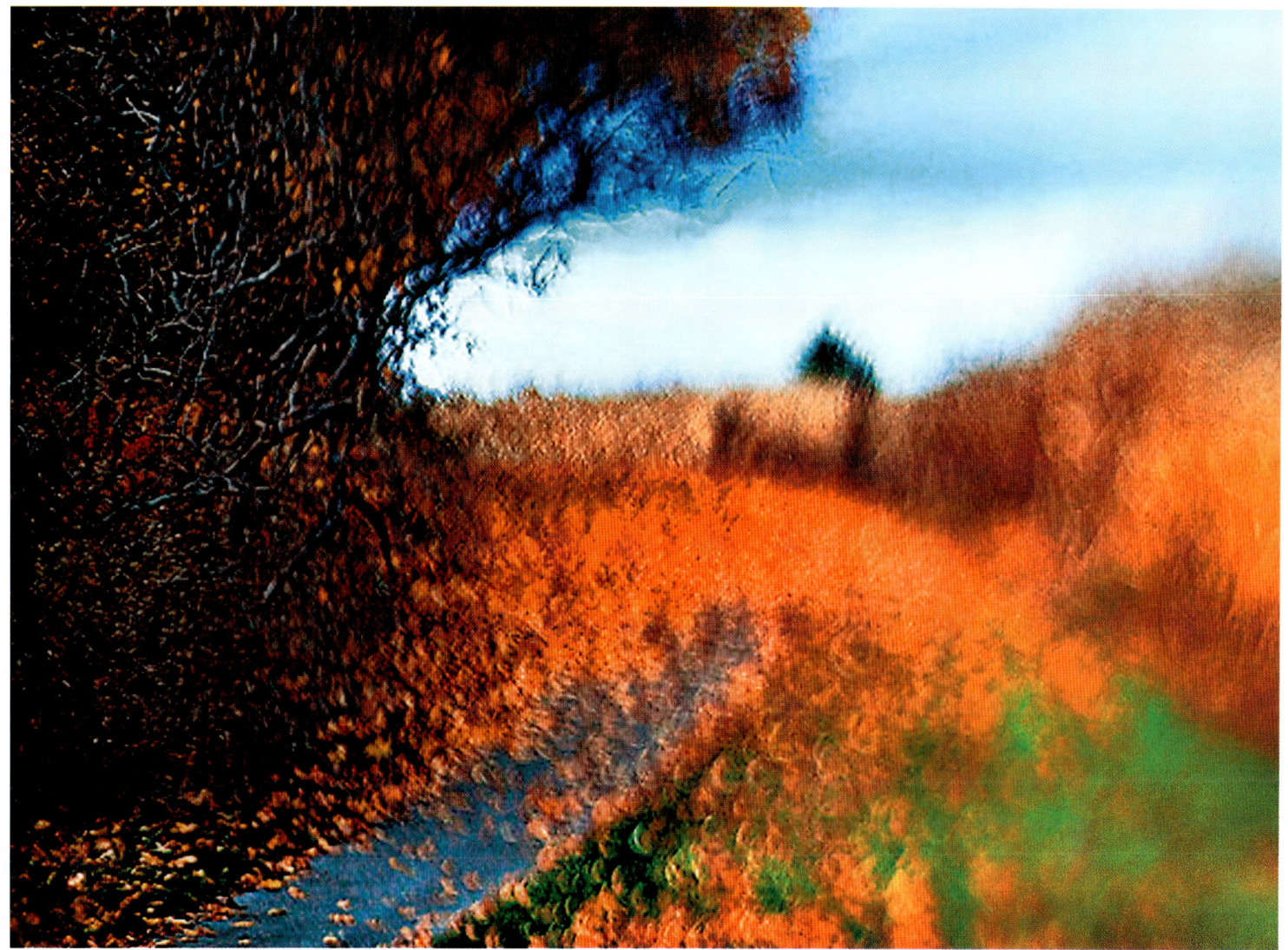

ABOVE: *The freelens technique and DIY tilt lenses can produce similar results. However, while they are fun to use, they are not as precise as real tilt-shift lenses or lens adaptors, and the result is never really repeatable if you need to focus precisely.*

However, there are a few drawbacks with this method that should be discussed. The biggest problem is that the sensor will be open to dust, dirt, moisture, and extraneous light, which can cause undesirable effects to the image. For some photographers, including this one, the chances are worth taking as long as it isn't my main camera—I usually freelens using a digital camera that I don't mind getting a little dirty. An inexpensive, pre-owned camera would be a great choice.

Although you can use just about any focal length lens, the best lenses for this technique are those that are made for a larger format camera. So, as with tilt-shift lens adapters, a medium-format lens would be a good choice for DSLR users, while full-frame lenses will work well on smaller format mirrorless cameras. In each instance, this means that you can hold the lens a bit farther away from the front of your camera, making it less likely to damage the lens mount or, worse, the mirror.

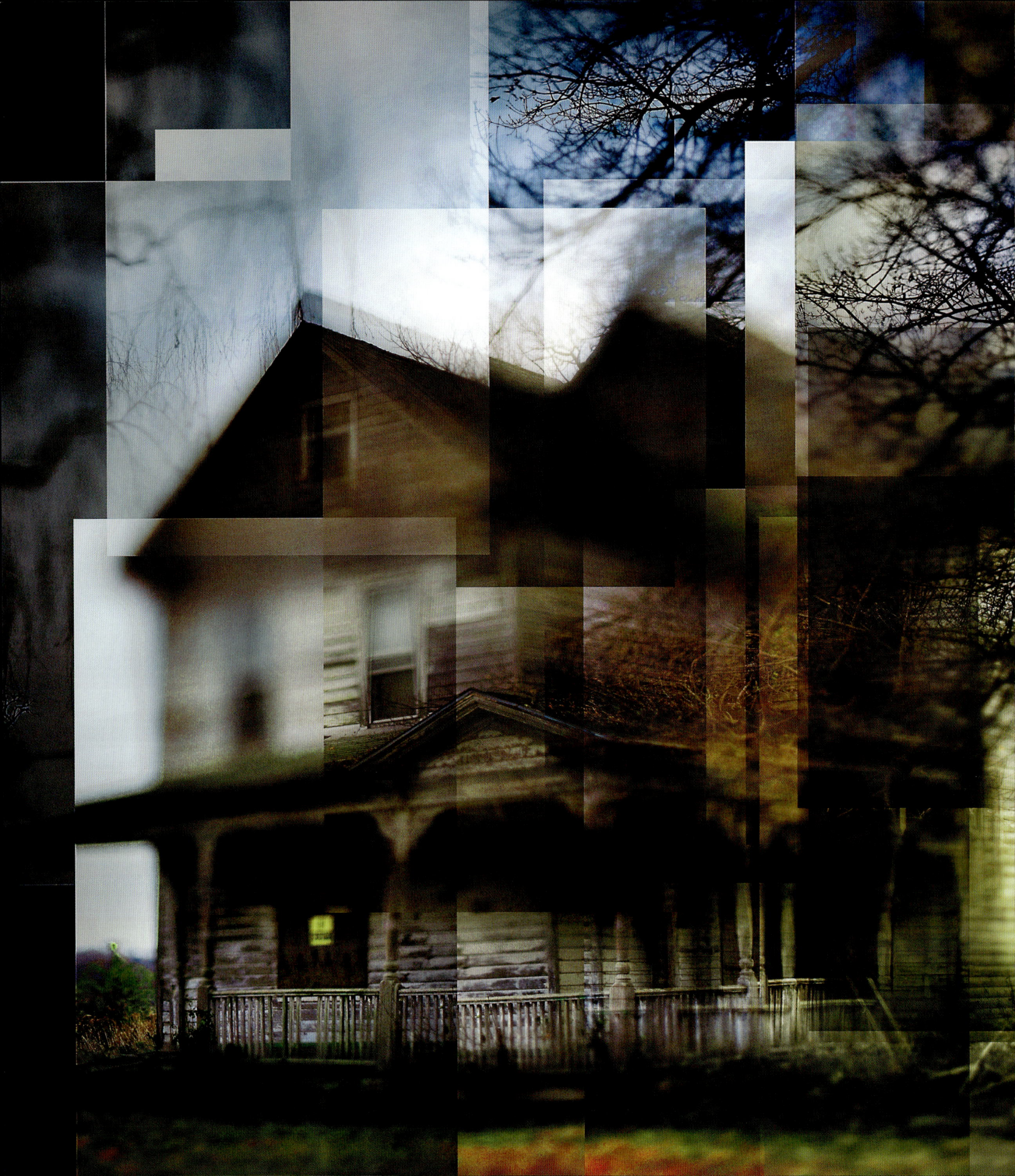

03 // FREELENSING // OPTICS & EQUIPMENT

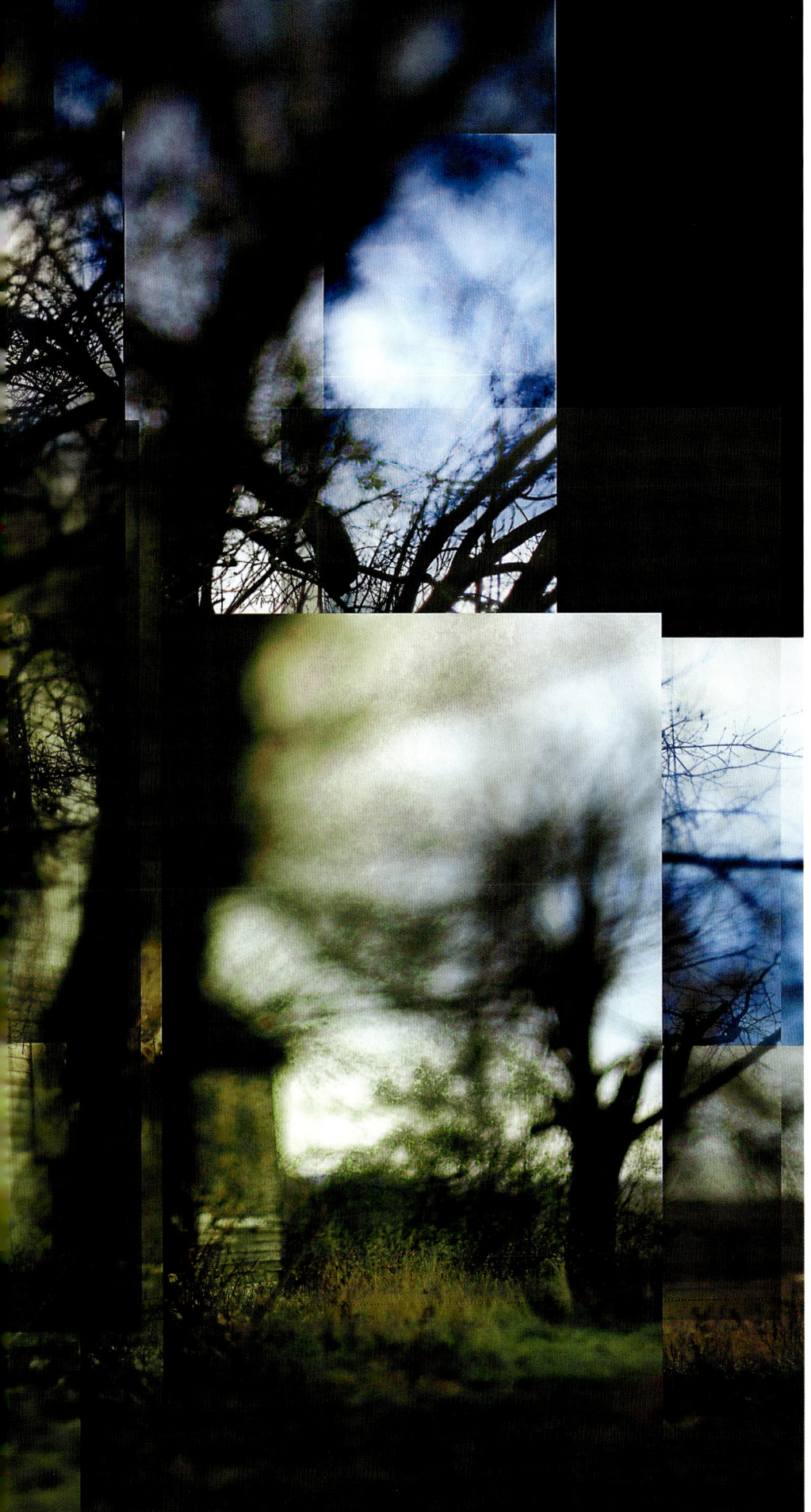

LEFT: *Using a freelens in different orientations produced a patchwork of images containing various in- and out-of-focus elements. The individual frames were stitched together by hand in Photoshop.*

Tripods

Although the lens is the main component used for creating sharpness, a tripod can help you produce much sharper results with many subjects.

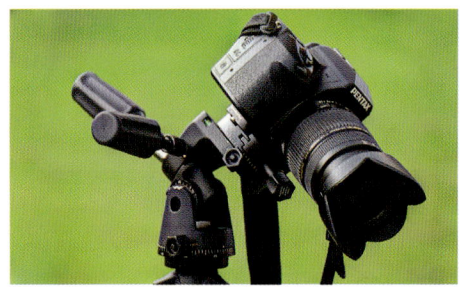 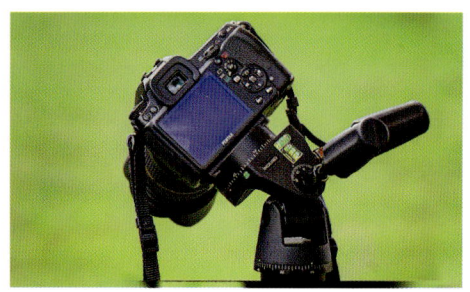

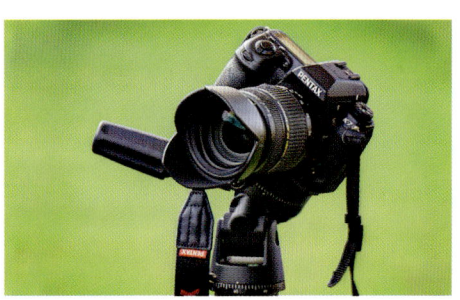 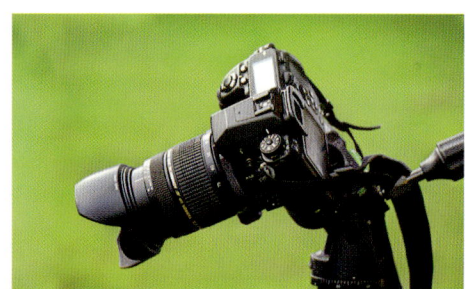

If you are shooting long exposures, or an image needs to be repeated (when you are shooting an HDR sequence, for example), a tripod is essential if you want to keep the camera steady. It can also help you frame your subject precisely.

A great tripod is light, but sturdy, and adaptable to many different shooting situations; the best ones are made from lightweight alloy or carbon fiber. A good, medium-priced tripod with a quick-release head that can be rotated and locked in any position can be a great asset to most photographers.

Photographers are usually very fussy about what tripods they use, because not all tripods are created equally. When looking for a tripod, buy something that suits your shooting technique and purpose. For me, the ideal tripod should be easy to set up, light weight, sturdy, and strong. A proper head can make it easy to set a camera at various angles and hold it in place for the duration of a photographic session.

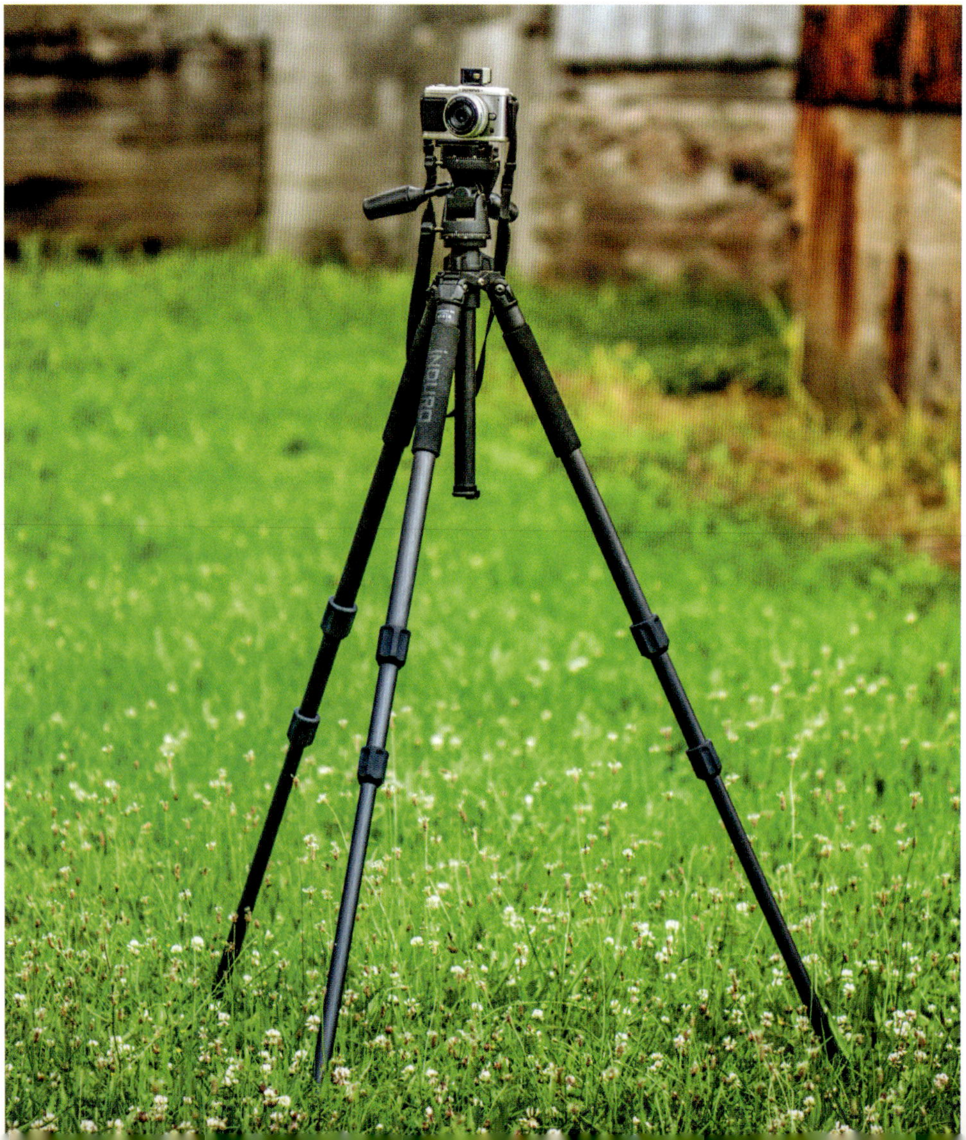

ABOVE RIGHT: *A sturdy tripod with a good head will serve most photographers well.*

RIGHT: *A light camera needs to be held in place so as not to move, whereas a heavy camera's weight helps it maintain a degree of steadiness. Rather counterintuitively, this means that it is best to use a well-made, sturdy, and heavier tripod in order to maintain the highest degree of support, even (or especially) with a light camera.*

HANDHELD EXPOSURES

The general rule for shooting pictures handheld is that the shorter the focal length, the longer the camera can be held steady for the exposure to occur without blurring.

The traditional advice that is often given is to use a shutter speed that corresponds to the focal length of the lens, so a 135mm lens on a full-frame sensor camera requires a shutter speed of at least 1/125 second to avoid camera shake, while a 24mm lens on the same camera would allow a much longer time of roughly 1/30 second to achieve a relative sharp image. Of course, other factors need to be considered, such as the steadiness of the user, any subject movement, and the light source being used, but generally speaking it is always best to use the fastest shutter speed allowable by your subject and lighting.

However, many of today's digital cameras and lenses have some sort of vibration control or image stabilization system. This allows you to handhold the camera at much slower shutter speeds than would usually be recommended, and still maintain sharp focus. The control must be turned on in order to use it, although it is not recommended for use when the camera is mounted to a tripod (ironically, the stabilization system can actually cause blur in this situation).

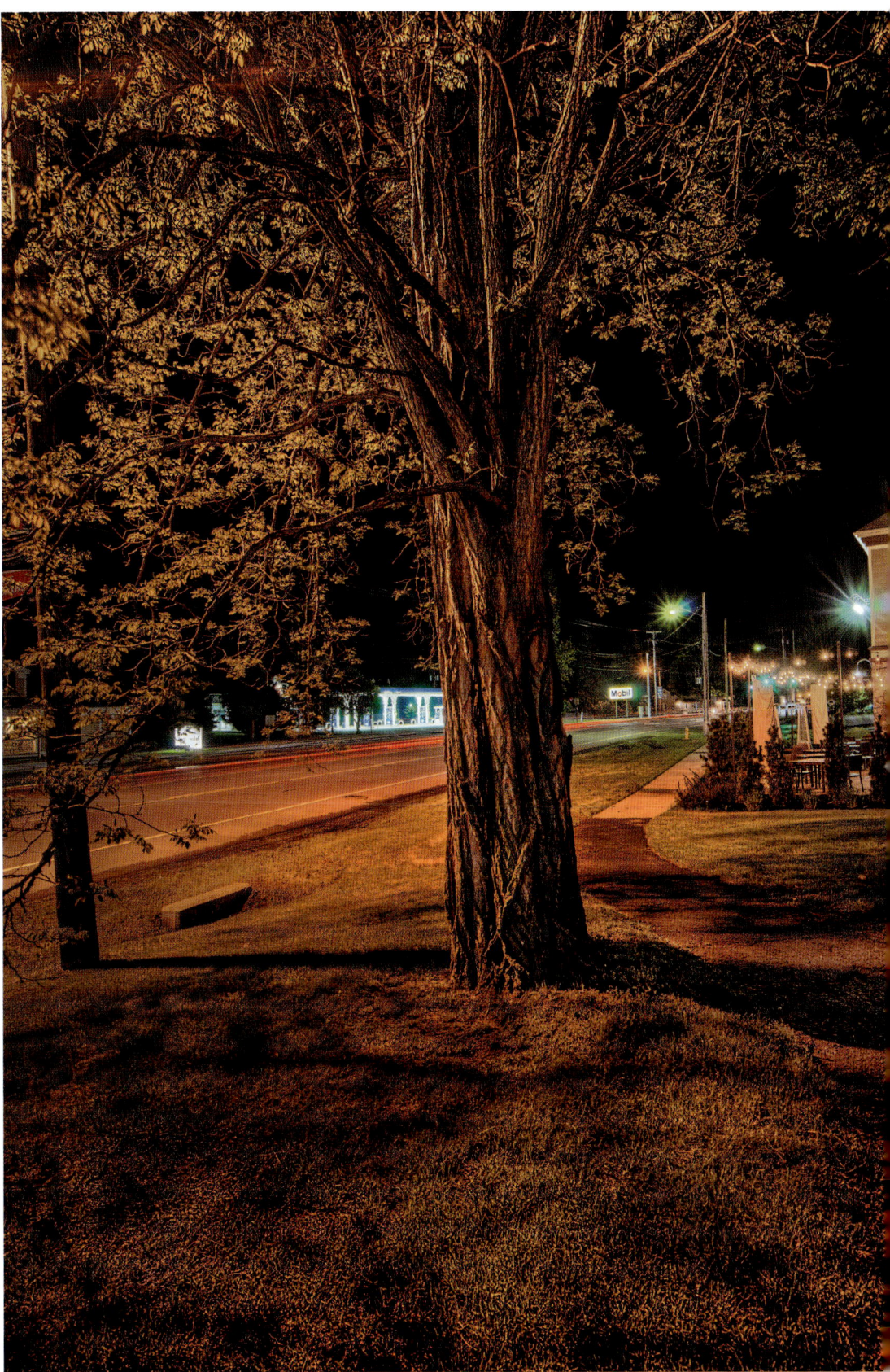

RIGHT: *Night shots like this absolutely require a tripod—especially in order to capture streaks of light from passing cars.*

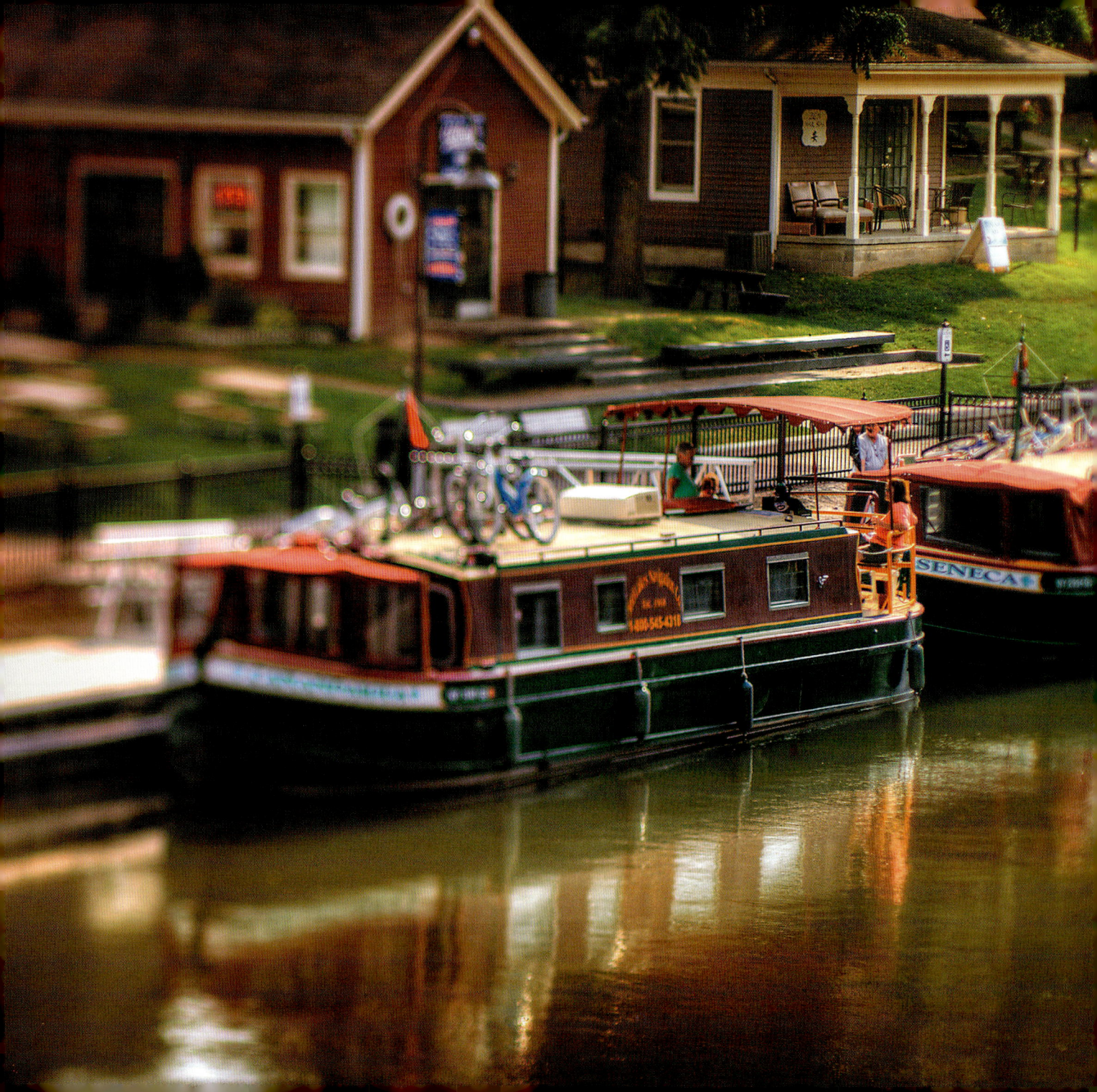

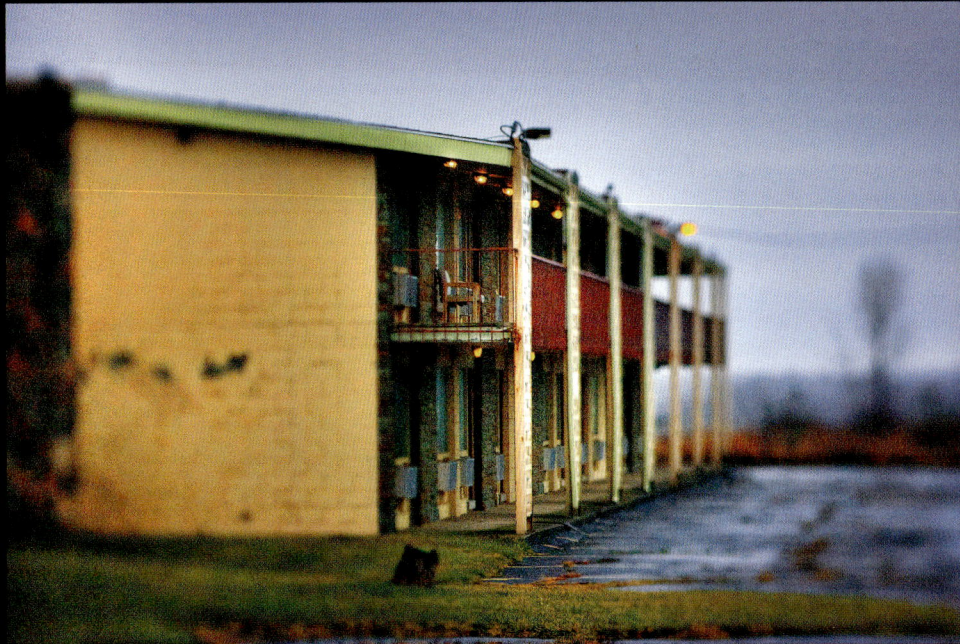

ABOVE: *Using a Zörk MFS allowed me to set the focus on the front corner of this old motel.*

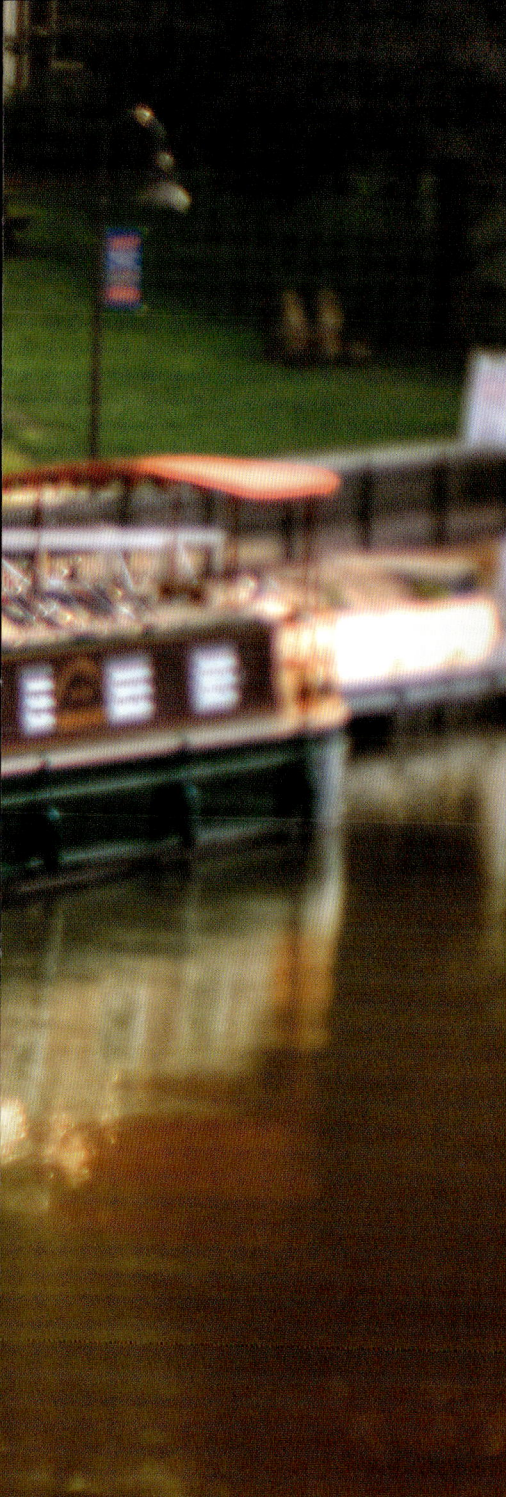

LEFT: *I chose to place the focus on the rear of the first old canal barge in this scene. I used a Nikkor 85mm perspective control lens to tilt the lens to the right, until the plane of focus ran as a vertical strip.*

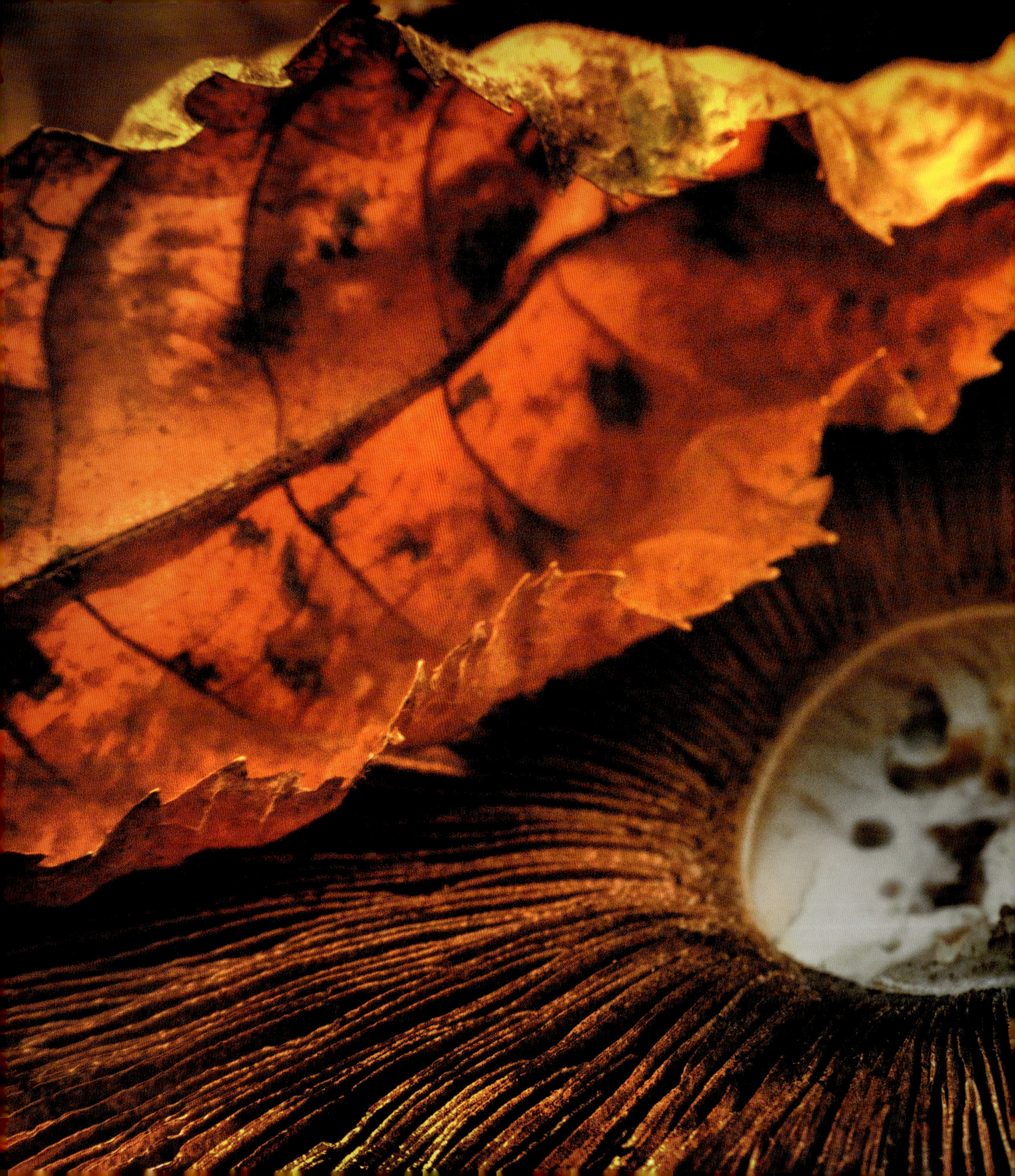

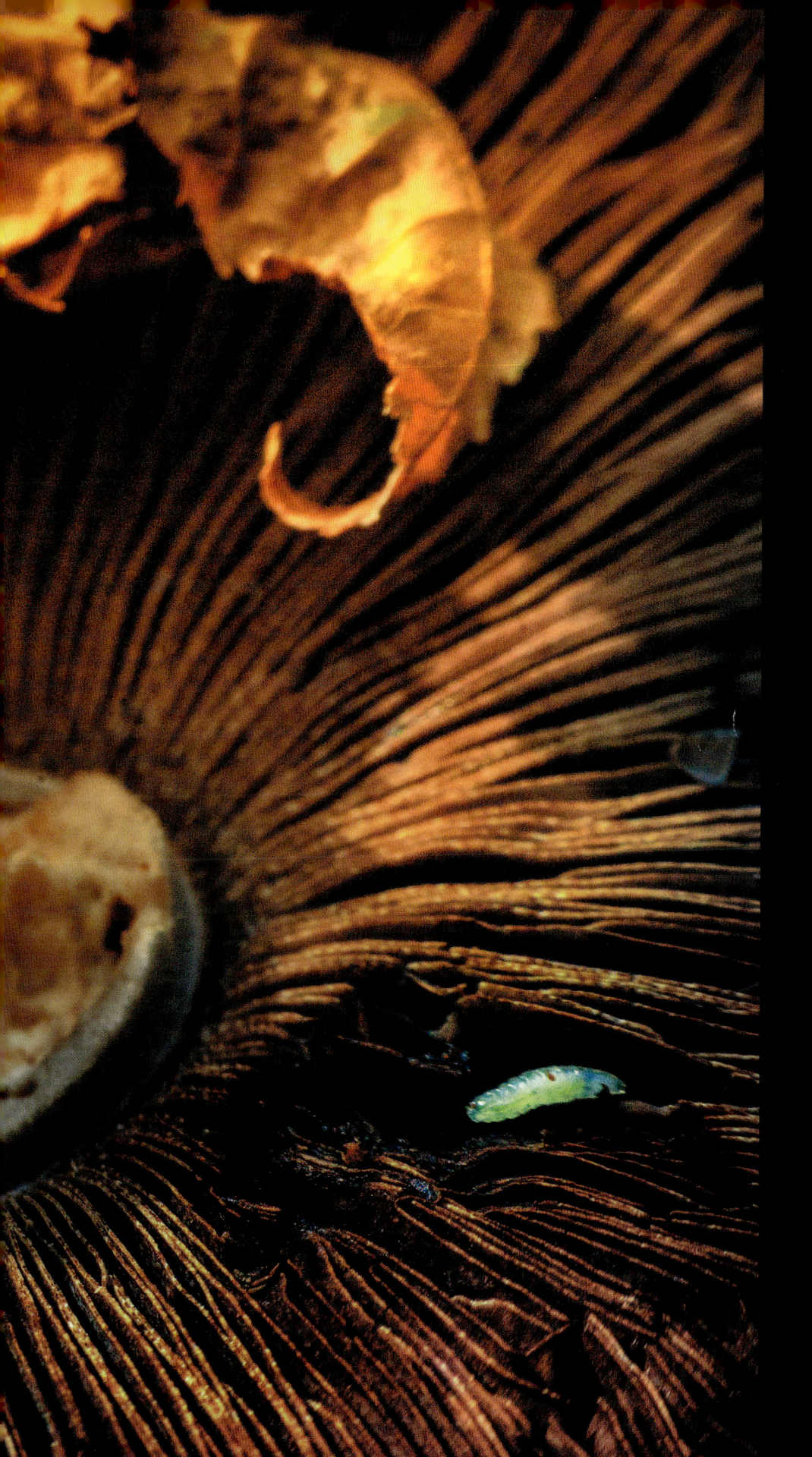

04 // CLOSE-UP

Getting Up Close

Most lens manufacturers make lenses that have both long-range as well as macro focusing capabilities. Macro photography has become increasingly popular, as digital cameras have made it much easier to perform. Today, it is pretty easy to shoot close-up images of almost anything.

Most compact, fixed-lens digital cameras have the capability for macro built into the camera; usually, all it takes is a setting on the lens or in the cameras menu. However, if you're using a mirrorless camera or DSLR, it is not quite so straightforward: you will typically need to invest in a more specialist lens or other solution that will enable you to explore the macro world.

Macro Lenses

Although many zoom lenses boast a "macro" capability, dedicated macro lenses with a fixed focal length are the best lenses for this type of close-up work, as they offer superior image quality and "life-size" (1:1) reproduction of the subject. This type of lens is available from most of the major camera manufacturers (for their own

BELOW: *This Tamron macro lens has excellent optics for close-up and macro work. It produces a beautiful bokeh effect as well.*

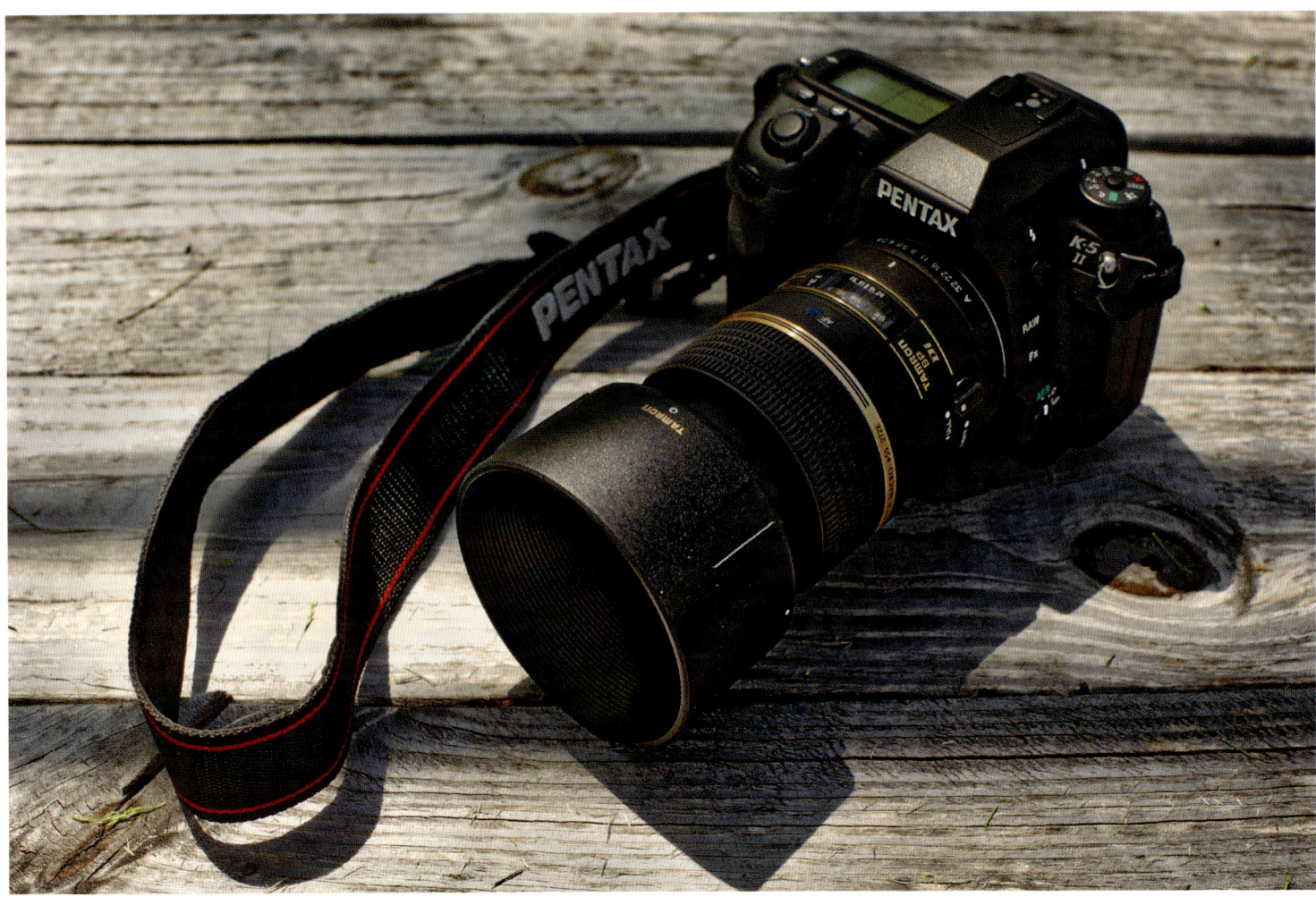

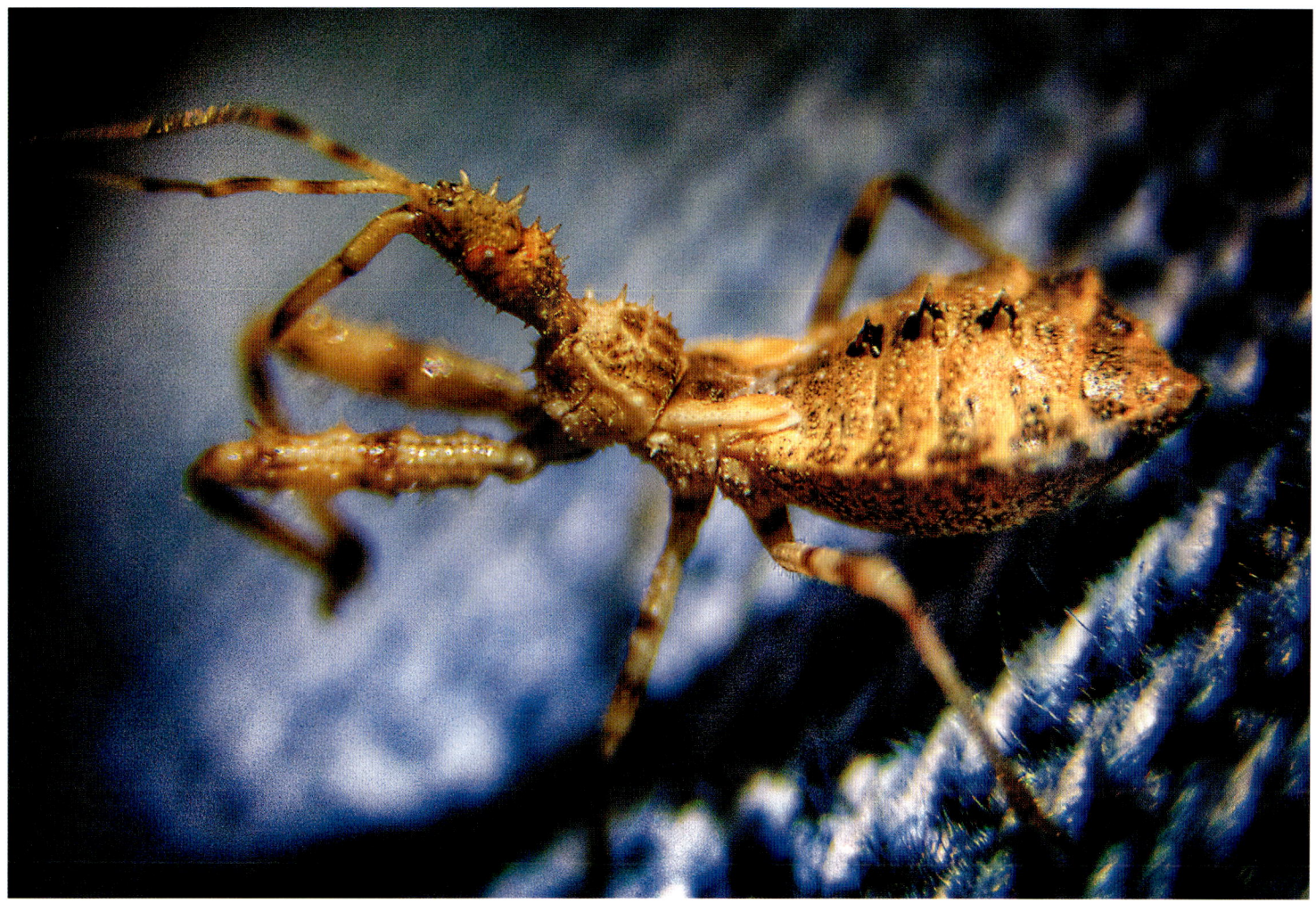

ABOVE: *This insect was shot using LiveView on the camera's rear LCD, rather than looking through the viewfinder. Macro shots often require very odd angles, where the viewfinder can be difficult to access.*

camera systems), as well as third-party lens makers such as Tamron, Tokina, and Sigma.

Macro lenses are available with focal lengths ranging from 40mm to 180mm, and the simple rule is that the longer the focal length, the farther you can be from your subject and still get a large magnification. This is known as the "working distance," and a greater working distance is helpful when you can't get close to the subject and/ or don't want to scare a living subject away.

Most macro lenses will give at least a 1:1 image to subject ratio. That means that the subject will appear to be life-size in relationship to the image sensor. Some lenses can give even greater magnification.

Extension Tubes

There are many different ways to obtain high degrees of image magnification, without investing in a dedicated lens. One of the simplest is to use extension tubes.

Extension tubes fit between the camera and a conventional lens, moving the lens farther from the sensor. This allows the lens to focus closer to the subject and produce a greater magnification of the subject: the farther the lens is moved from the sensor, the greater the magnification.

Bear in mind that a lot of the Canon, Minolta, Nikon, Olympus, and Pentax macro equipment made in the last 20 or so years can usually be used on the same company's DSLR and mirrorless counterparts (although you may need an adaptor), so you can save money by purchasing used equipment. Older extension tubes and other macro photography items are available from used camera dealers, as well as online sellers.

The best (and most expensive) extension tubes contain electrical contacts that retain automatic aperture control over the attached lens and automatic focus. This means that you can continue to use your camera's automatic TTL exposure control and focusing systems.

Many inexpensive extension tubes would restrict you to setting the aperture manually and would not allow for auto focusing. Therefore you will need to use a lens with an aperture ring that you can adjust manually, and shoot in Manual mode.

Extension bellows work in the same way as extension tubes, but their flexible design enables you to adjust them more precisely, and usually across a greater range. However, they are typically more expensive, bulkier, less robust, and much slower to use.

In either case, extension tubes and bellows are best used with a prime lens, rather than with a zoom.

NOTE

If you are planning to purchase a set of extension tubes, be aware of the cheap plastic tubes that you will find on eBay. These tubes are hardly usable for serious macro photography; it is much better to purchase quality tubes made from metal.

RIGHT: *Particularly when you start attaching focusing accessories like extension tubes, it can sometimes be easier to ignore autofocus altgether and simply move the camera closer to or farther from the subject, until what you want is in sharp focus.*

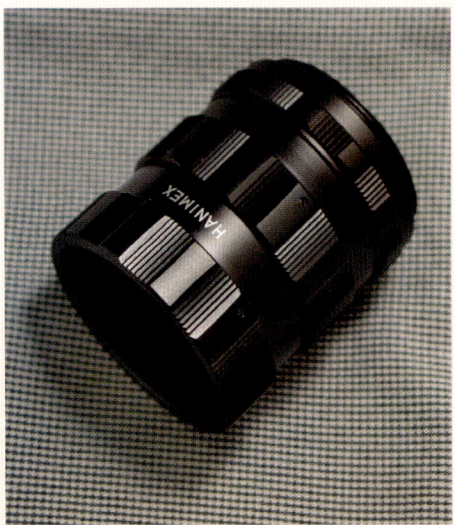

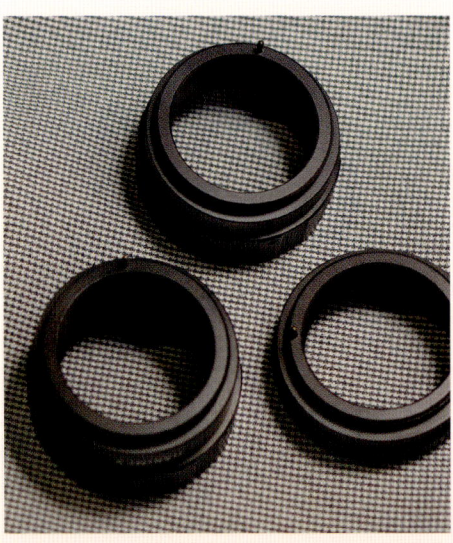

EXTENSION TUBES

These M42 mount extension tubes were originally meant for a Pentax 35mm film SLR, but with the relevant adaptor I can use them on a Canon (or other brand) DSLR instead.

All functions are manual using this arrangement, but it makes for a compact and light kit to carry. In use, the tubes can be stacked together or used separately to create a variety of magnifications. The combination of the lens and tube length will determine the magnification of a subject.

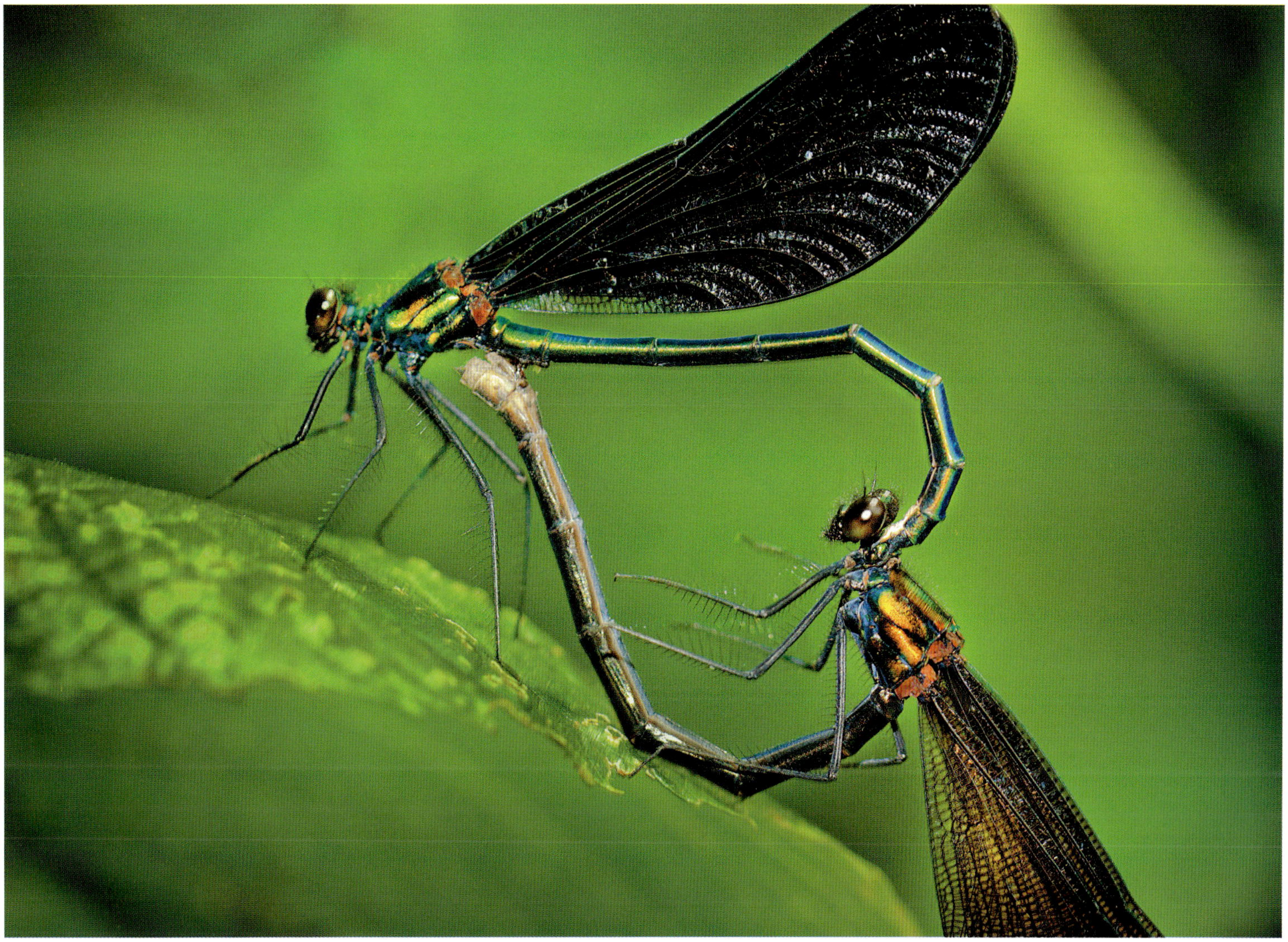

CLOSE-UP LENSES

Another inexpensive way to shoot close-up subjects is with a close-up lens. These look like filters (and fit to the filter thread of a regular lens) and work like reading glasses in that they allow the lens to focus at a closer distance than normal.

Close-up lenses come in various strengths, which are measured in "diopters." The higher the diopter figure, the greater the magnification of the lens, although you can also use multiple lenses to increase the magnification.

However, while close-up lenses have some use, they are considered the bottom tier of useful macro equipment. The image quality is not as good as a macro lens (especially if you fit them to a low-cost zoom lens), and it falls off considerably if you start stacking the lenses together.

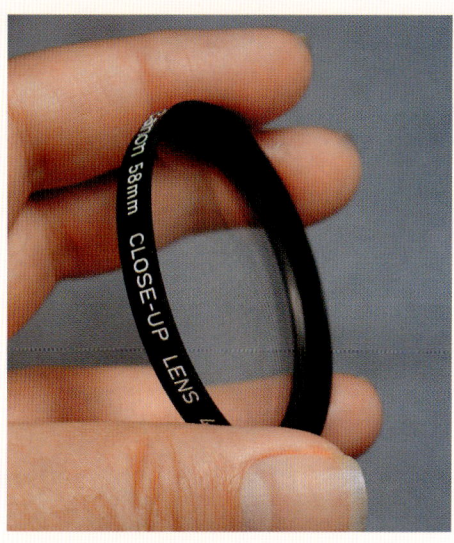

Lens Reversal

The least expensive way to shoot macro images is to buy an inexpensive adaptor that will allow you to mount a lens in reverse. The adaptor has a bayonet lens mount compatible with your camera on one side, and a male filter thread on the other side: you screw the adaptor into the filter thread on the front of the lens and then attach it to your camera. Depending on the lens used, the magnification can be better than 1:1.

The main problem with reverse-mounting conventional lenses is that you cannot focus at infinity as you might when using a real macro lens.

Lens reversal is much better if the lens you are using has the capability to stop down the aperture manually. Many newer zoom lenses (and some prime lenses) need the aperture to be set by the camera, so can only be used "wide open" when the lens is reversed. You could introduce paper, thin card, or other types of apertures into the light path (using the same principle as waterhouse stops), and this can be useful for controlling depth of field. However, these makeshift apertures can make it difficult to see through the viewfinder and therefore focus on the subject.

A simpler solution is to use an older, manual-focus lens with an aperture ring. There are countless options available through both camera dealers and Ebay, and a 50mm prime lens makes a good (affordable) start point. As the lens isn't being attached by the lens mount, you don't even need to get a lens that is designed for your camera—all you need is a reversing adaptor that matches its filter thread size.

Two-Lens Macro

A "macro coupler" is a ring that allows two lenses to be connected face to face. The adaptor has two male threads so that it can be screwed into the filter ring of each lens; one of the lenses is then attached to the camera.

The advantage of using two lenses (rather than a single reversed lens) is that you can create a magnification greater than 1:1 without the need for a macro lens.

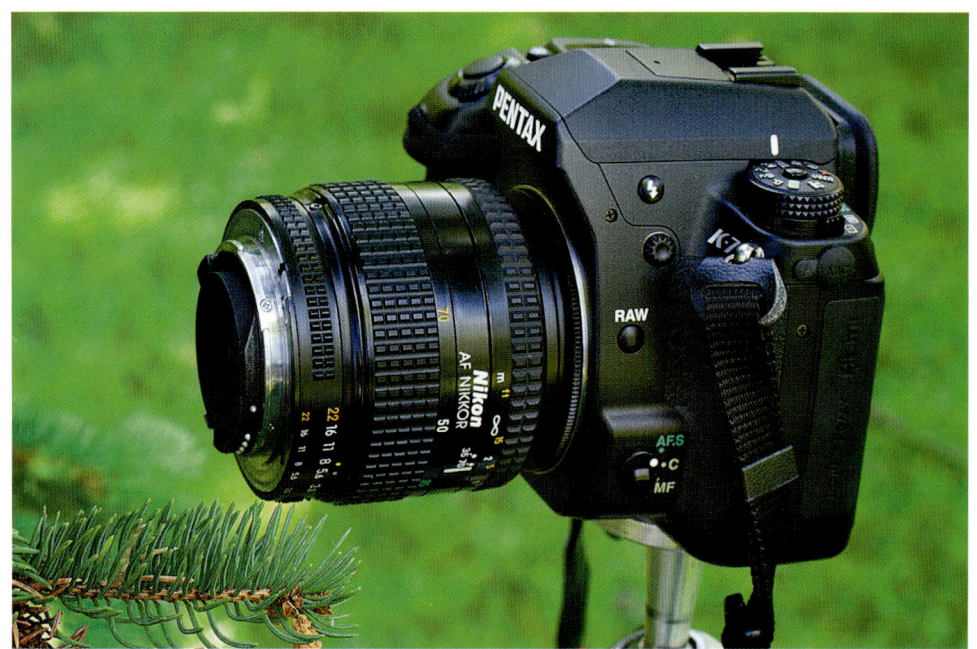

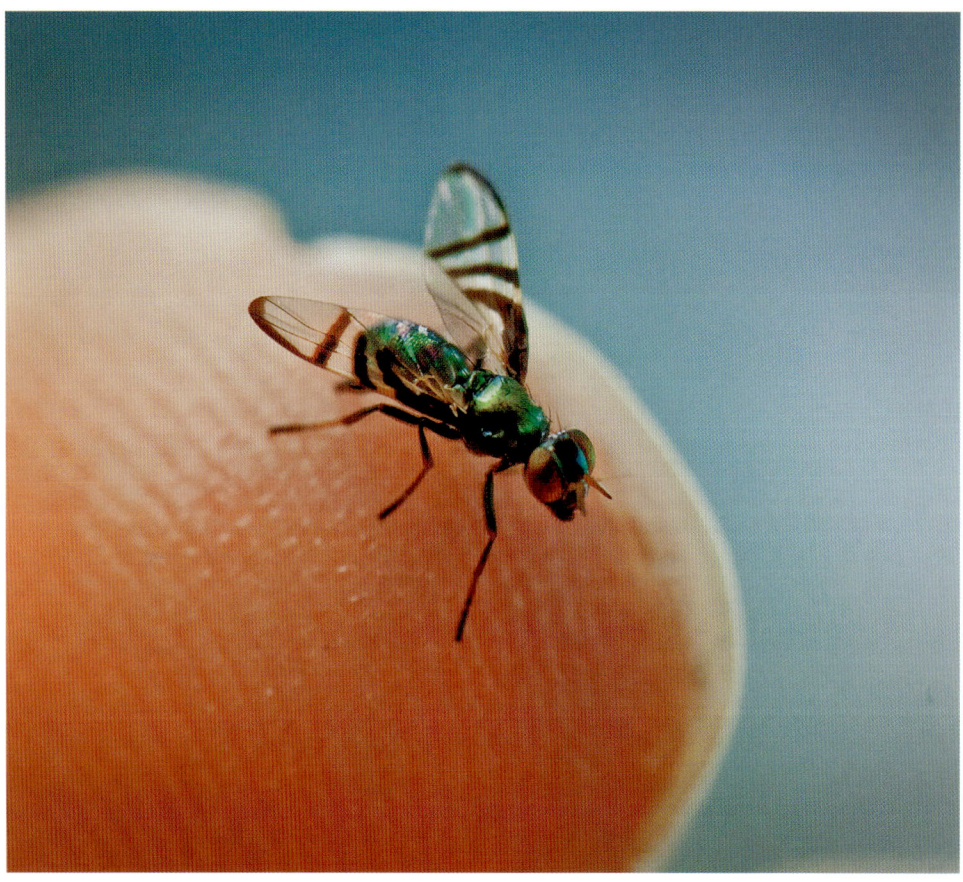

TOP: *This short Nikon zoom has been mounted in reverse on a Pentax K7 DSLR camera.*

ABOVE: *And that lens and camera combination was then used to capture this tiny fly!*

04 // GETTING UP CLOSE // CLOSE-UP

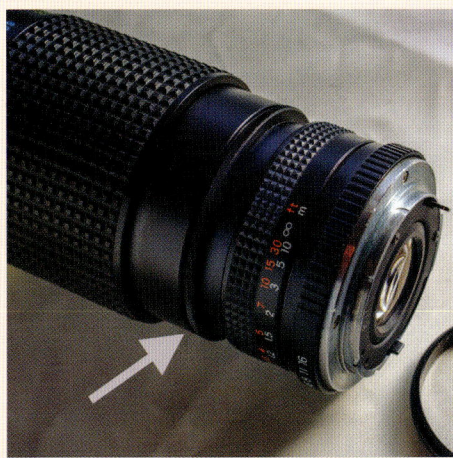

ABOVE: *Here, a 50mm prime lens is attached to a mid-range zoom lens using a macro coupler (indicated by the arrow). The zoom lens is attached to the camera and the prime lens is used to control the aperture.*

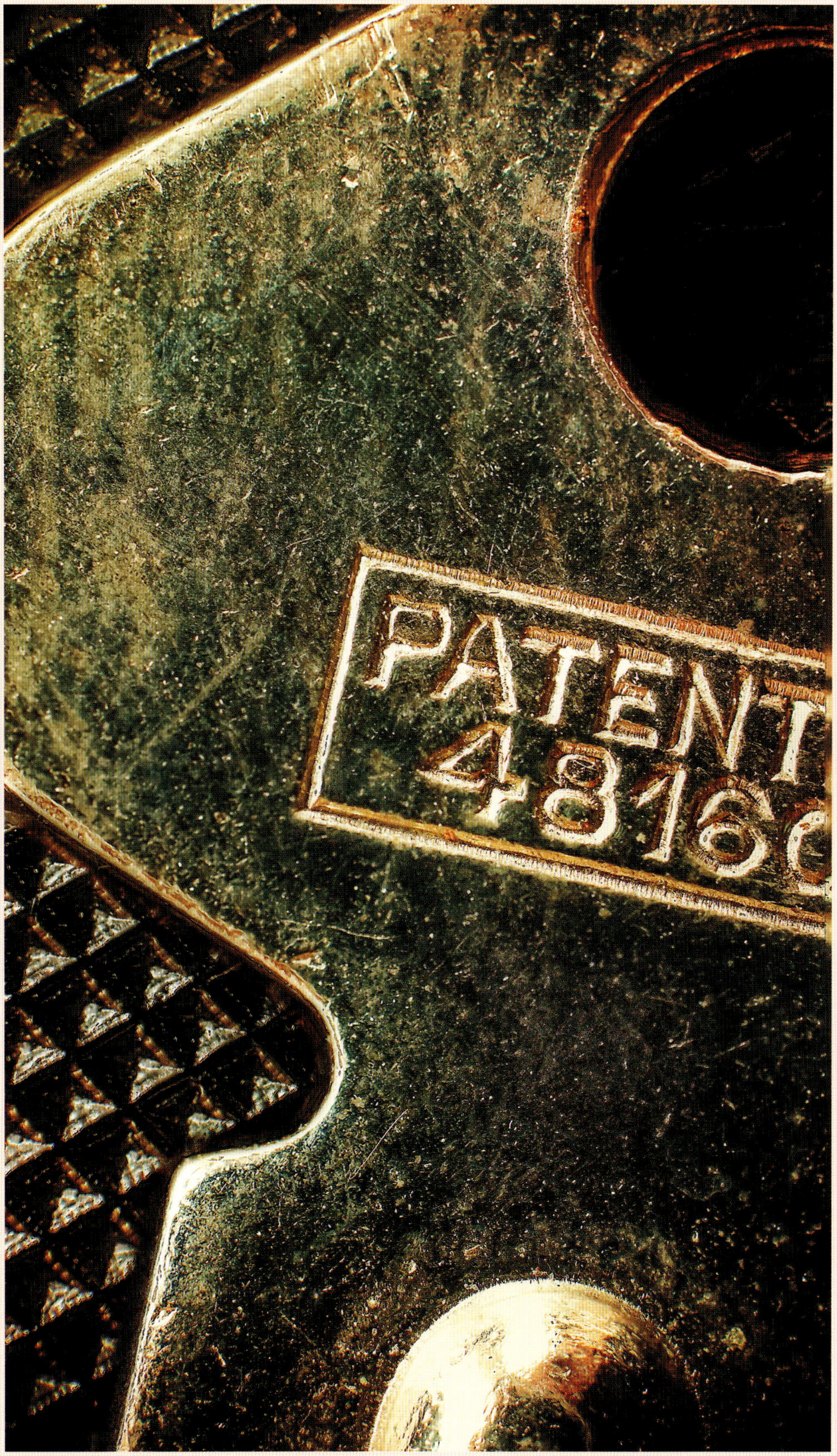

RIGHT: *This detail tiny on a key was shot using a setup similar to the one shown above. The actual key was approximately an inch in length. The image was captured using focus stacking and HDR.*

Focusing Rails

A focusing rail like the one shown is a great tool for macro photography, it will allow you to fine-focus through your subject. Many of these devices have micro adjustment scales marked on the rail that will allow you to return to a previous point of focus.

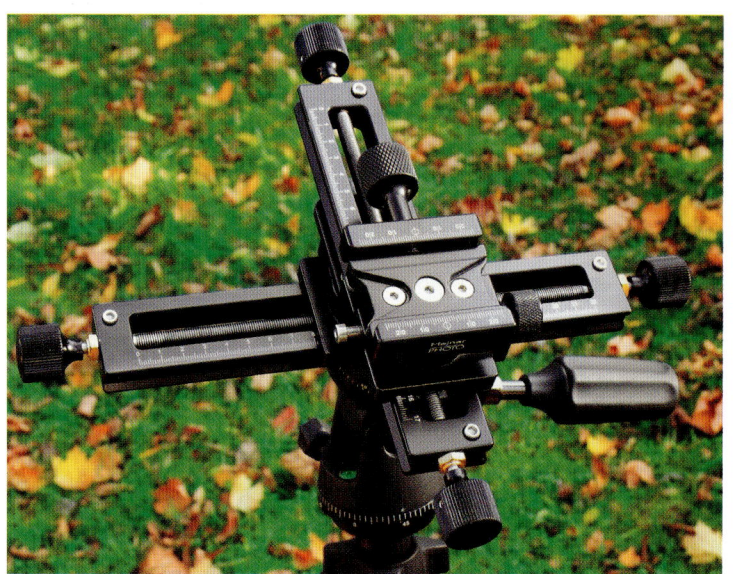

THIS PAGE: *This two-way macro rail made by Hejnar Photo can be adjusted horizontally, as well as forward and backward, without the need to move the tripod. The screws are calibrated to move at the rate of 1mm per full rotation, which gives extremely fine movements. This is ideal for many macro imaging applications, including focus stacking, which we will explore in Chapter 5.*

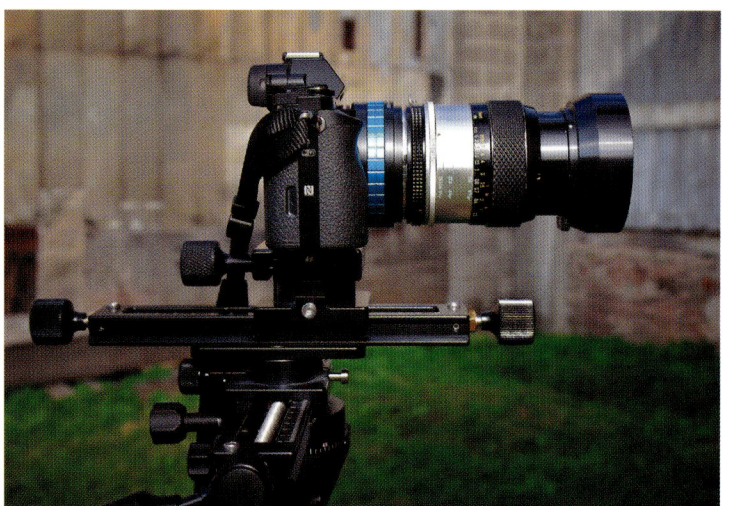

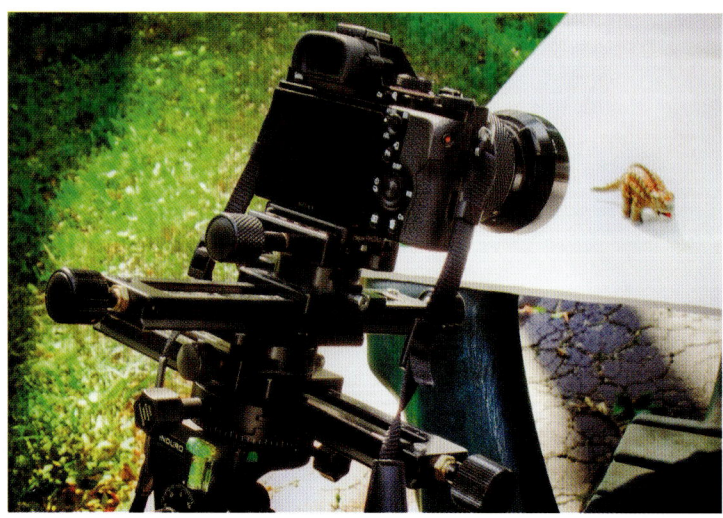

04 // GETTING UP CLOSE // CLOSE-UP

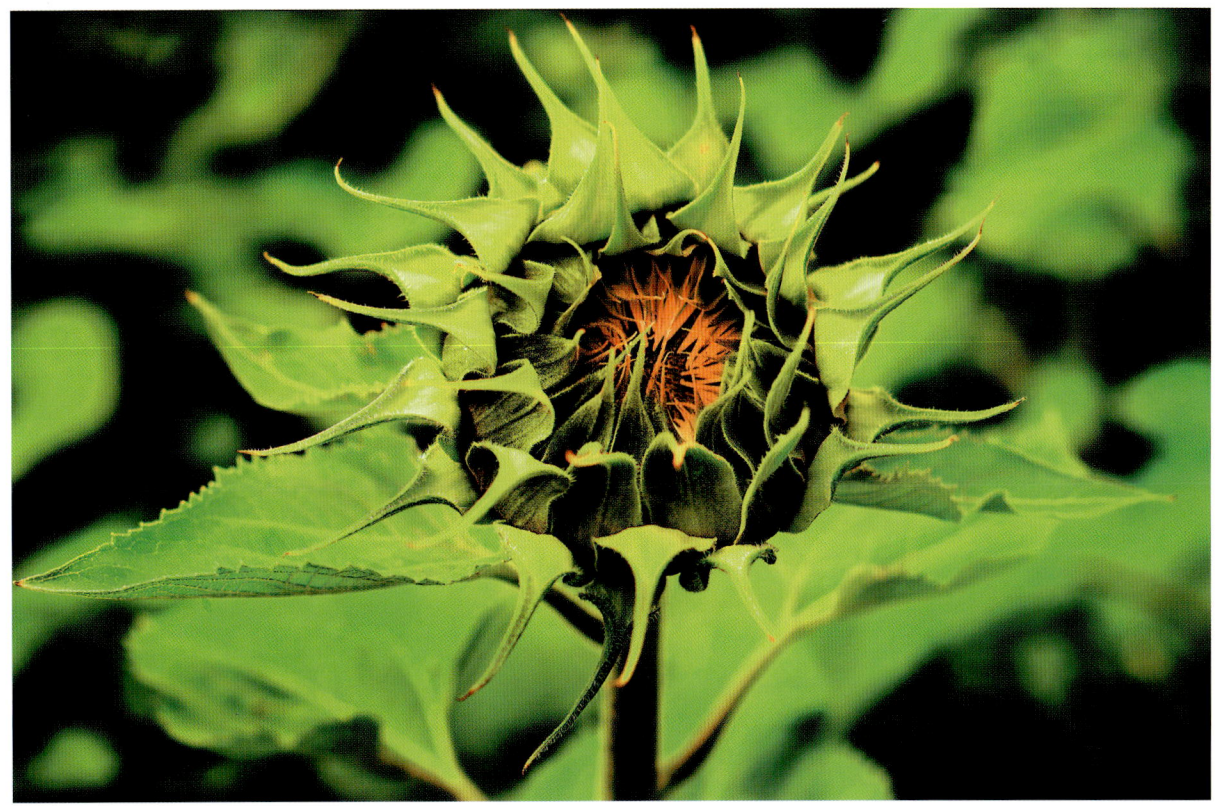

LEFT: *Very small subjects benefit from using focusing rails, because the depth of field can be vanishingly thin, and focus needs to be placed with as much precision as possible.*

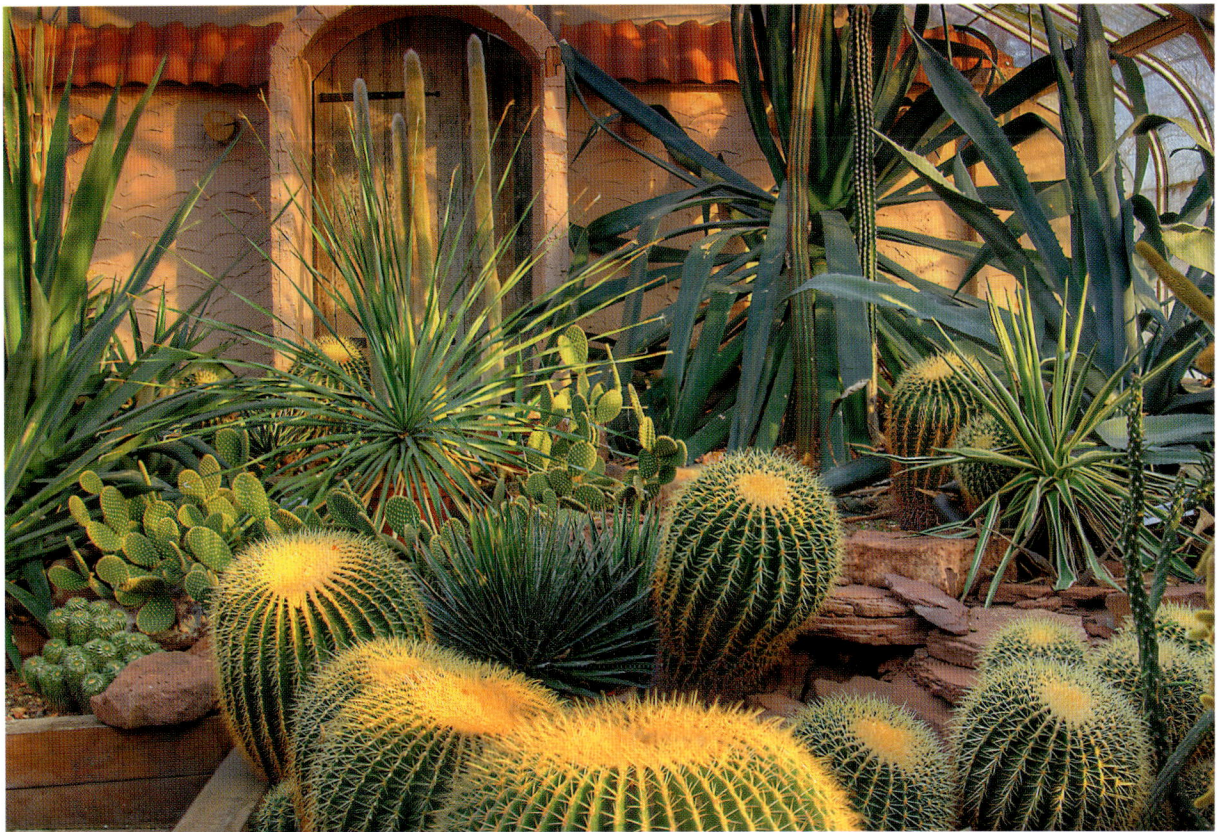

LEFT: *This light was fading fast, requiring a somewhat wide aperture, so the only way to get it sharp from foreground to background was to take multiple images using focusing rails, and stack them together.*

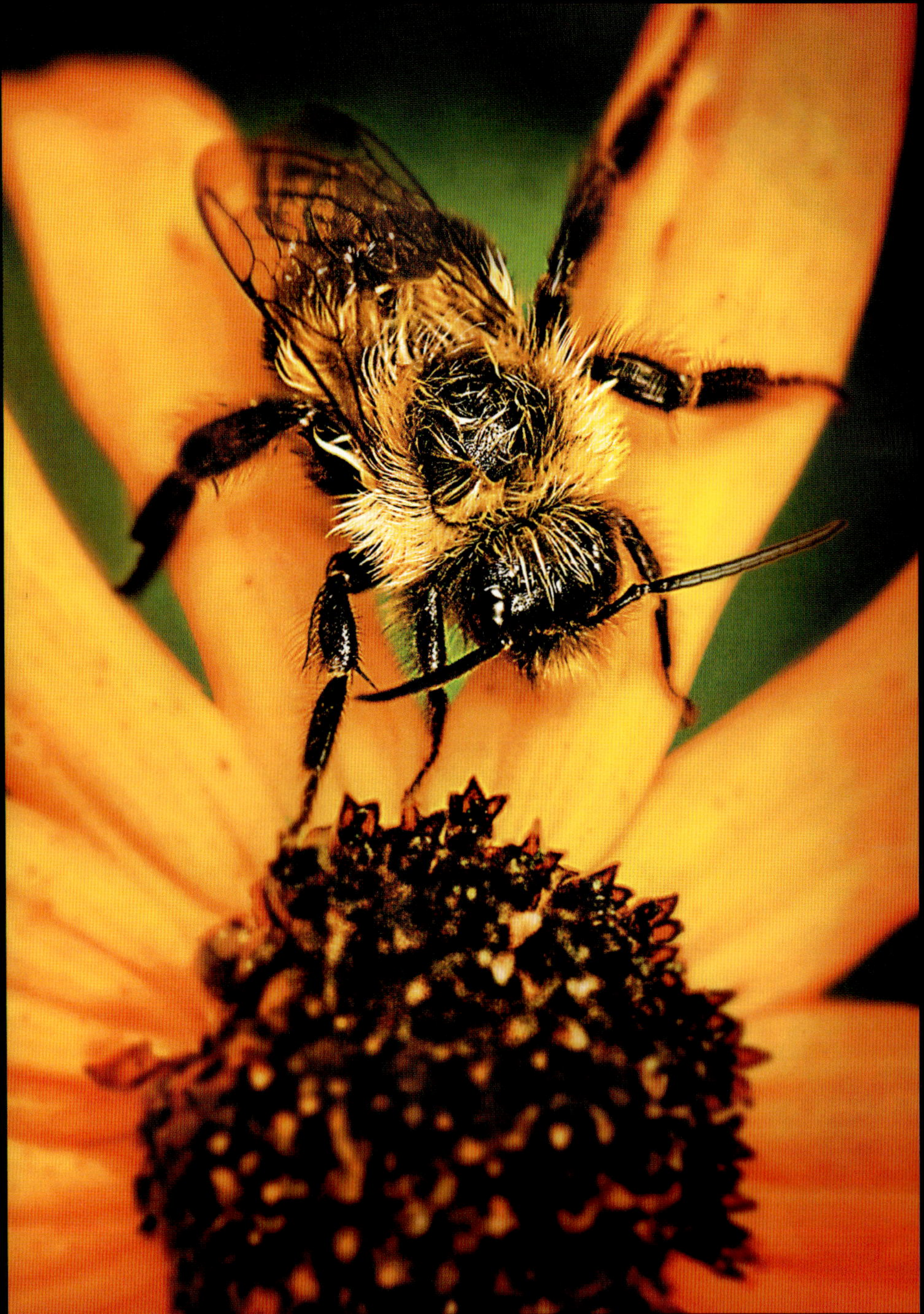

Gallery | Close-Up

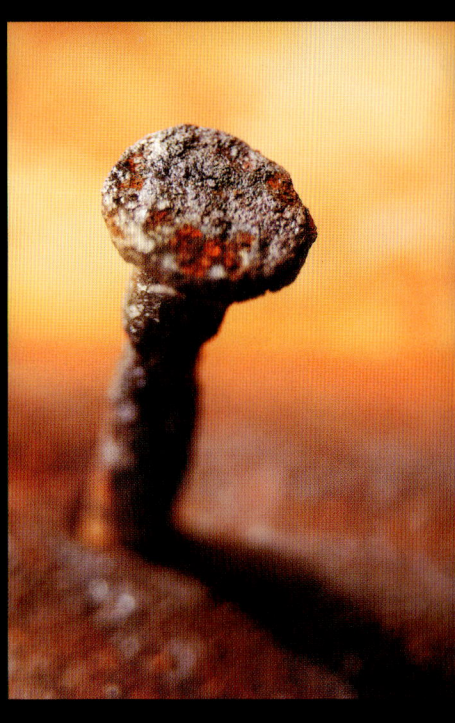

ABOVE: *You don't necessarily need expensive or specialist equipment to take great close-up shots. This nail head was photographed with a simple lens taken from a single-use camera, which I mounted to a DSLR. The nature of the lens means that it can be used only for close-up work.*

RIGHT: *Using a shallow depth of field has helped to create a simple backdrop for these berries.*

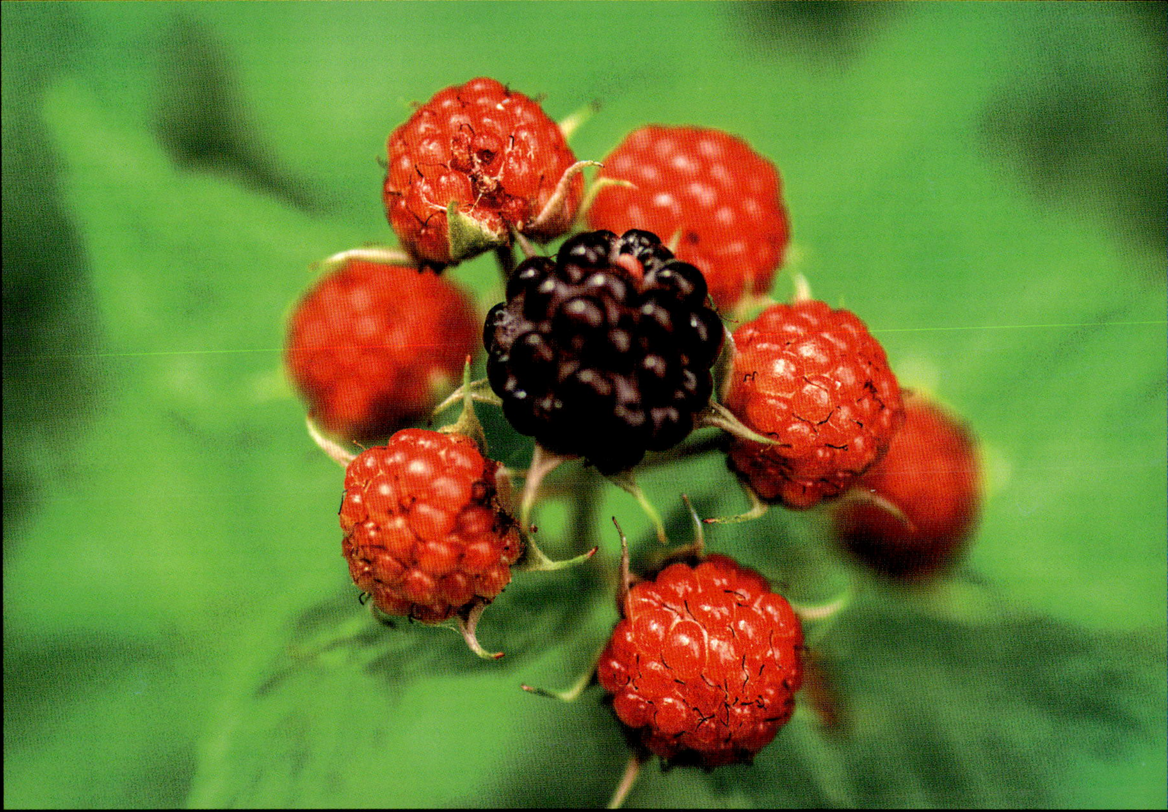

RIGHT: *Subjects such as this beetle can be difficult to see against a sharply focused background. The softness of focus helps to separate the main subject while creating a normal- looking close-up view of a small subject. It matches what we might see in the real world.*

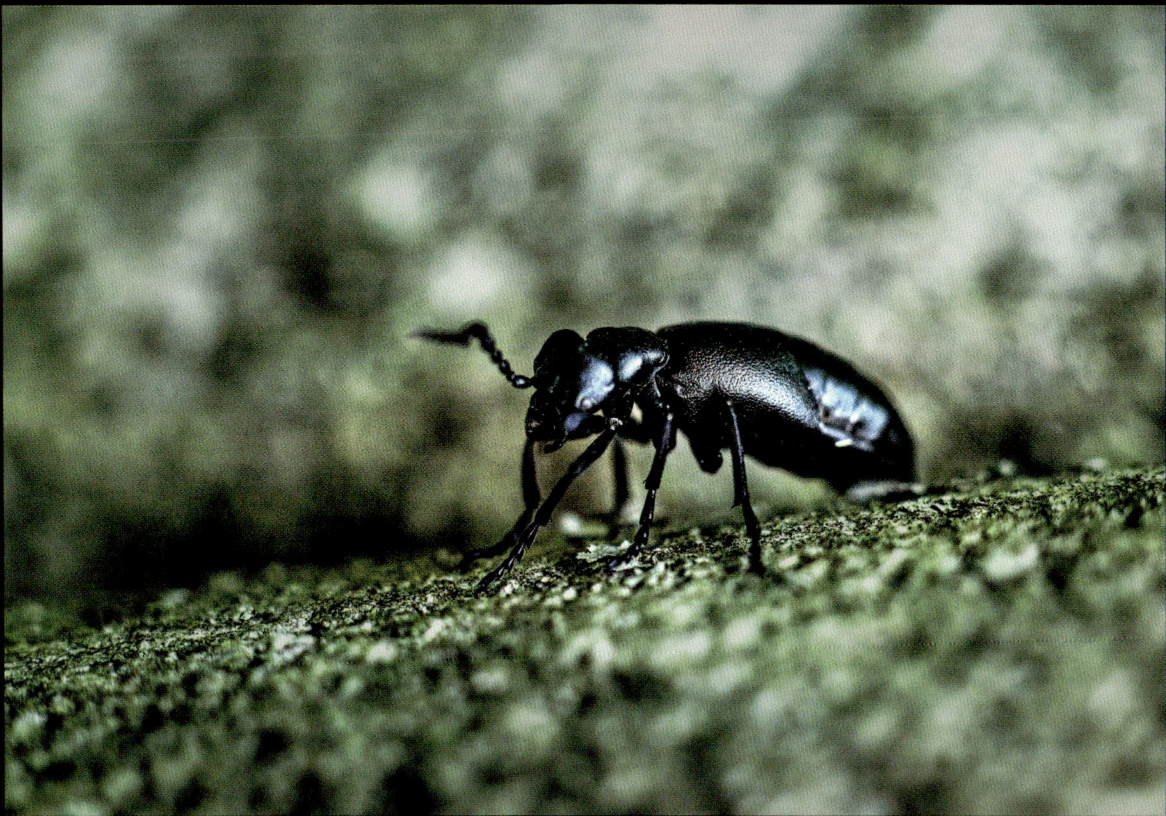

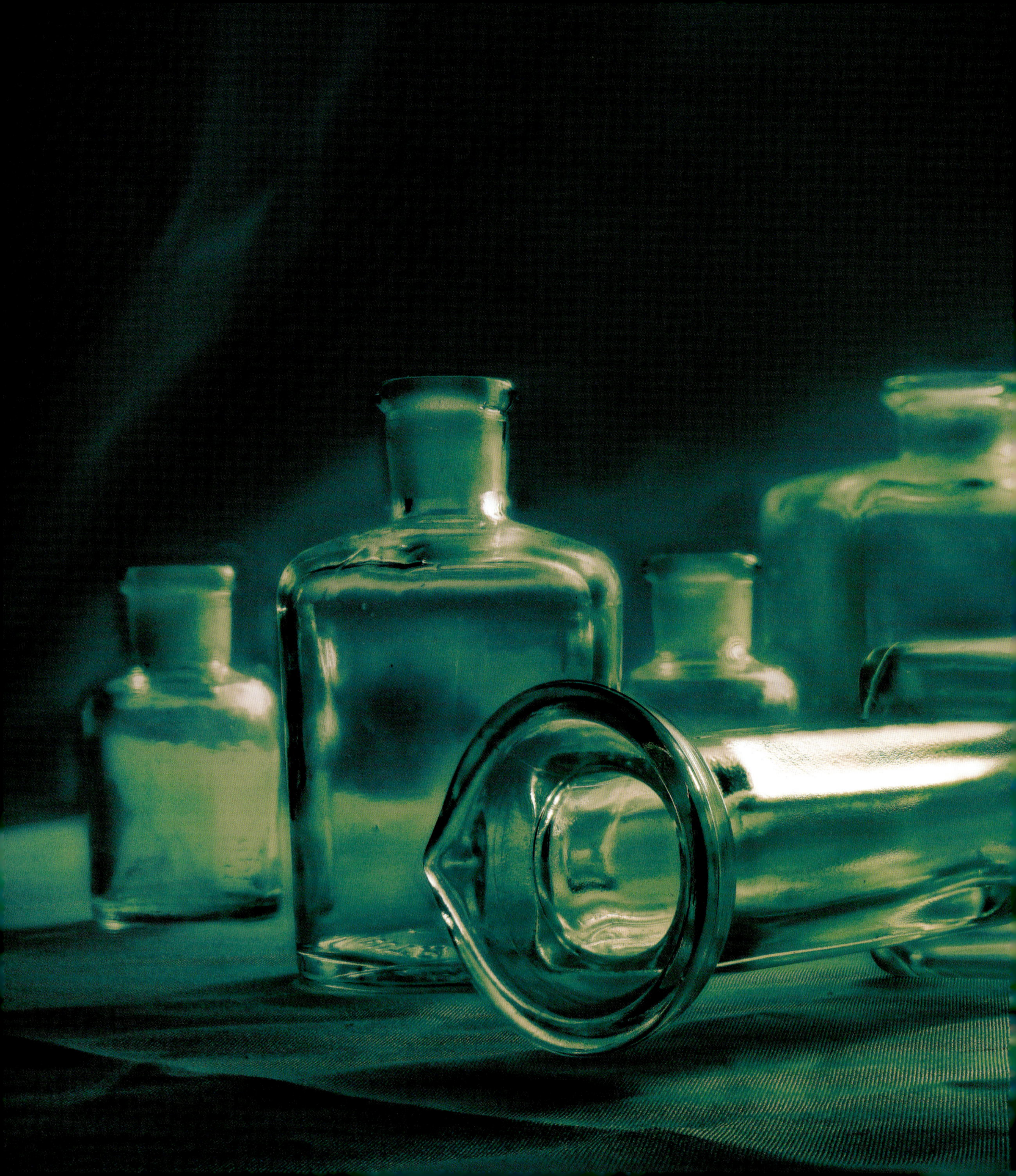

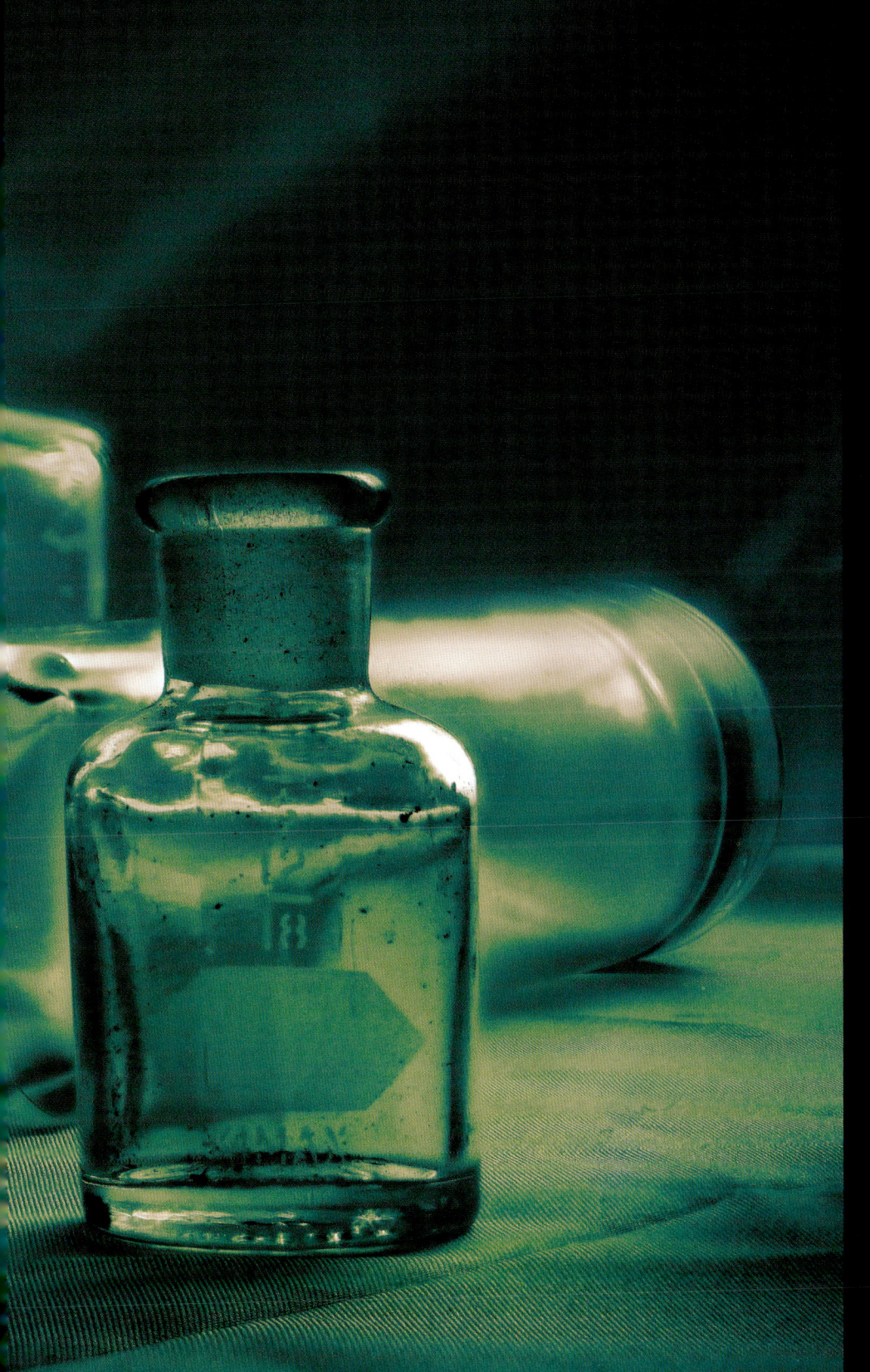

05 // FOCUS STACKING

Focus Stacking Explained

Can you imagine infinite depth of field using a maximum aperture? How about macro photographs that show amazing detail throughout the subject? Well, that's what focus stacking offers.

As we have seen previously, there is only a single plane of focus in a photograph. Every point that is not on the plane of focus is in "relative" focus, with depth of field determining what does and does not appear "sharp." However, focus stacking can turn this on its head.

At its most basic level, focus stacking combines a number of exposures of the same subject. With each exposure, the focus is shifted slightly, to create a newly focused slice of the subject. This means you end up with a sequence of similar images, each with slightly different focus. These images are "stacked" using software on your computer to combine the in-focus areas of each and produce a single composite photograph with dramatically extended depth of field.

In macro imaging, the depth of field is extremely shallow, even at small apertures. For this reason, focus stacking is generally thought of as a macro-imaging technique. However, insects, flowers, and fruit are not the only things that can be focus-stacked—almost anything can be treated in this manner to achieve incredible depth of field, using what I like to think of as a "super depth-of-field" technique.

Focus stacking can also be used to overcome technical challenges. Normally, anytime you want to achieve sharpness from the foreground to the background, you would select a small aperture to achieve the results. This also means using a slow shutter speed and/or high ISO setting, which in some cases could be problematic. However, focus stacking allows you to produce a greater depth of field while using wider apertures. This could be useful under low light conditions, for example, enabling you to use a slower ISO setting or faster shutter speed.

Focus stacking also offers unparalleled control over depth of field. As the software combines only the focused areas of the stacked images, you can choose what appears sharp by choosing where to start your in-focus sequence and where to end it. In this way, you can capture the exact depth of field that you want or need, regardless of the camera-to-subject distance, focal length, or aperture setting.

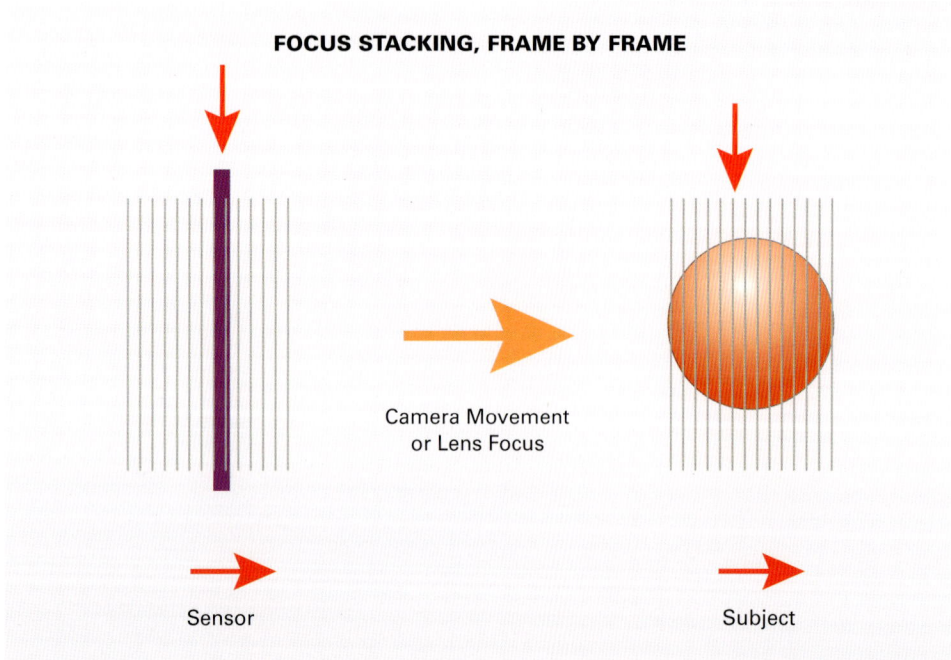

LEFT: *Focus stacking relies on the point of focus being shifted across a sequence of images, so you end up with a range of shots all focused at slightly different points. The focus shift can be created either by manually adjusting the focus of the lens or by moving the camera along a focus rail. Using a focus rail is best for close-up subjects.*

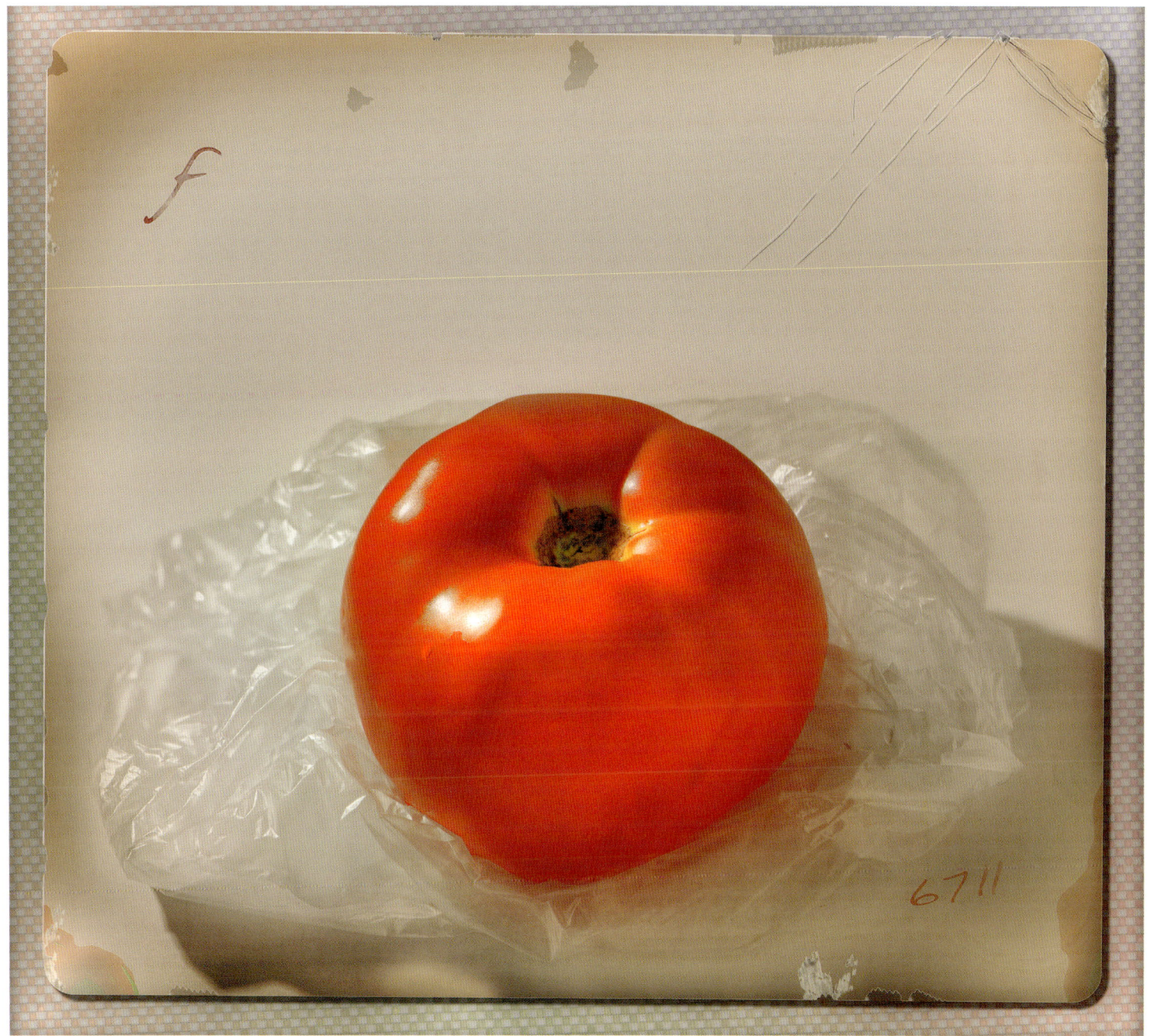

Image-Stacking Software

While focus stacking can be accomplished in Photoshop and other general image-editing programs, I find that there are better, dedicated programs to do this work.

Zerene Stacker and Helicon Focus are a couple of programs that I have used to create excellent focusing results. Both can process the sequence and blend it into a single image with an extended range of focus. When done correctly, the results can be truly amazing.

ABOVE: *This tomato was shot in four sections, which were focus-stacked and combined to produce a highly detailed image that can be printed at 40 x 40 inches (100 x 100cm).*

Focus Stacking in Practice

As with any multi-shot technique, focus stacking requires a precise and methodical approach, with particular attention needed when it comes to setting the focus.

The key to successful focus stacking is to be fairly precise as to where to place the focus for each shot in your sequence. You need to focus manually in small overlapping increments, or adjust the camera perpendicular to the subject, and this makes a tripod essential. For close-up photography, a focusing rail (as shown on page 112) is also useful, and you generally need to move the camera roughly the same distance as your intended focus distance. For example, if you want the focus to cover a distance of 100mm from the front to the back focus point, you would move the camera about that distance.

However, when shooting a landscape a focusing rail just doesn't have enough physical length to move the focus to a new point in the scene. In this instance, I will use several different methods, depending on the scene I am photographing.

My first method is to move the camera along a slider (this is normally used in video to capture a smooth camera movement). At one end of the rail, I will make an exposure focused on a close subject, and then I will gradually move the camera forward along the slide rail in order to produce at least three or four shots focused at different distances away from the camera. The number of shots is determined by the focal length of the lens and by the amount of depth of field. Toward the end of the rail's travel, I may also use some focus adjustment in order to "reach out" farther into the scene. Wide-angle lenses need less overall movement than a short telephoto because of their already reduced apertures.

In the second method, I use a similar technique of simply changing the focus of the lens manually in order to focus on the details that I want to include as sharp. In a landscape, the focus points might be a nearby subject, a middle subject, and infinity. By using a small aperture, the DOF will be extended throughout the total of the focus points used.

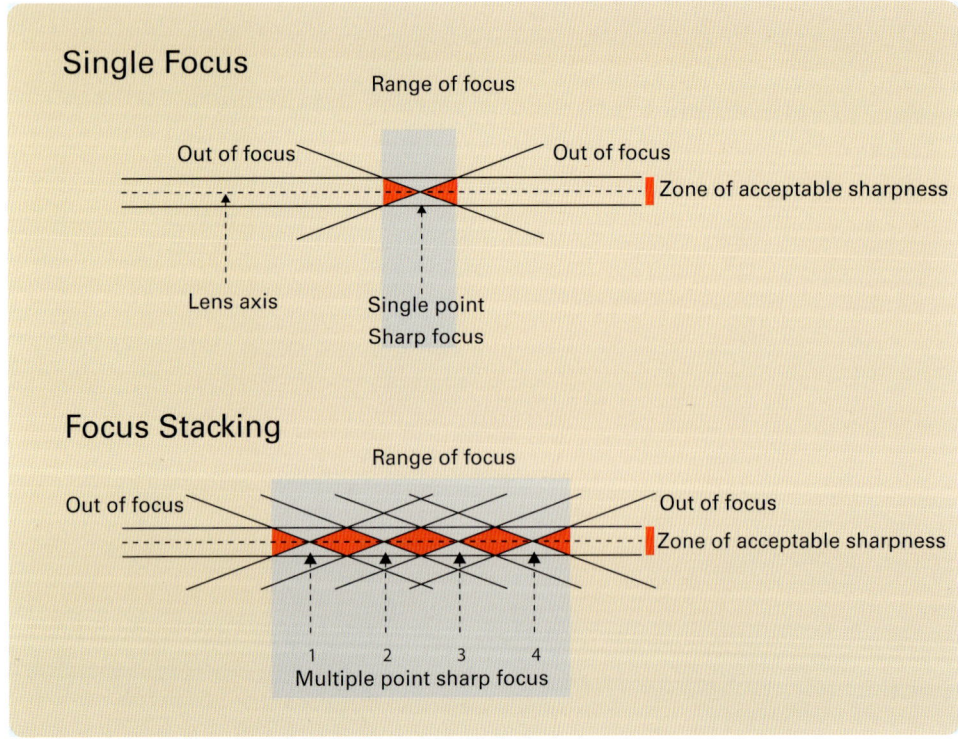

LEFT: *When working outdoors, the focus points can be spread further apart as the distance increases. The simple rule is that the further the focus point is from the camera, the greater the distance covered by the depth of field.*

05 // FOCUS STACKING IN PRACTICE // FOCUS STACKING

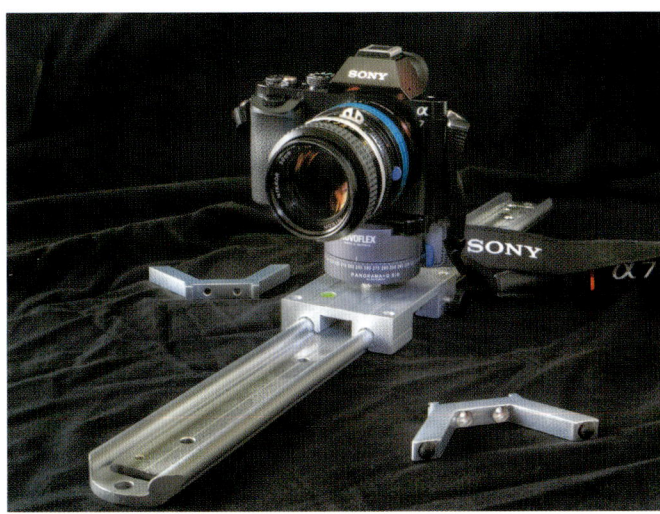

ABOVE: *A slider like this is normally used as a means of creating smooth motion in video production, but it can also be useful for doing focus stacking in the field. The slider can be used mounted to a tripod, or on a surface by attaching the V-shaped leg supports shown.*

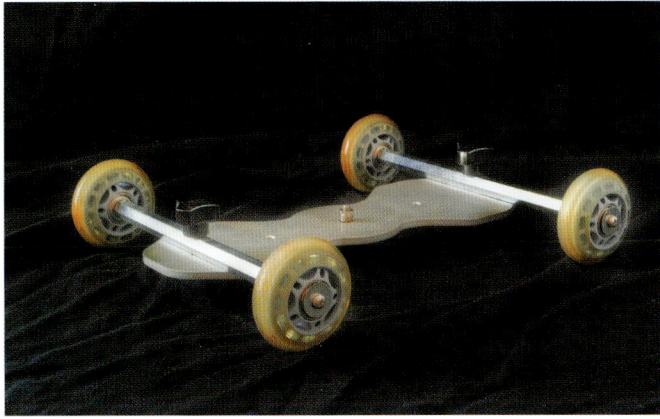

ABOVE: *As an alternative to a slider, you can also use a wheeled camera mount. For focus stacking, the wheels need to be set in a straight line and the camera needs to be mounted at the center of the platform on a tripod head that is tall enough so the wheels don't appear in shot.*

RIGHT: *Approximately 20 different focus points were needed to capture all the details shown here. As a rule, the closer the subject is to the camera, the shallower the depth of field will be, so you will need a greater number of focus points to extend the overall zone of sharpness in your stacked composite.*

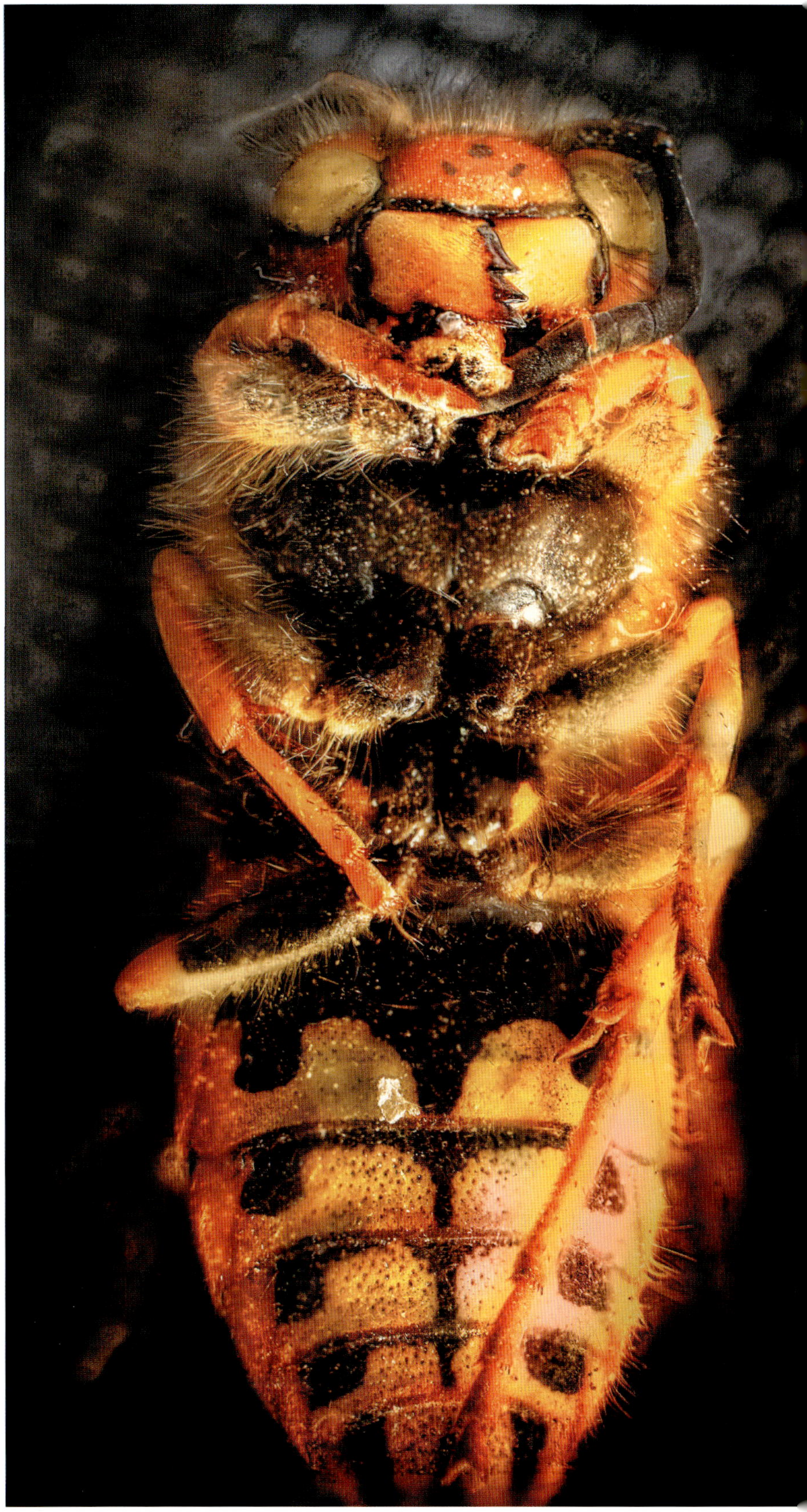

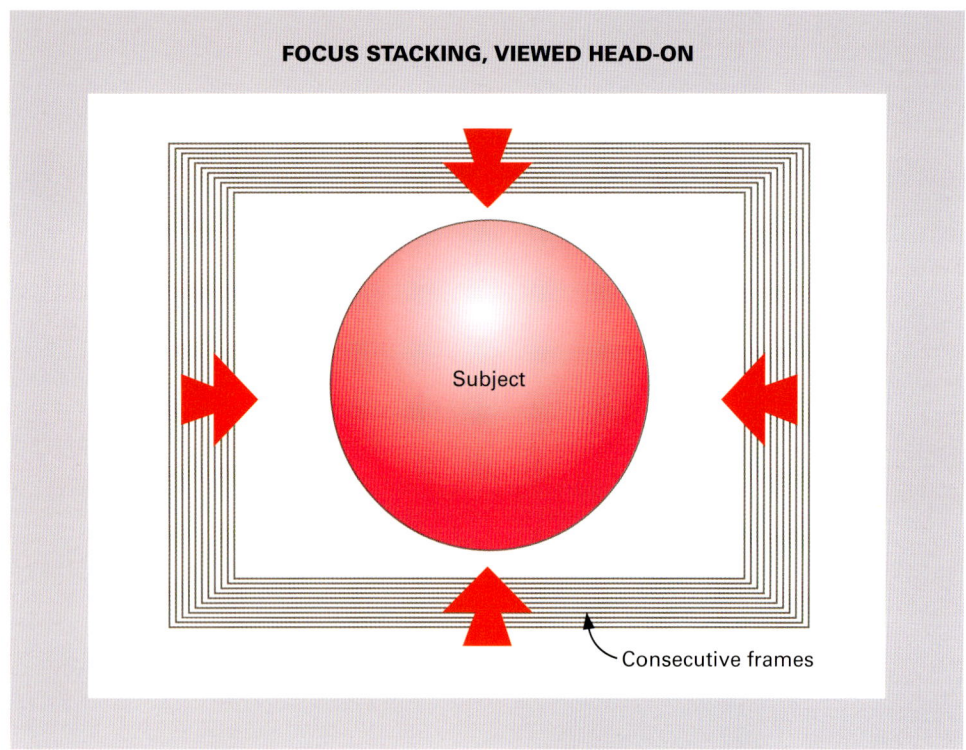

FOCUS STACKING, VIEWED HEAD-ON

Subject — Consecutive frames

LEFT: *Moving the camera toward the subject produces an enlargement of the subject with each progression. Therefore it is important to allow extra space around your subject before starting the stacking process. This diagram shows the effect of changing the distance on the sensor. In my own work, I often start the shooting session with the focus set at the farthest distance and move the camera away from the object with each new focus point. This way, I avoid the problem of magnification.*

OPPOSITE (FULL PAGE): *Focus stacking is the opposite of shallow depth of field miniaturization (see page 92), in that it makes things seem much larger than they actually are. Our brain interprets increased sharpness as signifying an object that is as large or larger than we are—it is one of the ways that we determine scale. This bird's skull measured just 1½ inches (3.8cm) across, but in a focus-stacked photograph we perceive it as being much larger. Here, the image received further treatment in Photoshop to create the aged appearance.*

Obviously, when doing stacking, there is a blooming effect that happens due to the changes in camera position or focus points. By blooming, I mean a reduction in the size of the final image, as the software blends the layers together. Each successive frame will be added in such a way as to crop a portion at the edge. It is important to consider this before starting the process, and allow a bit of room around your subject when setting up the shot; the framing can be tightened by cropping during post-production. Alternatively, you may find it helpful to shoot the sequence of images in reverse, so starting with the focus at the back and working forward. Doing so will allow the image to grow proportionately, rather than to shrink, so each shot effectively becomes slightly wider. This avoids the problem of the image frame becoming too tight. As well as taking care with the focus, you need to make sure that the exposure and color do not change between shots. Set your camera to Manual mode—so the aperture, shutter speed, and ISO are consistent throughout—and a custom white balance.

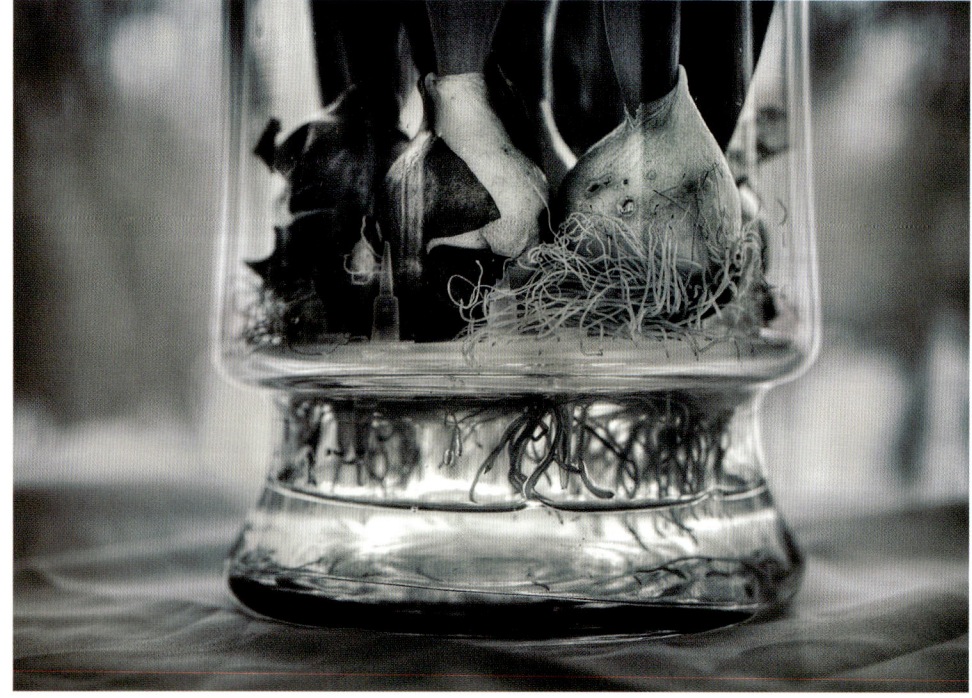

ABOVE: *At times, only a few images are needed to obtain the desired outcome. Here, the focus points were kept to a minimum, in order to show the roots and the two bulbs at the front as sharp. While this can be accomplished by simply using a wide aperture, the use of focus stacking allows for more precise placement of the focus.*

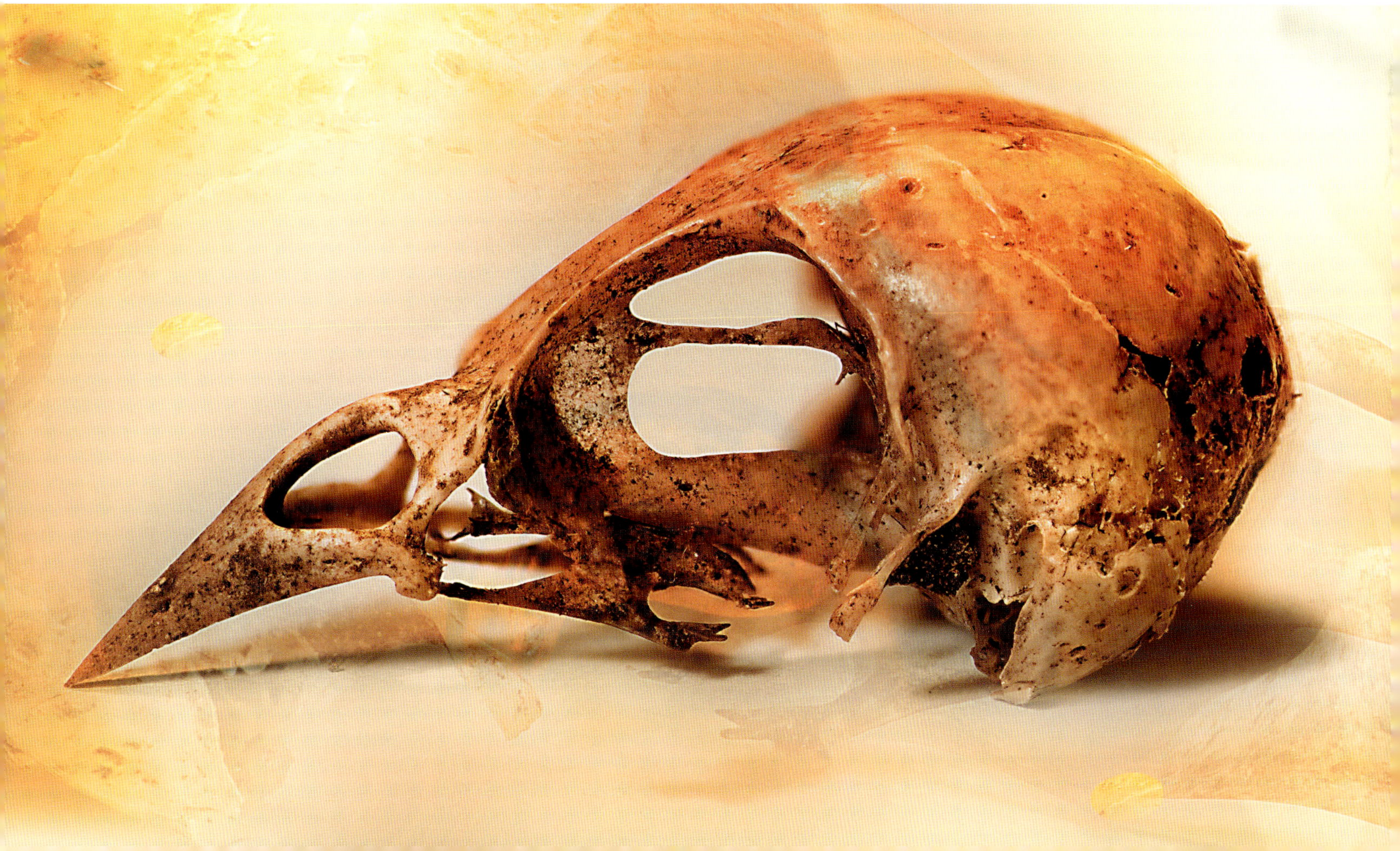

05 // FOCUS STACKING IN PRACTICE // FOCUS STACKING

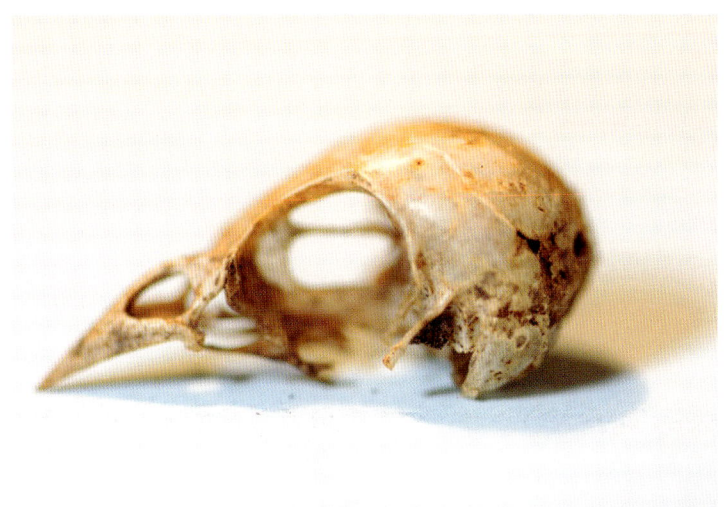
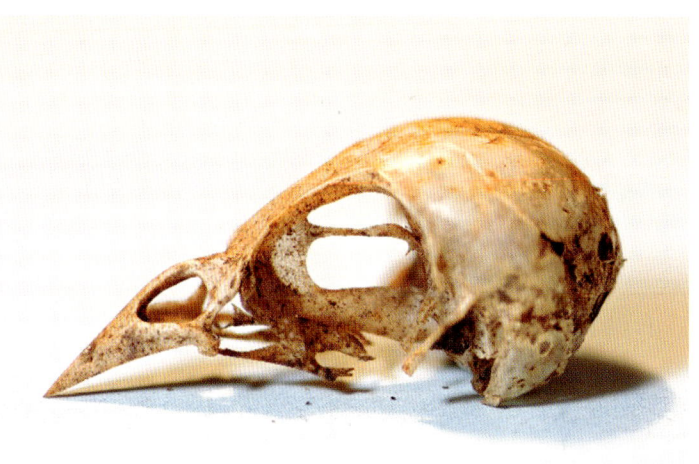

Focus-stacking Walk-throughs

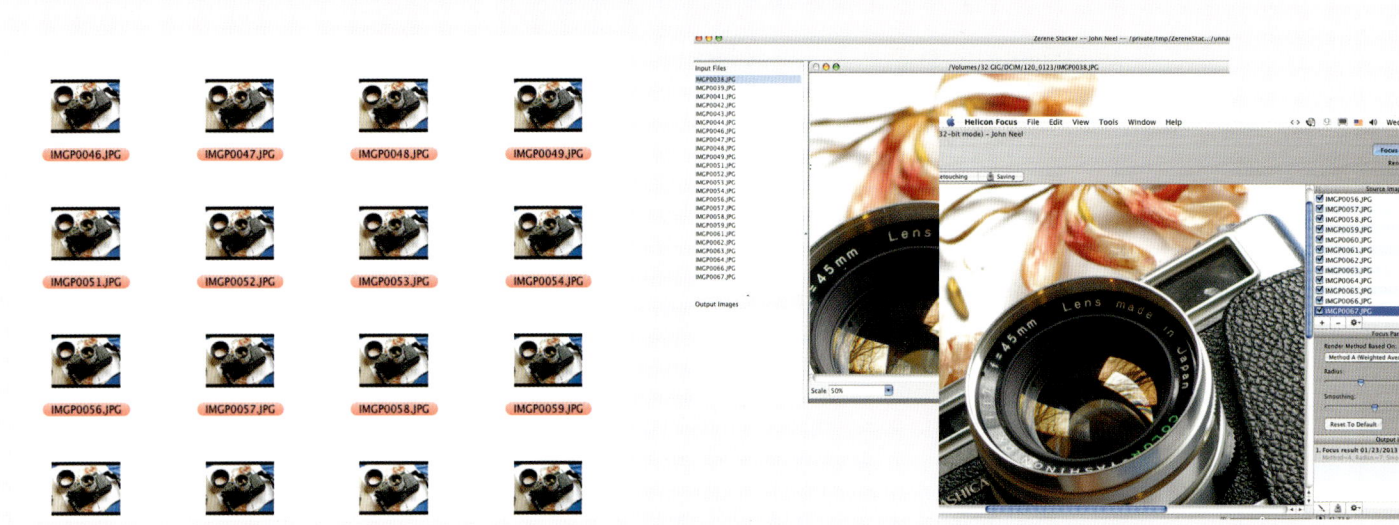

ABOVE: *Over 30 shots were taken at different focus points to achieve this amazingly sharp image of an old Yashica film camera. The use of focus stacking actually enhances the sharpness due to the overlapping of the aperture cones.*

ABOVE: *Although ZereneStacker and Helicon Focus do similar stacking operations, they offer slightly different algorithms and user interfaces.*

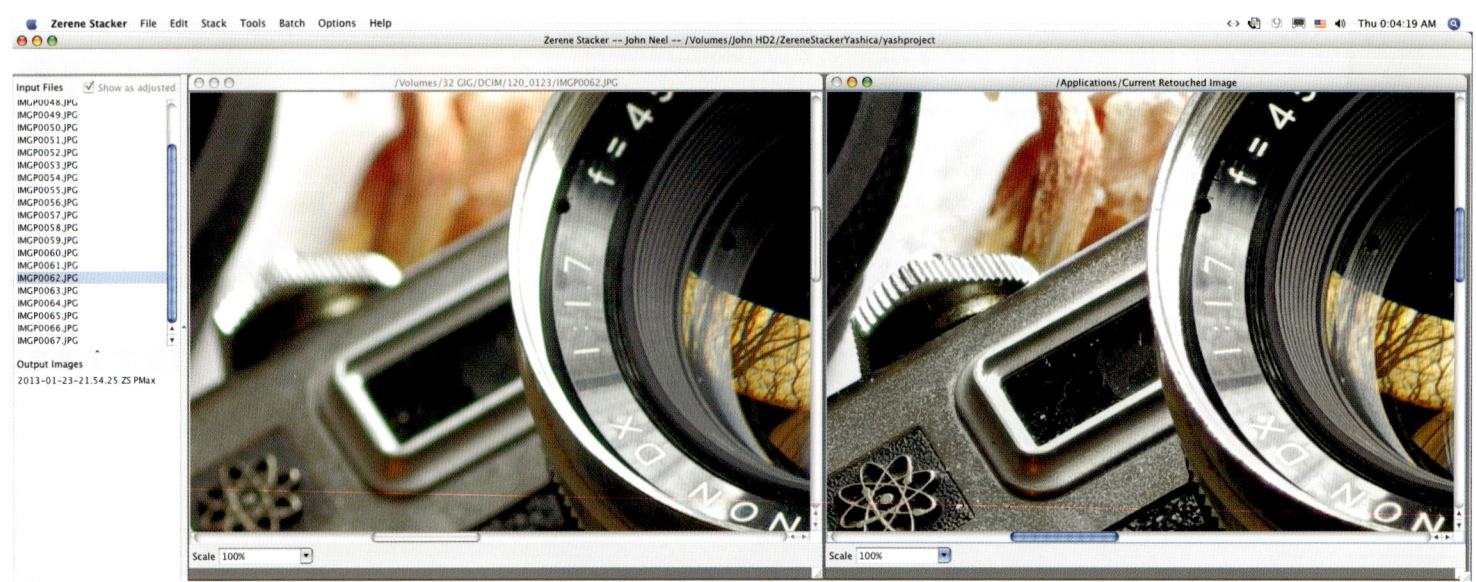

ABOVE: *This is Zerene Stacker showing "before" and "after" previews. The image on the left shows a single image from the stack, while the image at the right shows the result as it is being processed. The list of images used is at the far left. Notice the dramatic difference in focus between the two preview images.*

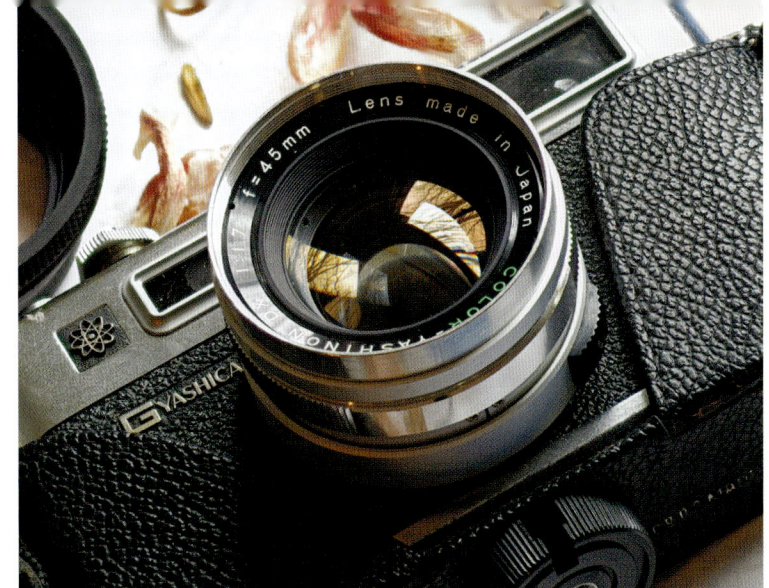

LEFT: *This is a detail of the image before finishing in Photoshop, showing the range of overall sharpness produced through focus stacking.*

BELOW: *The final focus-stacked image before finishing in Photoshop.*

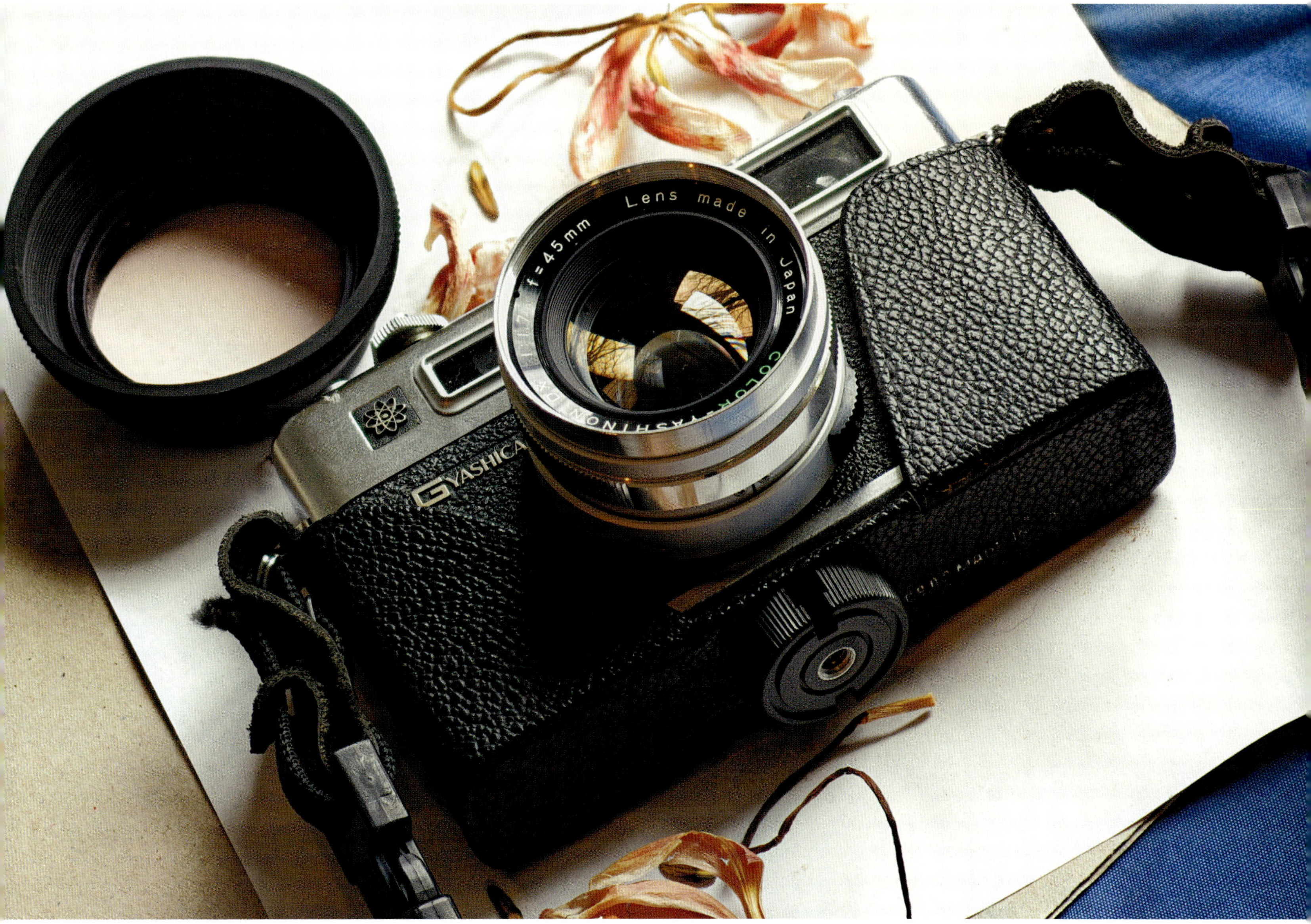

RIGHT: *I decided to shoot the peach image shown opposite in four sections, in order to produce a large-scale final print. These four peach sections could then be stitched together to create my final, large-scale image.*

BELOW: *Each section of the peach was shot using the same set of multiple focus points—in this case, a series of 12 exposures was made for each section. Each section was stacked and processed separately prior to stitching. After I had combined the four stacked image sections, I produced a tone-mapped image using Photomatix Pro.*

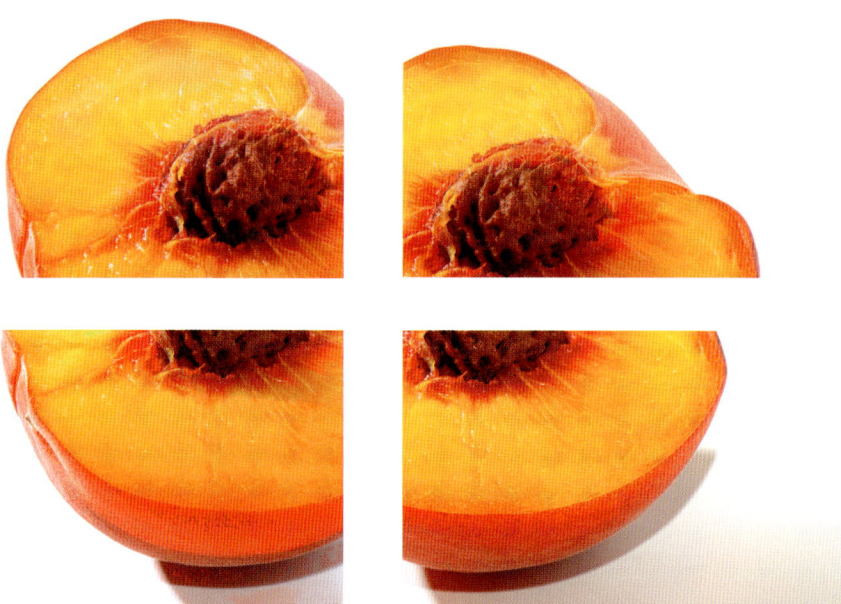

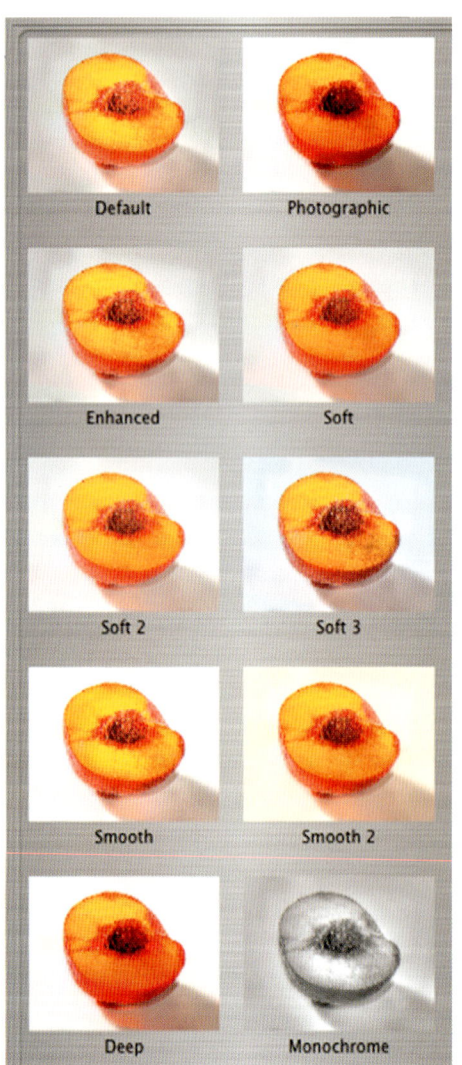

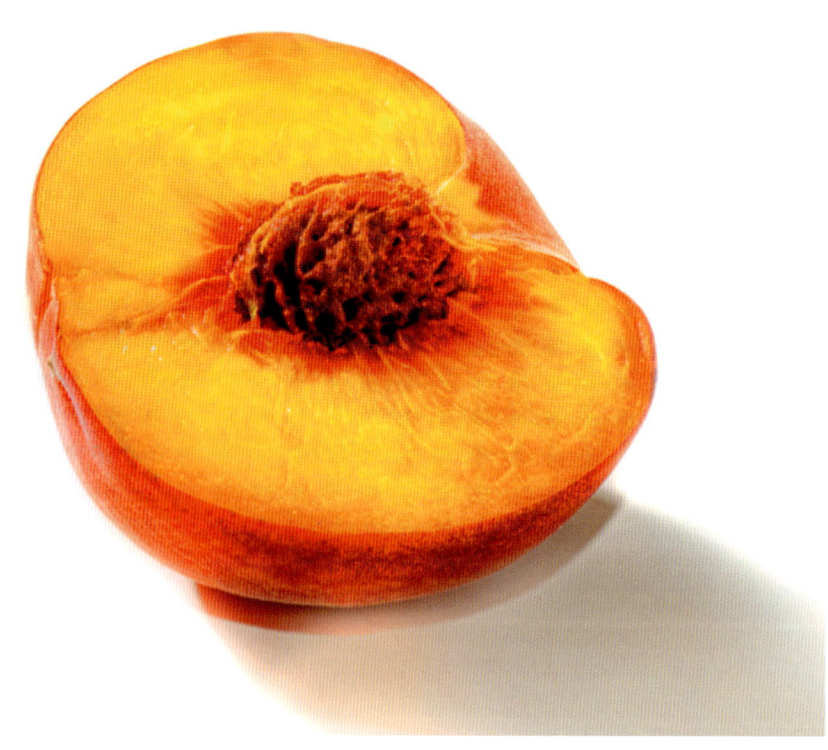

ABOVE: *This is the result of the stacking, stitching, and tone-mapping processes, prior to the image being taken into Photoshop for final retouching and color enhancements.*

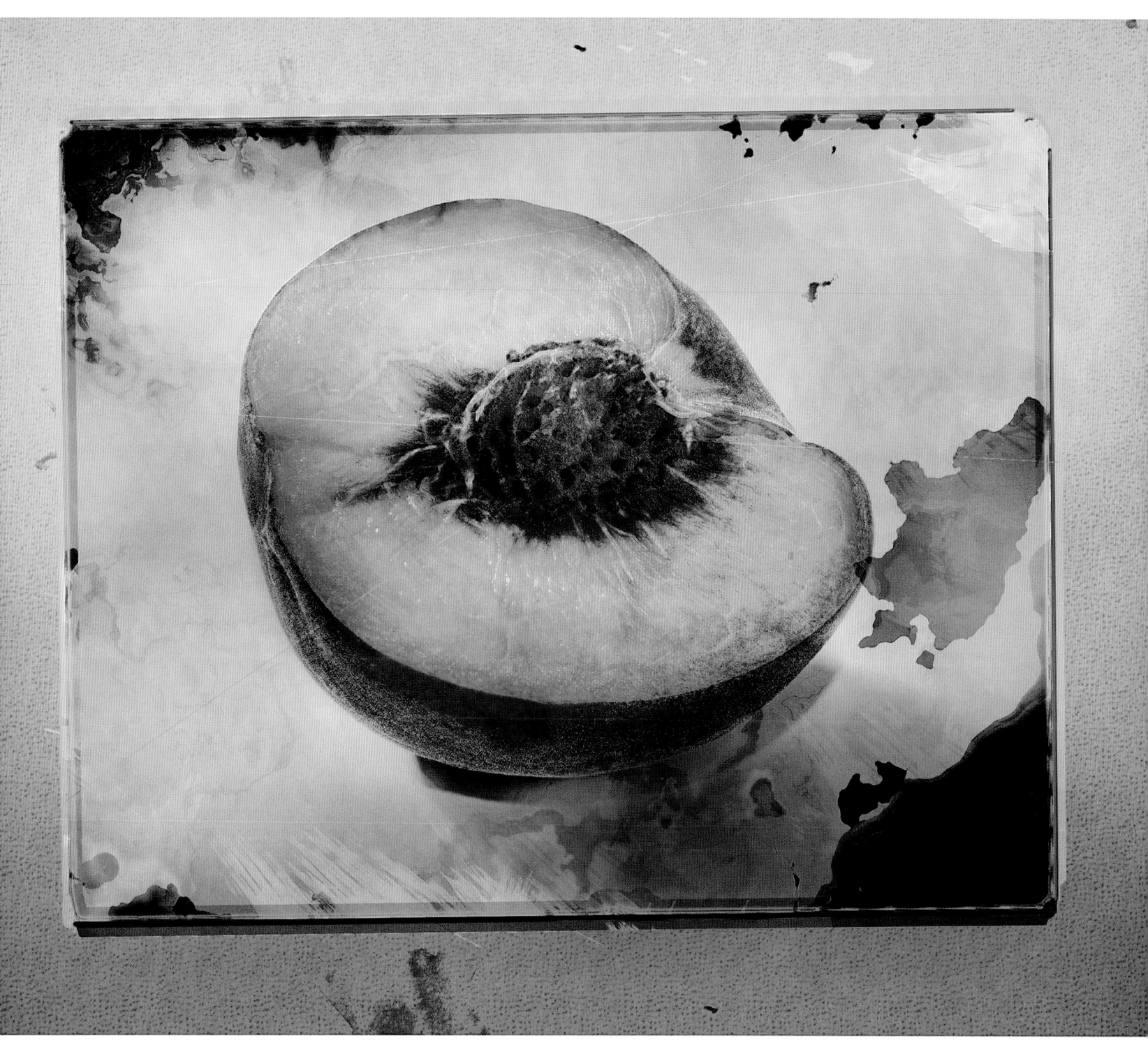

ABOVE: *As a result of the multiple section treatment, the highly detailed image ended up at roughly 30 x 40 inches (75 x 100cm) at 300 ppi. This monochrome version was made to mimic an aged glass positive.*

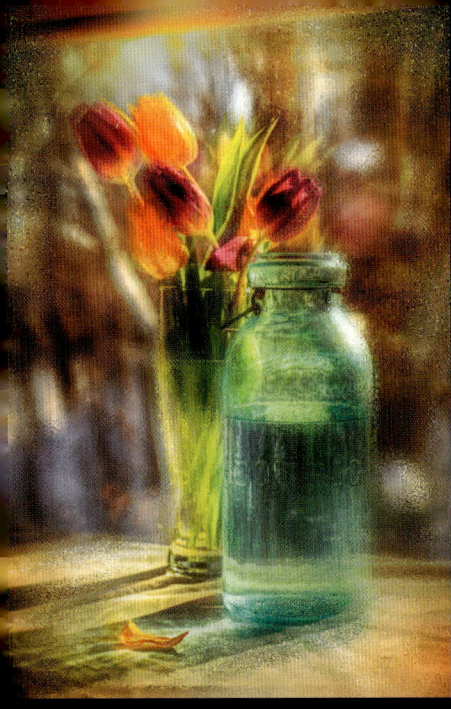

LEFT: *In this example, a painterly image was first stacked to ensure that the background and foreground had different levels of sharpness—the top of the bottle, the fallen petal, and the front of the flowers were all made sharp. The image was then altered in Photoshop using a combination of texture blending and brushwork to soften and color.*

RIGHT: *These dead bees are pretty much equally sharp across the entire table, due to the use of focus stacking.*

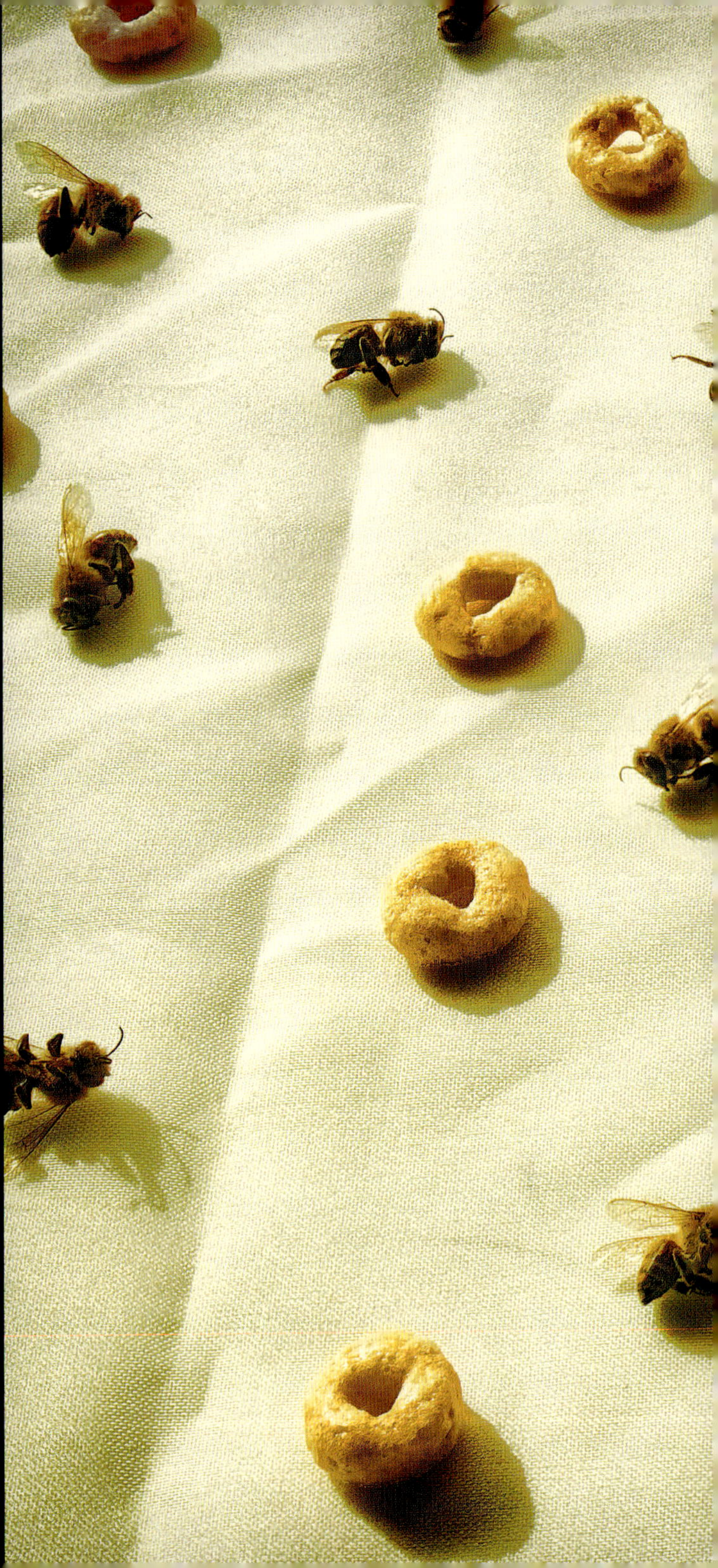

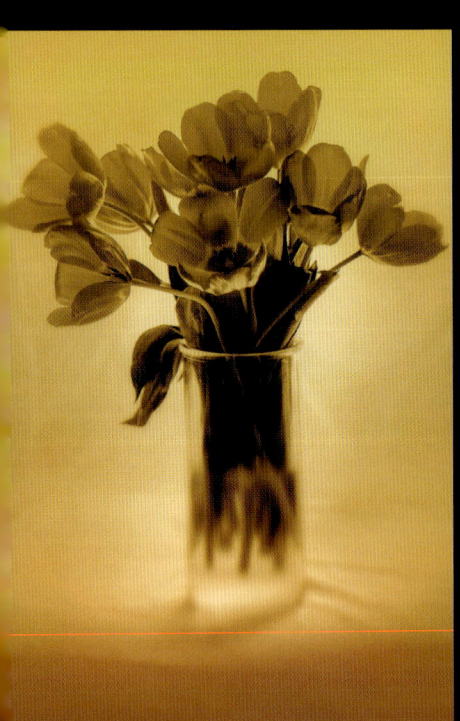

ABOVE: *Focusing the sharpness on the flowers, the vase was deliberately made out of focus for effect.*

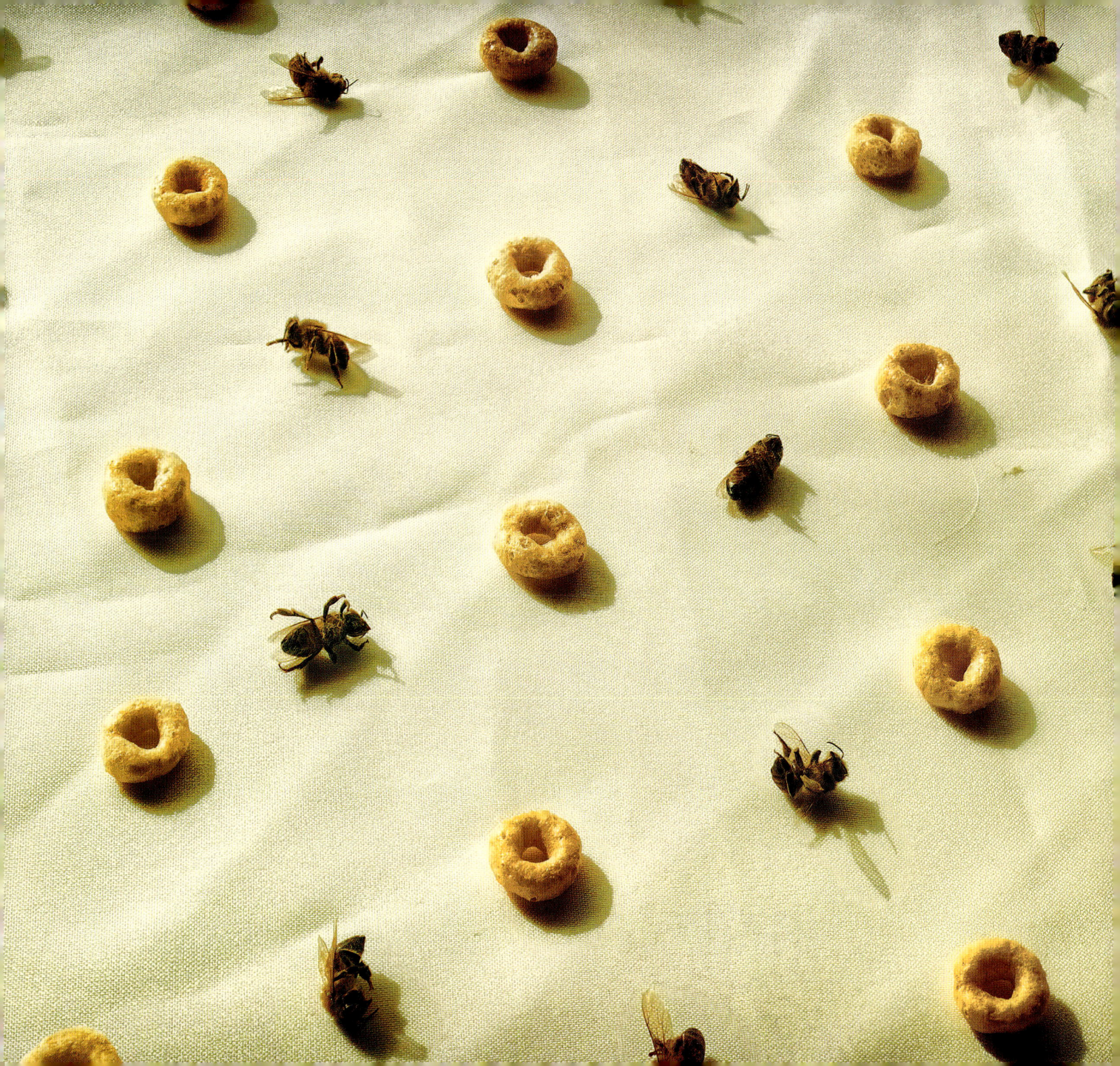

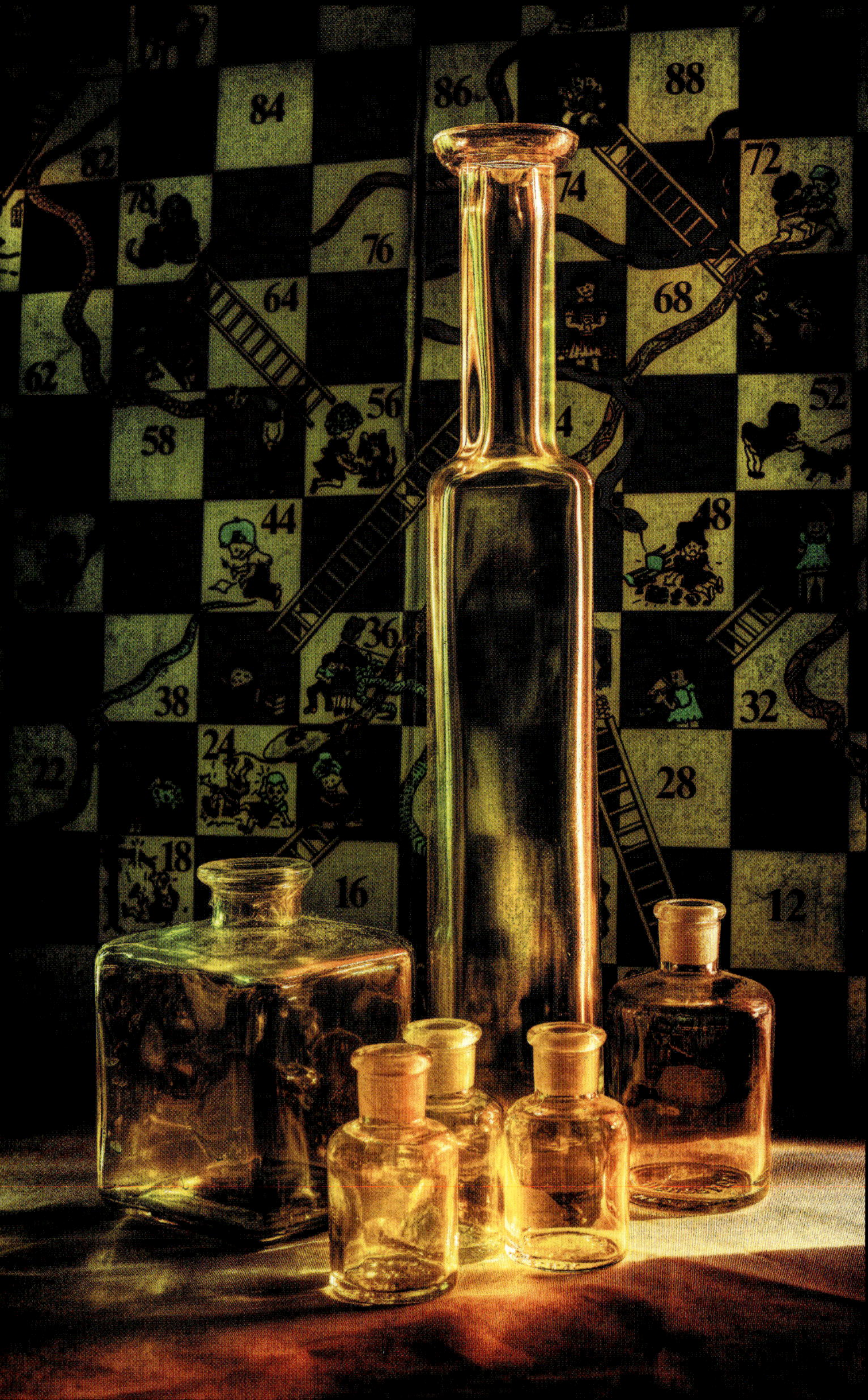

LEFT: *Focus stacking allows for amazingly precise control over depth of field, which can increase the focus potential of any lens.*

BELOW: *This tabletop still life of a deer's skull was made sharp from the front to the back of the horns using focus stacking.*

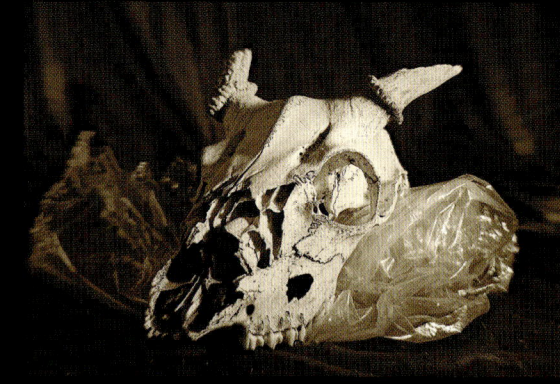

05 // GALLERY // FOCUS STACKING

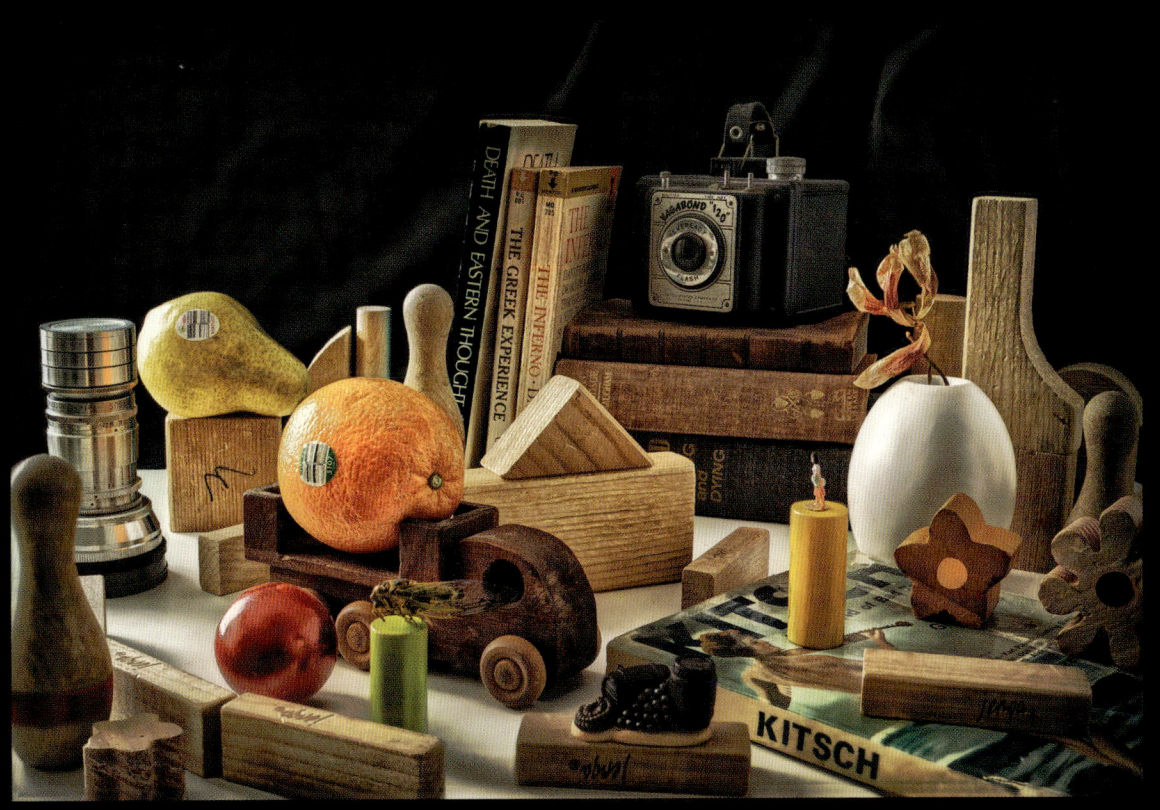

LEFT: *The process of focus stacking can be a great option for tabletop photography, as it makes everything sharp. This has the opposite effect to the miniaturization techniques explored in Chapter 3.*

BELOW: *Both of these objects were shot separately using focus stacking. They were then combined in Photoshop, where they received some blending and brushwork using a variety of custom brushes.*

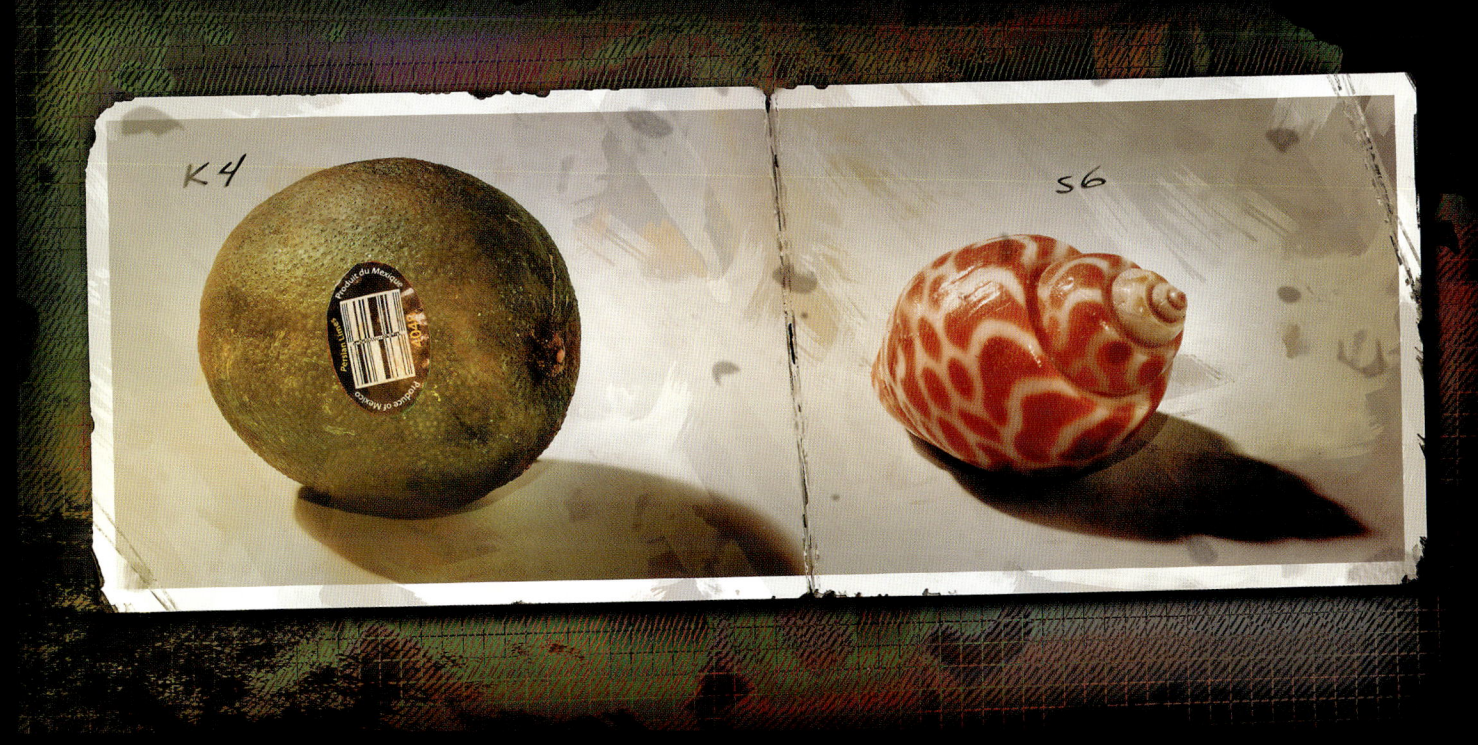

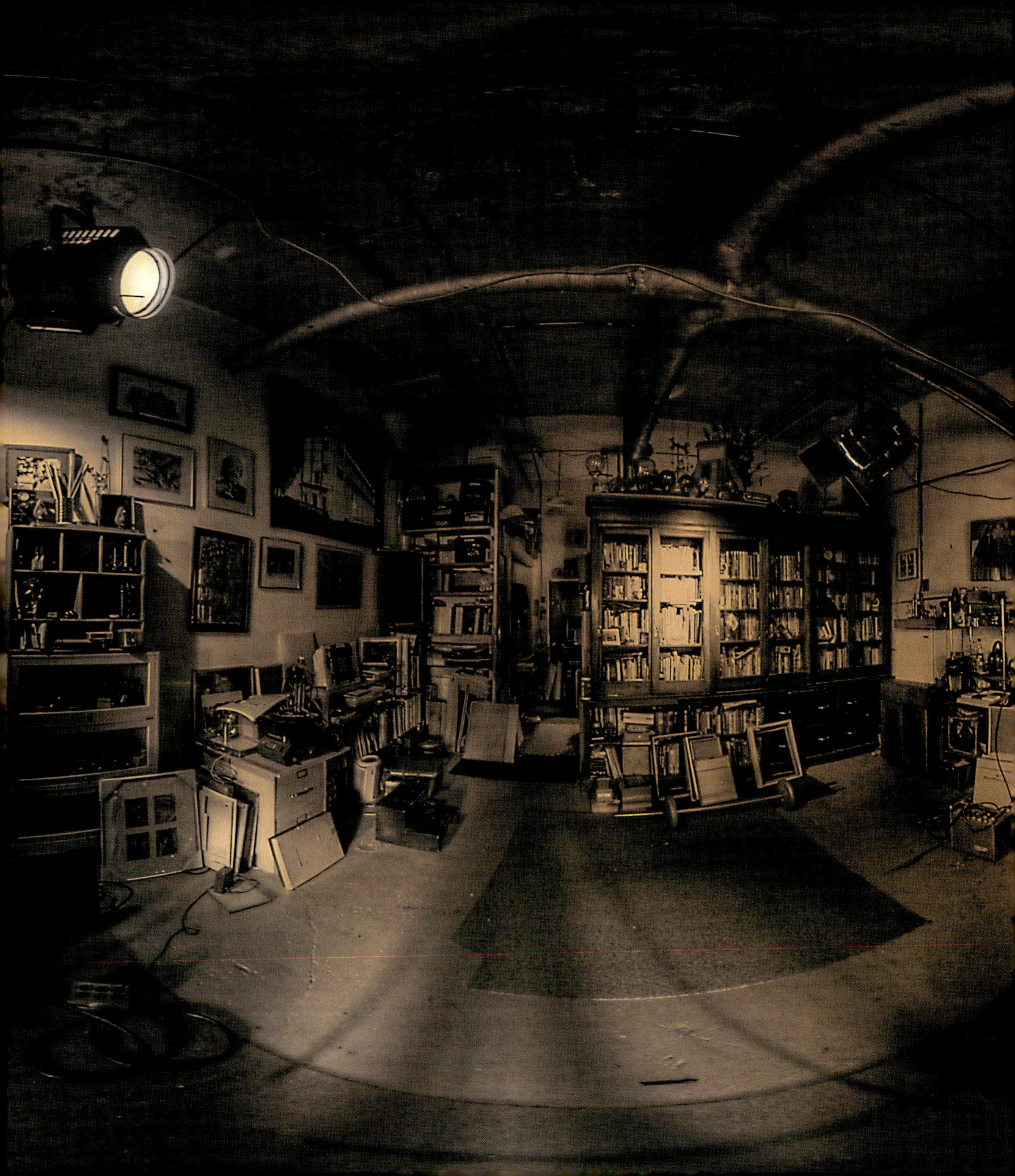

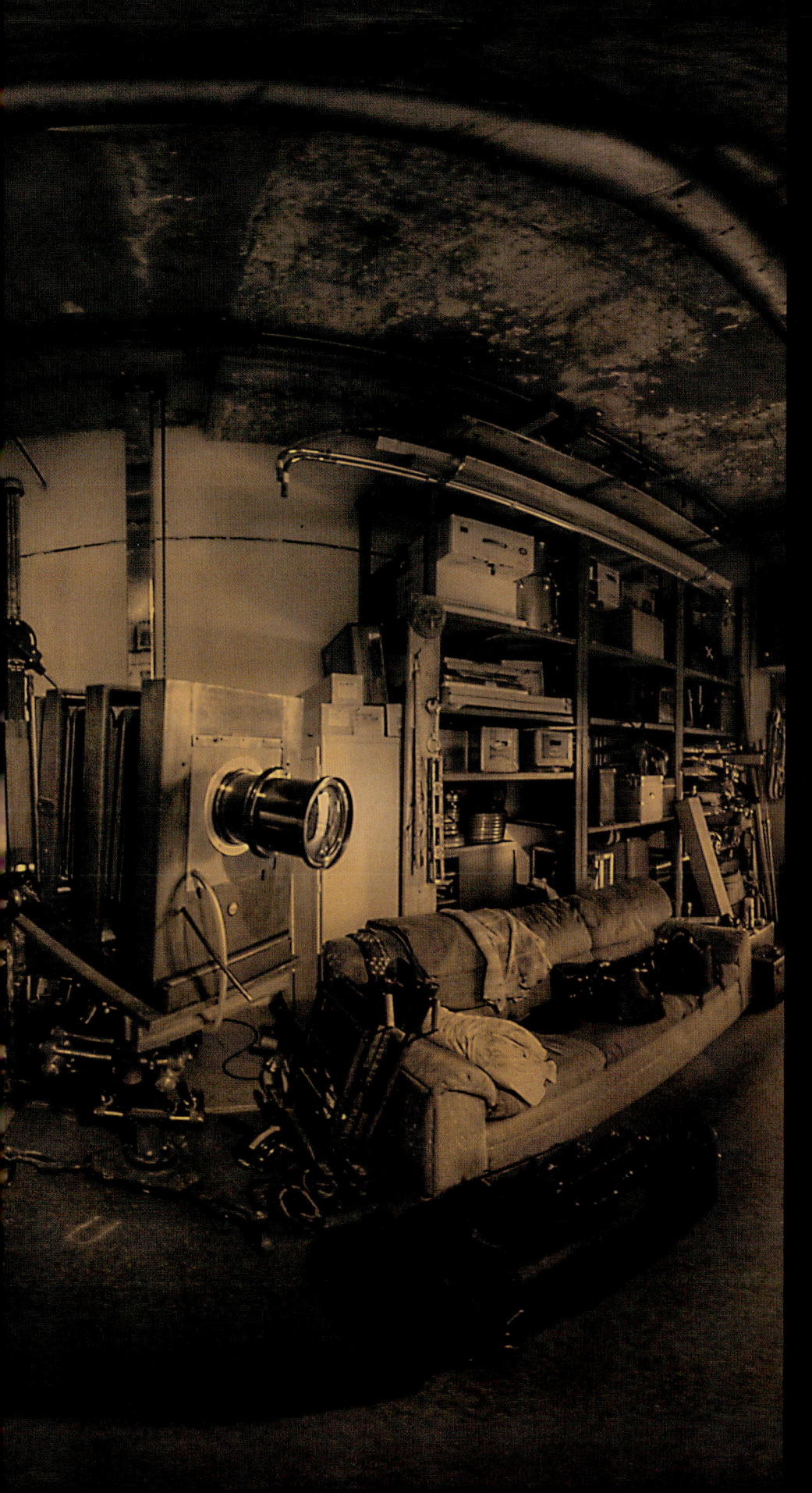

06 // PANORAMAS

What is a Panorama?

Traditionally, a panoramic image is one that has a width that is at least twice as wide as it is tall. The format is generally used for making landscape images, in order to capture a broad view of a scene.

The panoramic image is a unique type of photographic image that has been in existence since the very early days of photography. Panoramas are typically used to depict expansive views, such as the skyline of New York City, the Grand Canyon, or a view of the Golden Gate Bridge, where the classic 3:2 ratio of 35mm film or a full-frame sensor might lead to excessive amounts of sky when the subject is wide, but not necessarily tall. By contrast, a panoramic format elongates the picture space, concentrating attention on the subject itself. In some ways, they are like dioramas, in that we can scan over the scene to see new details, just as we might scan the scene itself.

Today, however, the panoramic format is used for a much greater range of photographic genres, including still life, portraiture, large groups of people, and architectural interiors. To me, a panoramic format is simply another option for shooting almost any kind of subject in any situation and in any orientation. I have created panoramas that have been shot vertically, horizontally, and even diagonally, and I have shot the interiors of buildings and studios, street-views, landscapes, and pinhole and macro subjects. To me, choosing the format to shoot a certain kind of subject is as fundamental a choice as choosing a lens.

Image Stitching

The world of image stitching (the process used to create a panoramic image) can be thought of as rows and columns of overlapping images. However, not all stitched images need to be panoramas: a mosaic of images can be stitched together to produce nearly any square or rectangular format, so the technique can be used to create not only panoramic photographs but also images with a much higher resolution than a single shot.

In fact, one of the main reasons why I use image stitching is to create high-resolution images. This is not just because

BELOW: *Stringing three in-camera panoramas together produced this multi-panel panorama. The camera was passed from left to right in a vertical orientation for each of the individual shots.*

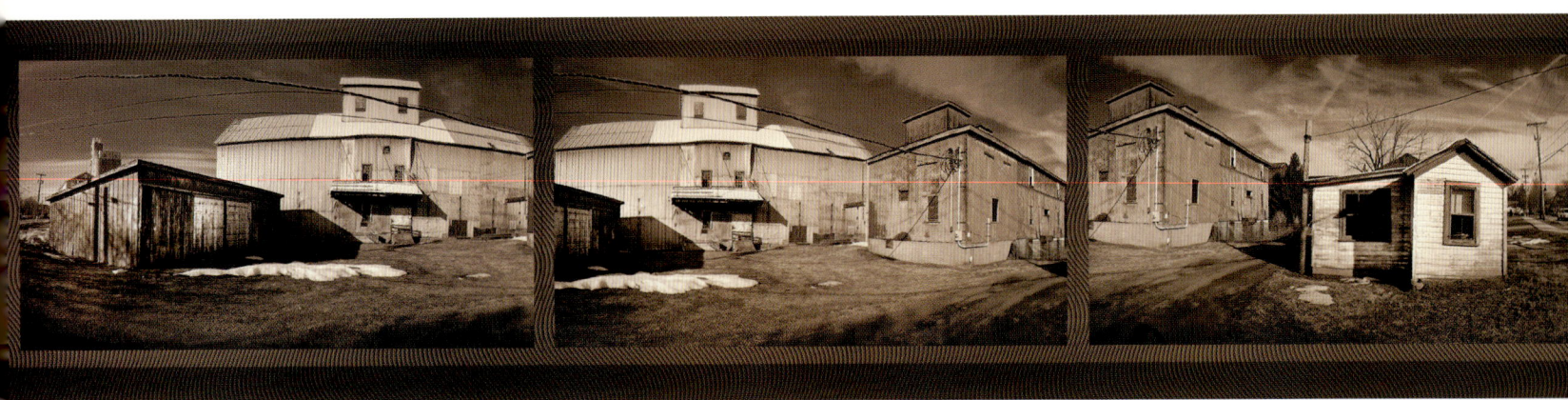

I always make big prints, but because the images have a different look to them due to their increased resolution. Even when printed to small dimensions, photographs look sharper, details are enhanced, and the image looks cleaner and more realistic as gradations are smoother with far less tendency to show banding, or other anomalies such as noise, grain, and "stair stepping" (pixelation). To me, it is the difference that used to exist between an image created with a 35mm SLR and one created using a large-format camera.

Regardless of the format, image stitching usually requires you to use a tripod in order to get the best overlaps, to keep the camera level, and to maintain the same height during the capture. However, great images can be produced handheld, as today's stitching software is capable of identifying the details in slightly mismatched images and creating a convincing stitch.

While it is possible to make panoramas using almost any lens, in most cases it is best to use a wide-angle lens. The general rule says that the wider the lens coverage, the fewer images you need to make the panorama, and this is especially important if you are capturing anything containing movement. Any technique that requires several shots to be taken will show a difference in anything that moves at the time of exposure at the point where stitching is required. In this case, the moving element is likely produce an unwanted result.

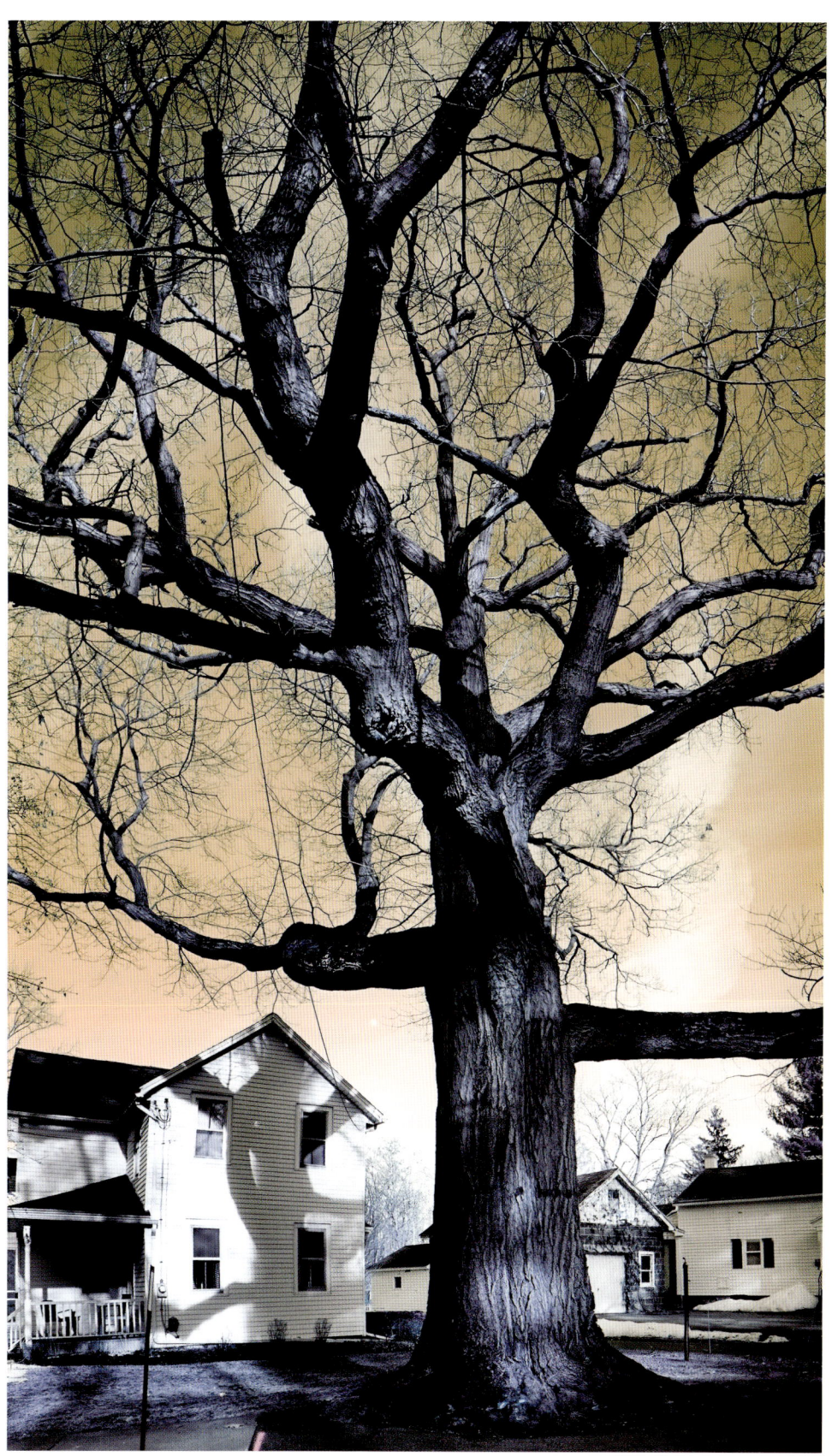

RIGHT: *Panoramas don't have to be "landscape" format—vertical panoramas can be created using many of the techniques discussed in this chapter. This image was shot using a Sony A7's "sweep" panorama mode, moving the camera upward, rather than sideways.*

In-Camera Panoramas

Many cameras have some sort of built-in panoramic shooting option, which may require you to do little more than rotate the camera across the scene you want to record. However, this is not necessarily the best way to create your panoramic images.

It is possible to get some fantastic results from your camera's built-in panoramic feature. One technology that is increasingly popular is the "sweep" panorama, which simply requires you to move the camera in a sweeping motion along a circular trajectory. This usually means rotating the camera a certain distance, in order to capture a broad "sweep" of the scene.

However, there are limitations. For a start, the camera takes away a lot of the work involved, which for many photographers removes some of the creativity and pride in producing an image. It is also not easy to control the start and stop points precisely, and the accuracy of the final panoramic image depends on the speed at which you sweep, among other factors.

Cameras with this function often create the panorama by taking a series of low-resolution images that are strung together or "stitched" by the camera's internal software. They use an on-board algorithm to process the frames into a stitched panorama, with the individual images used to create the panorama lost in the process. In other cases, the images used are derived from video frames, which are also low in resolution.

In both cases, the resulting file is typically output as a JPEG file. While this can be ideal for display on a computer screen or printing at a small size, they will not necessarily enlarge well without a noticeable reduction in sharpness and detail.

In other instances, the panoramic mode may simply crop a "full-size" image, again leading to a lower-resolution result with a limited print size.

Thankfully, however, there are many ways to create panoramic shots that are far more accurate and creative than the built-in options, and that also have a much higher resolution.

To start with, to create high-resolution images and to maintain all of the dynamic range, you should shoot your panoramas as individual images, which can be any format (including Raw). You can then stitch your frames together as you please, knowing that you will also have all of the images for use in another project. Above all, you will have the satisfaction of knowing that you made the image yourself.

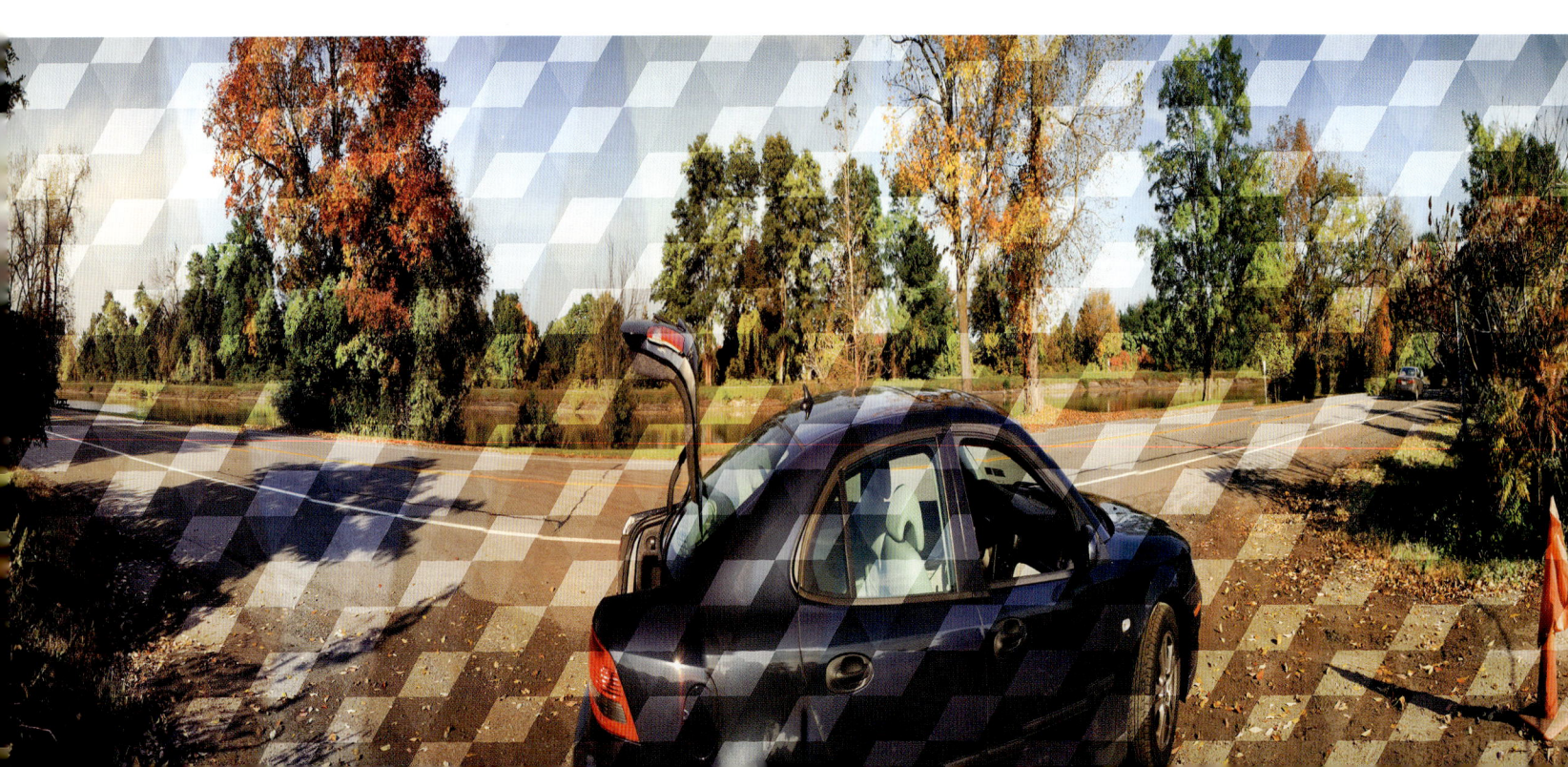

06 // IN-CAMERA PANORAMAS // PANORAMAS

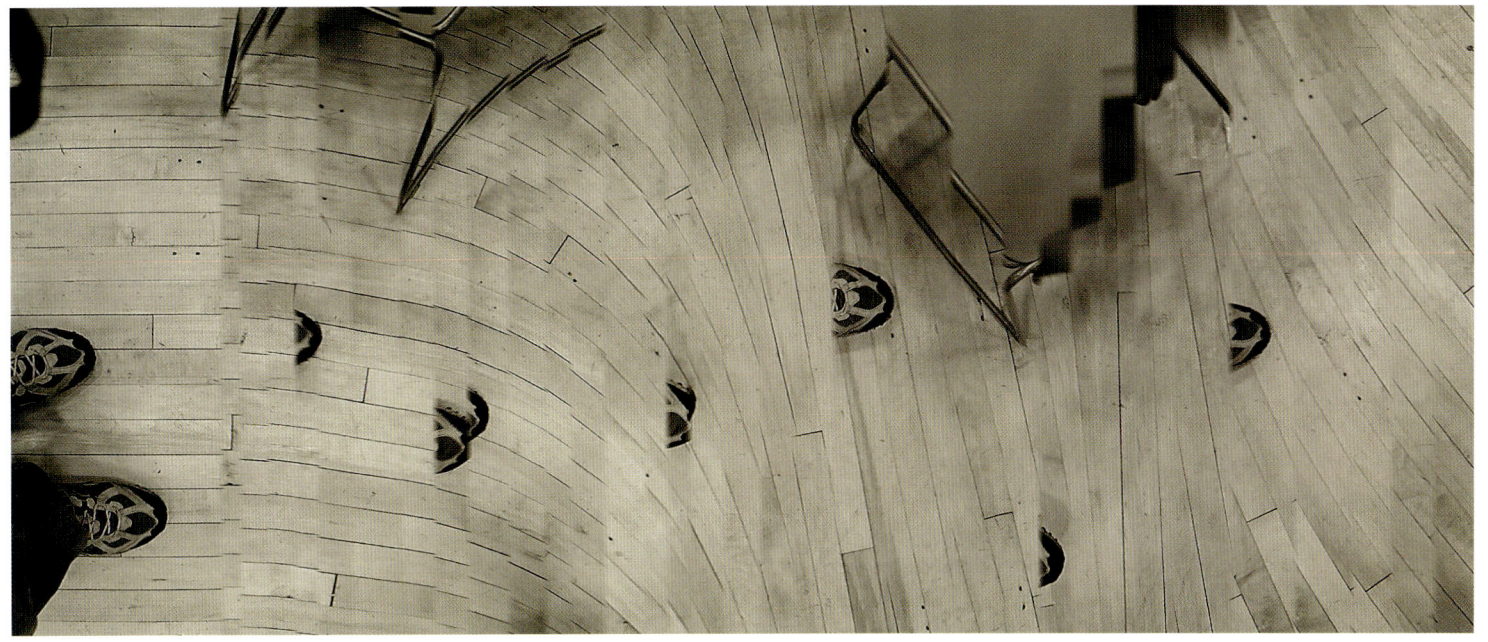

BELOW: *Panoramic images can be produced with nearly any lens and in numerous creative ways. Post-production can also allow you to create your own, unique results.*

ABOVE: *A built-in "sweep" panorama mode was used to create this image. The exposure was started while I walked from one side of a room to another, rather than sweeping the camera. You can see here the separate images that were taken in sequence, which the camera has attempted to align.*

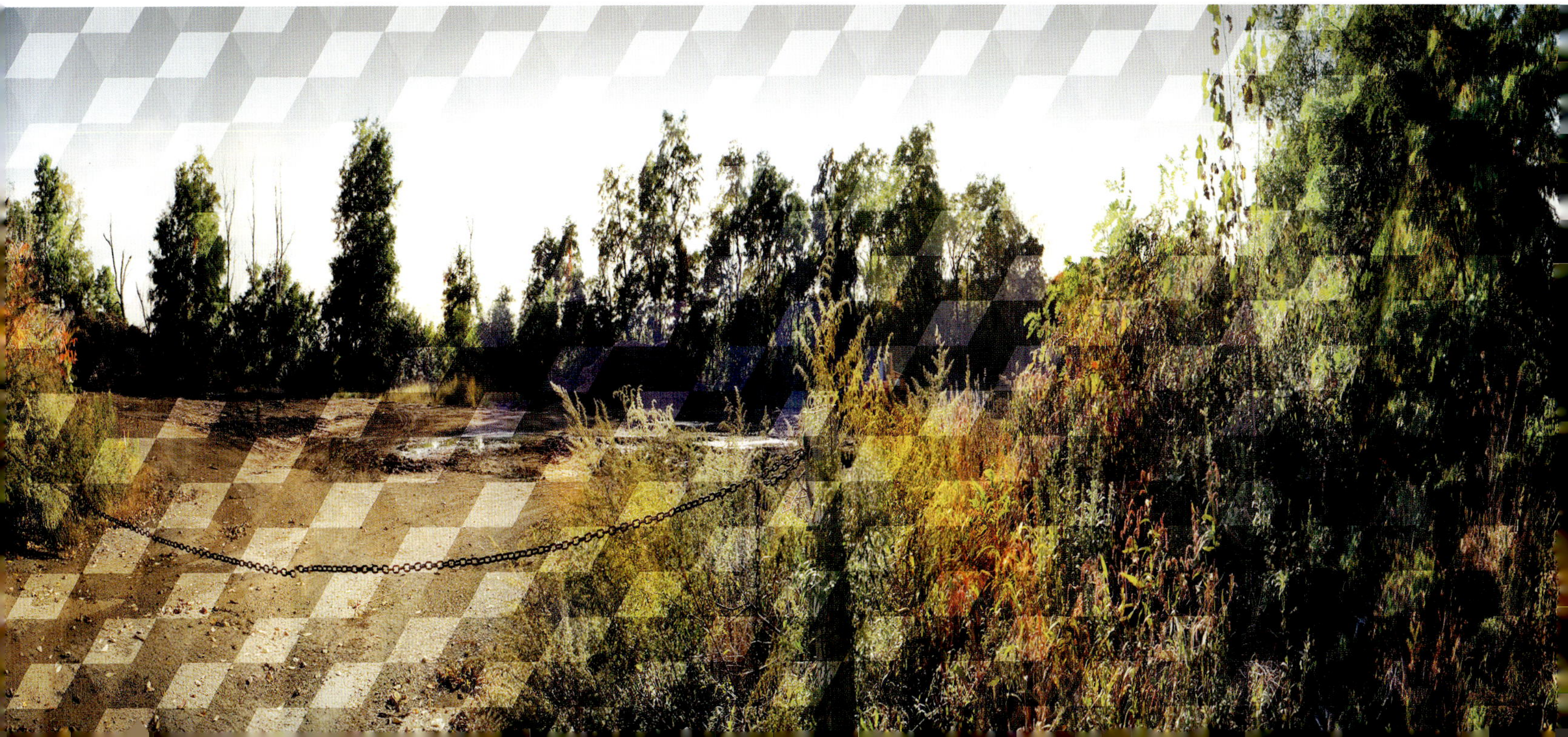

Multi-Shot Panorama

There are numerous reasons why you might choose to shoot a panorama: because it best fits the shape of your subject; to avoid a low-resolution result; or when the lens you have just isn't wide enough for the shot you would like to take.

I was driving home from a meeting when a beautiful red barn caught my eye. I immediately turned around and drove back, parking my car across the highway and getting out to shoot. The problem was that the only camera I had with me was a Pentax K7 with a Tamron 90mm telephoto attached. The 90mm lens on the K7's APS-size sensor is equivalent to a 135mm lens on a full-frame camera, and this meant that I could get only a small portion of the subject into the frame from where I stood. Obviously, I was not going to make this image with a single shot.

In order to capture the image I wanted, I had to shoot a series of overlapping shots that I could stitch together. However, I also wanted to capture details in both the highlights and the shadows, so I decided to shoot the scene using a high dynamic range (HDR) capture. This meant making at least three exposures for each portion of the image: one at the "correct" exposure setting; one darker to hold the highlights; and one lighter to retain detail in the shadows. To automate this process, I set the camera's AEB (Automatic Exposure Bracketing) so that it would capture three shots at ±2EV.

There needed to be enough overlap for the eventual stitching of similar details, so I needed to overlap the shots by about 20% horizontally and vertically. I shot by dividing the subject into a series of frames and then, starting at the top, I worked my way around the scene in a clockwise fashion with each shot overlapping the previous one. By the time I had finished shooting, I had shot 30 frames in total (three different exposures for ten overlapping sections), which took about 3–4 minutes in total. But I was confident that I had the exposures and the alignment that I needed to produce the image.

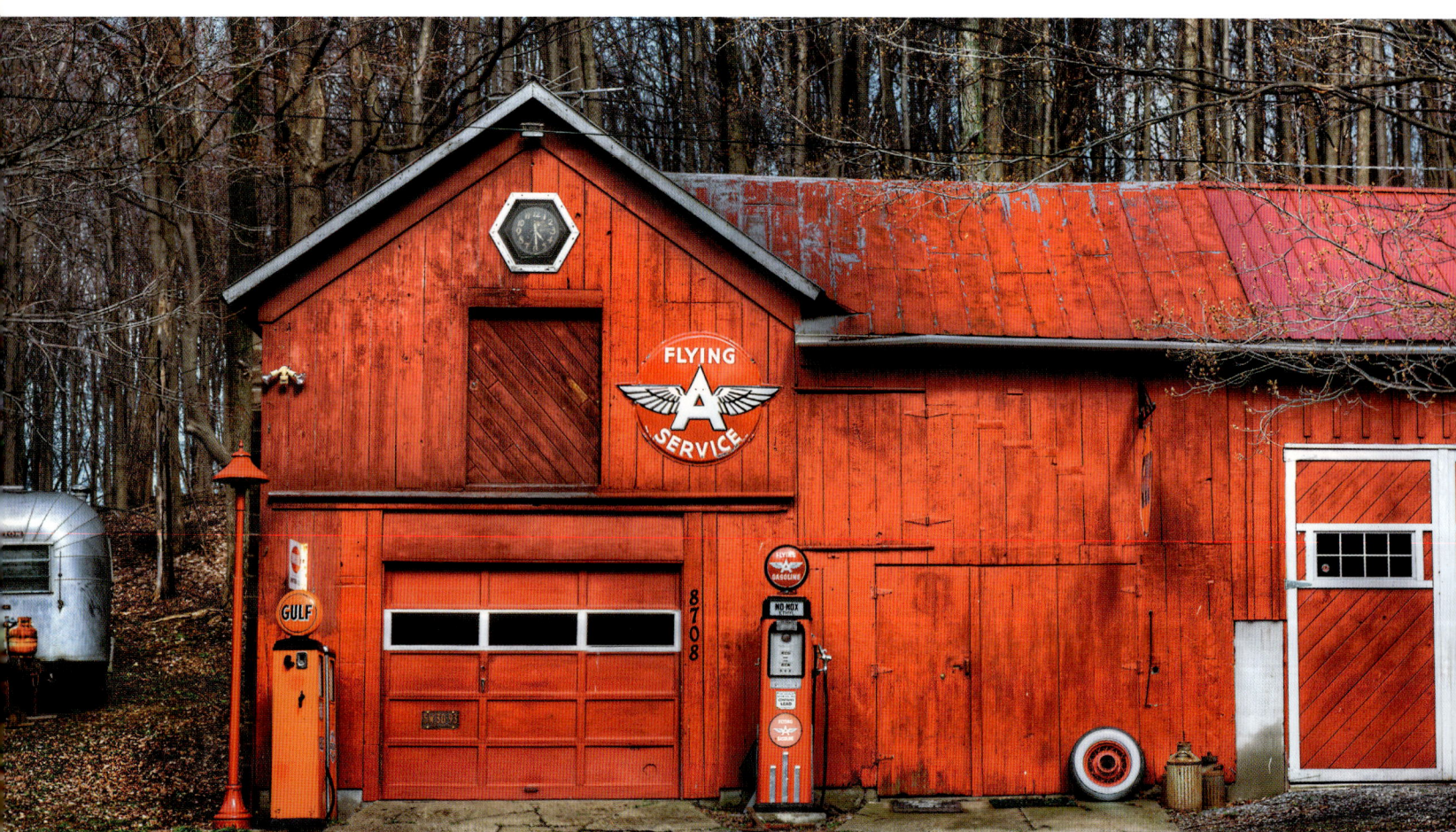

06 // MULTI-SHOT PANORAMAS // PANORAMAS

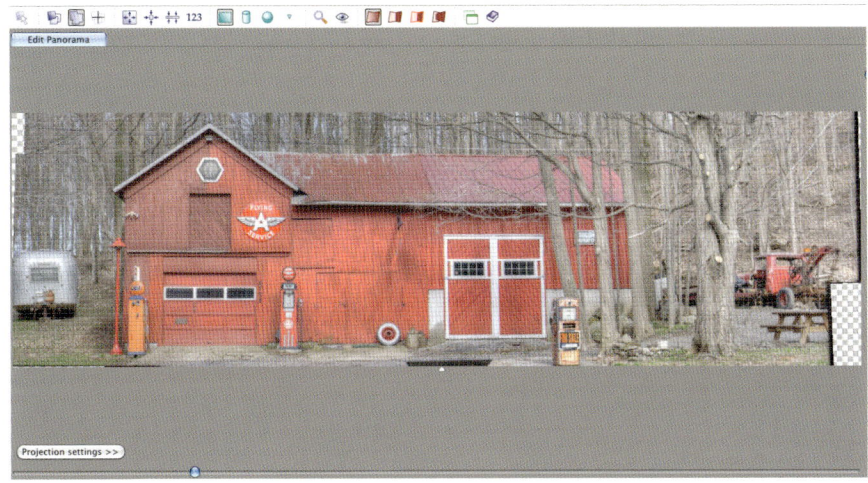

ABOVE: *Here is an example of an image that has been shot using a handheld approach.*

When I returned home, I moved the files to the computer where I batch-processed the images using Photomatix Pro to produce HDR versions of each of the ten frames that would be stitched together. These ten files were then stitched together using PTGui stitching software, which produced an absolutely flawless stitch.

If I had a wide-angle lens with me, then I could perhaps have made a single HDR exposure sequence. The result, however, would have been very different. The perspective would have been more angular, rather than flat, and the depth of field would have been greater. The final image file would also have been much smaller—after cropping in Photoshop, the image ended up at almost 13,000 pixels wide, with extremely fine detail. This would easily be suitable for printing at over 40 inches (100cm) wide at 300ppi.

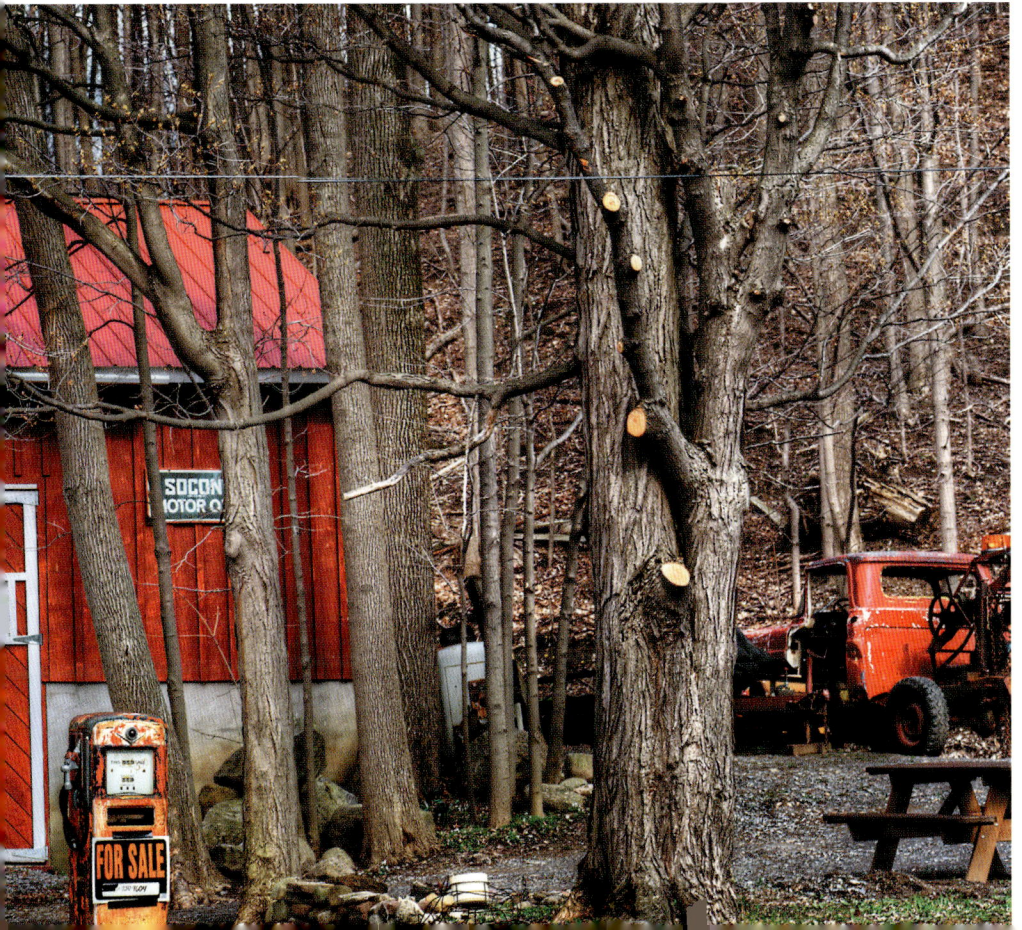

LEFT: *The final photograph is made up of 30 separate exposures, which has resulted in a detail-rich, high-resolution image.*

Parallax

When multiple frames are captured for panorama stitching, there are discrepancies caused by the lens used and the angles that the camera has to pan for the shots. This variation, which is caused by a number of factors, is one reason we need to overlap the images.

Software needs the detail information of adjacent images in order to find suitable stitching points, so it can align the individual frames accurately. Misalignment can also be caused by movement of subjects such as cars, people, and trees in the wind, but it can also be caused by "parallax." The dictionary definition for parallax is "the effect whereby the position or direction of an object appears to differ when viewed from different positions, e.g., through the viewfinder and the lens of a camera." It is similar to what is perceived when we view things with one eye versus the other.

Parallax occurs in a number of photographic situations, but in creating a multi-shot image it is the offset alignment of objects in the images that are to be joined through the stitching process that causes us problems. Views through open doorways and the space between objects can cause some major problems for stitching software, and images with the least amount of parallax are more likely to stitch without encountering any problems.

No Parallax Point

What we are actually interested in is the "no parallax point" (NPP), sometimes called the "nodal point." The NPP is where you will get a much more precise placement for rotation, which will yield the best possible panorama results. To confuse the issue slightly, the NPP is also called the "entrance pupil," which is a virtual aperture that also the center of perspective. Strangely, the entrance pupil can be completely outside of the lens' optics.

Unfortunately, there are no markings on the lens to indicate the NPP on the lens barrel, which is hardly surprising when you consider that a zoom lens can have a moving NPP that changes with the focal length as the lens is zoomed. For that reason, the NPP should be recalculated with each new setting of the focal length.

Thankfully, the point of rotation is easily identified through simple trial and error. If you are a stickler for precision, many charts can be found online that will help you find the exact location of the NPP

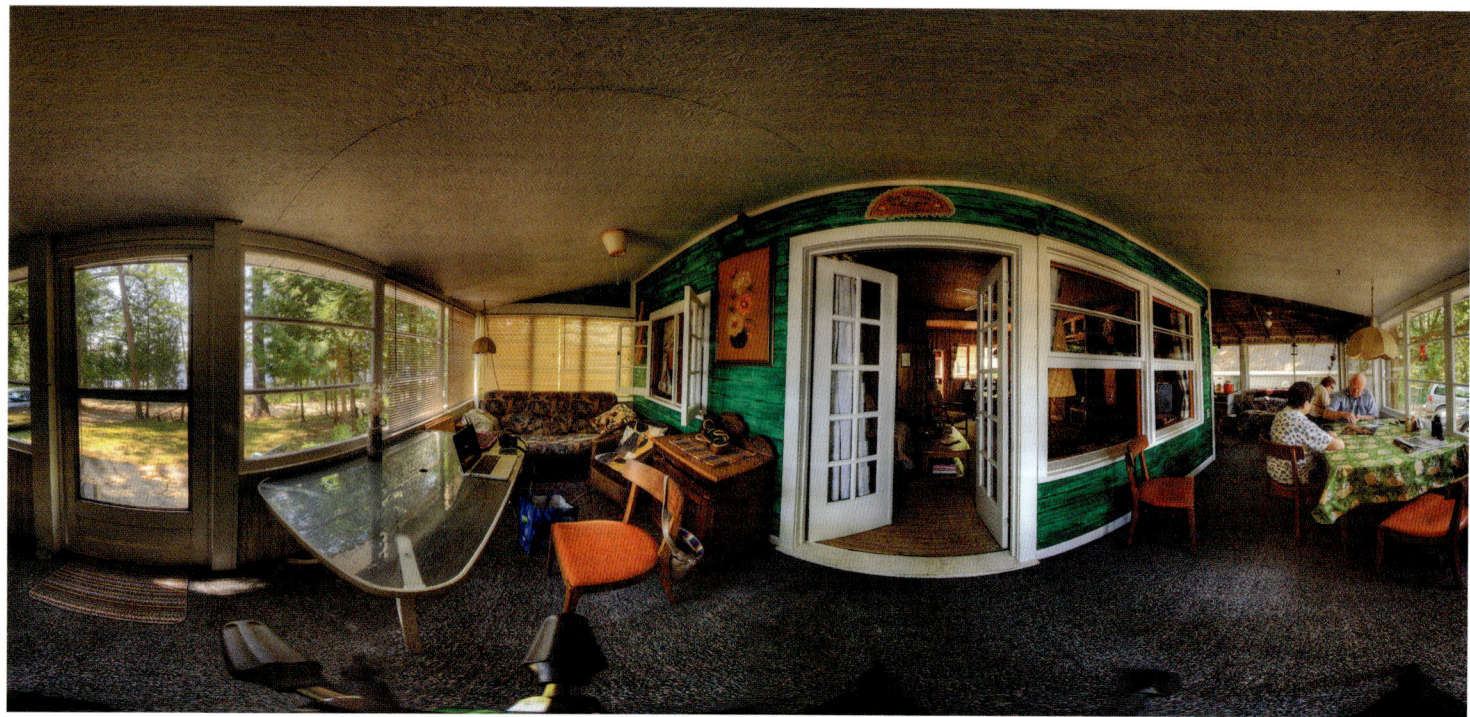

for a particular lens/camera combination. Personally, I use the simple technique discussed in the box (right).

Ultimately, the camera needs to rotate around a precise XY position. For this reason, most newer mirrorless and DSLR cameras have a tripod screw mount located directly in line with the lens axis (X). As long as the camera is centered along the X-axis, the camera can easily be set to the NPP by adjusting its position forward or backward (by mounting it on a specialist VR tripod head) until test targets are aligned when rotating the camera. Once alignment is set, it can be recorded and marked for future reference.

Most VR-mounting systems have metric markings, which can be used to remount a particular camera and lens to the correct position at any time. If you use a number of different lenses (and perhaps different cameras) to make your panoramas, you would need to use different mounting points. You should also be aware that multi-row panoramas may need to be corrected for vertical parallax as well as for horizontal parallax. This relies on centering the lens vertically around the X-axis once the horizontal parallax is resolved.

RIGHT: *The "no parallax point" (NPP) can be found through simple trial and error. The correct position will produce transitions from adjacent rotations where there is no appreciable misalignment of the elements in the frame. In this illustration, A (in red) shows a discrepancy between the alignment of the two objects when the lens is rotated; image B (in green) shows the result of correct placement of the NPP.*

LEFT: *It's easy enough to casually shoot a handheld panorama for distant subjects, but in close quarters like this screen porch, parallax errors will be immediately evident if the NPP isn't properly set.*

LOCATING THE NO PARALLAX POINT

1) Look through your camera's viewfinder and locate two vertical subjects. One should be close to you, and the other in the distance. Adjust your camera so that these objects line up in the viewfinder.

2) Level your equipment, with the camera over the center of rotation of the tripod (the axis of rotation).

3) Once you feel that the camera is level and centered along the lens axis, pan to the left.

4) Using the front object as a marker, note how the distant object shifts relative to it.

5) If the distant object shifts to the left, the lens is in front of the NPP. Move the lens backward and repeat the process.

6) If the distant object shifts to the right, the lens is behind the NPP. Move the lens forward and repeat the process.

7) When the distant object does not shift relative to the front object, you have located the NPP; the optical center of the lens is directly over the axis of rotation.

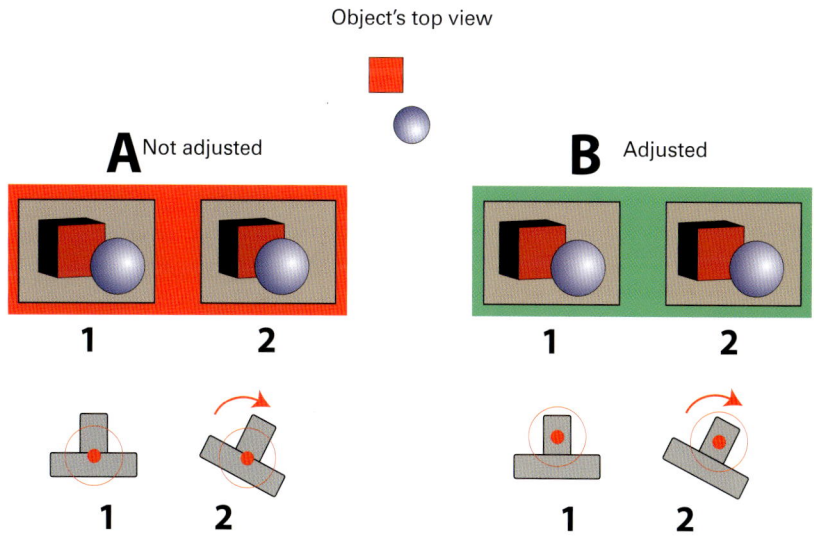

Panoramic Equipment

When creating a panorama, it is best to use a tripod equipped with a specialist panorama head. These are available from various manufacturers and come in a variety of different types, ranging from simple heads that are marked with degrees, through to those that can center the lens' nodal point or "No Parallax Point."

A VR rig is a good way to ensure that the images you shoot for a panoramic photograph align perfectly. The VR stands for "virtual reality" and for many users it is a way of producing "virtual tour" movies. However, the same rigs can be used for making panoramic images.

While there are many different brands of VR devices, the basic principle is the same: they allow each image to be captured at different angles using the nodal point, or "no parallax point," of the lens. Using modular components, a VR panorama system allows many different configurations, including rotating bases and adjustable stages that can be configured for precise camera requirements. Although expensive, the benefit of using a system like this is that, once the nodal point or NPP has been determined for a particular camera/lens combination, the same settings can be used for future shots.

Then, all that is required is to make each exposure exactly the same using a manual setting on the camera. Camera features such as autofocus, auto exposure and auto white balance need to be turned off so that the exposures are consistent throughout the panorama sequence. Maintaining focus throughout the panorama sequence is also important to the stitching process. The stitching software needs to be able to locate sharp details that match in the adjoining images in a sequence. In most cases, the software needs to identify three or more points that can be used to push and pull the image and create a seamless panorama.

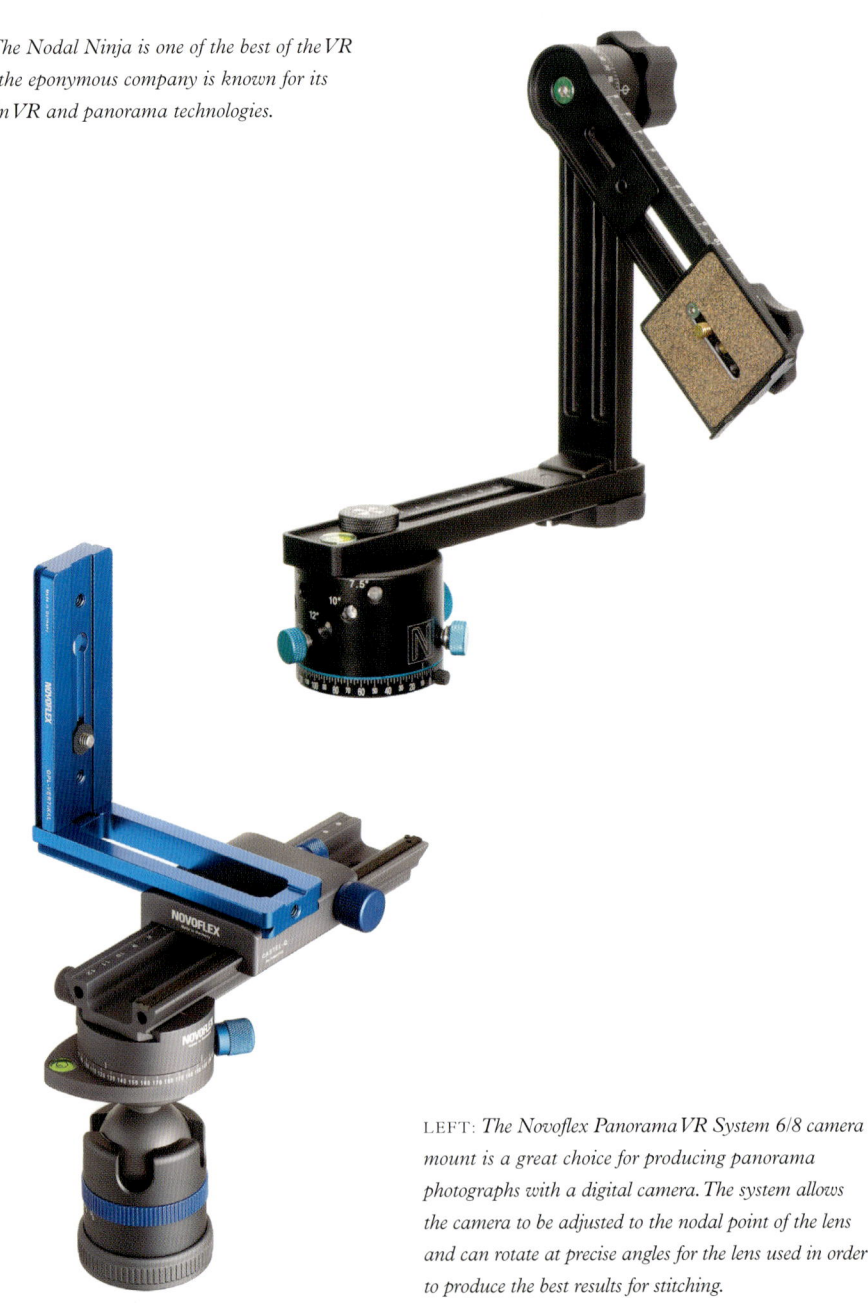

RIGHT: *The Nodal Ninja is one of the best of the VR systems—the eponymous company is known for its expertise in VR and panorama technologies.*

LEFT: *The Novoflex Panorama VR System 6/8 camera mount is a great choice for producing panorama photographs with a digital camera. The system allows the camera to be adjusted to the nodal point of the lens and can rotate at precise angles for the lens used in order to produce the best results for stitching.*

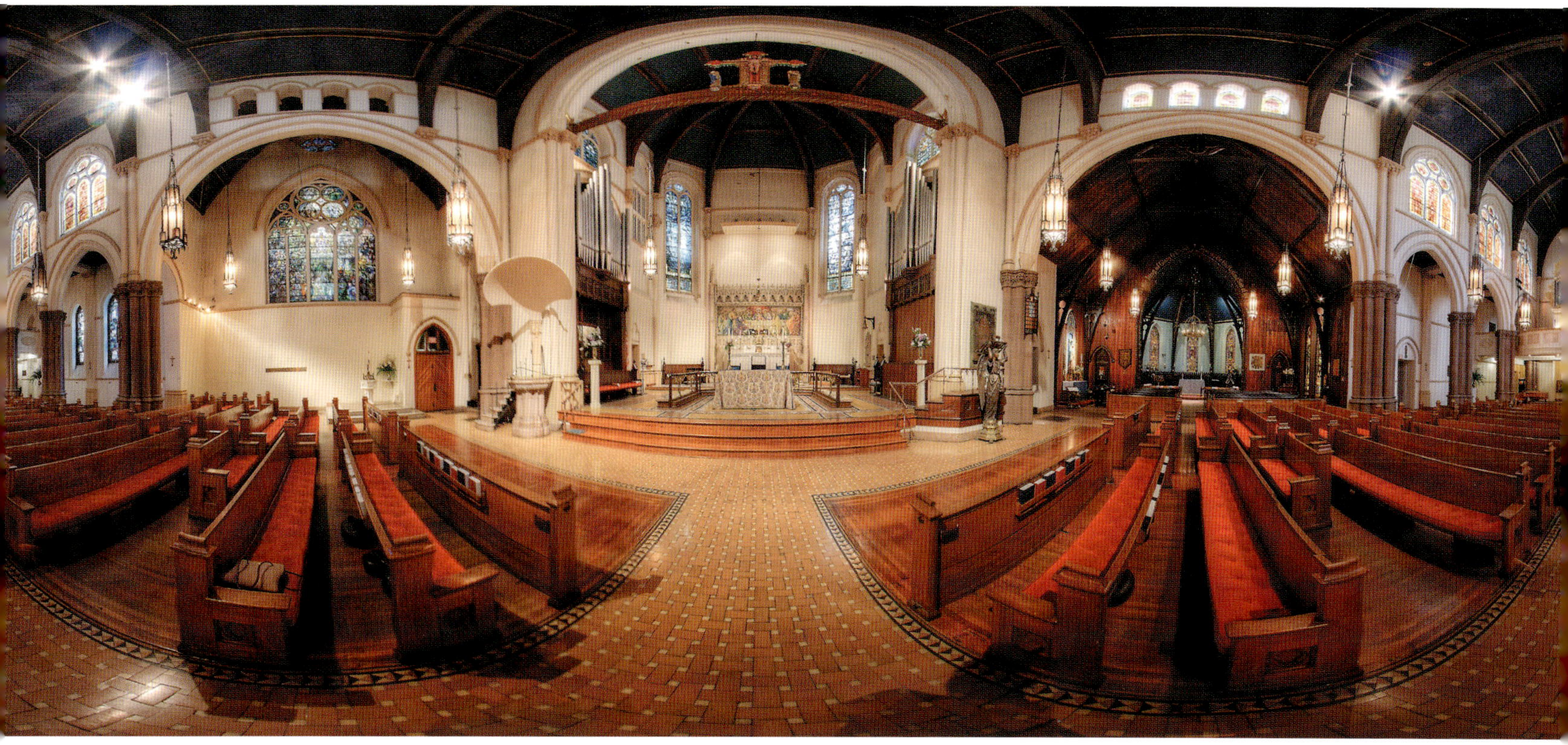

06 // PANORAMIC EQUIPMENT // PANORAMAS

ABOVE: *It is possible to make a 360° photograph with just two shots if you use a fisheye lens with a 180° angle of view. However, it is best to shoot using overlapping image frames, so I usually use at least four camera positions when shooting this type of image.*

BELOW: *Four different shooting angles were used to capture this back room at a gallery. A 180° Fisheye lens was used with a Nodal Ninja to produce the 360° panorama.*

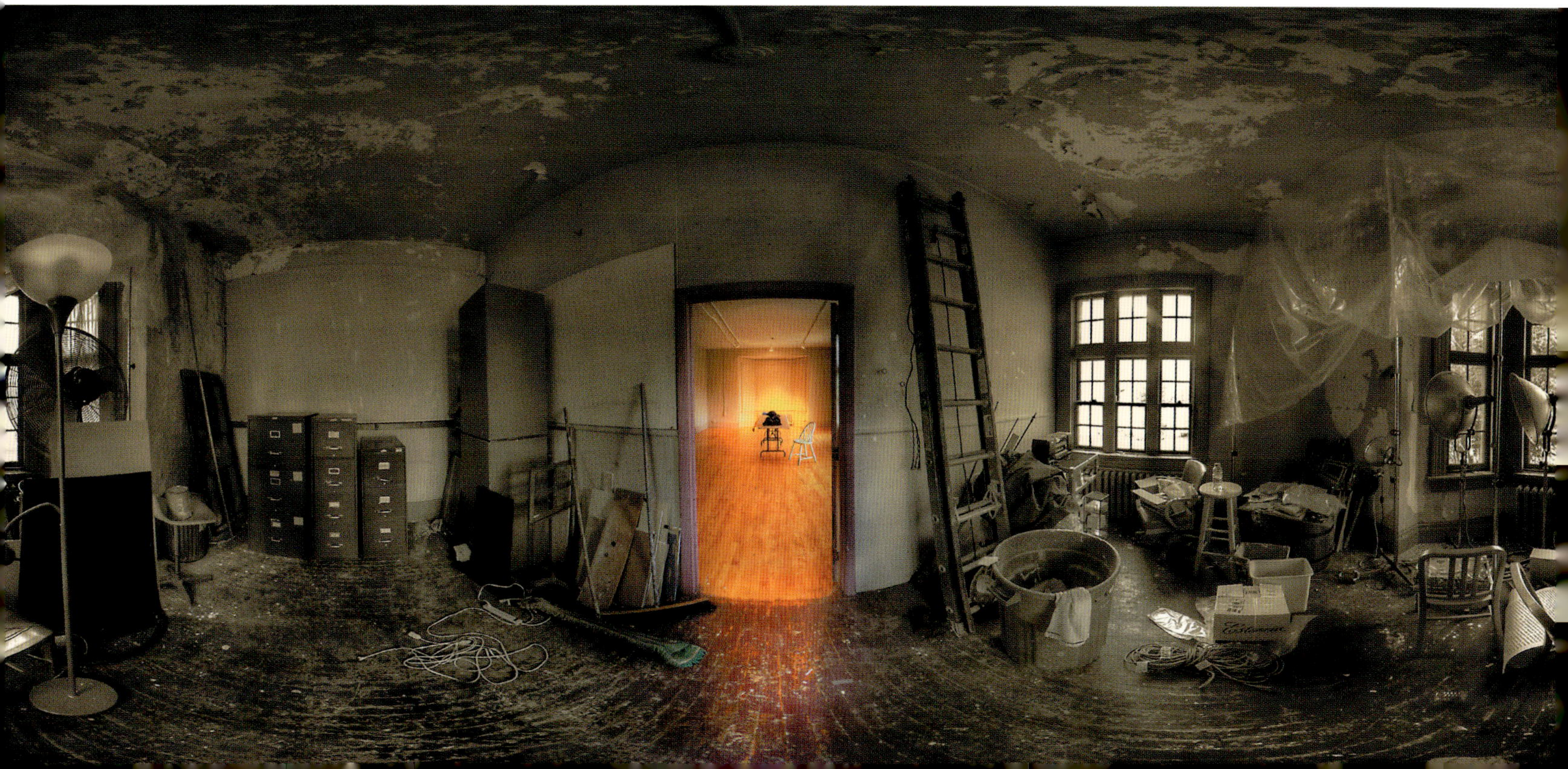

GigaPan Panoramas

If you're serious about shooting panoramic images then GigaPan's range of motor-driven, computerized mounts will help you to create panoramas on a truly epic scale.

The beauty of GigaPan's EPIC system of camera mounts is that it can take all of the camera variables—such as lens, focal length, and shutter speed—and calculate the number of images and the amount of overlap needed to produce a mega-panorama. As this often results in hundreds of images, the file sizes can easily grow to several gigabytes in size, but the final image will contain high-resolution detail of subjects that are far off into the distance. You can see many examples of this process at the GigaPan website (http://gigapan.com/), where you can zoom right into the images, and then zoom out to see the wider view.

BELOW: *The unit has a computerized control at the base, which can be programmed in the field to make any number of shots automatically. The device will then move the camera you mount on it through a series of overlapping rows and columns, with the option to fire the shutter automatically at each image location.*

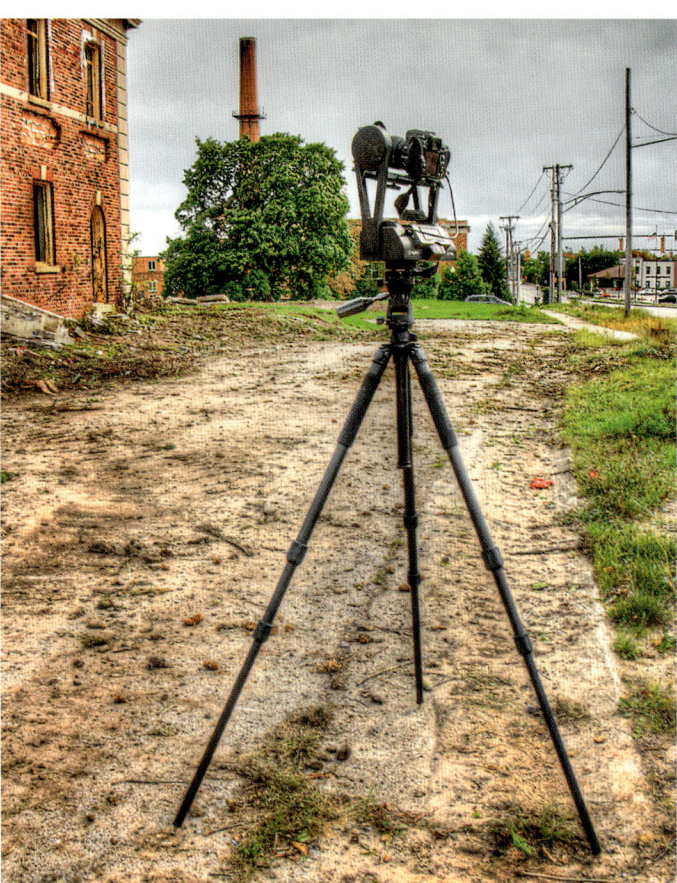

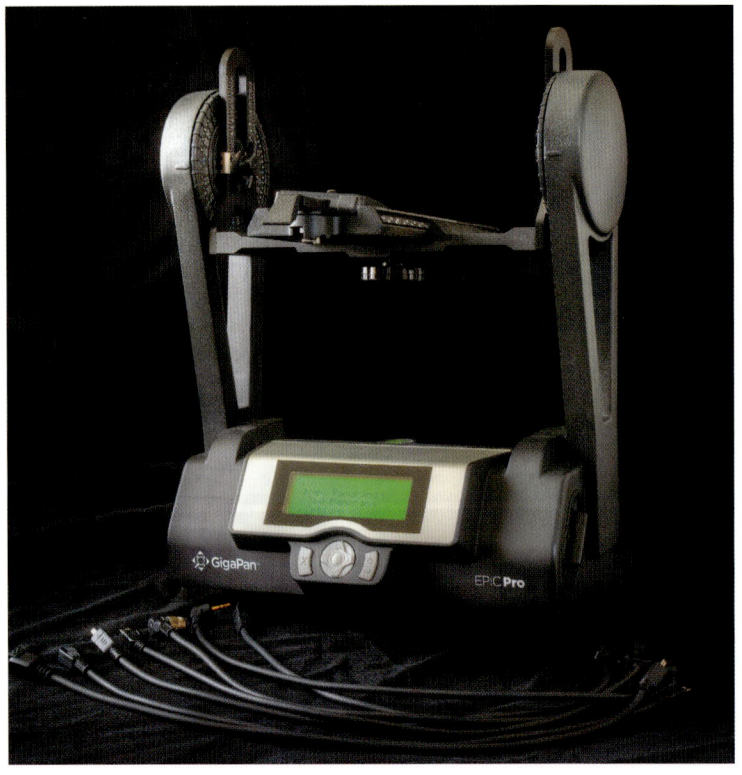

ABOVE: *A GigaPan rig is mounted to a tripod where it is set to move automatically through as series of exposures, which are calculated in rows and columns for the best overlap of a panoramic scene. The amount of overlap is determined by the focal length of the lens used, sensor size, and the total area of the scene desired. The built-in software programs the unit to produce the proper sequence. The user simply locates the starting position as well as the end position.*

RIGHT: *A GigaPan EPIC Pro was used to produce this multi-shot image of my best friend sitting for a portrait near his favorite tree. Not all GigaPan images need to be panoramic.*

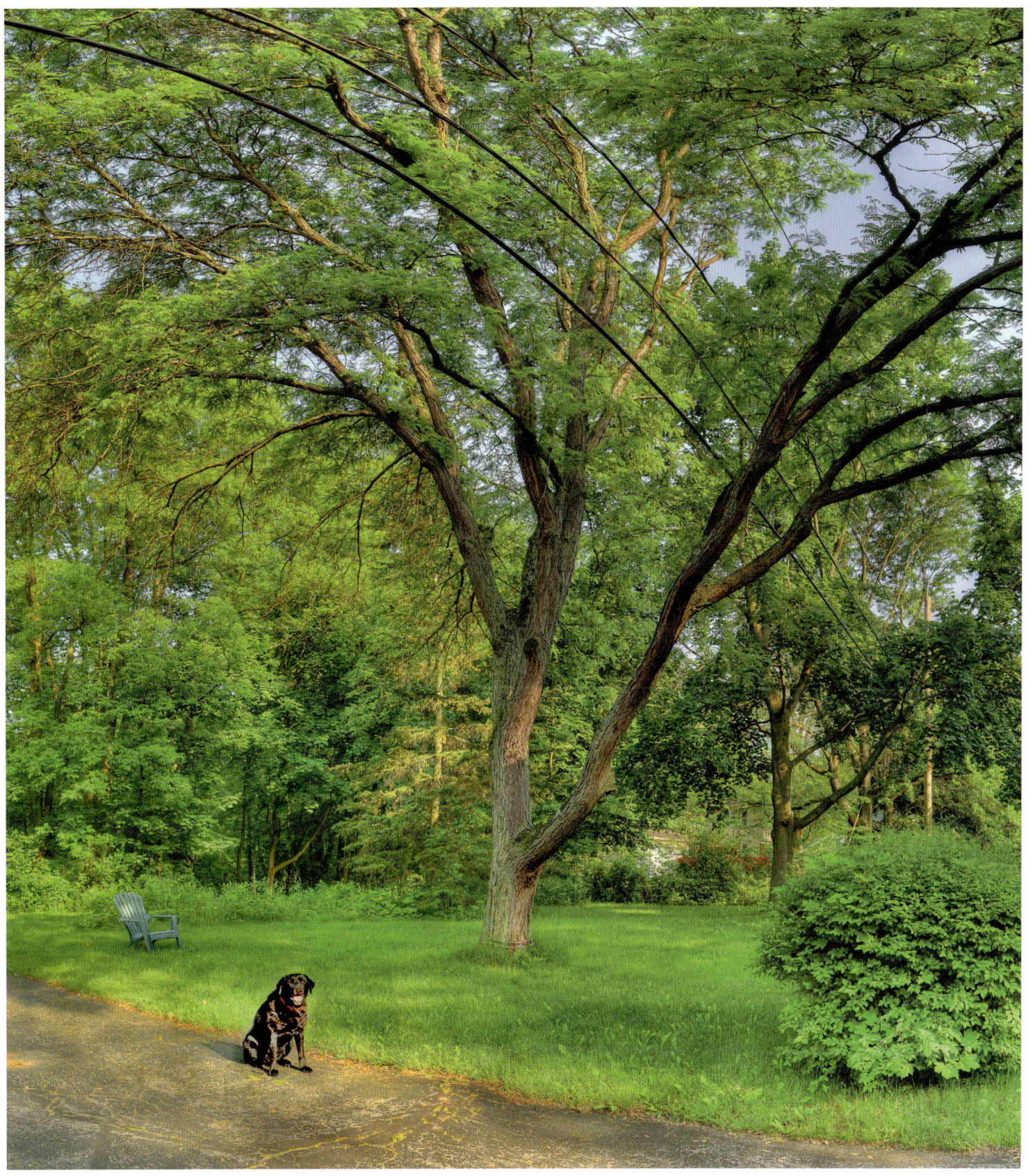

Gallery | Panoramas

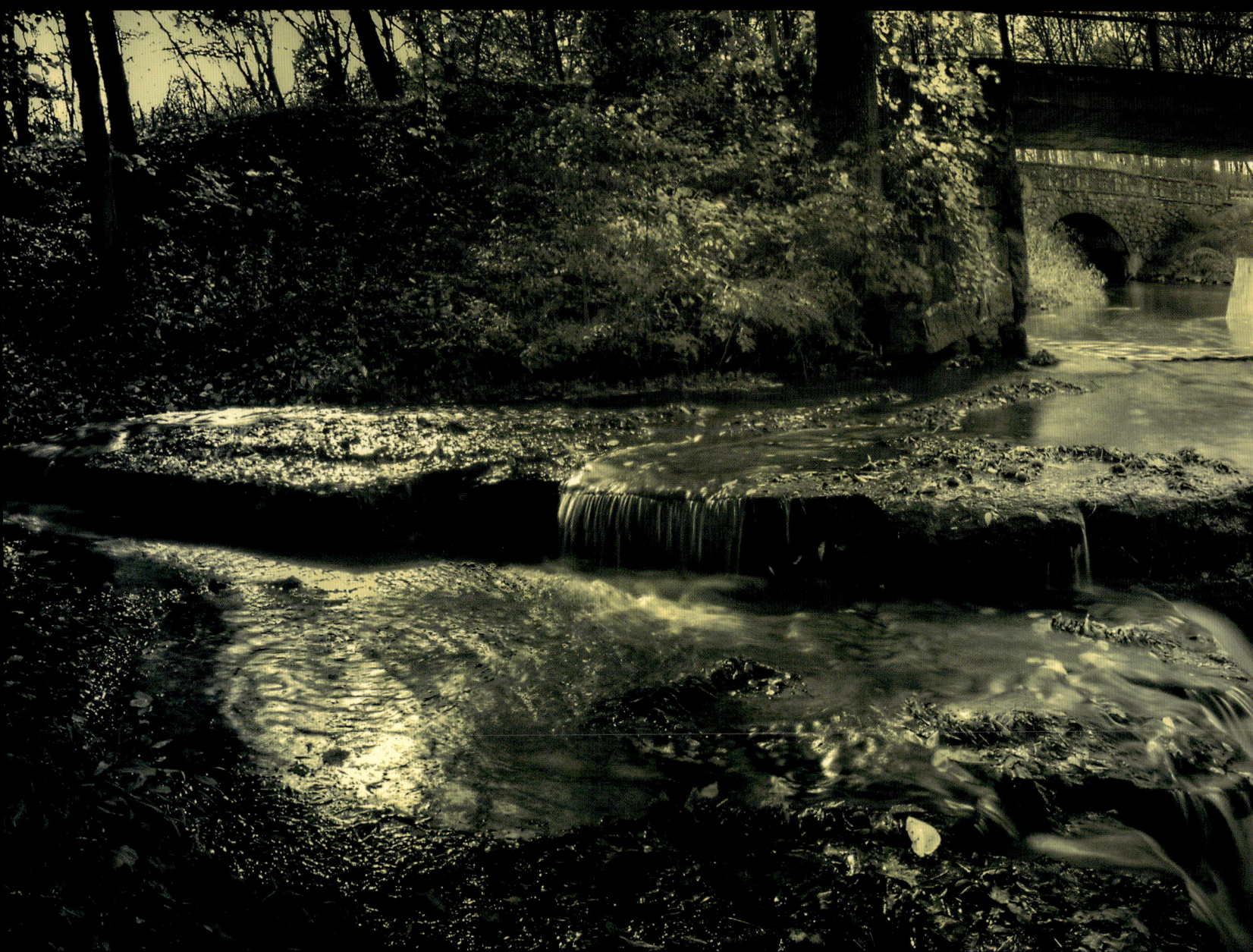

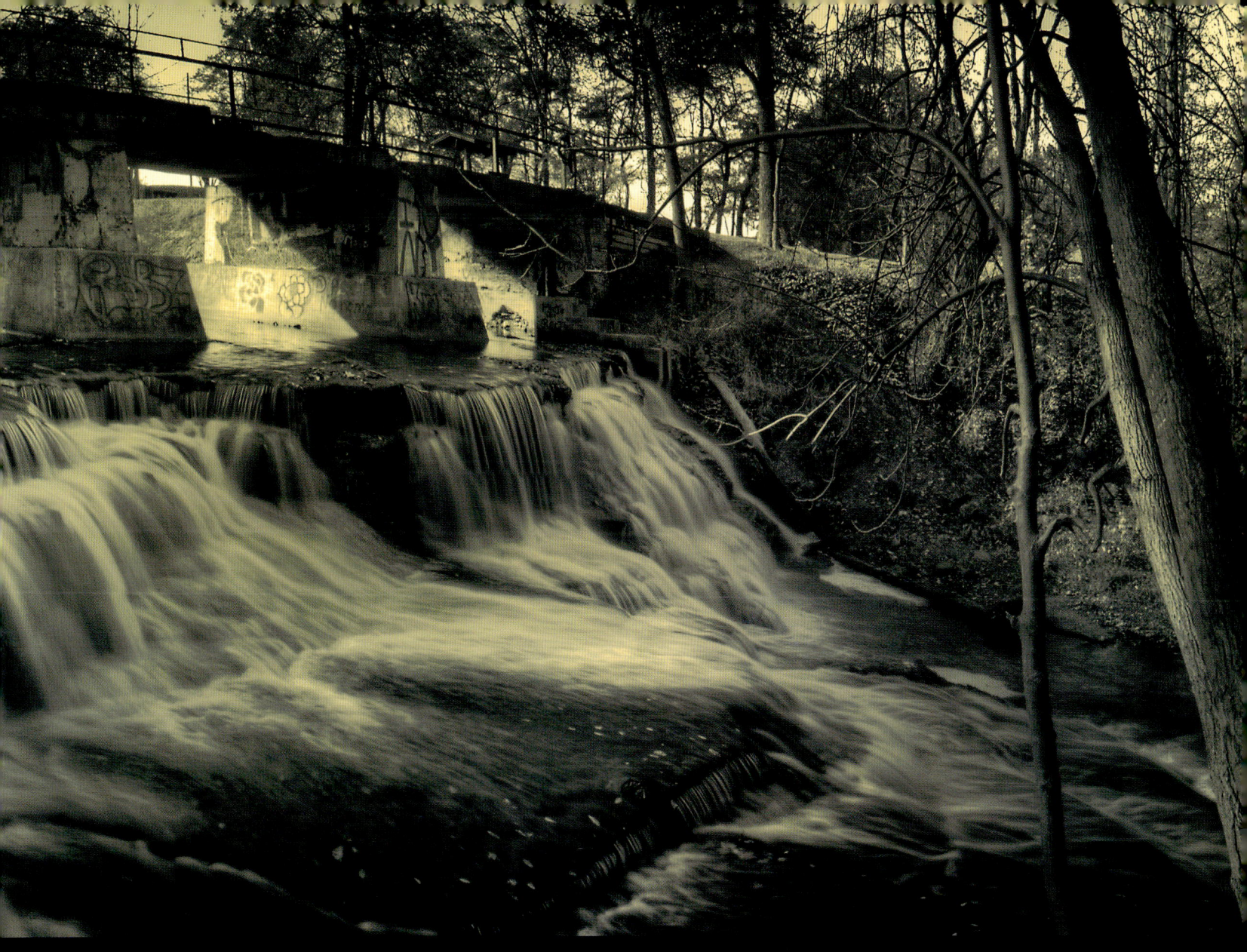

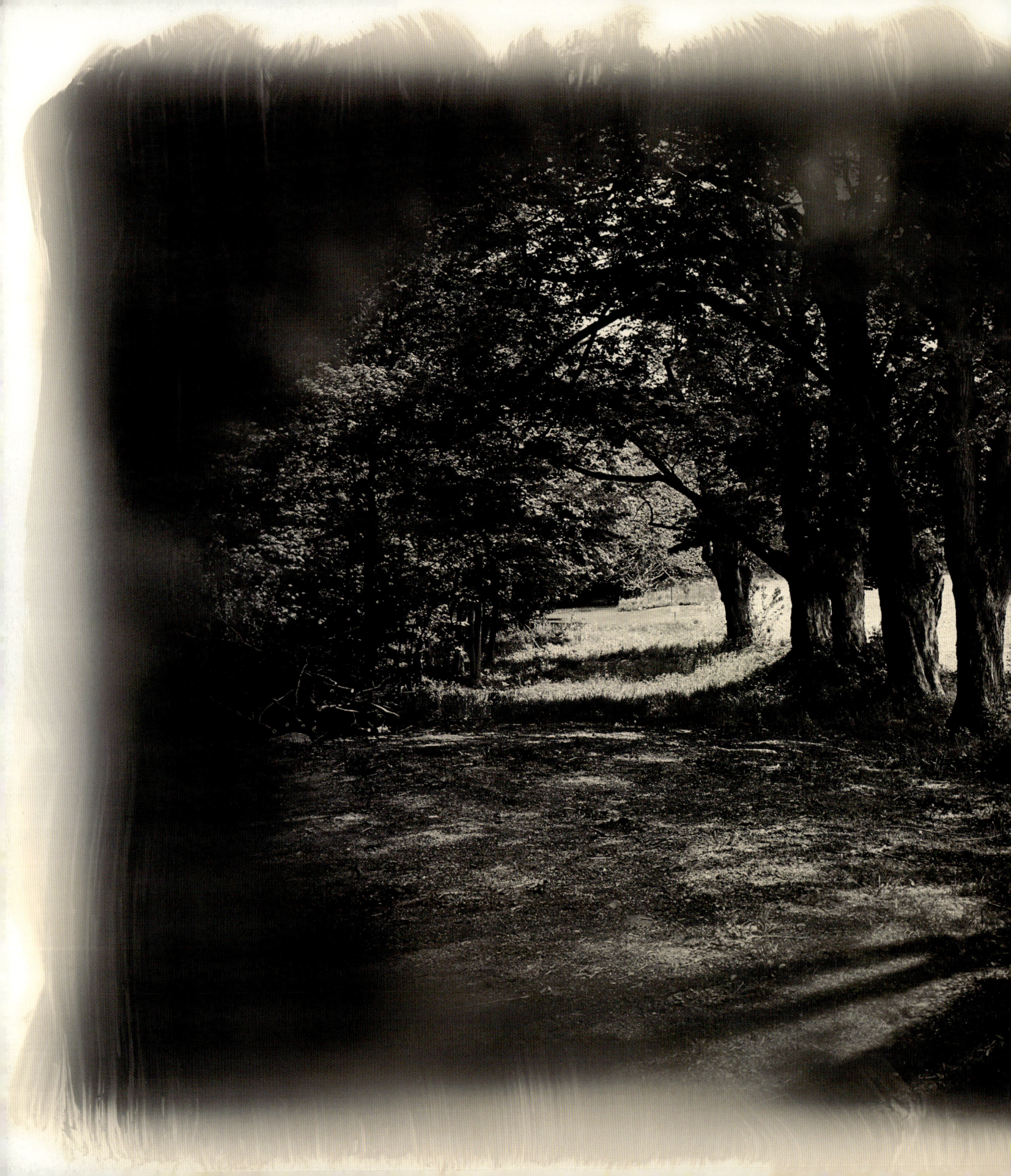

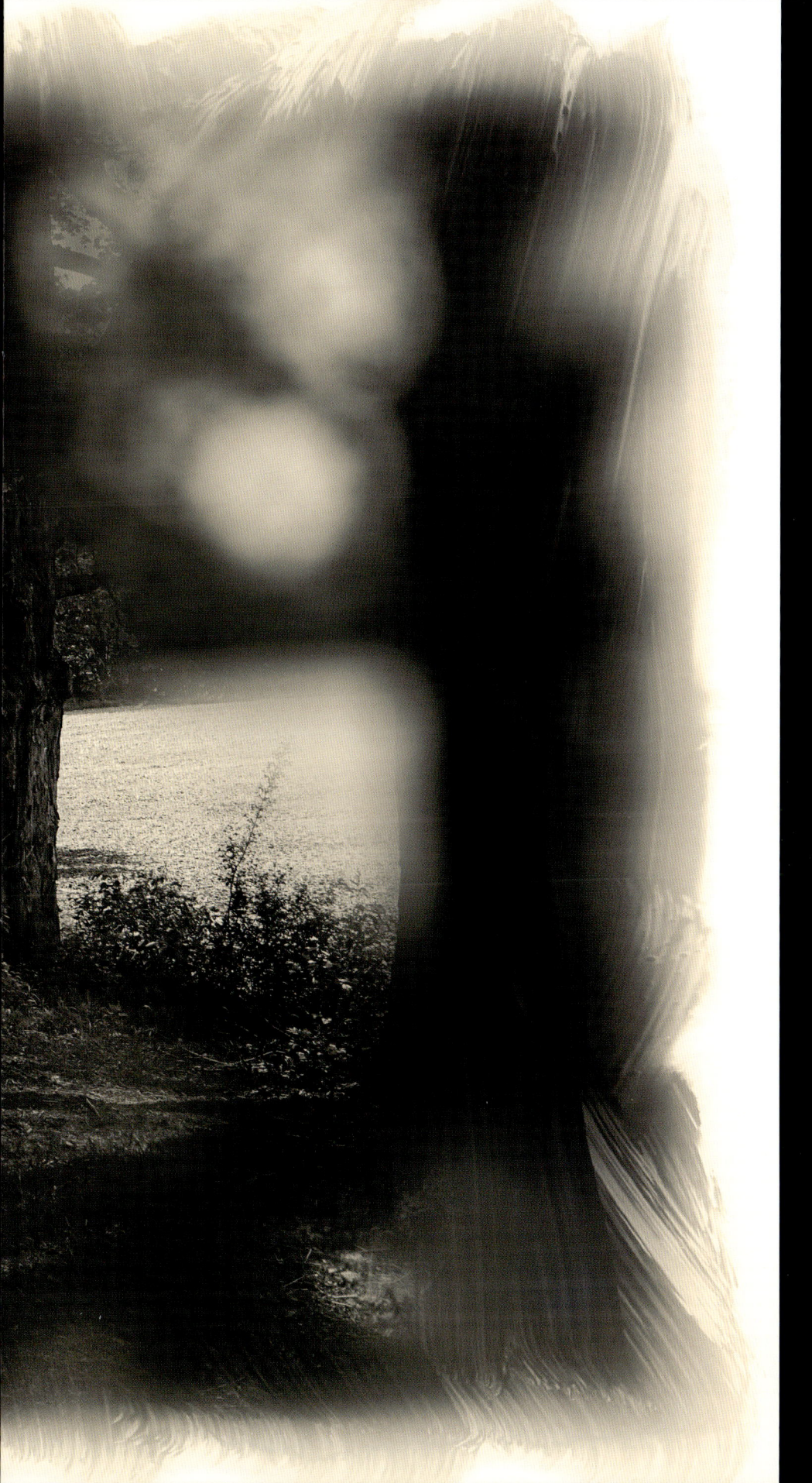

07 // SOFTWARE

Alien Skin Exposure X

Alien Skin's Exposure X now includes their Bokeh plugin. This addition allows for many more image manipulations within the same software. The images here have been processed through a number of programs such as Photoshop, Macphun's Aurora HDR, and Photoshop before receiving a bokeh treatment in Alien Skin Exposure X.

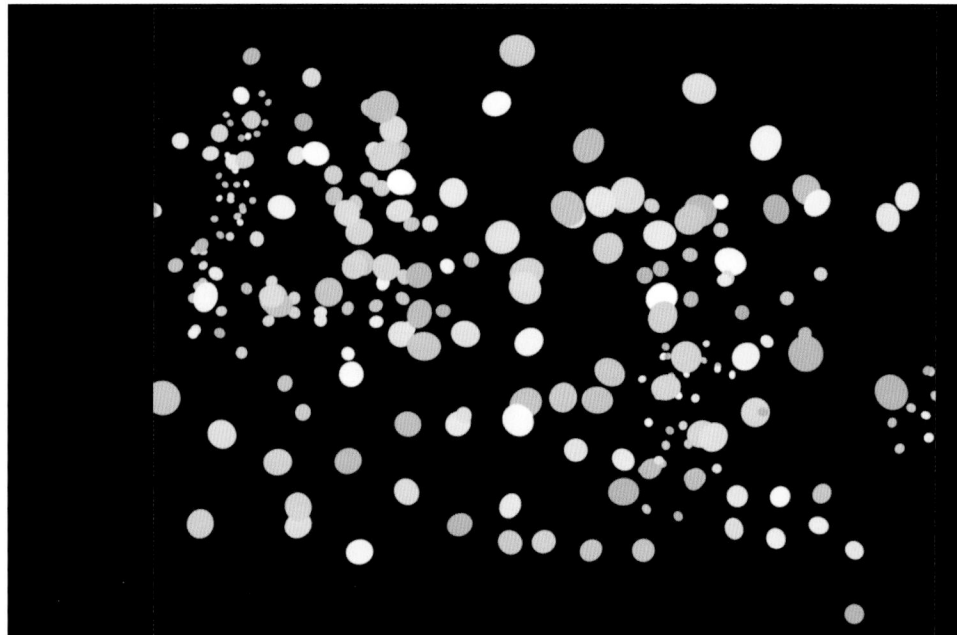

LEFT: *A series of random dots were painted in Photoshop using a random airbrush to create a base for an eventual Photoshop bokeh mask that will first be prepared using Exposure X.*

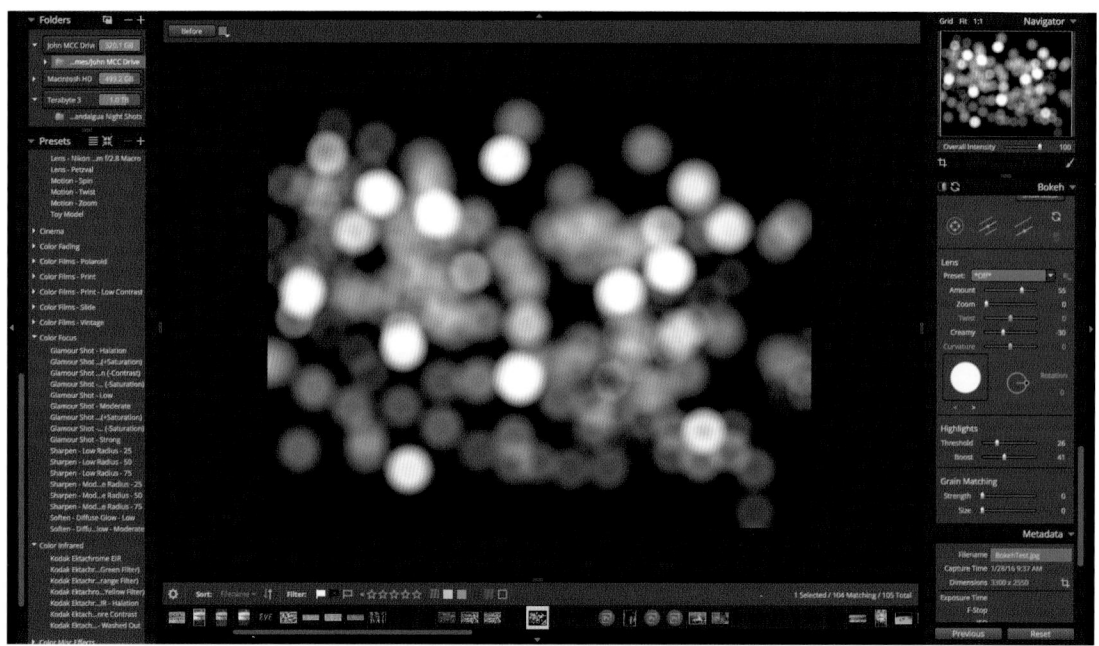

RIGHT: *Rather than subject the entire image to a soft bokeh effect, a brush was used to produce a random grouping of white and grey circles, which were blurred using Exposure V's Bokeh panel. The advantage for doing this is that it can be used as a layer mask to add a bokeh effect within Photoshop.*

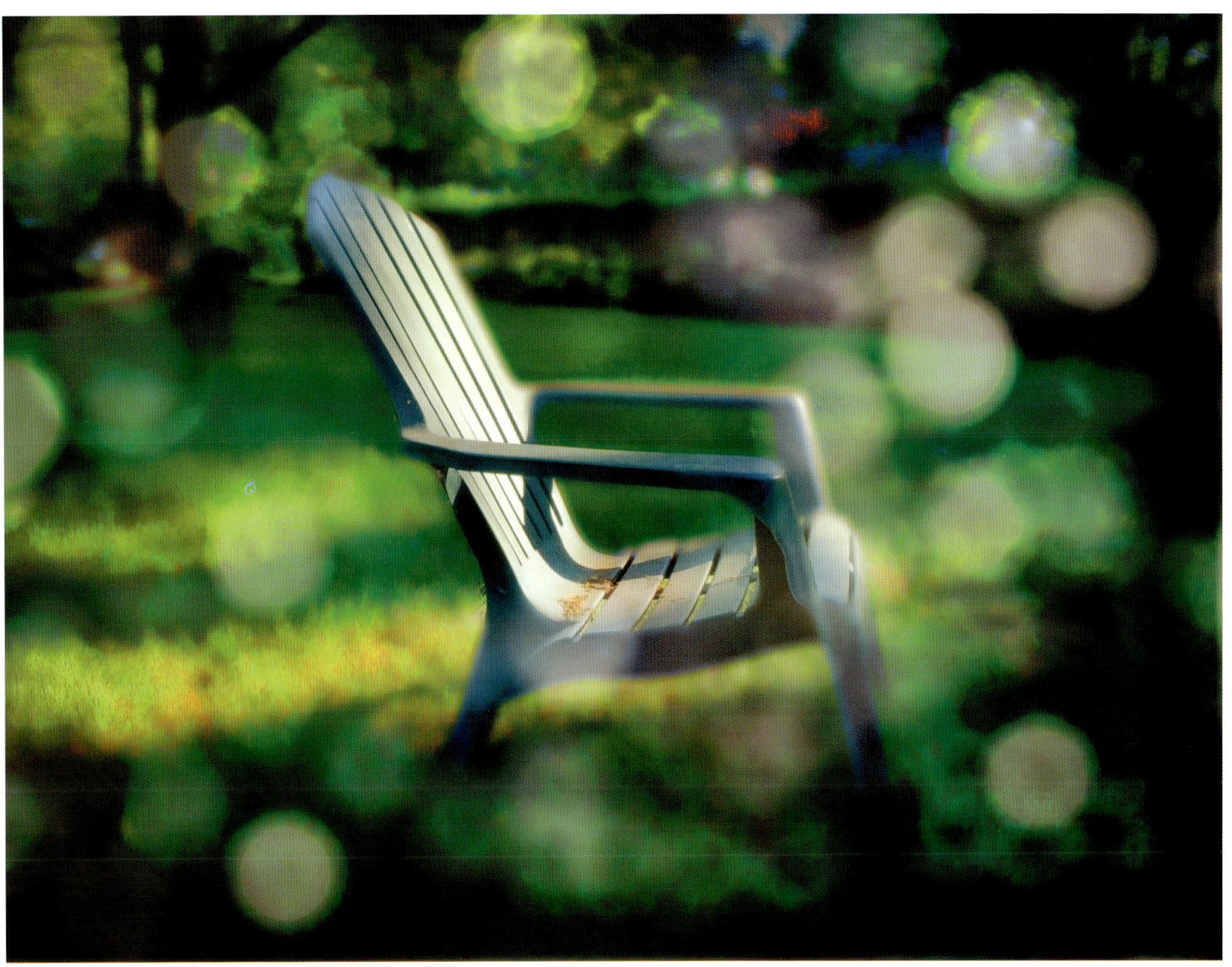

ABOVE: *Photoshop was the source for this Bokeh effect. However, to get a more natural look, the image was further processed in Exposure X.*

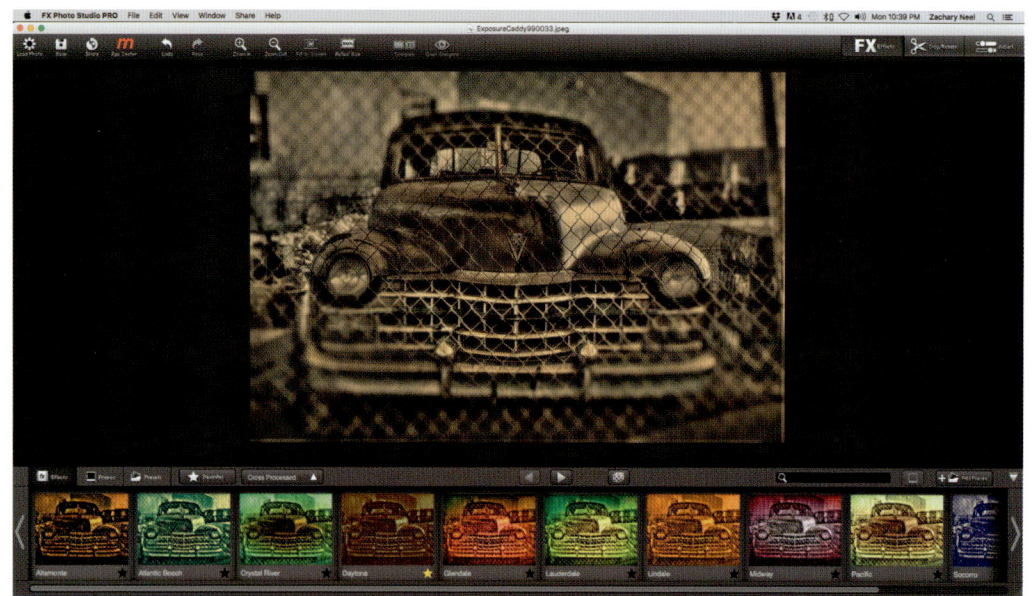

LEFT: *Alien Skin's Exposure X now includes their Bokeh plug-in. This addition allows for many more image manipulations within the same software. The image here has been processed through a number of programs such as Photoshop, Macphun's Aurora HDR, and Photoshop before receiving a bokeh treatment in Alien Skin Exposure X.*

BELOW: *Alien Skin Exposure X was used to create a soft bokeh effect around the interesting bumper of the old Cadillac.*

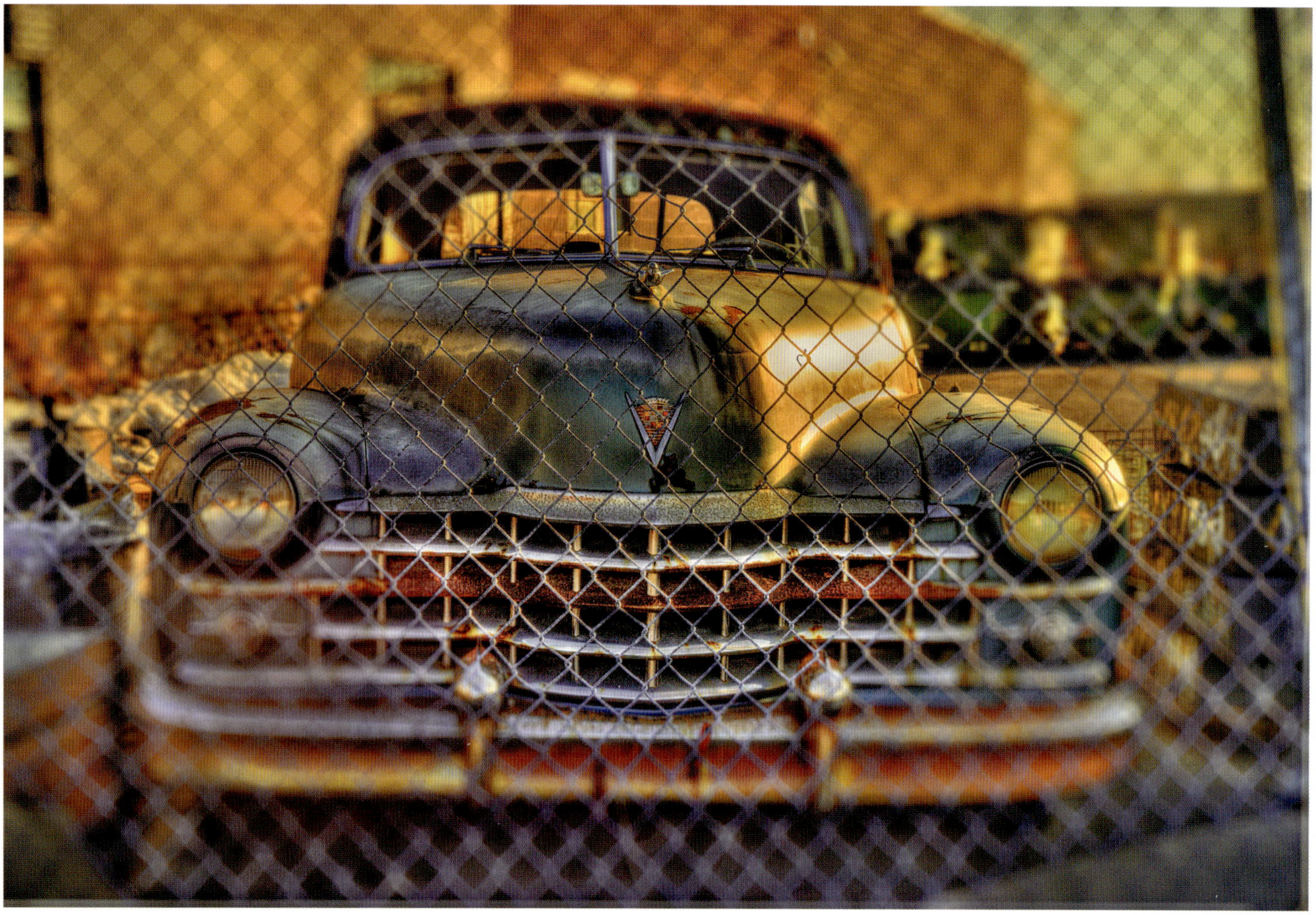

07 // ALIEN SKIN EXPOSURE X // SOFTWARE

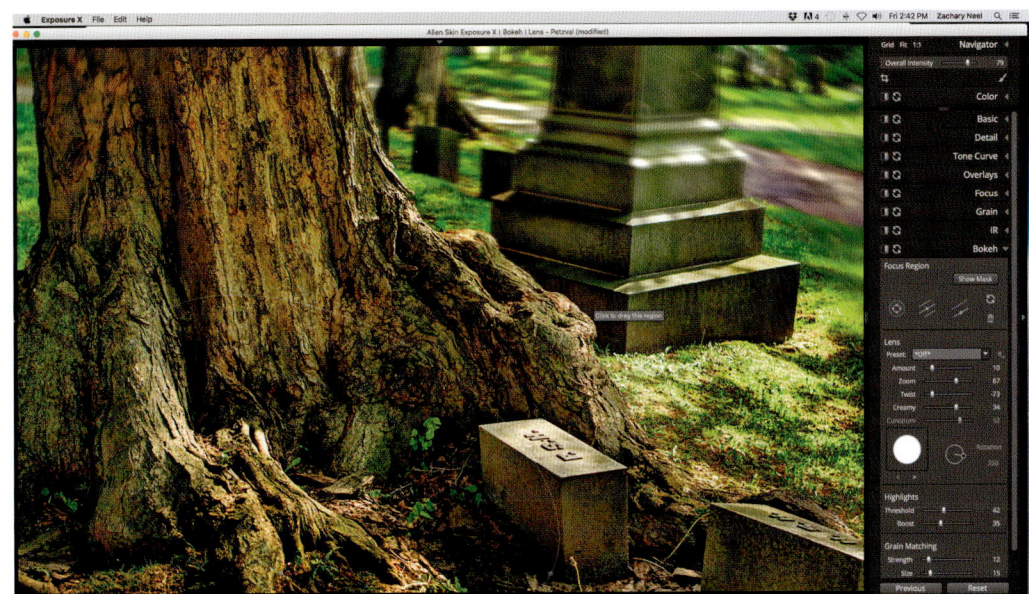

LEFT: *The Bokeh panel of Exposure X shows the sliders that control the bokeh parameters.*

BELOW: *A moderately light amount of the Bokeh effect was applied to the very near foreground as well as to the details behind the tree.*

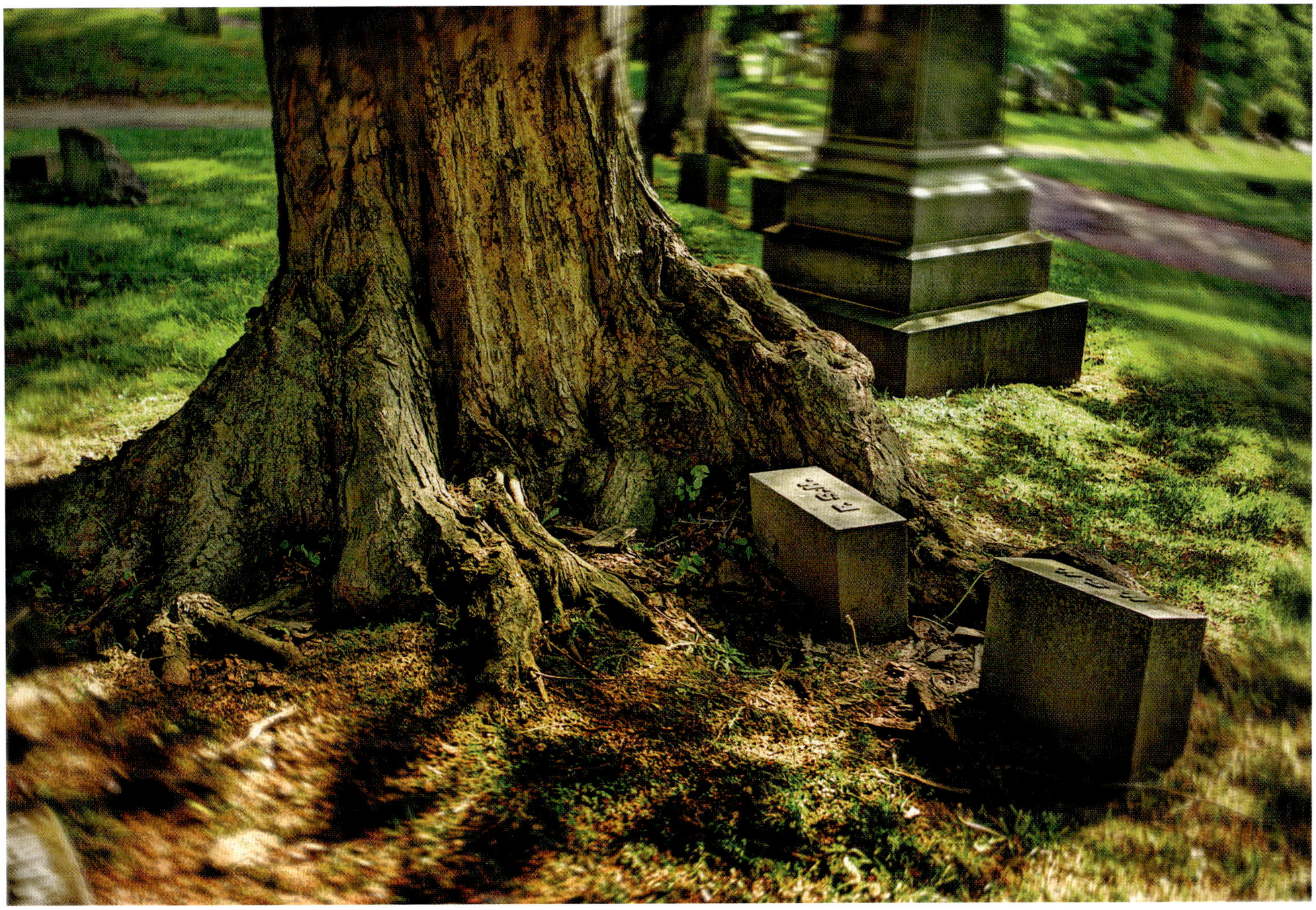

152 // 153

Tonality Pro & Intensify Pro

Intensify Pro and Tonality Pro are a great programs from Macphun Software. Their main function is to improve the image by adding either presets that alter the image contrast, saturation, sharpness or luminosity using various sliders. The software works as a plugin in Photoshop or as a standalone software package.

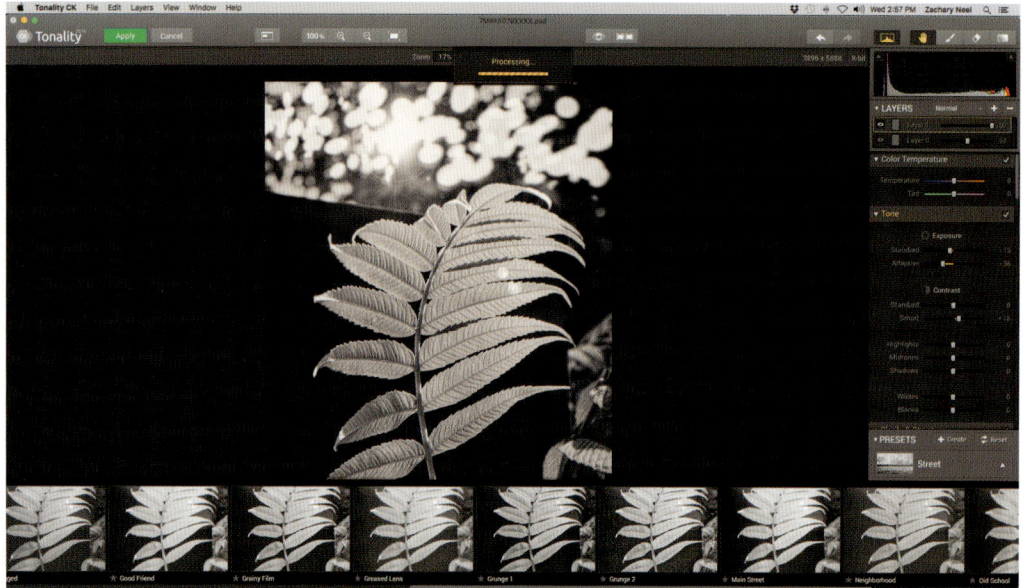

LEFT: *This fern image was created using Photoshop brushes and masks. It was later run through Macphun's Tonality Pro, which uses presets that can be applied at different densities using built in layers and brushes.*

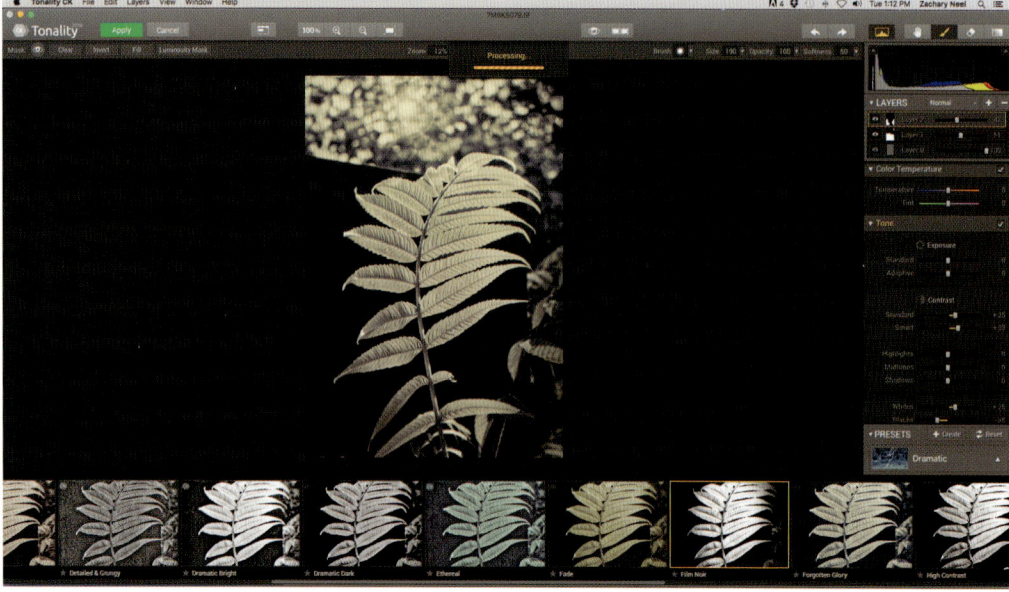

LEFT: *Tonality Pro can be useful for adding color tones and contrast to an image.*

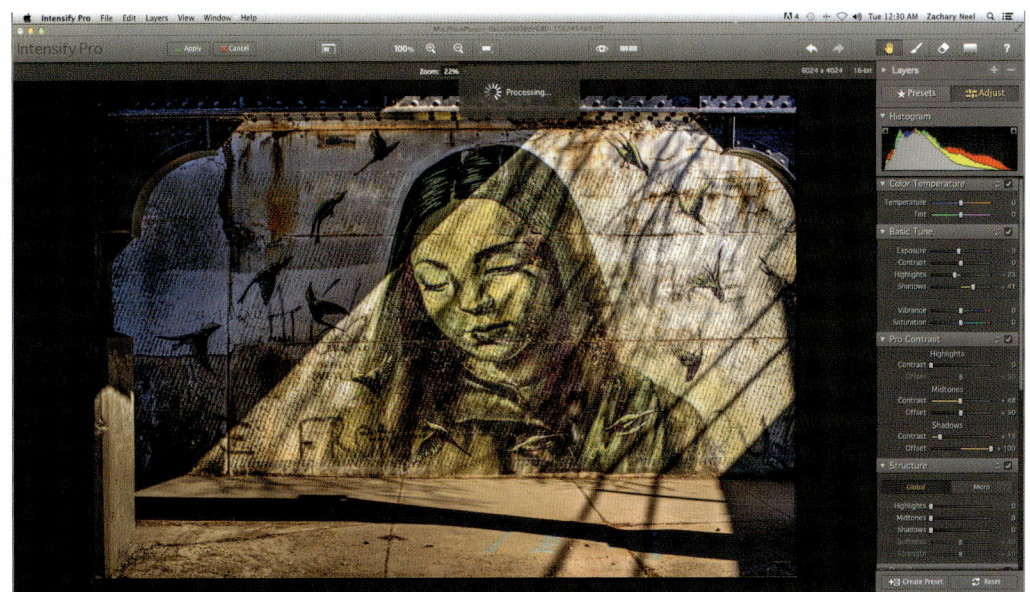

LEFT: *One of the things I've learned is that the entire image need not receive the full effect of the software. In fact in much of my work, the plug-in is only used where I need to modify the image for problems such as exposure, saturation, sharpness adjustments and when noise is present in a portion of the scene. The great thing about Macphun software is that most of the interfaces have layers and brushes that can be used to mask the results where you want them.*

BELOW: *This way, I can maintain all of the lens characteristics of sharpness and detail, while correcting the areas that might require further consideration. Rarely do I apply a single effect to the entire image. Instead, I selectively alter what I need to rework.*

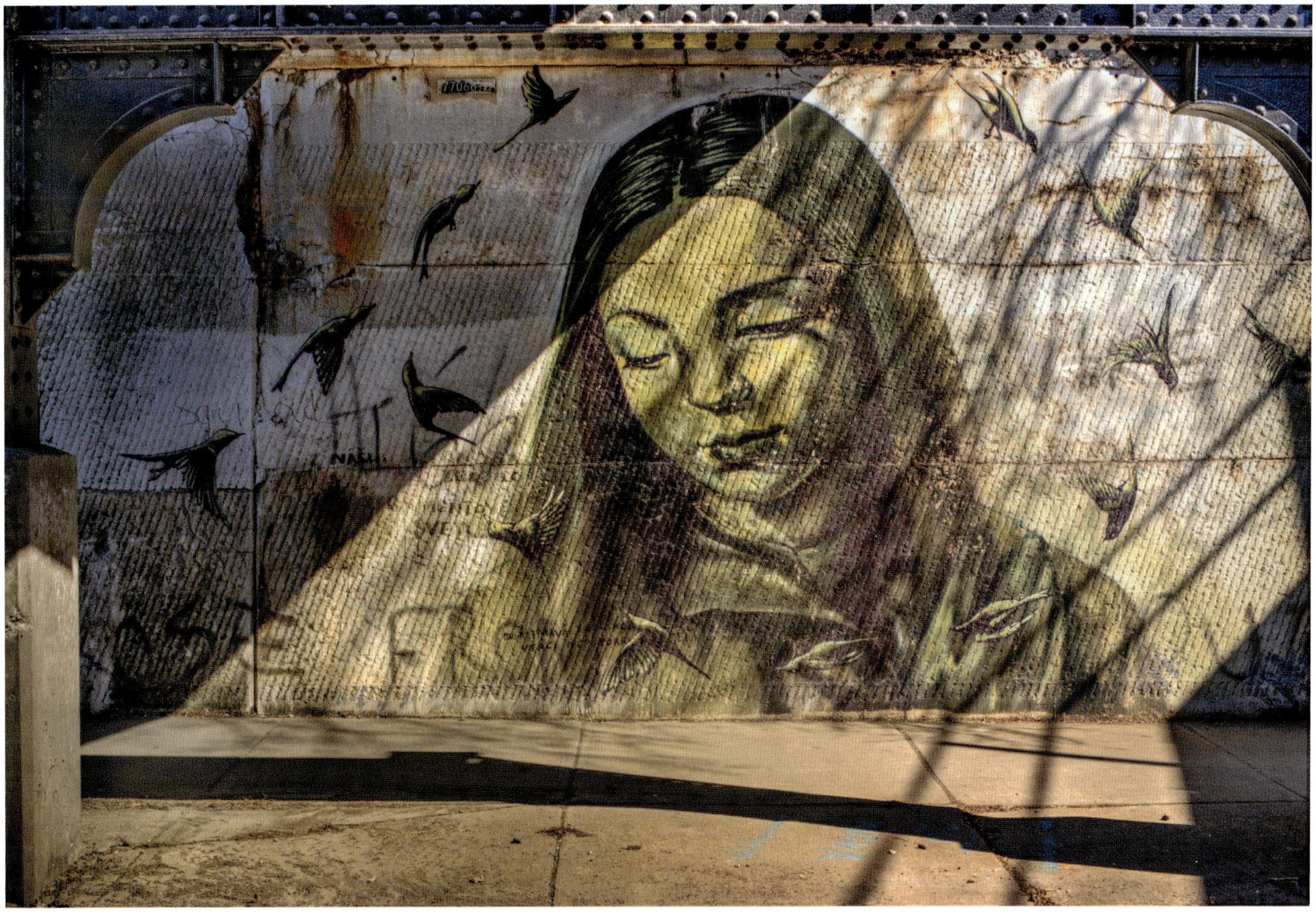

Noiseless

Noiseless is another very useful product of Macphun Software and works as both a standalone or as a plugin. Noiseless does pretty much what it says it will do: It does a great job of removing noise from images that have been subjected to long or underexposure, which often contains grainy-looking digital noise.

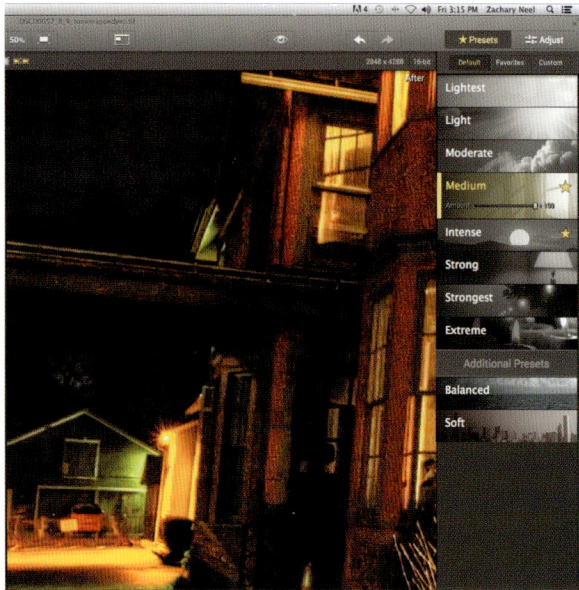

ABOVE: *Noiseless uses advanced noise reduction technology in order to remove both color and luminance noise from affected images. The program contains a large selection of presets that can be individually selected and modified to the taste of the user. The range of presets can tackle noise that would otherwise be out of range of most other software such as Photoshop. Even light noise is in my opinion best tackled with this kind of software.*

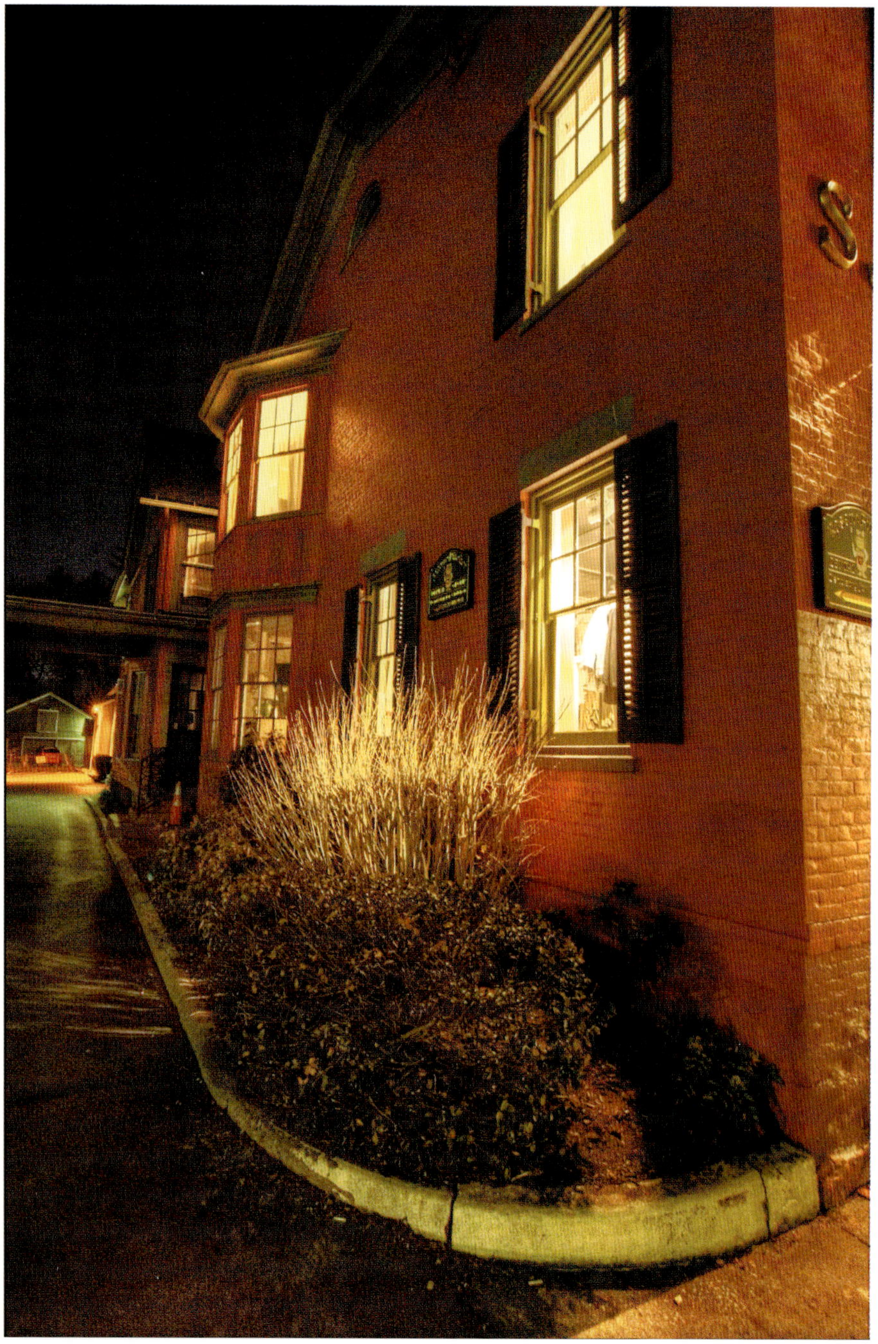

RIGHT: *Over the years of working with plug-ins such as Noiseless, I've learned to use the software usually within Photoshop to produce the effect on a single layer. This allows me to add the effect into the original layer as necessary.*

07 // NOISELESS // SOFTWARE

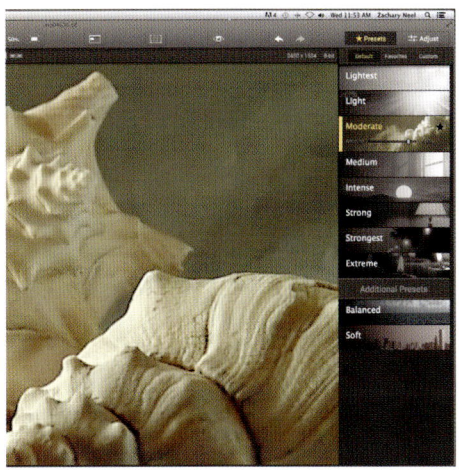 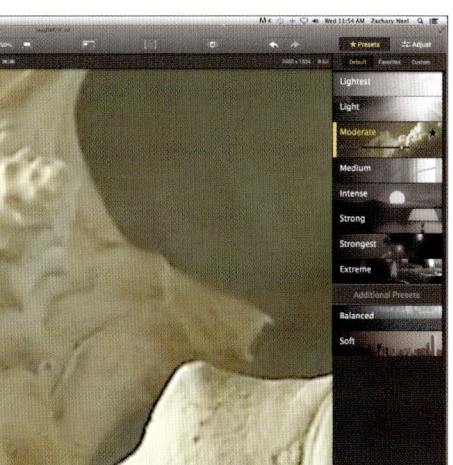 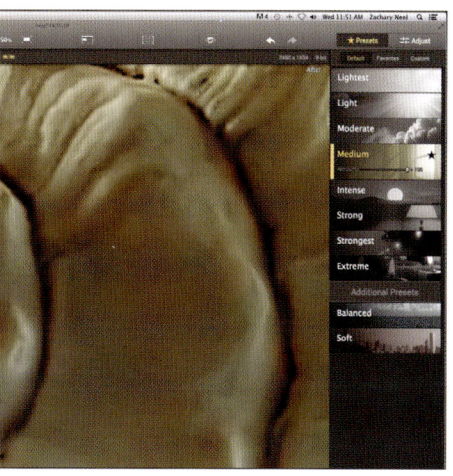

ABOVE ROW: *The original file contained some noise in the shadows. Noiseless was used to virtually eliminate the granular structure, producing a very acceptable result.*

BELOW: *Digital noise is not a good thing to have in any image. However, when it occurs, it can be remedied as long as it is not too severe.*

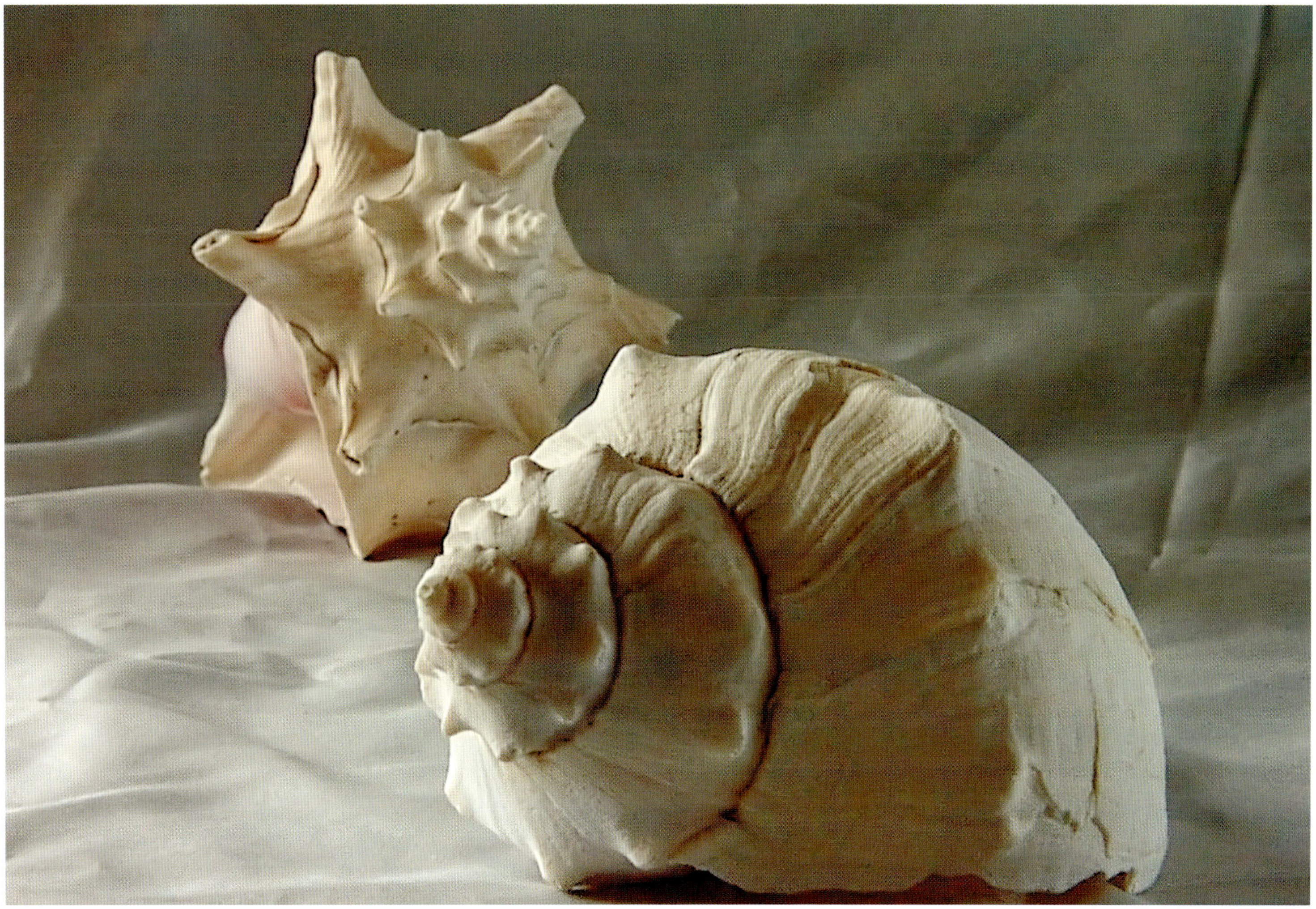

Piccure+

One of my favorite new pieces of software is Piccure+. This software was designed to improve upon the look of a lens to make the image appear to have been shot with much higher end glass. That means that it attempts to produce a higher degree of sharpness throughout the entire image. The software claims to improve the image sharpness by correcting aberrations, increasing sharpness, and fixing camera shake. I've been using this program for a while and have been extremely impressed with the results it can produce.

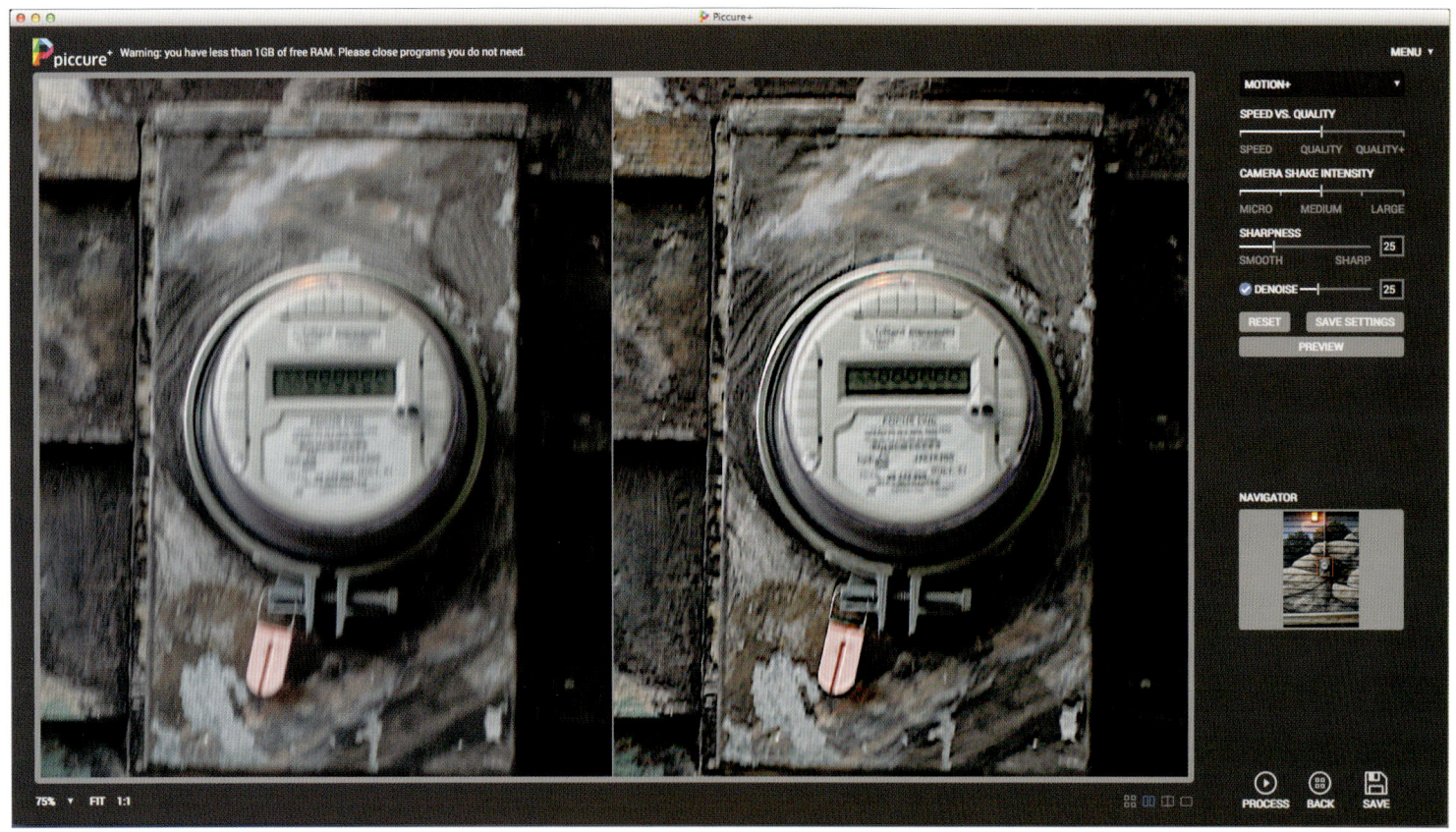

ABOVE: *The best way to appreciate Piccure+ is to see the before and after results as side-by-side comparisons. The image on the right has been sharpened. Shot in low light handheld, the image showed some movement had occurred while shooting. Piccure+ was used to correct the motion to a point that made the image much more acceptable – making the result printable to a large size.*

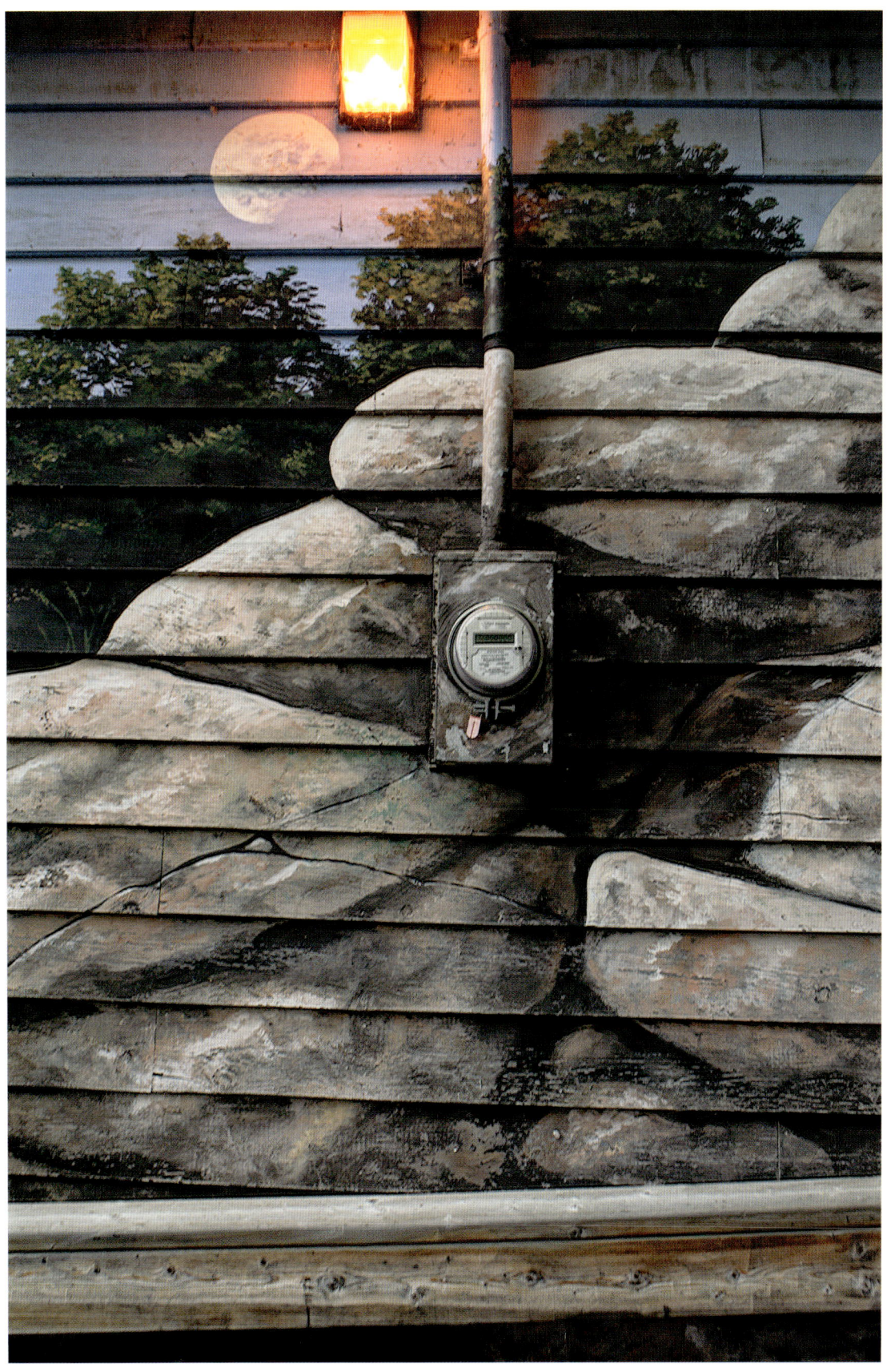

LEFT: *This is the final image after running Piccure+ using both the motion and sharpening tools separately. I first ran the motion part of the program and then I added the sharpening. Piccure+ runs as either a standalone program or as a plug-in in Photoshop. I prefer to use the plug-in version as it can be used to enhance a layer, which can then be layer blended with other Photoshop layers.*

Photoshop Bokeh Effects

Photoshop was created for artistically skilled image-makers for the purpose of creating almost any kind of visual effect. Not only can it be used to enhance image color or contrast, it is also a paint program.

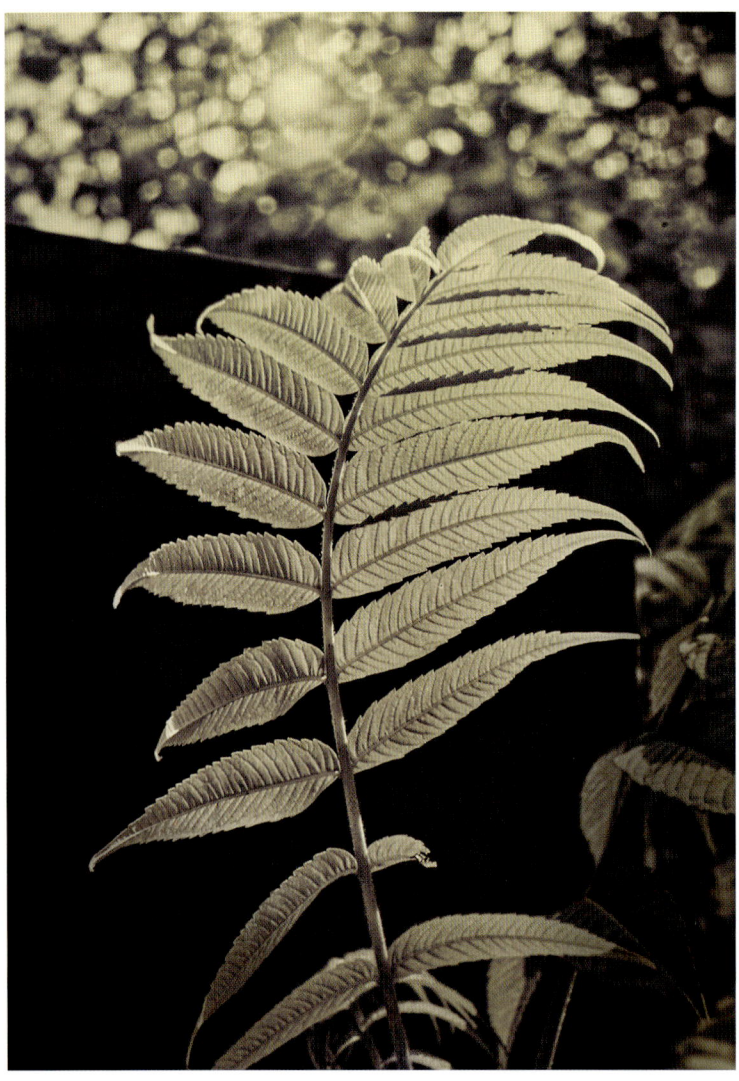

ABOVE: *The Bokeh simulation at the top of his image was created using a scatter brush in Photoshop.*

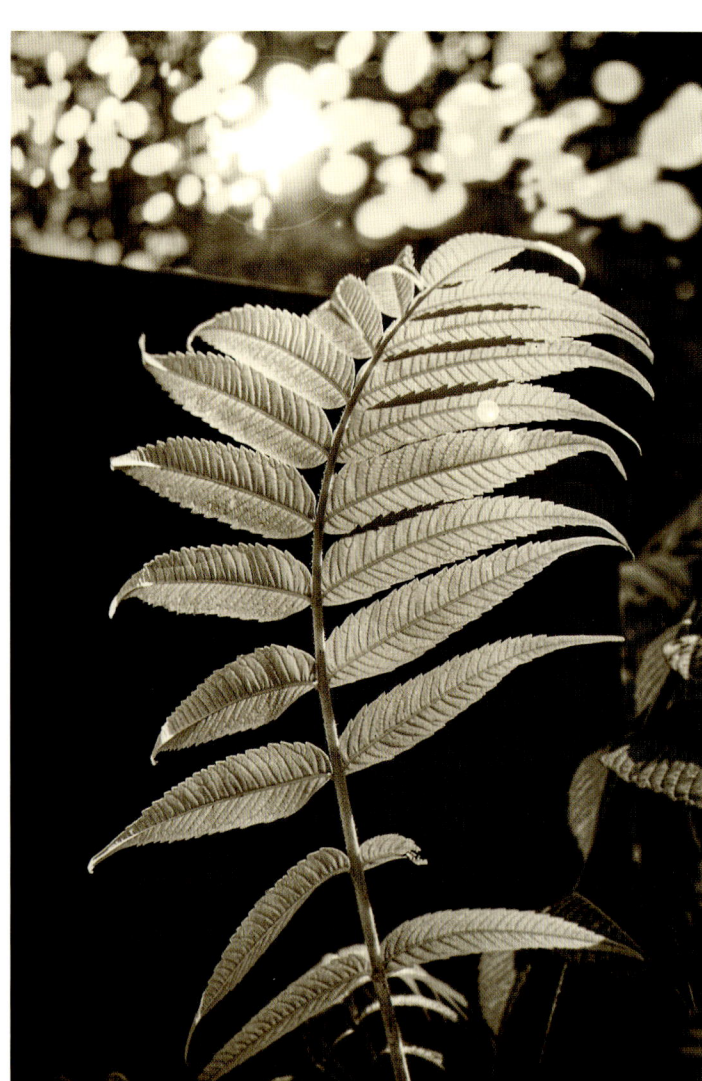

ABOVE: *The Bokeh at the top of his image was created using a scatter brush in Photoshop. Both this and the last versions also have simulated flare produced with the Lens Flare filter in Photoshop.*

07 // PHOTOSHOP BOKEH EFFECTS // SOFTWARE

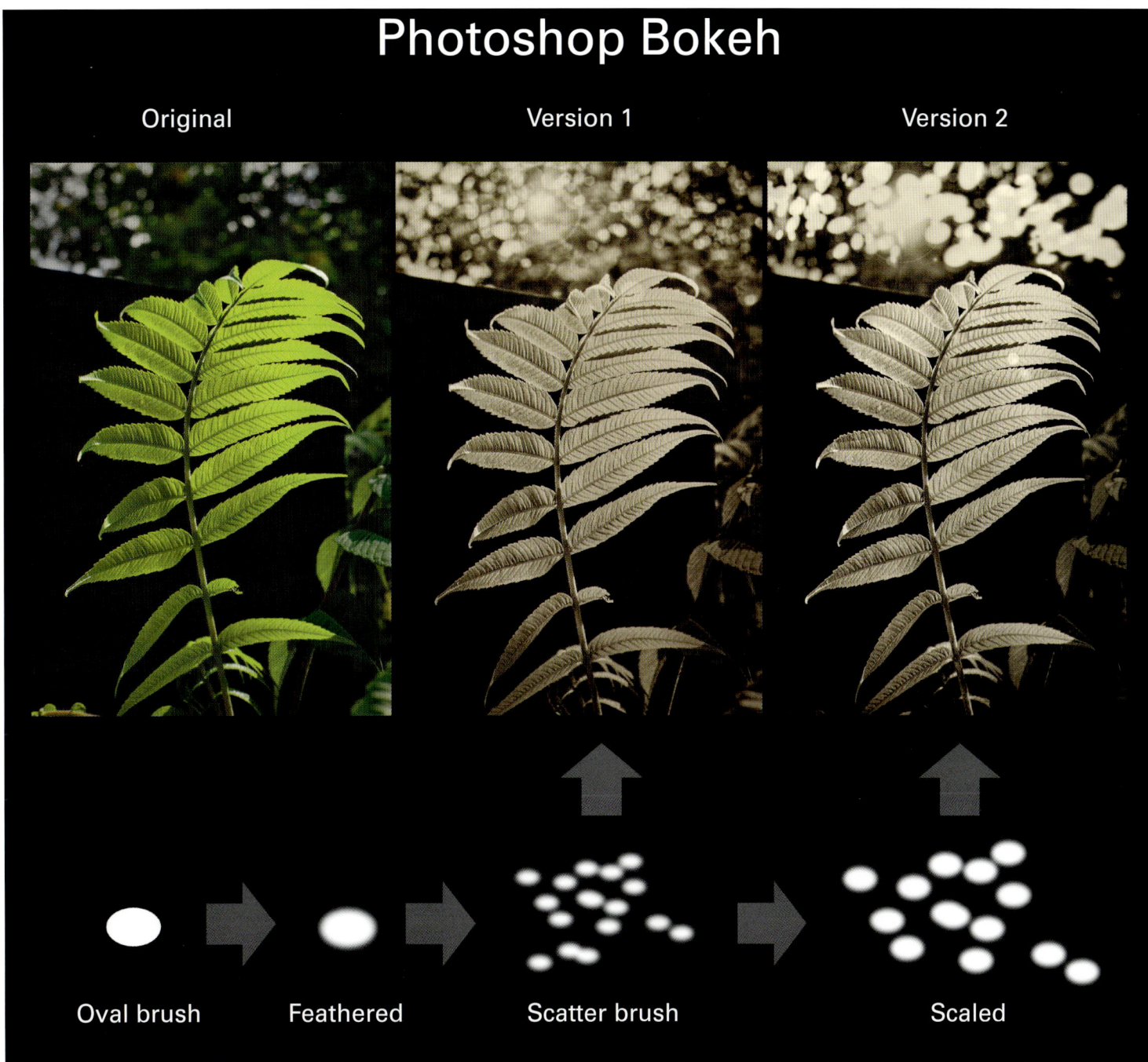

ABOVE: *To create additional Bokeh in this image, an oval shaped brush was created and softened using a blur. The brush was modified using shape dynamics, scattering as well as scale and rotation, which was brushed into the area at the top. The main difference between versions 1 and 2 is the scale of the brush used.*

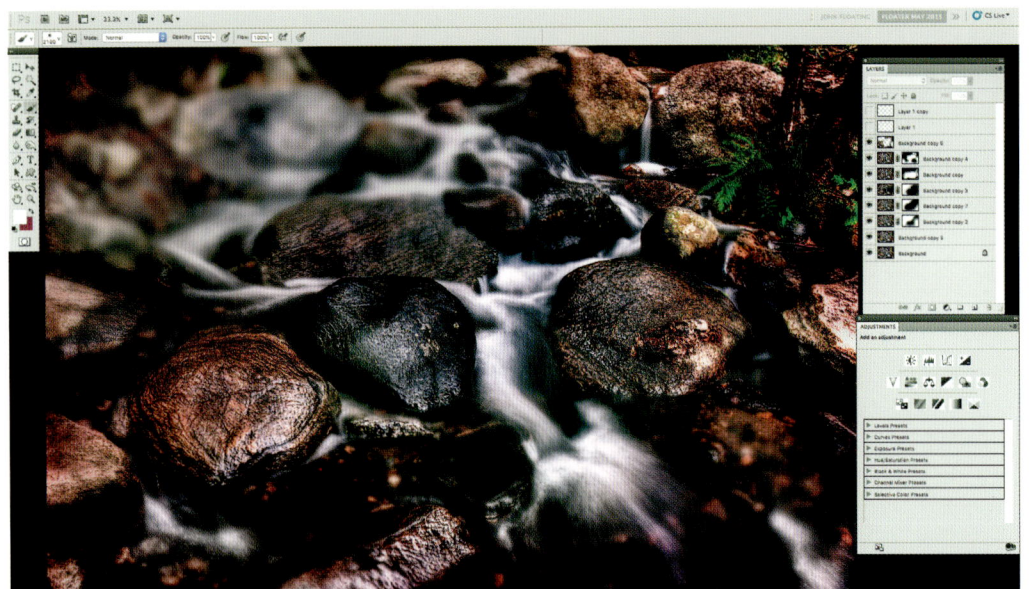

LEFT: *Creating a convincing tilt focus effect in Photoshop, involves a series of masks and blend layers. The idea is to soften the focus gradually.*

BELOW: *Created with gradations and brushed masking, Photoshop was the only tool used to produce the out of focus results in this stream. The results resemble some of the lens effects discussed in this book. In the case of this image, the DOF in the original image was such that the rocks and details were sharp from the foreground to background.*

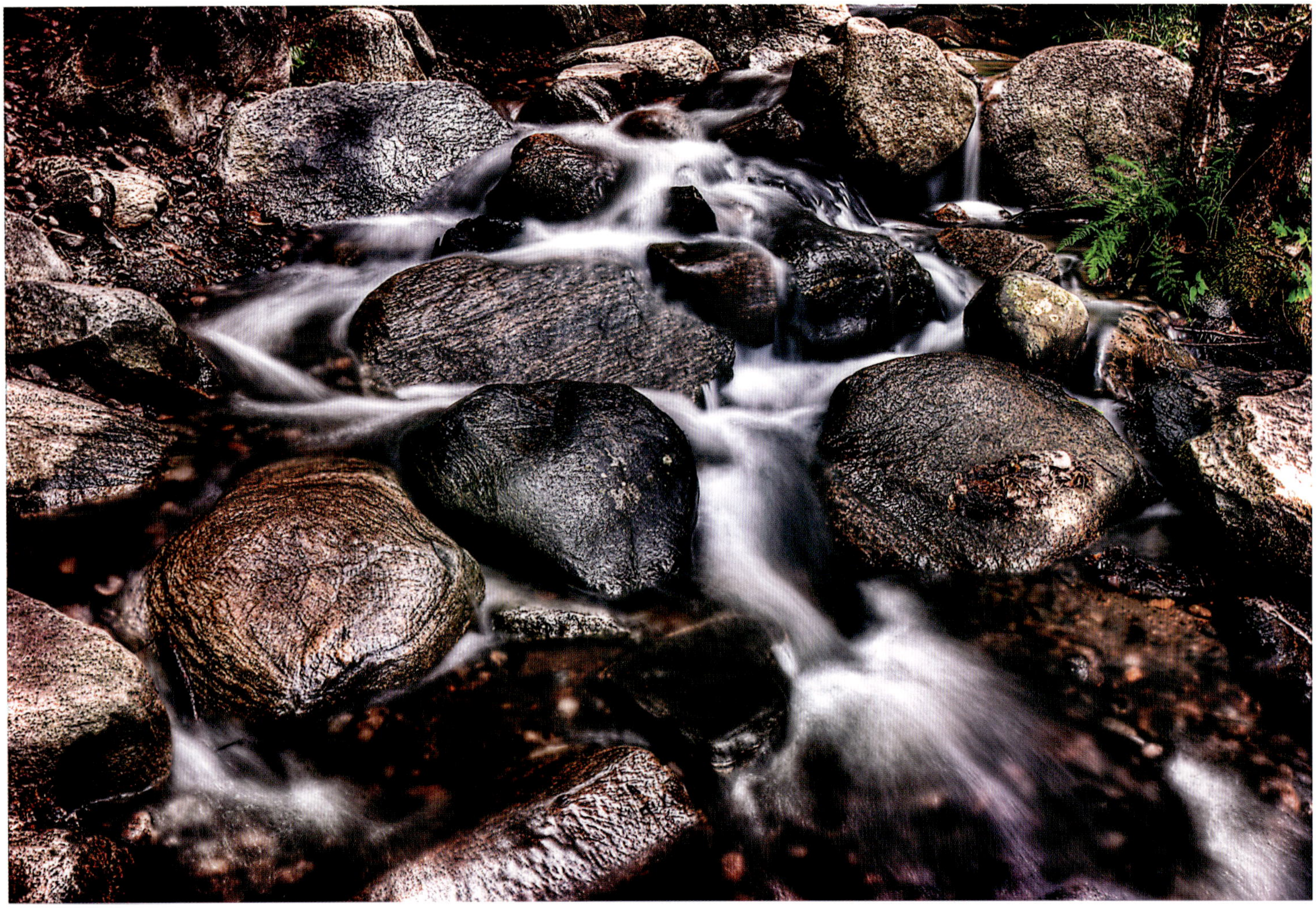

07 // PHOTOSHOP BOKEH EFFECTS // SOFTWARE

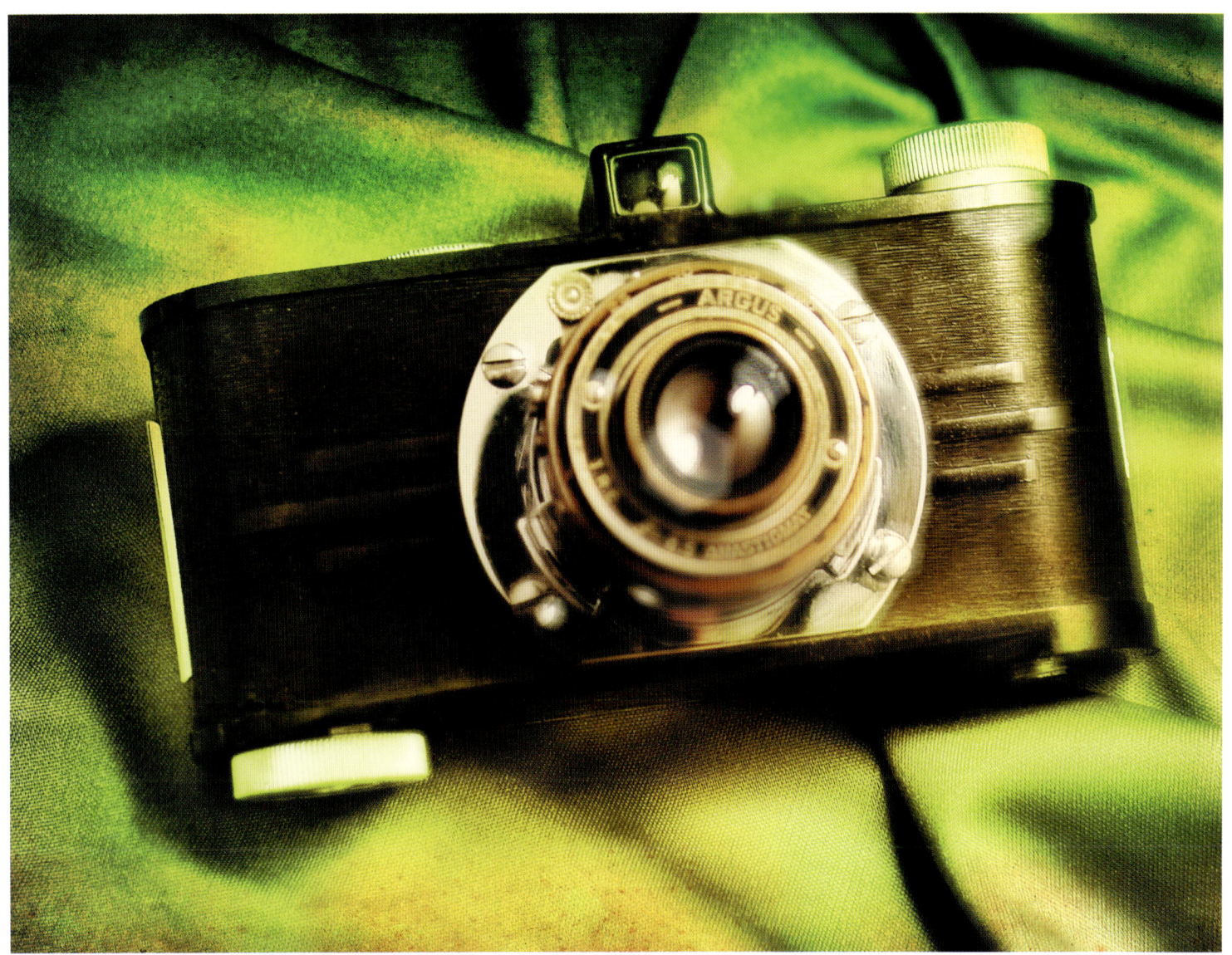

ABOVE: *A hexagonal shaped brush was used to create the lens flare on this old Argus camera. The out of focus areas were produced with gradation layer masks. Both effects were created in Photoshop.*

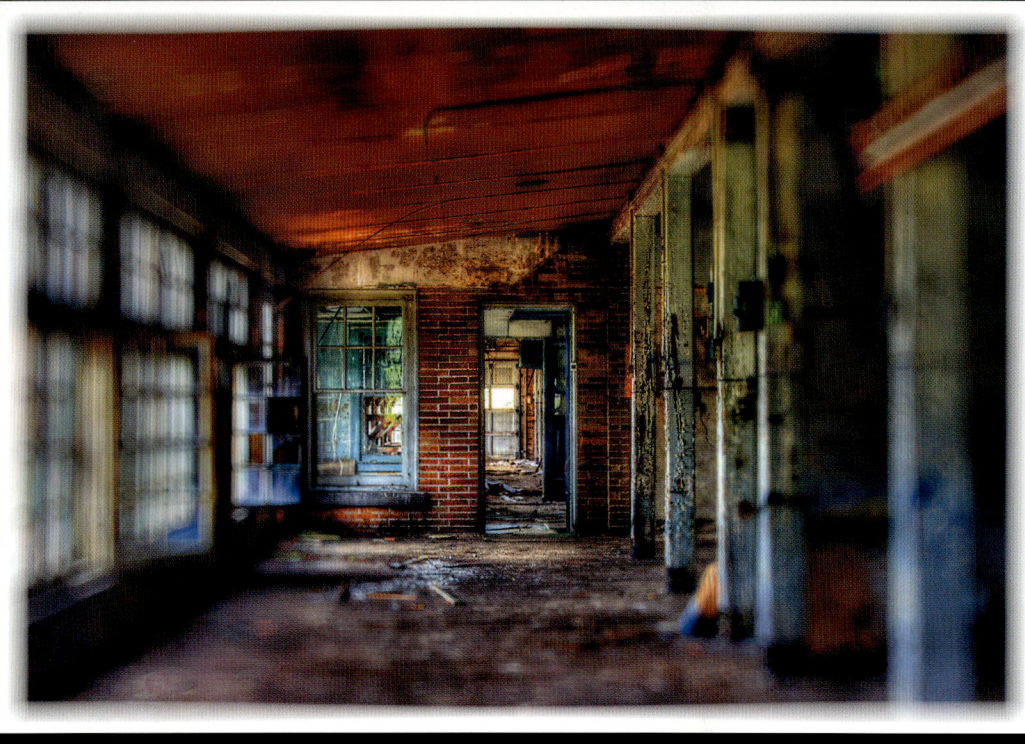

LEFT: *Made from a single Exposure X preset after the image was first processed as an HDR using Photomatics Pro.*

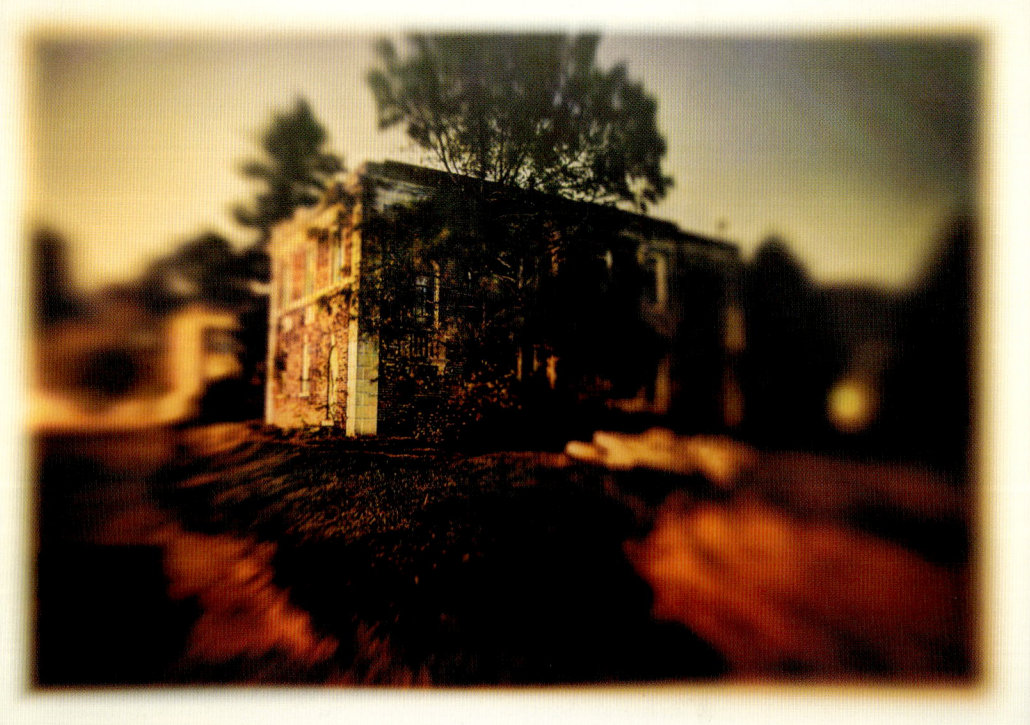

LEFT: *Toy camera, reversed lens, and dreamlike results can be created easily using the Bokeh presets found in Exposure X. Though the same software can also be used to create distinctively new focus effects.*

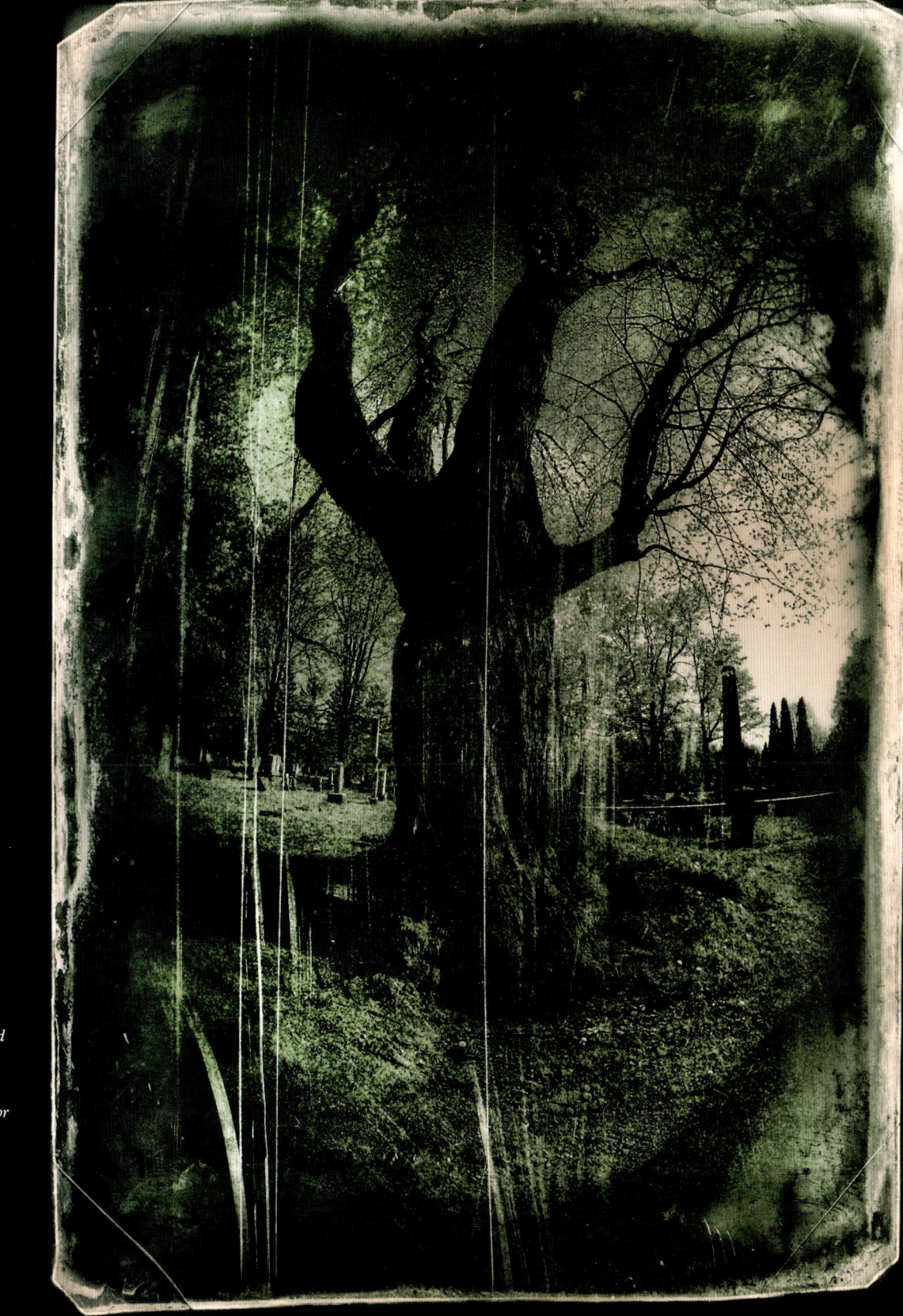

RIGHT: *Exposure X Bokeh was used along with some preset overlays to create a worn and scratched appearance common to that of an old daguerreotype. The resemblance to a real Dag is not currently possible as the original process produced a mirror effect that was actually a negative image that, when held at the right angle to the light, became a positive. Strictly speaking, the simulation that is possible with software only represents an image that might be printed from a daguerreotype reproduction.*

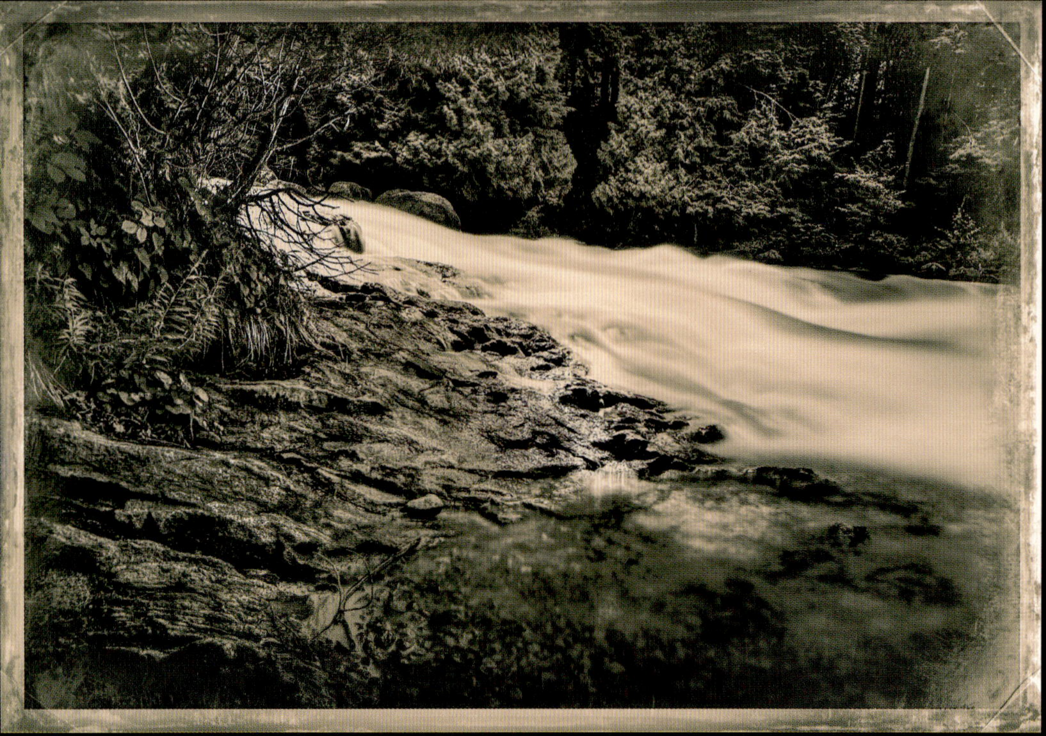

LEFT: *A built-in Exposure X preset was all that was used to create the look of an very old and worn-looking photographic result.*

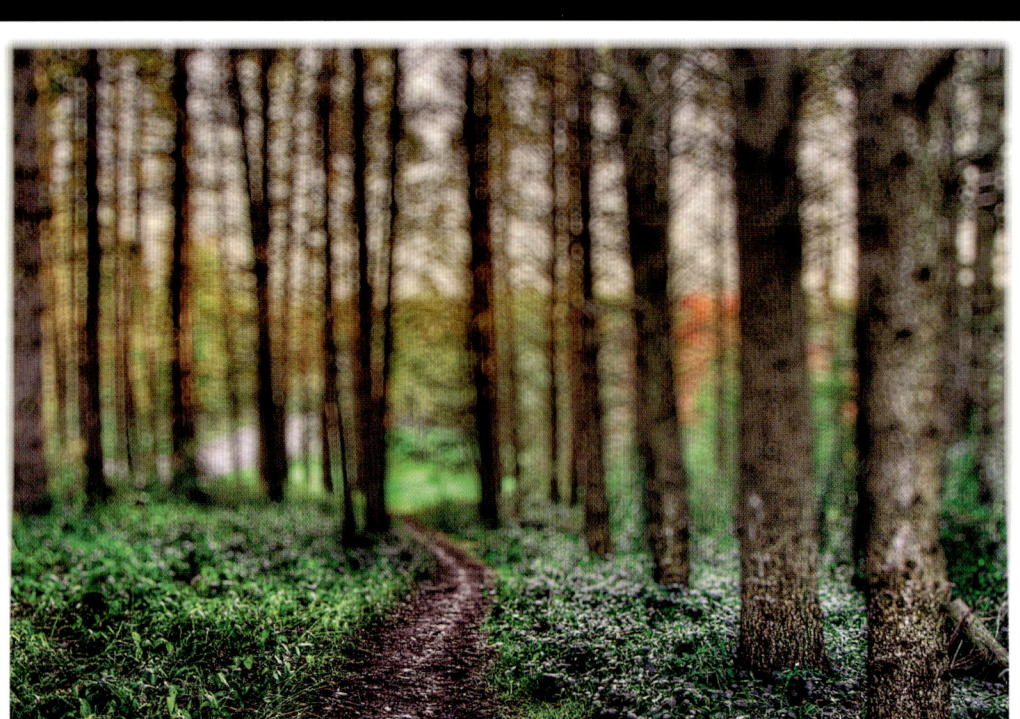

LEFT: *The Bokeh Panel in Exposure X has a number of built in settings that are meant to produce the effects of particular lenses. This one simulates a Nikkor 50mm at f/1.8.*

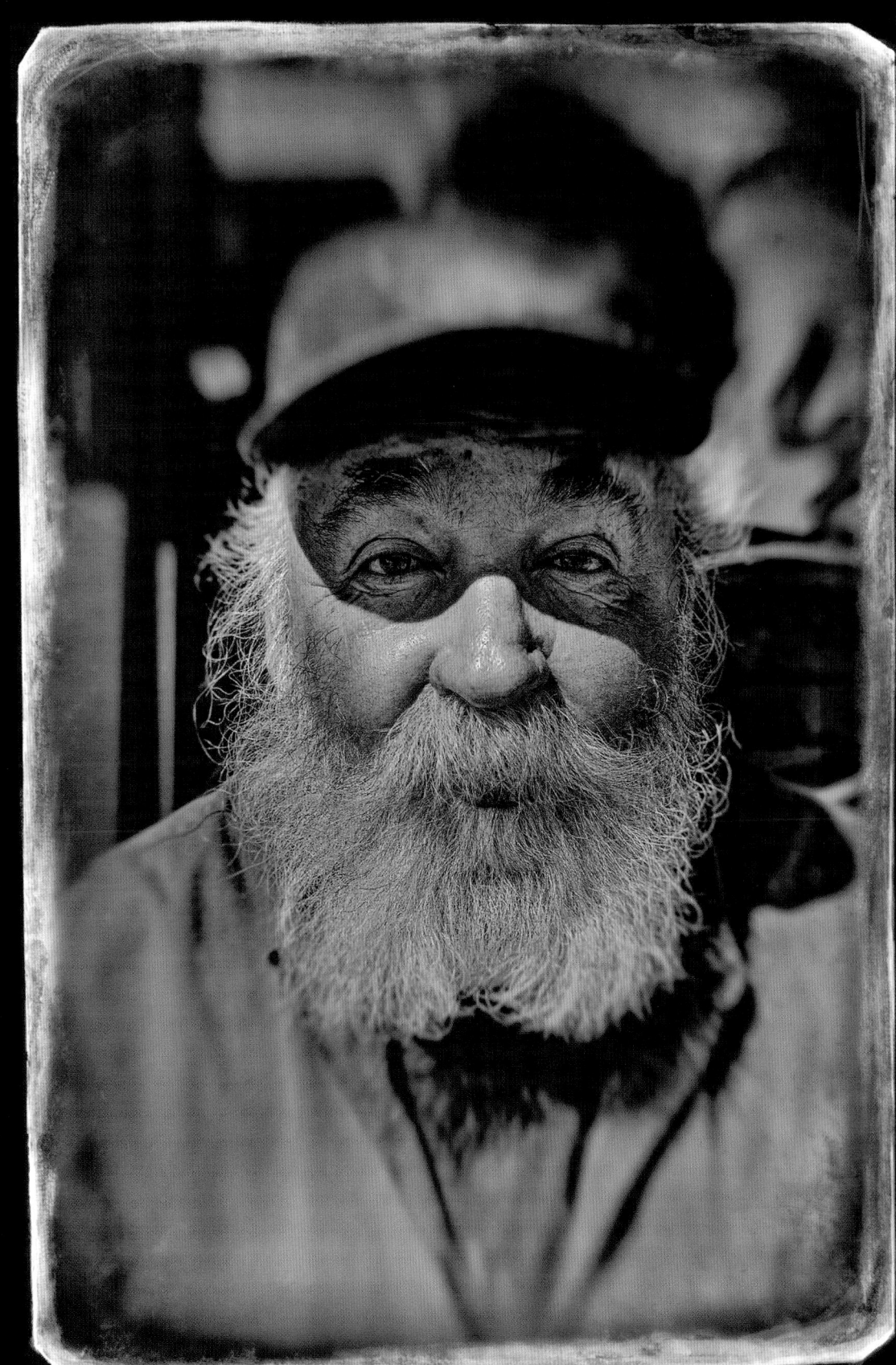

RIGHT: *Another Exposure X preset was used to create this modern portrait that resembles a wet plate. Like most old processes, original Wet-plate images have a distinctive appearance caused by the result of the process.*

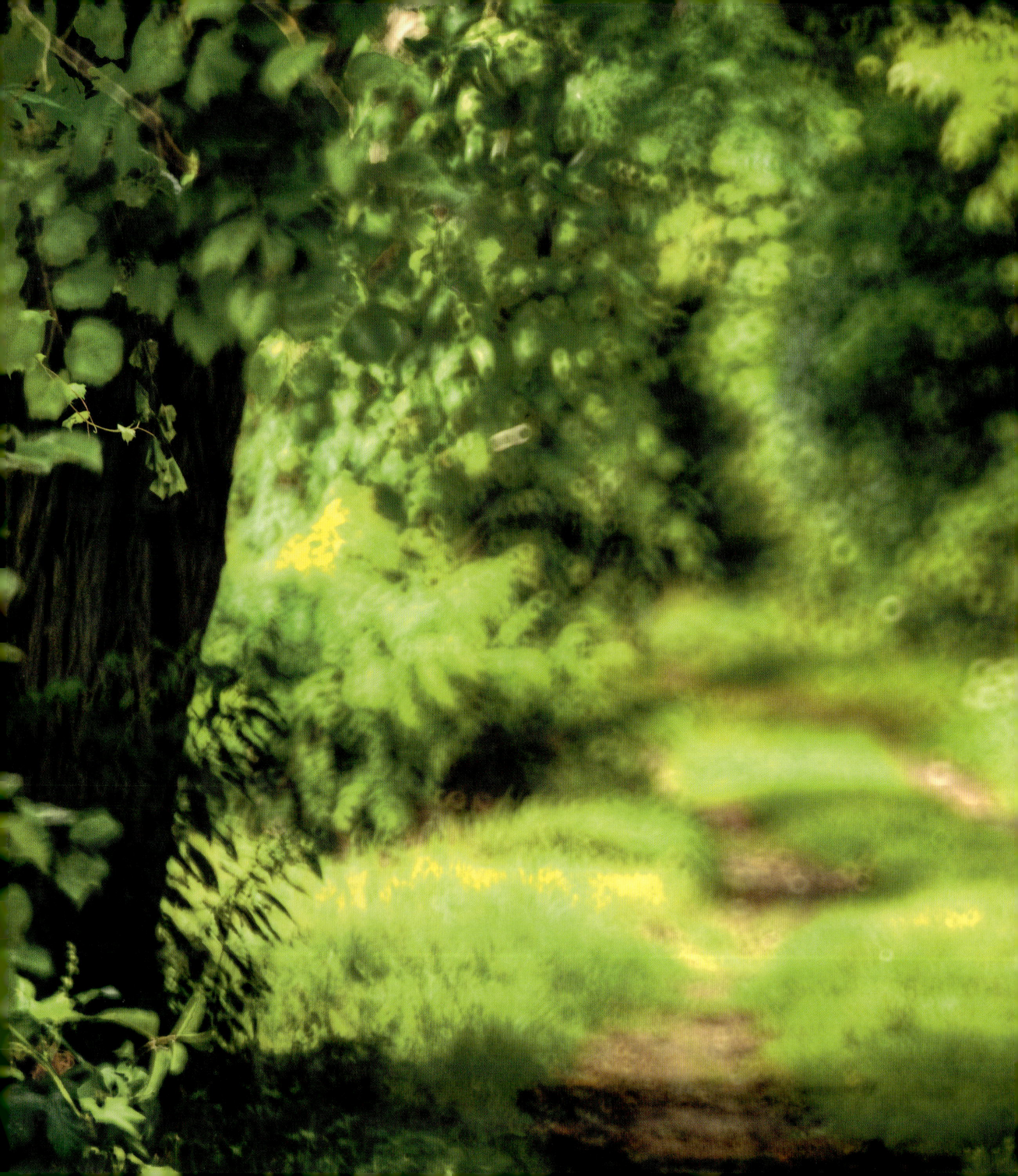

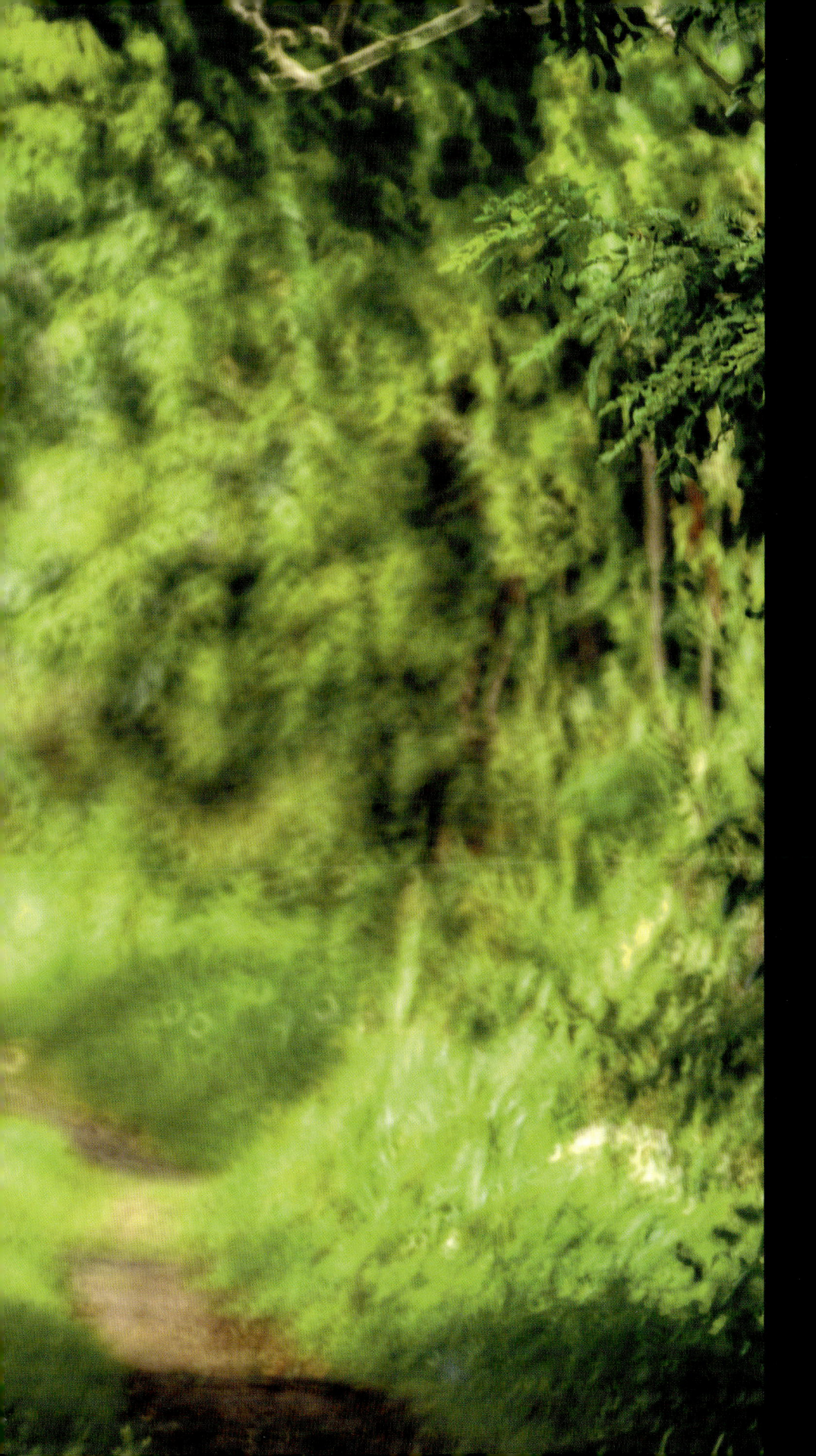

08 // APPENDICES

Glossary

angle of view The area of a scene that a lens "sees," determined by a combination of the focal length of the lens and the film format. It is conventionally measured in degrees across the diagonal of the film format.

aperture The opening behind the camera lens through which the imaging light passes en route to the film plane. Usually described using f-numbers: the larger the f-number, the smaller the opening.

astigmatism Aberration where off-axis points are smeared in either the radial or tangential directions. It is only possible to focus one—focusing tangential elements will cause greater smearing of the radial. This aberration is not identical to astigmatism in the human eye.

blooming Optical term for the process of applying an anti-reflective coating to camera lenses (and other optical equipment). Such lenses are then said to be bloomed.

catadioptric lens A lens in which reflective elements and lens elements feature. Typical designs feature mirror lens design along with a supplementary lens (usually at the aperture) that corrects aberrations in the prime mirror. The Schmidt design, for example, uses a simple (and cheap) spherical mirror coupled with a lens of complex form to remove spherical aberrations from the mirror. Maksutov lenses use a concave lens for similar effect. The optical alignment and construction tends to make for a more delicate lens system; such lenses may not be so resilient to rough handling. The use of catadioptric lenses, like mirror lenses, is often betrayed on an image by the presence of a doughnut-shaped highlight, an artefact of the annular mirror. Though obvious, this can be used to creative effect.

circle of confusion Illuminated area when a lens images a point source of light. Parts of the image can be incorrectly focused leading to overlapping circles of confusion and a blurred result.

close-up lens A subsidiary lens fitted to the filter ring of a conventional lens to enable close-up shots to be taken at a distance less than that which the lens alone would allow. Available in a range of "strengths" denoted by dioptres.

closest focusing Distance from the film plane at which the lens can focus when set to the minimum focus position.

coma A photographic lens aberration which causes blurring at the edge of a picture. Off-axis highlights tend to grow radial tails (rather like comets, hence the name) and are due to differential magnification at the centre and edge of the image.

compound lens A camera lens comprising more than one lens (elements). The use of compound lenses enables the lens to be optically adjusted for aberrations and distortion.

contrast detection Technique employed by passive autofocus systems to achieve correct focus.

depth of field The distance in front of, and behind, the point of focus in a photograph in which the subject remains acceptably sharp or focused. By altering the lens aperture, the depth of field can be altered: the smaller the aperture, the greater the depth of field or sharpness and vice versa.

depth-of-field preview Camera or lens control that closes the aperture to the user or an automatically selected setting to enable the photographer to gauge the depth of field in the image.

depth-of-field scale Scale engraved on the barrel of some lenses, or provided as a separate diagrammatic table that indicates the depth of field for a particular aperture.

diaphragm The opening, or "aperture," behind or within a camera lens which can be adjusted to control the amount of light that reaches the film. The aperture opening is calibrated on the camera lens by f-stop numbers. Also called an "iris diaphragm."

diffraction When a beam of light passes through a lens or aperture it spreads out; the degree of spreading depends on the size of the aperture. Diffraction will ultimately determine how sharp an image can be formed by a lens.

f-number/f-value/f-stop The calibration of the aperture size of a photographic lens. This is the ratio of the focal length ("f" = focal) to the diameter of the aperture. The numbers are marked on the equipment. For example, a camera lens normally calibrated in a standard series would include the following numbers: $f/1$, $f/1.4$, $f/4$, $f/4.$, $f/4$, $f/5.6$, $f/8$, $f/11$, $f/16$, $f/42$, $f/32$ and so on, and these set the aperture size. The maximum amount of light that can be transmitted through a lens determines the "speed" of a lens—a lens with a minimum aperture of, e.g., $f/1$ is a "fast lens" (it lets in more light), whereas a lens with a minimum aperture of $f/3.5$ is described as a "slow lens."

field curvature A lens aberration in which the plane of sharpest focus is curved rather than the flat surface needed at the film plane.

fish-eye lens A camera lens with an extremely wide angle of view, producing a distorted image with an exaggerated apparent curve. In the 35 mm format lenses of focal length 8 mm provide a full, circular fish-eye, 16 mm give a full frame fish-eye.

fixed focus Description of a lens (or camera) which has a fixed, predetermined focus set for a particular subject distance (normally around 3 metres), in order to have group shots and middle-distance objects in best focus. The use of small apertures on such cameras generally means there is reasonable depth of field.

fixed-focus lens A photographic lens offering no focus adjustment. Usually found on basic cameras or those for specialist applications.

flare A bright streak, disc or other bright artefact seen through the viewfinder, or on an image, due to extraneous light entering the camera lens. Usually the use of a lens hood can reduce the extent of flare.

focal length The distance between the optical centre of a lens and its point of focus (usually the film plane) when the lens is focused on infinity. It is normally measured in millimetres.

focal plane The plane at which a camera lens forms a sharp image; also the "film plane," the point at which the image is recorded.

focal range The range over which a camera or lens is able to focus (or be manually focused) on a subject. On interchangeable lenses the range is usually marked on the lens barrel and might be, for example, 0.5 m to infinity.

focus The adjustment of the distance setting (either manually or automatically) in an autofocus camera to produce the sharpest definition across an image plane. Also the point at which light rays converge to produce the sharpest image.

focus lock A method of fixing the focus of an autofocus camera at a particular point. Usually achieved by light pressure on the shutter release or by pressing a separate button. Useful for focusing on a non-central subject.

hyperfocal distance The closest distance at which a lens records a subject sharply when focused at infinity. Will vary with aperture. If the camera is set to the hyperfocal distance, the region from half that distance to infinity will be in focus.

infinity In photographic terms, the notional point of the most extreme distant focus.

lens The name describing a cylindrical tube containing one or more glass "elements" which collect and focus light rays to create an image. Also the name given to an individual element within a lens assembly.

lens aberration A deficiency in a photographic lens wherein light rays do not pass "correctly" through the lens, causing degraded images. This can be due to faults or shortcomings in the optical construction. With chromatic aberration, light of different colors comes to different focal planes, resulting in colored haloes around objects. In spherical aberration, imprecise (or incorrect) curvature of the lens surface prevents light from coming to a single focal point; instead there is a focal patch from which the "best point of focus" must be selected. Certain lens distortions are also classed with aberrations. Barrel distortion causes objects to "bulge," with rectangles appearing barrel-like. Pincushion distortion is the converse, with rectangles appearing "pinched" along their sides.

lens hood Integral or accessory unit that shades the front of the lens from extraneous light. The most effective are rectangular or square in section (depending on the film format), and allow only that part of the scene which will comprise the recorded image on the film to pass through. A good lens hood will minimize flare, even when bright light sources are forward of the camera.

lens speed The widest setting to which a lens can be set. Corresponds to the smallest f-number.

macro lens Lens with a focusing range from infinity to extreme close-up. Normally macro lenses are capable of reproducing objects at a 1:1 scale on film (i.e., life size). Some macro lenses use supplementary close-up lenses to achieve even greater magnifications.

macro mode A mode offered by some lenses (and some cameras) that enables focusing in the macro range. Selecting the macro mode results in changes to the internal configuration of the lens elements and groups to make close focusing possible. Where indication is possible (such as on a camera's LCD display) macro mode is often denoted by a tulip icon.

minimum aperture The smallest aperture that can be set on a lens. In a 35 mm format lens this is typically $f/42$ or $f/16$.

mirror lens A camera lens that forms an image by reflecting it from curved mirrors rather than by refraction through a series of lenses. A mirror lens is more compact than a traditional lens of the same focal length (a telephoto lens, for example) but may not be capable of the same optical performance.

optical axis An imaginary line through the centre of lens elements through which a light passes from a central subject. Light passing through other parts of the lens is described as off-axis.

1.228 optical zoom Term used mainly with digital cameras and digital video cameras to denote a conventional zoom lens where the position of lens elements is altered to achieve different focal lengths. "Optical" is used to distinguish this from the "digital" zoom also found on many of these cameras.

optimum aperture Lens designs tend to offer the best performance (in terms of achieving a good focus and suppressing aberrations) at an optimum aperture. This is usually two or three f-stops down from the maximum aperture. When the highest quality is sought this aperture should be used, although being stopped down will mean that exposure times are substantially longer than at full aperture.

parallax error A subject-framing error found with non-SLR cameras (such as compacts, rangefinders and twin lens reflex cameras). As the viewfinder and the taking lens are slightly offset, their view is also slightly different. This becomes a problem at close subject distances where a degree of compensation needs to be introduced. Many camera viewfinders either adjust their view at this range or feature "parallax marks."

perspective control (PC) lens A camera lens used mainly to correct converging verticals in architectural photography. Also called a "shift lens." The lens can be moved laterally with respect to the film plane and also tilted to achieve corrective results.

perspective correction Adjusting an image geometry so that converging verticals (for example, when photographing buildings from a low viewpoint) are compensated for to give "straight" verticals. Can also be used to correct other perspective effects and usually achieved on 35 mm and medium format cameras with a perspective control (PC) lens. Large format cameras usually feature a camera back that can be tilted or moved relative to the lens to achieve a similar result.

portrait lens Generally a term applied to lenses of between 90 mm and 110 mm focal length (in the 35 mm format) used for portraiture work. Lenses of this length give a face or head and shoulder view in correct perspective (anything shorter tends to over-emphasize the nose) and give a shallow depth of field useful for isolating the subject from the background. Specialist portrait lenses feature integral soft focus filtration that can be dialled in or out from the lens barrel when required.

prime lens Fixed focal length lens. Though a zoom lens may replace several prime lenses, these lenses are usually capable of better optical performance and are to be preferred for exacting work.

resolving power The ability of a lens (or, sometimes, photographic emulsion) to record fineness of detail.

rotating lens Term usually applied to a lens whose front element rotates when the focus is adjusted or, where appropriate, the zoom mechanism is adjusted. Although this does not affect the optical performance, the rotating front will cause any mounted filters to rotate similarly. The action of certain filters (polarizers and graduated) will be adversely affected by such movement.

sharpness A measure of the clarity of focus present in a photographic image.

short-focus lens A camera lens with a focal length shorter than the diagonal measurement of the film format. Thus for 35 mm film, a lens shorter than 35 mm is short-focus.

soft focus An effect which "softens" or slightly diffuses the lines and edges of an image without altering the actual focus. Slightly opaque "softening" filters are employed to confer a "romantic" feel to portraits and landscapes, but are also useful for hiding minor skin blemishes. Filters with stronger effects are termed diffusers.

spherical aberration The failure of a lens to exactly focus light rays at its centre and at its edges.

standard lens The fixed focus lens normally sold with SLR cameras and boasting a focal length of between 45 mm and 55 mm. This gives a view that most closely echoes the proportions and perspective of the original scene, although it often has too narrow a field of view for use with interiors and is not selective enough for longer range views. Also known as a "normal lens."

standard zoom A zoom lens including the range of a standard lens (around 50 mm) in its focal range. Although this might apply to some of the "super-zooms" (with focal ranges from 28 mm to 300 mm) it normally applies to more modest ranges (typically 28–80 mm, for example).

stop The aperture size of a camera lens.

stop down The action of closing down the aperture of a lens.

teleconverter A negative lens placed between a camera body and lens to increase the effective focal length of that lens. Typical teleconverters multiply the focal length of the lens by 1.4, 2 or 3 times. Teleconverters tend to degrade image quality to a degree: this degree tends to increase with the value of the multiplier. The highest quality teleconverters are matched to a specific lens. Sometimes (historically) described as a "Barlow lens" or, for a dedicated lens, a "matched multiplier."

telephoto lens A photographic lens with a long focal length that enables distant objects to be enlarged. Telephoto lenses have a limited angle of view and offer limited depth of field for a given f-number.

vignetting A reduction in the light levels at the edge of an image or print due to deficiencies in the lens used for taking or enlarging the print. The use of an incorrect lens hood or too many filters can also cause vignetting.

wide-angle lens A photographic lens with wider field of view than a standard lens, so that more of the subject can be included. For 35 mm cameras the term wide angle usually applies to focal lengths of 35 mm or less. The widest wide angles have focal lengths of around 14 mm. Normally the term wide angle denotes lenses that do not introduce obvious distortion. Those that are wider and make no attempt at correcting distortions are described as fish-eye lenses. Wide-angle lenses are ideal for including sweeping landscapes and capturing small interiors.

zoom lens A camera lens with a focal length that can be adjusted over a range of focal lengths giving, in effect, a set of lenses of different focal length in one body. Useful for framing a subject, but generally a zoom lens is likely to have a smaller maximum aperture, suffer more aberrations and distortion. Wide-angle zooms provide a range of focal lengths that cover several equivalent wide-angle lenses (such as 24 mm to 35 mm in 35 mm format). Standard zooms give a range that includes the "standard" 50 mm focal length.

Index

#
3D 10, 94

A
Adobe Illustrator 69
Adobe Photoshop 69, 119, 150, 154, 156, 160–163
Alien Skin Exposure X 68, 150–153
aperture 14, 26, 29, 36, 38, 40, 53, 54, 55, 56, 57, 58, 59, 62, 63, 66, 67, 110, 118
artifacts 34
Aurora HDR 150, 152
autofocus 45, 108

B
background 29, 41, 44, 52, 53, 54, 62, 64, 68, 69, 118
barrel distortion 35
black-and-white photography 47
blur 13, 45, 52, 58, 68, 70, 101
bokeh 36, 50–73, 79, 150–153, 160–163, 164, 165, 166

C
Canon 108
catadioptric lens (see mirror lens)
chromatic aberration 21, 27, 34
circles of confusion 36–37, 38, 52, 70
close-up photography 27, 52, 104–115, 118, 120
color theory 20
composition 64, 77
Contax 82
contrast 8, 34, 154, 160
creativity 12, 14
cropping 80, 81, 122, 136

D
Deardorff 84
defocusing 58, 62, 72, 77, 92
depth of field 14, 21, 28, 30, 38–41, 53, 59, 61, 72, 79, 80, 85, 86, 110, 118
dispersion 27

E
Eastman Kodak Company 8, 11
electromagnetic radiation 20
entrance pupil (see no parallax point)
exposure 44, 45, 46, 100, 101, 122, 138, 142, 156
extension tubes 95, 96, 108

F
filters 42–49
 close-up lenses 109
 colored filters 47
 color gradient filters 47
 extreme ND filters 45
 graduated ND filters 46, 47
 neutral density (ND) filters 44–45
 polarizer filter 43
 variable ND (VND) filters 45
flare (see lens flare)
flash 44, 57
focal length 21, 31, 35, 38, 39, 40, 53, 59, 60, 61, 78–81, 101, 106, 107, 118, 120, 140, 144
focal plane (see plane of focus)
focal point 33, 38
focus distance 40, 89, 120
focus peaking 41
focus plane (see plane of focus)
focus stacking 116–131
focusing rail 112–113, 120
foreground 33, 38, 46, 47, 53, 64, 78, 87, 92, 128, 153
framing 14, 29, 45, 122
freelensing 55, 96–99
Fujifilm 41, 82, 83

G
gamma rays 20
gel 42
GigaPan 144–145
glare 43
glycerin 42
grain 135, 156

H
handheld photography 101, 135, 141, 158
Hasselblad 82
HDR 16, 78, 82, 100, 111, 138, 139, 150, 152, 164
Hejnar Photo 112
Helicon Focus 118, 124
highlights 52, 66, 67, 138
horizon 35, 46
hue 20, 22, 23
human eye 28–29, 36, 38
hyperfocal distance 14, 39, 40

I
image circle 31, 56, 70, 80, 81, 85, 86, 87, 90
image stitching 134–135
image-stacking software 119
infrared radiation 20
Intensify Pro 154–155
invisible radiation 20
ISO 118

K
keystone effect 86, 88

L
large-format cameras 14, 84–89, 90, 94
layering 69
lens adaptors 90, 93, 108, 110
lens flare 34, 57, 160, 163
lens movements 86–87
lens reversal 110–111
lens shade 34, 45
lenses
 DIY lens 92, 94–95, 97
 enlarging lens 90, 92
 fast lenses 53, 59, 79
 fisheye lens 35, 80, 143
 found lenses 72
 macro lens 106–107, 109, 110
 mirror lens 60–61

normal lens 78, 79
perspective-control lens (see tilt-shift lens)
plastic lens 63, 72
prime lens 35, 41, 79, 108, 110, 111
telephoto lens 31, 35, 60, 78, 79, 80, 120
tilt-shift lens 89, 90–93 94, 95, 97
wide-angle lens 31, 35, 43, 55, 79, 80, 81, 86, 135
zoom lens 35, 40, 79, 106, 109, 110, 111, 140
light
 artificial light 49, 57
 direct light 34

M
Macphun Software 150, 152, 154, 155
macro coupler 110, 111
macro imaging 72, 112, 118
magnification 80, 107, 108, 109, 110, 122
Mamiya 82
medium-format cameras 24, 90
miniaturization 92–93
Minolta 108
mirrorless cameras 82–83, 90, 91, 93, 97, 106, 141
motion 34, 45, 93, 158

N
Nikkor lenses 61, 91, 103, 166
Nikon 78, 90, 95, 108, 110
no parallax point (NPP) 140, 141, 142
Nodal Ninja 142, 143
nodal point (see no parallax point)
noise 46, 135, 155, 156, 157
Noiseless 156–157

O
Olympus 82, 108

P
panoramic photography 132–147
parallax 140–141
Pentax 82, 108, 110, 138
petroleum jelly 42
Piccure + 158–159
pincushion distortion 35
pinhole cameras 11, 24, 25, 26, 32, 63, 70–71
plane of focus 17, 33, 36, 53, 84, 89, 90, 103, 118
point of focus (see focal point)
primary colors of light 20
printing 119, 126, 135, 136, 139, 158

R
resolution 83, 134, 136, 138, 139, 144
rising front 88

S
Scheimpflug principle 89
selective focus 76, 85, 86, 92
sensor
 APS-C sensor 25, 81, 138
 full-frame sensor 79, 81, 83, 90, 101, 134, 138
 micro four-thirds sensor 81, 82, 90
shadows 42, 138, 157
sharpness 21, 28, 30, 37, 38, 76–77, 80, 91, 100, 118, 121, 122, 124, 125, 128, 136, 158
shift 84, 86, 87, 91, 96, 118
shutter speed 13, 44, 45, 79, 101, 118
single-use camera 63, 72, 114
sky 16, 43, 46, 47, 134
slider 120
soft focus 11, 42–43, 94
Sony 10, 78, 82, 90, 91, 135
standard lens (see normal lens)
sunlight 16, 20, 34, 44, 47, 48, 63

T
Tamron 106, 107, 138
tilt 17, 84, 86, 89, 90, 91, 92, 94
Tonality Pro 154–155
tone 154
tone mapping 126
toy cameras 164
tripod 78, 91, 92, 100–101, 120, 135, 141, 142, 144, 146

U
ultraviolet radiation 20
underexposure 156

V
vignetting 55
visible light 20
Voigtlander 82
VR rig 142

W
waterhouse stop 62, 66, 110
wheeled camera mount 121
white balance 122, 142
white light 20, 22, 27, 47

X
X-rays 20

Z
Zerene Stacker 119, 124
Zork 90, 91, 92, 103

Acknowledgments

Many thanks are due to all those who have helped me understand the process and value of photography over the years, including numerous teachers and students. My deepest thanks go to my family, who have provided their love, support, patience, and friendship over the years as I have developed my career in photography and teaching.

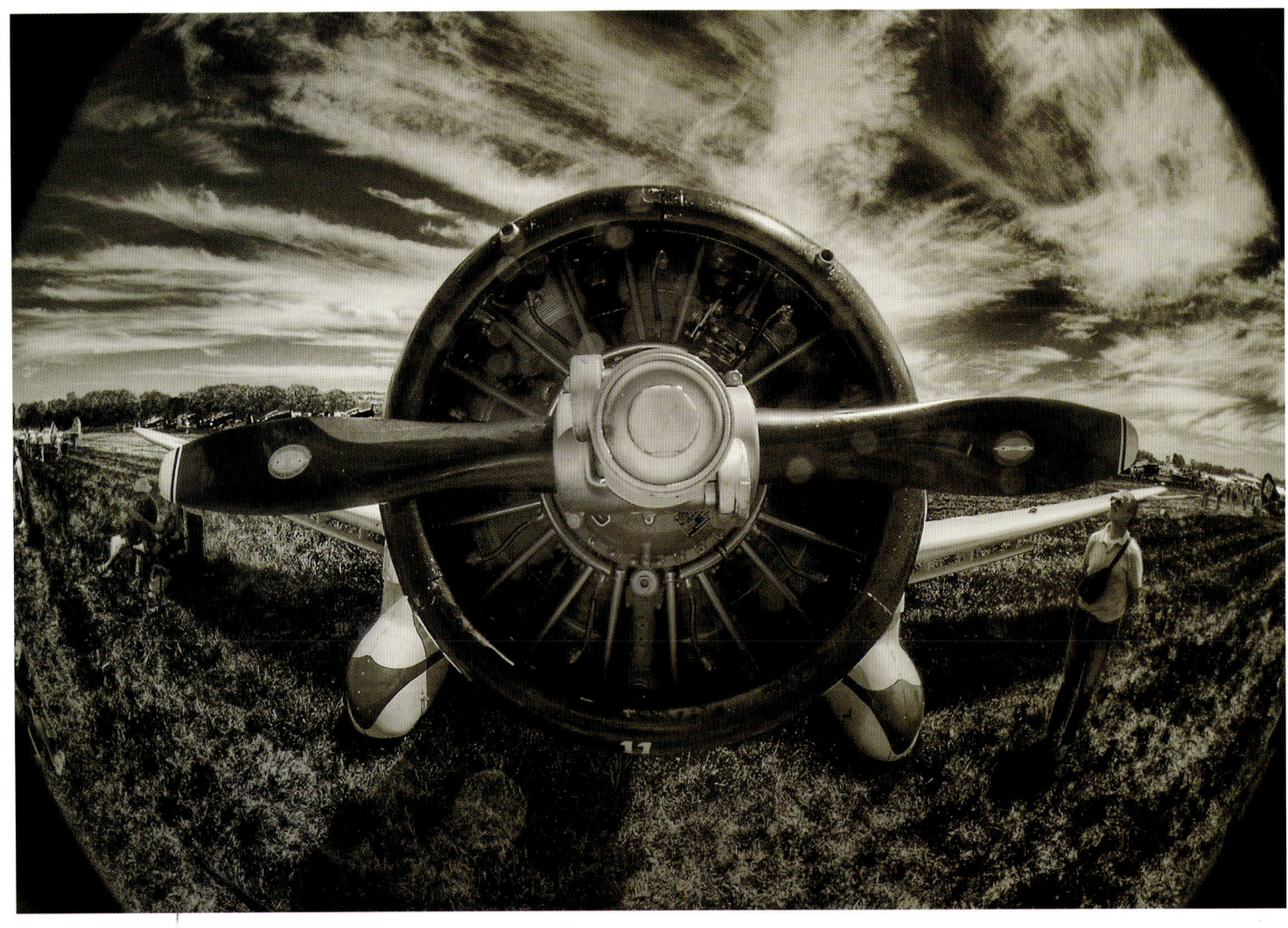